WHAT THEY SAY ABOUT
THE JOB BANK SERIES...

"If you are looking for a job...before you go to the newspapers and the help-wanted ads, listen to Bob Adams, editor of The Metropolitan New York JobBank."

-Tom Brokaw
NBC TELEVISION

"...A superior series of job hunt directories."

-Cornell University
Career Center
WHERE TO START

"Help on the job hunt...Anyone who is job-hunting in the New York area can find a lot of useful ideas in a new paperback called The Metropolitan New York JobBank..."

-Angela Taylor
THE NEW YORK TIMES

"A timely book for Chicago job hunters follows books from the same publisher that were well received in New York and Boston...A fine tool for job hunters..."

-Clarence Petersen
THE CHICAGO TRIBUNE

"Job hunting is never fun, but this book can ease the ordeal...[The Los Angeles JobBank] will help allay fears, build confidence, and avoid wheel-spinning."

-Robert W. Ross
THE LOS ANGELES TIMES

"This well-researched, well-edited job hunter's aid includes most major businesses and institutional entities in the New York metropolitan area...Highly recommended."

-Cheryl Gregory-Pindell
LIBRARY JOURNAL

"Here's the book for your job hunt...Trying to get a job in New York? I would recommend a good look through the Metropolitan New York JobBank..."

-Maxwell Norton
NEW YORK POST

"No longer can jobseekers feel secure about finding employment just through want ads. With the tough competition in the job market, particularly in the Boston area, they need much more help. For this reason, The Boston JobBank will have a wide and appreciative audience of new graduates, job changers, and people relocating to Boston. It provides a good place to start a search for entry-level professional positions."

-from a review in
THE JOURNAL OF
COLLEGE PLACEMENT

C0-ALV-862

What makes
The JobBank Series
the nation's premier
line of employment guides?

With vital employment information on thousands of employers across the nation, the JobBank Series is the most comprehensive and authoritative set of career directories available today.

Each book in the series provides information on **OVER THIRTY DIFFERENT INDUSTRIES** in a given city or area, with the primary employer listings providing contact information, telephone numbers, addresses, a thumbnail sketch of the firm's business, and in many cases descriptions of the firm's typical professional job categories, the principal educational backgrounds sought, and the fringe benefits offered.

In addition to the **DETAILED PRIMARY EMPLOYER LISTINGS,** the new 1993 JobBank books--for the first time--also give contact information, telephone numbers, and addresses for hundreds of other large employers as well as for **THOUSANDS OF SMALLER AND MEDIUM SIZED EMPLOYERS.**

All of the reference information in the JobBank Series is as up-to-date and accurate as possible. Every year, the entire database is thoroughly researched and verified, first by mail and then by telephone. Bob Adams Inc. publishes **MORE LOCAL JOBBANK BOOKS MORE OFTEN** than any other publisher of career directories.

In addition, the JobBank Series features important information about the local job scene--FORECASTS ON WHICH INDUSTRIES ARE THE HOTTEST, OVERVIEWS OF LOCAL ECONOMIC TRENDS, and even LISTS OF MAJOR PROFESSIONAL ASSOCIATIONS, so you can get your job hunt started off right.

Hundreds of discussions with job hunters show they prefer information organized geographically, because most people look for jobs in specific areas. The JobBank Series offers EIGHTEEN REGIONAL TITLES, from Minneapolis to Houston, and from Washington, D.C., to San Francisco. The future employee moving to a particular area can review the local employment data not only for information on the type of industry most common to that region, but also for names of specific employers.

A condensed, but thorough, review of the entire job search process is presented in the chapter "THE BASICS OF JOB WINNING," a feature which has received many compliments from career counselors. In addition, each JobBank directory is completed by a section on RESUMES AND COVER LETTERS The New York Times has acclaimed as "excellent."

The JobBank Series gives job hunters the most comprehensive, most timely, and most accurate career information, organized and indexed to facilitate the job search. An entire career reference library, JobBank books are the consummate employment guides.

Published by Bob Adams, Inc.
260 Center Street, Holbrook MA 02343

Copyright © 1993 by Bob Adams, Inc. All rights reserved. No part of the material printed may be reproduced or utilized in any form or by any means, electronic or mechanical, including photo-copying, recording, or by any information storage retrieval system without written permission from the publisher.

The Denver JobBank and its cover design are trademarks of Bob Adams, Inc.

Brand name products mentioned in the employer listings are proprietary property of the applicable firm, subject to trademark protection, and registered with government offices.

While the publisher has made every reasonable attempt to obtain accurate information and to verify same, occasional errors are inevitable due to the magnitude of the data base. Should you discover an error, please write to the publisher so that corrections may be made in future editions.

The appearance of a listing anywhere in this book does not constitute an endorsement from the publisher.

Cover design by Peter Weiss.

ISBN:1-55850-264-5

The Denver JobBank
5th Edition

Managing Editor
Carter Smith

Associate Editor
Steven Graber

Editorial Assistants
Kenny Brooks
Lynne A. Griffin
Keith Moore

Top career publications from Bob Adams, Inc:

THE JOBBANK SERIES:

The Atlanta JobBank ($15.95)
The Boston JobBank ($15.95)
The Carolina JobBank ($15.95)
The Chicago JobBank ($15.95)
The Dallas-Ft. Worth JobBank ($15.95)
The Denver JobBank ($15.95)
The Detroit JobBank ($15.95)
The Florida JobBank ($15.95)
The Houston JobBank ($15.95)
The Los Angeles JobBank ($15.95)
The Minneapolis-St. Paul JobBank ($15.95)
The New York JobBank ($15.95)
The Ohio JobBank ($15.95)
The Philadelphia JobBank ($15.95)
The Phoenix JobBank ($15.95)
The San Francisco Bay Area JobBank ($15.95)
The Seattle JobBank ($15.95)
The St. Louis JobBank ($15.95)
The Tennessee JobBank ($15.95)
The Washington DC JobBank ($15.95)

The National JobBank
 (Covers 50 states: $240.00)

The JobBank Guide to Employment Services
 (Covers 50 states: $140.00)

OTHER CAREER TITLES:

America's Fastest Growing Employers ($15.95)
Careers and the College Grad ($9.95)
Careers and the Engineer ($9.95)
Careers and the MBA ($9.95)
Cold Calling Techniques that Really Work ($6.95)

Cover Letters that Knock'em Dead ($12.95)
The Elements of Job Hunting ($4.95)
Harvard Guide to Careers in the Mass Media ($7.95)
High Impact Telephone Networking for Job Hunters ($6.95)
How to Become Successfully Self Employed ($15.95)
How to Get a Job in Education ($6.95)
Job Search Handbook ($6.95)
Knock 'em Dead: The Ultimate Job Seeker's Handbook ($7.95)
The Minority Career Book ($9.95)
Resume Handbook ($5.95)
Resumes that Knock 'em Dead ($12.95)
300 New Ways to Get A Better Job ($7.95)

To order these books or additional copies of this book, send check or money order (including $3.75 for postage) to:

Bob Adams, Inc., 260 Center Street, Holbrook MA 02343

Ordering by credit card?
Just call 1-800-USA-JOBS
(In Massachusetts, call 617-767-8100)

How To Use This Book

A copy of *The Denver JobBank* book is one of the most effective tools you can use in your professional job hunt. In this guide you will find the most up-to-date information available on over ten thousand businesses throughout the Denver area. This book will supply you with specific addresses, phone numbers, and personnel contact information--and often much more than that--for companies which employ over 50 people.

Separate yourself from the flock of candidates who rely on help-wanted advertisements as their main job hunting strategy. The method this book offers, direct employer contact, boasts twice the success rate of any other. Exploit it.

Read and use *The Denver JobBank* to uncover new opportunities. Here's how:

--Read the introductory economic overview in order to gain insights on what the overall trends are for Denver's economy.

--Map out your job-seeking strategy by reading the "Basics of Job Winning" section. This section gives a condensed version of the most effective job search methods.

--Write a winning resume and learn how to sell yourself most effectively on paper, using the "Resumes and Cover Letters" section.

--Within each industry you will find detailed information on "Primary Denver Employers." These primary listings give contact information, a telephone number, an address, a thumbnail sketch of the firm, and in many cases descriptions of the firm's typical professional categories, the principal educational backgrounds sought, and the fringe benefits offered. Formulate a target list of the potential employers in your field by selecting appropriate companies from the "Primary Denver Employers" section of each industry. Use the detailed information provided in this section to supplement your own research on the major local employers in your area--so you'll be knowledgeable about each firm before your interview. Then expand your list of target employers by consulting the "Additional Denver Employers" and the "Small to Medium Sized Employers" section within each industry. These listings provide contact information, telephone numbers, and addresses.

--Increase your knowledge of your field, as well as your connections within it, by using our major professional and trade associations.

Whether you are just out of college and starting your first job search, looking for a new position in your current field, or entering an entirely new sector of the job market, *The Denver JobBank* will give you an idea of the range and diversity of employment possibilities throughout the state. Your ultimate success will depend on how rigorously you use the information provided here. This one-of-a-kind employment guide can lead you to a company, and a job, that would otherwise have remained undiscovered. With a willingness to apply yourself, a positive attitude, and the research within these covers, you can attain your career objective.

TABLE OF CONTENTS

Introduction/11
A complete and informative economic overview designed to help you understand all of the forces shaping the Colorado job market.

The Basics of Job Winning/15
A condensed review of the basic elements of a successful job search campaign. Includes advice on developing an effective strategy, time planning, preparing for interviews, interview techniques, etc.

Resumes and Cover Letters/29
Advice on creating a strong resume. Includes sample resumes and cover letters.

Primary Denver Employers/43
The Denver JobBank is organized according to industry. Many listings include the address and phone number of each major firm listed, along with a description of the company's basic product lines and services, and, in most cases, a contact name and other relevant hiring information. Also includes thousands of secondary listings providing addresses, numbers, and contact names for smaller and mid-sized firms.

Professional Employment Services & Executive Search Firms/315

Includes the address, phone number, description of each company's services, contact name, and a list of positions commonly filled.

Index/331

An alphabetical index of Denver's primary employer listings only. Due to space constraints, employers that fall under the headings "Large Employers", or "Small to Medium Sized Employers" are not indexed here.

INTRODUCTION

As energy declines, services rise

As Denver moves toward the mid-1990s, the only thing constant about the Mile High City economic picture is its changing shape. During the 1970s and early 1980s, Denver reaped the benefits of favorable oil prices. By the late '80s, the city suffered when the energy industry could no longer fuel the local economy. By the fall of 1992, the energy industry had lost 1,100 jobs in less than a year, specifically in oil and gas extraction. Fortunately, Denver has not been hit as hard as other energy-producing cities because it is not nearly as dependent upon energy to power its economy.

While Denver's energy-related jobs have been cut almost in half, the city's diversified economy has cushioned it against a more serious economic depression. In fact, Denver was cited in January, 1993 by the *Wall Street Journal's National Business Employment Weekly* as the nation's fourth fastest metro area in the generation of new jobs. Tourism, construction, real estate, transportation, services, and retail trade are all economic strengths. The service industry is the area's largest employer, followed by retail trade, government, manufacturing, and transportation. Of these, retail trade is the strongest, gaining 4,800 jobs in 1992.

Unemployment rate

Metro Denver's unemployment rate in November, 1992 was 5.3%, well below the national average. While the unemployment rate was as low as 4.9% during the previous month, the increase was due largely to declining construction work as the colder weather arrived.

Breaking all the records

Happily, the tourism industry has exploded in Denver. Outsiders travel to the metropolitan area year round. The summer of 1992 broke all the previous area tourism records, and by the winter of '92 the skiers hit the slopes in record numbers. Forecasters believe that 1993 may break all of the records again.

On the other hand, the state's tourism and convention industry suffered a potentially serious setback in the waning months of 1992. In response to the passage of Amendment 2, an antigay protection bill, a group called Boycott Colorado has launched a nationwide boycott of the state. Several major cities, including San Francisco, New York and Atlanta have also instituted prohibitions against city employees traveling to the state.

Although the long-term effect of the boycott on tourism is unclear, analysts project that the state lost at least $20 million between Election Day in November, 1992 and January, 1993.

New transportation and construction projects

Despite several mall construction cancellations and a winter slowdown, the seasonal construction industry was still one of the fastest growing industries in the state in 1992. Construction showed a 12-month gain of 4,800 jobs in Denver alone, and a total gain of 11,300 jobs throughout the state, according to the *Colorado Labor Force Review.*

During the '80s, the metro area's construction/real estate industry was hurt by over-expansion, leading to an abundance of vacant office space. New construction projects have included considerable highway construction throughout Colorado. Thousands of jobs have also been created due to huge construction projects such as Denver International Airport and Coors Stadium. The $3 billion Denver International Airport is expected to open by late 1993, just outside of Denver. The site employs 6,000-8,000 workers who are constructing what will be one of the largest airports in the United States. Included in this project will be a $55 million maintenance center to service the airport's planes.

A new major league baseball franchise, the Colorado Rockies, is set to begin action in the spring of 1993 at Mile High Stadium. Currently under construction is the future home of the Rockies, Coors Stadium, which is scheduled to be completed for the 1995 season.

The real estate market

Colorado's consumer real estate market is strong, with home sales increasing rapidly. On the commercial front, low rental rates for office space offer businesses strong incentives to relocate to Denver or to expand local facilities. **The Metropolitan Life Insurance Company** plans to lease a large amount of office space in Denver in early 1993. According to the *Colorado Labor Force Review*, the company plans to hire 200 new employees during the mid-1990's.

Services

As with most of the U.S., Colorado has experienced a huge increase in service-related jobs. There were 1,700 new jobs in Colorado's service sector by the summer of 1992. Metro Denver was no exception, gaining 1,300 such jobs. One weak link was business services, which had lost 1,800 jobs in Denver alone by September of 1992.

Retail

Denver averaged 1.3% annual population growth during the 1980's. In 1990, the population was 1.8 million. By early 1993, the population had risen by an additional 100,000. This growing population has boosted the area's retail sector. The fastest-growing area in retail has been at eating and drinking establishments.

As with many of Denver's industries, there is also some bad news. **Macy's** department store signed a letter of intent to be the anchor store for a $300 million downtown mall, but with the retail giant in bankruptcy, the project has been cancelled. Developers of the proposed Regency Fashion Centre had obtained financing for their mall and targeted **Nordstrom** as the anchor store, but have since cancelled their plans as well.

Energy

Although no longer a dominant industry in Denver, the energy sector is still important and high-paying. The impact of companies such as **Total Petroleum**, a Fortune 500 company, and **The Associated Natural Gas Company**, a fast-growing producer of natural gas and crude oil, have helped the industry regain some lost momentum.

Banking

Employment within Colorado's banking industry is stable with very few jobs being created. However, much else has changed at the state's largest banks. Out-of-state banks such as **Norwest** (Minnesota) and **Bank One** (Ohio) have purchased several Colorado banks, such as **Affiliated Bank**. Unfortunately, this has led to a dip in employment.

Problems

As in most areas of the country, Denver's economy has suffered due to the national recession, significant long-term defense budget cuts, and the instability of the high-tech field. In addition to the energy industry, regional economic concerns include defense, high-technology, health care, communications, and manufacturing.

Defense

Colorado's defense industry has been especially hard hit. **Lowry Air Force Base** is facing a phased shut down through to the end of 1994. Lowry's closing will mean the loss or transfer of 7,000 military and civilian personnel.

Computer Sciences Corporation has lost an Air Force contract which should lead to the transfer of up to 50 employees. The phased closure of **Rocky Flats**, the troubled plutonium plant employing more than 1,100, is yet another permanent closure expected by 1995.

High-tech.

While high-tech research and development in Denver is a big industry, it is not entirely stable. As in manufacturing, high-tech hiring has been very slow. In fact, America's high-tech capacity has come under increasing pressure as productivity has decreased, and the nation's technological advantage eroded. **Cray Computers** in Colorado Springs for example, thrived throughout the '80s, but announced to layoffs in 1992. Fortunately, several Denver area companies remain on the technological forefront. One of these is **Confertech International,** a manufacturer of teleconferencing equipment and services located in Golden.

Health care and communications.

Health services in Colorado registered a loss of 300 jobs midway through 1992. Symptomatic of this problem, **Marquest Medical Products, Inc.,** built a huge new plant in Parker, occupied it for a short period of time, and then moved back to Englewood because the Parker plant was too big. The return enabled Marquest to pay off some debts, and the company still plans on expanding its facilities, although in a more limited capacity.

Somatogen, Inc., manufactures genetically engineered blood, and has begun construction on a $45 million facility in nearby Boulder. This new facility is expected to add 150 new jobs.

The communications industry is struggling in Denver, but is helped by Confertech International, as well as two rapidly growing cable television companies, **Tele-Communications** and **Triax Communications**.

THE BASICS OF JOB WINNING:
A CONDENSED REVIEW

The best way to obtain a better professional job is to contact the employer directly. Broad-based statistical studies by the Department of Labor show that job seekers find jobs more successfully by contacting employers directly than by using any other method.

However, given the diversity and the increasingly specialized nature of both industries and job tasks, in some situations other job seeking methods may also be successful. Three of the other most commonly used methods are: relying on personal contacts, using employment services, and following up help wanted advertisements. Many professionals have been successful in finding better jobs using one of these methods. However, the Direct Contact method boasts twice the success rate of any other method, and is used successfully by many more professionals. So unless you have specific reasons to believe that another method would work best for you, the Direct Contact method should form the foundation of your job search.

The Objective

With any business task, you must develop a strategy for meeting a goal. This is especially true when it comes to obtaining a better job. First you need to clearly define your objectives.

The first step in beginning your job search is to clearly define your objectives.

Setting your job objectives is better known as career planning (or life planning for those who wish to emphasize the importance of combining the two). Career planning has become a field of study in and of itself. Since many of our readers are probably well-entrenched in their career path, we will touch on career planning only briefly.

If you are thinking of choosing or switching careers, we particularly emphasize two things. First, choose a career where you will enjoy most of the day-to-day tasks. This sounds obvious, but most of us have at one point or another been attracted by a glamour industry or a prestigious sounding job without thinking of the most important consideration: Would we enjoy performing the everyday tasks the position entailed?

The second key consideration is that you are not merely choosing a career, but also a lifestyle. Career counselors indicate that one of the most common problems people encounter in job seeking is that they fail to consider how well-suited they are for a particular position or career. For example, some people, attracted to management consulting by good salaries, early responsibility and high-level corporate exposure, do not adapt well to the long hours, heavy travel demands, and the constant pressure to produce. So be sure to ask yourself how you might adapt to not only the day-to-day duties and working environment that a specific position entails, but also how you might adapt to the demands of that career or industry choice as a whole.

The Strategy

Assuming that you've established your career objectives, the next step of the job search is to develop a strategy. If you don't take the time to develop a strategy and lay out a plan, you will find yourself going in circles after several weeks of random searching for opportunities that always seem just beyond your reach.

Your strategy can be thought of as having three simple elements:

1. Choosing a method of contacting employers.

2. Allocating your scarce resources. (In most job searches the key scarce resource will be time, but financial considerations will become important in some searches, too.)

3. Evaluating how the selected contact method is working and then considering adopting other methods.

We suggest you consider using the Direct Contact method exclusively. However, we realize it is human nature to avoid putting all your eggs in one basket. So if you prefer to use other methods as well, try to expend at least half your effort on the Direct Contact method, spending the rest on all of the other methods combined. Millions of other jobseekers have already proven that Direct Contact has been twice as effective in obtaining employment, so why not benefit from their effort?

With your strategy in mind, the next step is to work out the details. The most important detail is setting up a schedule. Of course, since job searches aren't something most people do regularly, it may be hard to estimate how long each step will take. Nonetheless, it is important to have a plan so that you can see yourself progressing.

When outlining your job search schedule, have a realistic time frame in mind. If you will be job searching full-time, your search will probably take at least two months. If you can only devote part-time effort, it will probably take four months.

You probably know a few people who seem to spend their whole lives searching for a better job in their spare time. Don't be one of them. Once you begin your job search on a part-time basis, give it your whole-hearted effort. If you don't feel like devoting a lot of energy to job seeking right now, then wait. Focus on enjoying your present position, performing your best on the job, and storing up energy for when you are really ready to begin your job search.

Those of you currently unemployed should remember that job hunting is tough work physically and emotionally. It is also intellectually demanding work that requires you to be at your best. So don't tire yourself out by working on your job campaign around the clock. At the same time, be sure to discipline yourself. The most logical way to manage your time while looking for a job is to keep your regular working hours.

Job hunting is intellectually demanding work that requires you to be at your best. So don't tire yourself out working around the clock.

For those of you who are still employed, job searching will be particularly tiring because it must be done in addition to your regular duties. So don't work yourself to the point where you show up to interviews looking exhausted and start to slip behind at your current job. On the other hand, don't be tempted to quit your current job! The long hours are worth it. Searching for a job while you have one puts you in a position of strength.

If you are searching full-time and have decided to choose several different contact methods, we recommend that you divide up each week allowing some time for each method. For instance, you might devote Mondays to following up newspaper ads because most of them appear in Sunday papers. Then you might devote Tuesdays, and Wednesday mornings to working and developing the personal contacts you have, in addition to trying a few employment services. Then you could devote the rest of the week to the Direct Contact method. This is just one plan that may succeed for you.

By trying several methods at once, job-searching will be more interesting, and you will be able to evaluate how promising each of the methods seems, altering your schedule accordingly. Be very careful in your evaluation, however, and don't judge the success of a particular method just by the sheer number of interviews you obtain. Positions advertised in the newspaper, for instance, are likely to generate many more interviews per opening than positions that are filled without being advertised.

If you are searching part-time and decide to try several different contact methods, we recommend that you try them sequentially. You simply won't have enough time to put a meaningful amount of effort into more than one method at once. So estimate the length of your job search, and then allocate so many weeks or months for each contact method you will use. (We suggest that you try Direct Contact first.)

If you're expected to be in your office during the business day, then you have an additional problem to deal with. How can you work interviews into the business day? And if you work in an open office, how can you even call to set up interviews? As much as possible you should keep up the effort and the appearances on your present job. So maximize your use of the lunch hour, early mornings and late afternoons for calling. If you keep trying you'll be surprised how often you will be able to reach the executive you are trying to contact during your out-of-office hours. Also you can catch people as early as 8 AM and as late as 6 PM on frequent occasions. Jot out a plan each night on how you will be using each minute of your precious lunch break.

Your inability to interview at any time other than lunch just might work to your advantage. If you can, try to set up as many interviews as possible for your lunch hour. This will go a long way to creating a relaxed rapport. (Who isn't happy when eating?) But be sure the interviews don't stray too far from the agenda on hand.

Try calling as early as 8 AM and as late as 6 PM. You'll be surprised how often you will be able to reach the executive you want during these times of the day.

Lunchtime interviews are much easier to obtain if you have substantial career experience. People with less experience will often find no alternative to taking time off for interviews. If you have to take time off, you have to take time off. But try to do this as little as possible. Try to take the whole day off in order to avoid being blatantly obvious about your job search. Try to schedule in two to three interviews for the same day. (It is very difficult to maintain an optimum level of energy at more than three interviews in one day.) Explain to the interviewer why you might have to juggle your interview schedule -- he/she should honor the respect you're showing your current employer by minimizing your days off and will probably appreciate the fact that another prospective employer is interested in you.

We want to stress that if you are searching for a job -- especially part-time -- get out there and do the necessary tasks to the best of your ability and get it over with. Don't let your job search drag on endlessly.

And remember that all schedules are meant to be broken. The purpose of a job search schedule is not to rush you to your goal but to help you map out the road ahead, and then to periodically evaluate how you're progressing.

The Direct Contact Method

Once you have scheduled your time, you are ready to begin your search in earnest. We'll limit discussion here to the Direct Contact method.

The first step in preparing for Direct Contact is to develop a check list for categorizing the types of firms for which you'd like to work. You might categorize firms by product line, size, customer-type (such as industrial or consumer), growth prospects, or, by geographical location. Your list of important criteria might be very short. If it is, good! The shorter it is, the easier it will be to locate the company that is right for you.

Consider where your skills might be in demand, the degree of competition for employment, and the employment outlook at each particular firm.

Next, try to decide at which firms you're most likely to be able to find a job. Try matching your skills with those that a specific job demands. Consider where your skills might be in demand, the degree of competition for employment, and the employment outlook at each particular firm.

Now you'll want to assemble your list of potential employers. Build up your list to at least 100 prospects. Then separate your prospect list into three groups. The first tier of around 25 firms will be your primary target group, the second tier of another 25 firms will be your secondary group, and the remaining names you can keep in reserve.

This book will help you greatly in developing your prospect list. Refer to our primary employers section. You'll notice that employer listings are arranged according to industry, beginning with "Accounting and Auditing", followed by "Advertising, Marketing, and Public Relations", and so on through to "Utilities."

If you know of a firm, but you're unsure of what industry it would be classified under, then refer to the alphabetical employer index at the rear of the book to find the page number that the firm's listing appears on.

After you form your prospect list begin work on your resume. Refer to the sample resumes included in the Resumes and Cover Letters section following this chapter in order to get ideas.

Once your resume is complete, begin researching your first batch of 25 prospective employers. You will want to determine whether you would be happy working at the firms you are researching and also get a better idea of what their employment needs might be. You also need to obtain enough information to sound highly informed about the company during phone conversations and in mail correspondence. But don't go all out on your research yet! At some of these firms you probably will not be able to arrange interviews, so save your big research effort until you start to arrange interviews. Nevertheless, you should plan to spend an average of three to four hours researching each firm. Do your research in batches to save time and energy. Use one resource at a time and find out what you can about each of the 25 firms in the batch. Start with the easiest resources to use (such as this book). Keep organized. Maintain a folder on each firm.

You should plan to spend an average of three or four hours researching each firm.

If you discover something that really disturbs you about the firm (they are about to close their only local office), or if you discover that your chances of getting a job there are practically nil (they have just instituted a hiring freeze), then cross them off your prospect list.

If possible, supplement your research efforts with contacts to individuals who know the firm well. Ideally you should make an informal contact with someone at the particular firm, but often a contact at a direct competitor, or a major supplier or customer will be able to supply you with just as much information. At the very least, try to obtain whatever printed information that the company has available, not just annual reports, but product brochures and any other printed material the firm may have to offer. The company might have printed information about career opportunities.

DEVELOPING YOUR CONTACTS

Some career counselors feel that the best route to a better job is through somebody you already know or through somebody to whom you can be introduced. The counselors recommend that you build your contact base beyond your current acquaintances by asking each one to introduce you, or refer you, to additional people in your field of interest.

The theory goes like this: You might start with 15 personal contacts, each of whom introduces you to three additional people, for a total of 45 additional contacts. Then each of these people introduces you to three additional people, which adds 135 additional contacts. Theoretically, you will soon know every person in the industry.

Of course, developing your personal contacts does not usually work quite as smoothly as the theory suggests because some people will not be able to introduce you to anyone. The further you stray from your initial contact base, the weaker your references may be. So, if you do try developing your own contacts, try to begin with as many people you know personally as you can. Dig into your personal phone book and your holiday greeting card list and locate old classmates from school. Be particularly sure to approach people who perform your personal business such as your lawyer, accountant, banker, doctor, stockbroker, and insurance agent. These people develop a very broad contact base due to the nature of their professions.

Getting The Interview

Now it is time to arrange an interview, time to make the Direct Contact. If you have read many books on job searching you may have noticed that most of these books tell you to avoid the personnel office like the plague. It is said that the personnel office never hires people, they just screen out candidates. Unfortunately, this is often the case, but there are other options available to you. If you can identify the appropriate manager with the authority to hire you, contact that person directly. This will take a lot of time in each case, and often you'll be bounced back to personnel despite your efforts. So we suggest that initially you begin your Direct Contact campaign through personnel offices. If it seems that the firms on your prospect list do little hiring through personnel, you might consider some alternative courses of action. The three obvious means of initiating Direct Contact are:

-Showing up unannounced
-Mail
-Phone calls

Cross out the first one right away. You should never show up to seek a professional position without an appointment. Even if you are somehow lucky enough to obtain an interview, you will appear so unprofessional that you will not be seriously considered.

Mail contact seems to be a good choice if you have not been in the job market for a while. You can take your time to prepare a letter, say exactly what you want, and of course include your resume. Remember that employers receive many resumes every day. Don't be surprised if you do not get a response to your inquiry, so don't spend weeks waiting for responses that may never come. If you do send a cover letter, follow it up (or precede it) with a phone call. This will increase your impact, and because of the initial research you did, will underscore both your familiarity and your interest in the firm.

Always include a cover letter with your resume even if you are not specifically asked to do so.

Another alternative is to make a "Cover Call." Your Cover Call should be just like your cover letter: concise. Your first sentence should interest the employer in you. Then try to subtly mention your familiarity with the firm. Don't be overbearing; keep your introduction to three sentences or less. Be pleasant, self-confident, and relaxed. This will greatly increase the chances of the person at the other end of the line developing the conversation. But don't press. When you are asked to follow up "with something in the mail", don't try to prolong the conversation once it has ended. Don't ask what they want to receive in the mail. Always send your resume and a highly personalized follow-up letter, reminding the addressee of the phone conversation. Always include a cover letter even if you are requested to send a resume. (It is assumed that you will send a cover letter, too.)

Unless you are in telephone sales, making smooth and relaxed cover calls will probably not come easily. Practice them on your own and then with your friends or relatives.

If you obtain an interview as a result of a telephone conversation, be sure to send a thank you note reiterating the points you made during the conversation. You will appear more professional and increase your impact.

However, unless specifically requested, don't mail your resume once an interview has been arranged. Take it with you to the interview instead.

Preparing For The Interview

Once the interview has been arranged, begin your in-depth research. You should arrive at an interview knowing the company upside down and inside out. You need to know the company's products, types of customers, subsidiaries, the parent company, principal locations, rank in the industry, sales and profit trends, type of ownership, size, current plans, and much more. By this time you have probably narrowed your job search to one industry. If you haven't then be familiar with the trends in the firm's industry, the firm's principal competitors and their relative performance, and the direction that the industry leaders are headed. Dig into every resource you can! Read the company literature, the trade press, the business press, and if the company is public, call your stockbroker (if you have one) and ask for additional information. If possible, speak to someone at the firm before the interview, or if not, speak to someone at a competing firm. The more time you spend, the better. Even if you feel extremely pressed for time, you should set aside at least 12 hours for pre-interview research.

You should arrive at an interview knowing the company upside down and inside out.

If you have been out of the job market for some time, don't be surprised if you find yourself tense during your first few interviews. It will probably happen every time you re-enter the market, not just when you seek your first job after getting out of school.

Tension is natural during an interview, but if you can be relaxed you will have an advantage. Knowing you have done a thorough research job should put you more at ease. Make a list of questions that you think might be asked in an interview. Think out your answers carefully; practice reviewing them with a friend. Tape record your responses to the problem questions. If you feel particularly unsure of your interviewing skills, arrange your first interviews at firms you are not as interested in. (But remember it is common courtesy to seem excited about the possibility of working for any firm at which you interview.) Practice again on your own after these first few interviews. Go over the difficult questions that you were asked.

DON'T BOTHER WITH MASS MAILINGS OR BARRAGES OF PHONE CALLS

Direct Contact does not mean burying every firm within a hundred miles with mail and phone calls. Mass mailings rarely work in the job hunt. This also applies to those letters that are personalized -- but dehumanized -- on an automatic typewriter. Don't waste your time or money on such a project; you will fool no one but yourself.

The worst part of sending out mass mailings or making unplanned phone calls is that you are likely to be remembered as someone with little genuine interest in the firm, who lacks sincerity, and as somebody that nobody wants to hire.

HELP WANTED ADVERTISEMENTS

Only a small fraction of professional job openings are advertised. Yet a majority of job seekers -- and a lot of people not in the job market -- spend a lot of time studying the help wanted ads. As a result, the competition for advertised openings is often very severe.

A moderate-sized Manhattan employer told us about an experience advertising in the help wanted section of a major Sunday newspaper:

It was a disaster. We had over 500 responses from this relatively small ad in just one week. We have only two phone lines in this office and one was totally knocked out. We'll never advertise for professional help again.

If you insist on following up on help wanted ads, then research a firm before you reply to an ad. Preliminary research might help to separate you from all of the other professionals responding to that ad, many of whom will only have a passing interest in the opportunity, and will give you insight about a particular firm to help you determine if it is potentially a good match. That said, your chances of obtaining a job through the want-ads are still much smaller than they are if you use the Direct Contact method.

How important is the proper dress for a job interview? Buying a complete wardrobe of Brooks Brothers pinstripes or Liz Claiborne suits, donning new wing tip shoes or pumps, and having your hair styled every morning is not enough to guarantee you a career position as an investment banker. But on the other hand, if you can't find a clean, conservative suit or a nice skirt and blouse, or won't take the time to wash your hair, then you are just wasting your time by interviewing at all.

The very beginning of the interview is the most important part because it determines the rapport for the rest of it.

Very rarely will the final selection of candidates for a job opening be determined by dress. So don't spend a fortune on a new wardrobe. But be sure that your clothes are adequate. Men applying for any professional position should wear a suit; women should either wear a dress or a suit (but not a pant suit). Your clothes should be at least as formal or slightly more formal and more conservative than the position would suggest.

Top personal grooming is more important than finding the perfect clothes for a job interview. Careful grooming indicates both a sense of thoroughness and self-confidence.

Be sure that your clothes fit well and that they are immaculate. Hair must be neat and clean. Shoes should be newly polished. Women need to avoid excessive jewelry and excessive makeup. Men should be freshly shaven, even if the interview is late in the day.

Be complete. Everyone needs a watch, a pen, and a notepad. Finally, a briefcase or a leather-bound folder (containing extra copies of your resume) will help complete the look of professionalism.

Sometimes the interviewer will be running behind schedule. Don't be upset, be sympathetic. There is often pressure to interview a lot of candidates and to quickly fill a demanding position. So be sure to come to your interview with good reading material to keep yourself occupied. This will help you to relax.

The Interview

The very beginning of the interview is the most important part because it determines the rapport for the rest of it. Those first few moments are especially crucial. Do you smile when you meet? Do you establish enough eye contact, but not too much? Do you walk into the office with a self-assured and confident stride? Do you shake hands firmly? Do you make small talk easily without being garrulous? It is human nature to judge people by that first impression, so make sure it is a good one. But most of all, try to be yourself.

SOME FAVORITE INTERVIEW QUESTIONS

Tell me about yourself...

Why did you leave your last job?

What excites you in your current job?

What are your career goals?

Where would you like to be in 5 years?

What are your greatest strengths?

What are your greatest weaknesses?

Why do you wish to work for this firm?

Where else are you seeking employment?

Why should we hire you?

Often the interviewer will begin, after the small talk, by telling you about the company, the division, the department, or perhaps, the position. Because of your detailed research, the information about the company should be repetitive for you and the interviewer would probably like nothing better than to avoid this regurgitation of the company biography. So if you can do so tactfully, indicate to the interviewer that you are very familiar with the firm. If he or she seems intent on providing you with background information, despite your hints, then acquiesce.

But be sure to remain attentive. If you can manage to generate a brief discussion of the company or the industry at this point, without being forceful, great. It will help to further build rapport, underscore your interests, and increase your impact.

Soon (if it didn't begin that way) the interviewer will begin the questions. This period of the interview falls into one of two categories (or somewhere in between): either a structured interview, where the interviewer has a prescribed set of questions to ask; or an unstructured interview, where the interviewer will ask only leading questions to get you to talk about yourself, your experiences and your goals. Try to sense as quickly as possible which direction the interviewer wishes to proceed. This will make the interviewer feel more relaxed and in control of the situation.

Many of the questions will be similar to the ones that you were expecting and have practiced. Remember to keep attuned to the interviewer and make the length of your answers appropriate to the situation. If you are really unsure as to how detailed a response the interviewer is seeking, then ask.

As the interview progresses, the interviewer will probably mention some of the most important responsibilities of the position. If applicable, draw parallels between your experience and the demands of the position as detailed by the interviewer. Describe your past experience in the same manner that you did on your resume: emphasizing results and achievements and not merely describing activities. If you listen carefully (listening is a very important part of the interviewing process) the interviewer might very well imply the skills needed for the position. Don't exaggerate. Be on the level about your abilities.

Try not to cover too much ground during the first interview. The interview is often the toughest, where many candidates are screened out. If you are interviewing for a very competitive position, you will have to make an impression that will last. Focus on a few of your greatest strengths that are relevant to the position. Develop these points carefully, state them again in other words, and then try to summarize them briefly at the end of the interview.

Often the interviewer will pause towards the end and ask if you have any questions. Particularly in a structured interview, this might be the one chance to really show your knowledge of and interest in the firm. Have a list prepared of specific questions that are of real interest to you. Let your questions subtly show your research and your knowledge of the firm's activities. It is wise to have an extensive list of questions, as several of them may be answered during the interview.

Do not turn your opportunity to ask questions into an interrogation. Avoid bringing your list of questions to the interview.

YOU'RE FIRED!!

You are not the first and will not be the last to go through this traumatic experience. Thousands of professionals are fired every week. Remember, being fired is not a reflection on you as a person. It is usually a reflection of your company's staffing needs and its perception of your recent job performance. Share the fact with your relatives and friends. Being fired is not something of which to be ashamed.

Don't start your job search with a flurry of unplanned activity. Start by choosing a strategy and working out a plan. Now is not the time for major changes in your life. If possible, remain in the same career and in the same geographical location, at least until you have been working again for a while. On the other hand, if the only industry for which you are trained is leaving, or is severely depressed in your area, then you should give prompt consideration to moving or switching careers.

Register for unemployment compensation immediately. A thorough job search could take months. After all, your employers have been contributing to unemployment insurance specifically for you ever since your first job. Don't be surprised to find other professionals collecting unemployment compensation as well. Unemployment compensation is for everybody who is between jobs.

Be prepared for the question, "Why were you fired?", during job interviews. Avoid mentioning you were fired while arranging interviews. Try especially hard not to speak negatively of your past employer and not to sound particularly worried about your status of being temporarily unemployed. But don't spend much time reflecting on why you were fired or how you might have avoided it. Learn from your mistakes and then look ahead. Think positively. And be sure to follow a careful plan during your job search.

Ask questions that you are fairly certain the interviewer can answer (remember how you feel when you cannot answer a question during an interview).

Even if you are unable to determine the salary range beforehand, do not ask about it during the first interview. You can always ask about it later. Above all, don't ask about fringe benefits until you have been offered a position. (Then be sure to get all the details.) You should be able to determine the company's policy on fringe benefits relatively easily before the interview.

Try not to be negative about anything during the interview. (Particularly any past employer or any previous job.) Be cheerful. Everyone likes to work with someone who seems to be happy.

Don't let a tough question throw you off base. If you don't know the answer to a question, say so simply -- do not apologize. Just smile. Nobody can answer every question -- particularly some of the questions that are asked in job interviews.

Before your first interview, you may be able to determine how many interviews there usually are for positions at your level. (Of course it may differ quite a bit even within the different levels of one firm.) Usually you can count on attending at least three or four interviews, although some firms, such as some of the professional partnerships, are well-known to give a minimum of six interviews for all professional positions. While you should be more relaxed as you return for subsequent interviews, the pressure will be on. The more prepared you are, the better.

Depending on what information you are able to obtain, you might want to vary your strategy quite a bit from interview to interview. For instance, if the first interview is a screening interview, then be sure a few of your strengths really stand out. On the other hand, if later interviews are primarily with people who are in a position to veto your hiring, but not to push it forward (and few people are weeded out at these stages), then you should primarily focus on building rapport as opposed to reiterating and developing your key strengths.

If it looks as though your skills and background do not match the position your interviewer was hoping to fill, ask him or her if there is another division or subsidiary that perhaps could profit from your talents.

After The Interview

Write a follow-up letter immediately after the interview, while it is still fresh in the interviewer's mind. Then, if you have not heard from the interviewer within seven days, call to stress your continued interest in the firm, and the position, and to request a second interview.

A parting word of advice. Again and again during your job search you will be rejected. You will be rejected when you apply for interviews. You will be rejected after interviews. For every job you finally receive, you will have probably been rejected a multitude of times. Don't let rejections slow you down. Keep reminding yourself that the sooner you go out and get started on your job search, and get those rejections flowing in, the closer you will be to obtaining the job you want.

RESUMES AND COVER LETTERS

THIS SECTION CONTAINS:

1. Resume Preparation
2. Resume Format
3. Resume Content
4. Should You Hire A Resume Writer?
5. Cover Letters
6. Sample Resumes
7. General Model For A Cover Letter
8. Sample Cover Letters
9. General Model For A Follow-up Letter

RESUMES/OVERVIEW

When filling a position, a recruiter will often have 100 plus applicants, but time to interview only the 5 or 10 most promising ones. So he or she will have to reject most applicants after a brief skimming of their resume.

Unless you have phoned and talked to the recruiter -- which you should do whenever you can -- you will be chosen or rejected for an interview entirely on the basis of your resume and cover letter. So your resume must be outstanding. (But remember -- a resume is no substitute for a job search campaign. YOU must seek a job. Your resume is only one tool.)

RESUME PREPARATION

One page, usually.

Unless you have an unusually strong background with many years of experience and a large diversity of outstanding achievements, prepare a one page resume. Recruiters dislike long resumes.

8 1/2 x 11 Size

Recruiters often get resumes in batches of hundreds. If your resume is on small sized paper it is likely to get lost in the pile. If oversized, it is likely to get crumpled at the edges, and won't fit in their files.

Typesetting

Modern photocomposition typesetting gives you the clearest, sharpest image, a wide variety of type styles and effects such as italics, bold facing, and book-like justified margins. Typesetting is the best resume preparation process, but is also the most expensive.

Word Processing

The most flexible way to get your resume typed is on a good quality word processor. With word processing, you can make changes almost instantly because your resume will be stored on a magnetic disk and the computer will do all the re-typing automatically. A word processing service will usually offer you a variety of type styles in both regular and proportional spacing. You can have bold facing for emphasis, justified margins, and clear, sharp copies.

Typing

Household typewriters and office typewriters with nylon or other cloth ribbons are NOT good for typing the resume you will have printed. If you can't get word processing or typesetting, hire a professional with a high quality office typewriter with a plastic ribbon (usually called a "carbon ribbon.")

Printing

Find the best quality offset printing process available. DO NOT make your copies on an office photocopier. Only the personnel office may see the resume you mail. Everyone else may see only a copy of it. Copies of copies quickly become unreadable. Some professionally maintained, extra-high-quality photocopiers are of adequate quality, if you are in a rush. But top quality offset printing is best.

Proofread your resume

Whether you typed it yourself or had it written, typed, or typeset, mistakes on resumes can be embarrassing, particularly when something obvious such as your name is misspelled. No matter how much you paid someone else to type or write or typeset your resume, YOU lose if there is a mistake. So proofread it as carefully as possible. Get a friend to help you. Read your draft aloud as your friend checks the proof copy. Then have your friend read aloud while you check. Next, read it letter by letter to check spelling and punctuation.

Functional Resume
(Prepared on a Word Processor and Letter-Quality Printer.)

Michelle Hughes
430 Miller's Crossing
Essex Junction, VT 05452
802/555-9354

Solid background in plate making, separations, color matching, background definition, printing, mechanicals, color corrections, and supervision of personnel. A highly motivated manager and effective communicator. Proven ability to:

* **Create Commercial Graphics**
* **Produce Embossing Drawings**
* **Color Separate**
* **Analyze Consumer Acceptance**

* **Meet Graphic Deadlines**
* **Control Quality**
* **Resolve Printing Problems**
* **Expedite Printing Operations**

Qualifications

Printing: Black and white and color. Can judge acceptability of color reproduction by comparing it with original. Can make four or five color corrections on all media. Have long developed ability to restyle already reproduced four-color artwork. Can create perfect tone for black and white match fill-ins for resume cover letters.

Customer Relations: Work with customers to assure specifications are met and customers are satisfied. Can guide work through entire production process and strike a balance between technical printing capabilities and need for customer approval.

Management: Schedule work to meet deadlines. Direct staff in production procedures. Maintain quality control from inception of project through final approval for printing.

Specialties: Make silk screen overlays for a multitude of processes. Velo bind, GBC bind, perfect bind. Have knowledge to prepare posters, flyers, and personalized stationery.

Personnel Supervision: Foster an atmosphere that encourages highly talented artists to balance high level creativity with a maximum of production. Meet or beat production deadlines. Am continually instructing new employees, apprentices and students in both artistry and technical operations.

Experience

Professor of Graphic Arts, University of Vermont, Burlington, VT (1977-present).
Assistant Production Manager, Artsign Digraphics, Burlington, VT (1981-present) Part time.

Education

Massachusetts Conservatory of Art, PhD 1977
University of Massachusetts, B.A. 1974

If you are having it typed or typeset by a resume service or a printer, and you can't bring a friend or take the time during the day to proof it, pay for it and take it home. Proof it there and bring it back later to get it corrected and printed.

RESUME FORMAT

(See samples)

Basic data

Your name, phone number, and a complete address should be at the top of your resume. (If you are a university student, you should also show your home address and phone number.)

Separate your education and work experience

In general, list your experience first. If you have recently graduated, list your education first, unless your experience is more important than your education. (For example, if you have just graduated from a teaching school, have some business experience and are applying for a job in business you would list your business experience first.) If you have two or more years of college, you don't need to list high schools.

Reverse chronological order

To a recruiter your last job and your latest schooling are the most important. So put the last first and list the rest going back in time.

Show dates and locations

Put the dates of your employment and education on the left of the page. Put the names of the companies you worked for and the schools you attended a few spaces to the right of the dates. Put the city and state or city and country where you studied or worked to the right of the page.

Avoid sentences and large blocks of type

Your resume will be scanned, not read. Short, concise phrases are much more effective than long-winded sentences. Keep everything easy to find. Avoid paragraphs longer than six lines. Never go ten or more lines in a paragraph. If you have more than six lines of information about one job or school, put it in two or more paragraphs.

RESUME CONTENT

Chronological Resume
(Prepared on a Word Processor and Laser Printer.)

WALLACE R. RECTORIAN
412 Maple Court
Seattle, WA 98404
206/555-6584

EXPERIENCE

1984-present   THE CENTER COMPANY, Seattle, WA
Systems Analyst, design systems for the manufacturing unit. Specifically, physical inventory, program specifications, studies of lease buy decisions, selection of hardware the outside contractors and inside users. Wrote On-Site Computer Terminal Operators Manual. Adapted product mix problems to the LASPSP (Logistical Alternative Product Synthesis Program).

As *Industrial Engineer* from February 1984 to February 1986, computerized system design. Evaluated manufacturing operations operator efficiency productivity index and budget allocations. Analyzed material waste and recommended solutions.

ADDITIONAL EXPERIENCE

1980-1984   *Graduate Research Assistant* at New York State Institute of Technology.

1978-1980   *Graduate Teaching Assistant* at Salem State University.

EDUCATION

1982-1984   NEW YORK STATE INSTITUTE OF TECHNOLOGY, Albany, NY
M.S. in Operations Research. GPA: 3.6. Graduate courses included Advanced Location and Queueing Theories, Forecasting, Inventory and Material Flow Systems, Linear and Nonlinear Determination Models, Engineering Economics and Integer Programming.

1980-1982   M.S. in Information and Computer Sciences. GPA: 3.8
Curriculum included Digital Computer Organization & Programming. Information Structure & Process. Mathematical Logic, Computer Systems, Logic Design and Switching Theory.

1976-1980   SALEM STATE UNIVERSITY, Salem, OR
B.A. in Mathematics. GPA: 3.6.

AFFILIATIONS
Member of the American Institute of Computer Programmers, Association for Computing Machinery and the Operations Research Society of America.

PERSONAL
Married, three dependents, able to relocate.

Be factual

In many companies, inaccurate information on a resume or other application material will get you fired as soon as the inaccuracy is discovered. Protect yourself.

Be positive

You are selling your skills and accomplishments in your resume. If you achieved something, say so. Put it in the best possible light. Don't hold back or be modest, no one else will. But don't exaggerate to the point of misrepresentation.

Be brief

Write down the important (and pertinent) things you have done, but do it in as few words as possible. The shorter your resume is, the more carefully it will be examined.

Work experience

Emphasize continued experience in a particular type of function or continued interest in a particular industry. De-emphasize irrelevant positions. Delete positions that you held for less than four months. (Unless you are a very recent college grad or still in school.)

Stress your results

Elaborate on how you contributed to your past employers. Did you increase sales, reduce costs, improve a product, implement a new program? Were you promoted?

Mention relevant skills and responsibilities

Be specific. Slant your past accomplishments toward the type of position that you hope to obtain. Example: Do you hope to supervise people? Then state how many people, performing what function, you have supervised.

Education

Keep it brief if you have more than two years of career experience. Elaborate more if you have less experience. Mention degrees received and any honors or special awards. Note individual courses or research projects that might be relevant for employers. For instance, if you are a liberal arts major, be sure to mention courses in such areas as: accounting, statistics, computer programming, or mathematics.

Chronological Resume
(Prepared on an Office-Quality Typewriter.)

Lorraine Avakian
70 Monback Avenue
Oshkosh, WI 54901
Phone: 414/555-4629

Business Experience

1984-1991 **NATIONAL PACKAGING PRODUCTS,** Princeton, WI

1989-1991 **District Sales Manager.** Improved 28-member sales group from a company rank in the bottom thirty percent to the top twenty percent. Complete responsibility for personnel, including recruiting, hiring and training. Developed a comprehensive sales improvement program and advised its implementation in eight additional sales districts.

1986-1988 **Marketing Associate.** Responsible for research, analysis, and presentation of marketing issues related to long-term corporate strategy. Developed marketing perspective for capital investment opportunities and acquisition candidates, which was instrumental in finalizing decisions to make two major acquisitions and to construct a $35 million canning plant.

1984-1986 **Salesperson, Paper Division.** Responsible for a four-county territory in central Wisconsin. Increased sales from $700,000 to over $1,050,000 annually in a 15 month period. Developed six new accounts with incremental sales potential of $800,000. Only internal candidate selected for new marketing program.

AMERICAN PAPER PRODUCTS, INC., Oshkosh, WI
1983-1984 **Sales Trainee.** Completed the intensive six month training program and was promoted to salesperson status. Received the President's Award for superior performance in the sales training program.

HENDUKKAR SPORTING GOODS, INC., Oshkosh, WI
1983 **Assistant Store Manager.** Supervised six employees on the evening shift. Handled accounts receivable.

Education
1977-1982 **BELOIT COLLEGE,** Beloit, WI
Received Bachelor of Science Degree in Business Administration in June 1982. Varsity Volleyball. Financed 50% of educational costs through part-time and co-op program employment.

Personal Background
Able to relocate; Excellent health; Active in community activities.

Job objective

Leave it out. Even if you are certain of exactly the type of job that you desire, the inclusion of a job objective might eliminate you from consideration for other positions that a recruiter feels are a better match for your qualifications.

Personal data

Keep it very brief. Two lines maximum. A one-word mention of commonly practiced activities such as golf, skiing, sailing, chess, bridge, tennis, etc. can prove to be good way to open up a conversation during an interview. Do not include your age, weight, height, etc.

SHOULD YOU HIRE A RESUME WRITER?

If you write reasonably well, there are some advantages to writing your resume yourself. To write it well, you will have to review your experience and figure out how to explain your accomplishments in clear, brief phrases. This will help you when you explain your work to interviewers.

If your write your resume, everything in it will be in your own words -- it will sound like you. It will say what you want it to say. And you will be much more familiar with the contents. If you are a good writer, know yourself well and have a good idea of what parts of your background employers are looking for, you may be able to write your own resume better than anyone else can. If you write your resume yourself, you should have someone who can be objective (preferably not a close relative) review it with you.

When should you have your resume professionally written?

If you have difficulty writing in "resume style" (which is quite unlike normal written language), if you are unsure of which parts of your background you should emphasize, or if you think your resume would make your case better if it did not follow the standard form outlined here or in a book on resumes, then you should have it professionally written.

There are two reasons even some professional resume writers we know have had their resumes written with the help of fellow professionals. First, when they need the help of someone who can be objective about their background, and second, when they want an experienced sounding board to help focus their thoughts.

Chronological Resume
(Prepared on a Word Processor and Laser Printer.)

Melvin Winter
43 Aspen Wall Lane
Wheaton, IL 60512
312/555-6923 (home)
312/555-3000 (work)

RELATED EXPERIENCE
1982-Present GREAT LAKES PUBLISHING COMPANY, Chicago, IL
Operations Supervisor (1986-present)
in the Engineering Division of this major trade publishing house, responsible for main-
taining on line computerized customer files, title files, accounts receivable, inventory
and sales files.

Organize department activities, establish priorities and train personnel. Provide corporate accounting with monthly reports of sales, earned income from journals, samples,
inventory levels/value and sales and tax data. Divisional sales average $3 million an-
nually.

Senior Customer Service Representative (1984-1986)
in the Construction Division. Answered customer service inquiries regarding orders and
accounts receivable, issued return and shortage credits and expedited special sales orders for direct mail and sales to trade schools.

Customer Service Representative (1982-1983)
in the International Division. Same duties as for construction division except that sales
were to retail stores and universities in Europe.

1980-1982 B. DALTON, BOOKSELLER, Salt Lake City, UT
Assistant Manager of this retail branch of a major domestic book seller, maintained all
paperback inventories at necessary levels, deposited receipts daily and created window
displays.

EDUCATION
1976-1980 UNIVERSITY OF MAINE, Orono, ME
Awarded a degree of Bachelor of Arts in French Literature.

LANGUAGES
Fluent in French. Able to write in French, German and Spanish.

PERSONAL
Willing to travel and relocate, particularly in Europe.

References available upon request.

If you decide to hire a resume writer

The best way to choose a writer is by reputation -- the recommendation of a friend, a personnel director, your school placement officer or someone else knowledgeable in the field.

You should ask, "If I'm not satisfied with what you write, will you go over it with me and change it?"

You should ask, "How long has the person who will write my resume been writing resumes?"

There is no sure relation between price and quality, except that you are unlikely to get a good writer for less than $50 for an uncomplicated resume and you shouldn't have to pay more than $300 unless your experience is very extensive or complicated. There will be additional charges for printing.

Few resume services will give you a firm price over the phone, simply because some people's resumes are too complicated and take too long to do at any predetermined price. Some services will quote you a price that applies to almost all of their customers. Be sure to do some comparative shopping. Obtain a firm price before you engage their services and find out how expensive minor changes will be.

COVER LETTERS

Always mail a cover letter with your resume. In a cover letter you can show an interest in the company that you can't show in a resume. You can point out one or two skills or accomplishments the company can put to good use.

Make it personal

The more personal you can get, the better. If someone known to the person you are writing has recommended that you contact the company, get permission to include his/her name in the letter. If you have the name of a person to send the letter to, make sure you have the name spelled correctly and address it directly to that person. Be sure to put the person's name and title on both the letter and envelope. This will ensure that your letter will get through to the proper person, even if a new person now occupies this position. But even if you are addressing it to the "Personnel Director" or the "Hiring Partner," send a letter.

Type cover letters in full. Don't try the cheap and easy ways like photocopying the body of your letter and typing in the inside address and salutation. You will give the impression that you are mailing to a multitude of companies and have no particular interest in any one. Have your letters fully typed and signed with a pen.

General Model for a Cover Letter

```
                                        Your Address
                                        Date


Contact Person Name
Title
Company
Address



Dear Mr./Ms._____:


Immediately explain why your background makes you the best can-
didate for the position that you are applying for. Keep the
first paragraph short and hard-hitting.

Detail what you could contribute to this company. Show how
your qualifications will benefit this firm. Remember to keep
this letter short; few recruiters will read a cover letter
longer than half a page.

Describe your interest in the corporation. Subtly emphasize
your knowledge about this firm (the result of your research ef-
fort) and your familiarity with the industry. It is common
courtesy to act extremely eager to work for any company that
you interview.

In the closing paragraph you should specifically request an in-
terview. Include your phone number and the hours when you can
be reached. Alternatively, you might prefer to mention that
you will follow up with a phone call (to arrange an interview
at a mutually convenient time within the next several days).



                                        Sincerely,

                                        (signature)

                                        Your full name (typed)
```

Phone

Precede or follow your mailing with a phone call.

Bring extra copies of your resume to the interview

If the person interviewing you doesn't have your resume, be prepared. Carry copies of your own. Even if you have already forwarded your resume, be sure to take extra copies to the interview, as someone other than the interviewer(s) might now have the first copy you sent.

General Model for a Follow-Up Letter

Your Address
Date

Contact Person's Name
Title
Company
Address

Dear Mr./Ms._____:

Remind the interviewer of the position for which you were interviewed, as well as the date. Thank him/her for the interview.

Confirm your interest in the opening and the organization. Use specifics to emphasize both that you have researched the firm in detail and considered how you would fit into the company and the position.

Like in your cover letter, emphasize one or two of your strongest qualifications and slant them toward the various points that the interviewer considered the most important for the position. Keep the letter brief, a half-page is plenty.

If appropriate, close with a suggestion for further action, such as a desire to have further interviews. Mention your phone number and the hours that you can best be reached. Alternatively, you may prefer to mention that you will follow up with a phone call in several days.

Sincerely yours,
(signature)
Your full name (typed)

ACCOUNTING AND AUDITING

Demand for accounting, auditing, and bookkeeping services is on the rise, which will result in higher industry receipts and employment. In times of recession, the accounting industry can actually benefit. Bankruptcies, for example, have more than doubled in the past decade, all of which means more business for accountants.

ARTHUR ANDERSEN & COMPANY
717 17th Street, Suite 1900, Denver CO 80202. 303/295-1900. **Contact:** Michael West, Personnel Director. **Description:** One of the largest certified public accounting organizations in the world, operating offices in more than 40 countries. Operates in the following divisions: Audit, Tax, and Management Information Consulting. The Audit Division offers assignments in a wide range of businesses and industries; company offers a highly recognized professional development program in all phases of the industry. The Tax Division offers assignments involving consultation and compliance in all areas of taxation, including home, estate, trust, and gift taxation, with client assignments providing exposure to a wide range of businesses and industries. The Management Information Consulting Division offers opportunities for both entry-level and experienced personnel in providing professional systems and consulting services to clients in a wide range of businesses and industries. Emphasis is on the design and installation of management information systems in the areas of finance, operations, and marketing. **Corporate headquarters:** Chicago, IL.

CLIFTON, GUNDERSON & COMPANY
11990 Grant Street, Suite 304, Denver CO 80233. 303/452-2008. **Contact:** William Petrie, Personnel Director. **Description:** An area accounting firm.

COOPERS & LYBRAND
370 17th Street, Suite 3300, Denver CO 80202. 303/573-2800. **Contact:** Personnel Director. **Description:** One of the largest certified public accounting firms, offering a wide range of accounting, auditing, tax, management consulting, emerging business, and actuarial consulting services. Maintains over 300 offices worldwide. **Corporate headquarters:** New York, NY.

GRANT THORNTON
1660 Lincoln Street, Suite 2600, Denver CO 80264. 303/861-5555. **Contact:** Personnel Director. **Description:** A national firm of accountants and management consultants. **Common positions:** Accountant. **Educational backgrounds sought:** Accounting; Computer Science. **Corporate headquarters:** Chicago, IL.

HAMMA & NELSON
370 17th Street, Suite 1350, Denver CO 80202. 303/825-7696. **Contact:** H.W. Nelson Jr., President. **Description:** An accounting firm.

PRICE WATERHOUSE
950 17th Street, Suite 2600, Denver CO 80202. 303/893-8100. **Contact:** H. W. Harnagel, Director of Personnel. **Description:** An international public accounting and consulting services organization with 458 offices in 110 countries with a total staff of 49,500. One of the Big 6 accounting firms, Price Waterhouse has 110 offices in the U.S. with a total staff of over 12,300. **Educational backgrounds sought:** accounting, information systems, and computer science. **Common Positions:** Auditor; Management Consultant; Tax Specialist. **Benefits:** medical, dental, and life insurance; pension plan; tuition assistance; disability coverage; savings plan. **Corporate headquarters:** New York, NY.

Additional large employers: 250+

ACCOUNTING, AUDITING, AND BOOKKEEPING SERVICES

Business Resources
6892 S Yosemite St, Englewood CO 80112-1419. 303/9306500. Employs: 250-499.

Additional small to medium sized employers: 50-249

ACCOUNTING, AUDITING, AND BOOKKEEPING SERVICES

1438 Florida Av, Longmont CO 80501-6352. 303/6517510. Employs: 50-99.

Bank Properties Services
109 E Centennial Ave, Englewood CO 80110-6711. 303/7621222. Employs: 100-249.

Duttons Enterprises Inc
6073 W 44th Ave, Suite 107, Wheat Ridge CO 80033-4702. 303/4217487. Employs: 100-249.

Coman Accounting
4604 Rusina Rd, Colorado Springs CO 80907-1721. 719/5997503. Employs: 100-249.

Personnel Systems Incorporated
650 S Cherry St, Denver CO 80222-1801. 303/3993180. Employs: 50-99.

Deloitte & Touche
1100 Holly Sugar Bldg, Colorado Springs CO 80903. 719/6365126. Employs: 50-99.

Ernst & Young
4300 Republic Plaza, Denver CO 80202. 303/5344300. Employs: 100-249.

Deloitte & Touche Accounting
1560 Broadway, Suite 1800, Denver CO 80202-5163. 303/8373000. Employs: 100-249.

Gelford Hochstadt Pangburn
370 17, Denver CO 80202. 303/5954000. Employs: 50-99.

Dental Management Systems

Wayne R Tucker
707 17, Denver CO 80202. 303/2962323. Employs: 100-249.

For more information on career opportunities in accounting and auditing:

Associations

AMERICAN ACCOUNTING ASSOCIATION
5717 Bessie Drive, Sarasota FL 34233. 813/921-7747.

AMERICAN INSTITUTE OF CERTIFIED PUBLIC ACCOUNTANTS
1211 Avenue of the Americas, New York NY 10036. 212/575-6200.

ASSOCIATION OF GOVERNMENT ACCOUNTANTS
2000 Mount Vernon Avenue, Alexandria VA 22301. 703/684-6931.

THE EDP AUDITORS FOUNDATION
455 Kehoe Boulevard, Suite 106, Carol Stream IL 60188. 708/682-1200.

INSTITUTE OF INTERNAL AUDITORS
P.O. Box 140099, Orlando FL 32889. 407/830-7600.

INTERNATIONAL CREDIT ASSOCIATION
Education Department, Box 419057, St. Louis MO 63141-1757. 314/991-3030.

INSTITUTE OF MANAGEMENT ACCOUNTING
10 Paragon Drive, Box 433, Montvale NJ 07645. 201/573-9000.

NATIONAL ASSOCIATION OF TAX CONSULTORS
454 North 13th Street, San Jose CA 92112. 408/298-1458.

NATIONAL ASSOCIATION OF TAX PRACTITIONERS
720 Association Drive, Appleton WI 54914. 414/749-1040.

NATIONAL SOCIETY OF PUBLIC ACCOUNTANTS
1010 North Fairfax Street, Alexandria VA 22314. 703/549-6400.

Directories

AICPA SURVEYS
American Institute of Certified Public Accountants, 1211 Avenue of the Americas, New York NY 10036. 212/575-6200.

ACCOUNTING FIRMS AND PRACTITIONERS
American Institute of Certified Public Accountants, 1211 Avenue of the Americas, New York NY 10036. 212/575-6200.

Magazines

ACCOUNTING NEWS
Warren, Gorham, and Lamont, Inc., 210 South Street, Boston MA 02111. 617/423-2020.

CPA JOURNAL
200 Park Avenue, New York NY 10166. 212/973-8300.

CPA LETTER
American Institute of Certified Public Accountants, 1211 Avenue of the Americas, New York NY 10036. 212/575-6200.

CORPORATE ACCOUNTING
Warren, Gorham, and Lamont, Inc., 210 South Street, Boston MA 02111. 617/423-2020.

JOURNAL OF ACCOUNTANCY
American Institute of Certified Public Accountants, 1211 Avenue of the Americas, New York NY 10036. 212/575-6200.

MANAGEMENT ACCOUNTING
Institute of Management Accounting, 10 Paragon Drive, Box 433, Montvale NJ 07645. 201/573-9000.

NATIONAL PUBLIC ACCOUNTANT
National Society of Public Accountants, 1010 North Fairfax Street, Alexandria VA 22314. 703/549-6400.

ADVERTISING, MARKETING AND PUBLIC RELATIONS

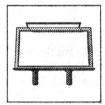

The long recession has put a continued damper on the advertising industry, as client companies put tighter reigns on their advertising budgets. Throughout the past ten years, mergers have played a major role, with advertising giants like Saatchi and Saatchi buying up competitors.
Another trend has been the emergence of in-house agencies, which means that more advertising jobs will be available in addition to the traditional advertising agencies. Overall, however, job prospects remain weak as many companies continue layoffs and job competition grows even fiercer.

AMERICOMM DIRECT MARKETING
10600 East 54 Avenue, Unit D, Denver CO 80239. 303/373-5323. **Contact:** Joy Annabal, Personnel Director. **Description:** A direct-mail processing company.

EVANS GROUP
1050 17th Street, Suite 700, Denver CO 80202. 303/770-2000. **Contact:** Jay Marks, Account Service Director. **Description:** A Denver-area advertising firm. **Common positions:** Advertising Worker; Commercial Artist; Public Relations Specialist. **Educational backgrounds sought:** Art/Design; Liberal Arts; Marketing. **Benefits:** medical insurance; life insurance; disability coverage; profit sharing. **Corporate headquarters:** This location. **Operations at this facility:** service.

INTERNATIONAL TECHNOLOGY
5600 Quebec, Englewood CO 80111. 303/793-5200. **Contact:** Human Resources Department. **Description:** A Denver-area management consulting and public relations firm.

KARSH & HAGEN, INC

5500 Greenwood Plaza Boulevard, Suite 200, Englewood CO 80111. 303/770-8088. **Contact:** Barbara Williams, Vice President. **Description:** An area advertising agency.

NEODATA

6707 Winchester Circle, Boulder CO 80301. 303/530-6715. **Contact:** Debbie Venrick, Personnel Administrator. **Description:** A company that provides direct-mail marketing services. **Common positions:** Accountant; Computer Programmer; **Educational backgrounds sought:** Computer Science; Data Processing. **Benefits:** medical insurance; dental insurance; pension plan; life insurance; tuition assistance; disability coverage. **Corporate headquarters:** This location. **Operations at this facility:** research/development; administration; service; sales. **Listed on:** New York Stock Exchange.

TALLANT, LAPOINTE AND PARTNERS, INC.

5200 DTC Parkway, Suite 400, Englewood CO 80111-3108. 303/771-0960. **Contact:** President. **Description:** A Denver-area advertising firm.

Additional large employers: 250+

PUBLIC RELATIONS SERVICES

United Tech Chem Sys Division

1495 W Garden Of The Gods Ste, Colorado Springs CO 80907. 7195947240. Employs: 500-999.

Additional small to medium sized employers: 50-249

ADVERTISING AGENCIES

The Advertising Consortium Inc
402 S Quebec St, Englewood CO 80111. 303/7719909. Employs: 50-99.

OUTDOOR ADVERTISING SERVICES

KWGN-Tv
6160 S Wabash Way, Englewood CO 80111-5108. 303/7402222. Employs: 100-249.

Fox 21 KXRM-Tv
560 Wooten Rd, Colorado Springs CO 80915-3524. 719/5962100. Employs: 50-99.

KDVR- Tv Fox 31
31 501 Wazee, Denver CO 80204. 303/5953131. Employs: 50-99.

Kusa Northern Bureau
419 Canyon Ave, Fort Collins CO 80521-2670. 303/4845332. Employs: 50-99.

KWHD-Tv 53
11203 E Peakview Ave, Englewood CO 80111-6812. 303/7925211. Employs: 50-99.

DIRECT MAIL ADVERTISING SERVICES

Marketing Communications Inc
2369 S Trenton Way Ste M, Denver CO 80231-3828. 303/7510433. Employs: 100-249.

Presort Incorporated
4725 Leyden St Suite A, Denver CO 80216-3301. 303/3319400. Employs: 100-249.

COMMERCIAL ECONOMIC, SOCIOLOGICAL, AND EDUCATIONAL RESEARCH

Marc Inc
14111 E Alameda Ave Suite 200, Aurora CO 80012-2509. 303/3678220. Employs: 100-249.

Colorado Market Research

2149 S Grape St, Denver CO 80222-5203. 303/7586424. Employs: 50-99.

PUBLIC RELATIONS SERVICES

Harmony Foundation Inc
1790 30th St Ste 315, Boulder CO 80301-1020. 303/5864491. Employs: 50-99.

For more information on career opportunities in advertising, marketing, and public relations:

Associations

ACADEMY OF MARKETING SCIENCE
School of Business Administration, University of Miami, Coral Gables FL 33124. 305/284-6673.

ADVERTISING RESEARCH FOUNDATION
Three East 54th Street, 15th Floor, New York NY 10022. 212/751-5656.

AFFILIATED ADVERTISING AGENCIES INTERNATIONAL
2280 South Xanadu Way, Suite 300 Aurora CO 80014. 303/671-8551.

AMERICAN ADVERTISING FEDERATION
1400 K Street NW, Suite 1000, Washington DC 20005. 202/898-0089.

AMERICAN ASSOCIATION OF ADVERTISING AGENCIES
666 Third Avenue, New York NY 10017. 212/682-2500.

AMERICAN MARKETING ASSOCIATION
250 South Wacker Drive, Suite 200, Chicago IL 60606. 312/648-0536.

BUSINESS-PROFESSIONAL ADVERTISING ASSOCIATION
901 N. Washington Street, Suite 206, Alexandria VA 22314. 703/683-2722.

DIRECT MARKETING ASSOCIATION
1101 17th St. NW, Washington DC 20036. 202/347-1222.

INTERNATIONAL ADVERTISING ASSOCIATION
342 Madison Avenue, Suite 2000, New York NY 10173-0073. 212/557-1133.

INTERNATIONAL MARKETING INSTITUTE
314 Hammond Street, Chestnut Hill MA 02167. 617/552-8690.

LEAGUE OF ADVERTISING AGENCIES
2 South End Avenue #4C, New York NY 10280. 212/945-4991.

MARKETING RESEARCH ASSOCIATION
2189 Silas Deane Highway, Suite #5, Rocky Hill CT 06067. 203/257-4008.

PUBLIC RELATIONS SOCIETY OF AMERICA
33 Irving Place, New York NY 10003. 212/995-2230.

**TELEVISION BUREAU OF
ADVERTISING**
477 Madison Avenue, 10th Floor,
New York NY 10022-5892.
212/486-1111.

Directories

**AAAA ROSTER AND
ORGANIZATION**
American Association of
Advertising Agencies, 666 Third
Avenue, New York NY 10017.
212/682-2500.

**DIRECTORY OF MINORITY
PUBLIC RELATIONS
PROFESSIONALS**
Public Relations Society of
America, 33 Irving Place, New
York NY 10003. 212/995-2230.

**O'DWYER'S DIRECTORY OF
PUBLIC RELATIONS FIRMS**
J. R. O'Dwyer Co., 271 Madison
Avenue, New York NY 10016.
212/679-2471.

**PUBLIC RELATIONS
CONSULTANTS DIRECTORY**
American Business Directories,
Division of American Business
Lists, 5707 South 86th Circle,
Omaha NE 68127. 402/331-7169.

**PUBLIC RELATIONS
JOURNAL
REGISTER ISSUE**
Public Relations Society of
America, 33 Irving Place, New
York NY 10003. 212/995-2230.

**STANDARD DIRECTORY OF
ADVERTISING AGENCIES**

National Register Publishing
Company, 3004 Glenview Road,
Wilmette IL 60091. 708/256-6067.

Magazines

ADVERTISING AGE
Crain Communications, 740 North
Rush Street, Chicago IL 60611.
312/649-5316.

ADWEEK
49 E. 21st Street, New York NY
10010. 212/529-5500.

BUSINESS MARKETING
Crain Communications, 740 Rush
Street, Chicago IL 60611. 312/649-
5260.

JOURNAL OF MARKETING
American Marketing Association,
250 South Wacker Drive, Suite
200, Chicago IL 60606. 312/648-
0536.

THE MARKETING NEWS
American Marketing Association,
250 South Wacker Drive, Suite
200, Chicago IL 60606. 312/648-
0536.

PR REPORTER
PR Publishing Co., P.O. Box 600,
Exeter NH 03833. 603/778-0514.

**PUBLIC RELATIONS
JOURNAL**
Public Relations Society of
America, 33 Irving Place, New
York NY 10003. 212/995-2230.

PUBLIC RELATIONS NEWS
Phillips Publishing Inc., 7811
Montrose Road, Potomac MD
20854. 301/340-2100.

AEROSPACE

Most analysts believe that while the commercial aerospace industry will continue to be hurt by the recession, the industry is well-poised for solid growth in the long run. Throughout the decade, air traffic is expected to rise rapidly, increasing the demand for new planes. That's good news for jobseekers, especially those with training in aerospace engineering.

BRANSON AIRCRAFT

3790 Wheeling Street, Denver CO 80239. 303/371-9112. **Contact:** John Haworth, Vice President. **Description:** An aircraft design company specializing in performing custom structural modifications for business jets. **Common positions:** Aerospace Engineer; Mechanical Engineer; Structural Engineer. **Educational backgrounds sought:** Engineering. **Benefits:** medical insurance; dental insurance; pension plan; life insurance; tuition assistance; disability coverage; profit sharing; savings plan. **Operations at this facility:** Manufacturing; Research and Development; Administration; Sales.

MARTIN MARIETTA CORPORATION
ASTRONAUTICS GROUP

P.O. Box 179, MP-DC1311, Denver CO 80201. 303/977-1178. **Contact:** Jeff Ross, University Relations Administrator. **Description:** Aerospace and technology company engaged in the design, manufacture, and management of systems and products in the field of space, defense, electronics, communications, information management, energy, and materials.

SUNDSTRAND AEROSPACE

2480 West 70th Avenue, Denver CO 80221. 303/428-3636. **Contact:** Martin M. Pocs, Manager, Human Resources. **Description:** Manufactures a wide range of aircraft components, systems, and subsystems. A subsidiary of Sundstrand Corporation (Rockford, IL), a manufacturer of aircraft systems, auxiliary power systems, fuel systems, actuator mechanisms, refrigeration systems, and many other products. International facilities. **Corporate headquarters:** This location.

Additional large employers: 250+

AIRCRAFT

Stanley Aviation Corporation
2501 Dallas St, Aurora CO 80010-1009. 303/3646411. Employs: 250-499.

MISC. AIRCRAFT PARTS AND AUXILIARY EQUIPMENT

Sundstrand Aviation Operations
2480 W 70th Ave, Denver CO 80221-2501. 303/4283636. Employs: 250-499.

GUIDED MISSILES AND SPACE VEHICLES

Barrios Technology
1155 Kelly Johnson Blvd, Colorado Springs CO 80920-3932. 7195985588. Employs: 500-999.

Boeing Aerospace Co
2862 S Circle Dr, Colorado Springs
CO 80906-4116. 7195768801.
Employs: 500-999.

Flight Refueling Ltd
2501 Dallas St, Aurora CO 80010-
1009. 303/3403446. Employs: 500-
999.

Jsa Aerospace Inc
4895 Joliet St, Denver CO 80239-
2525. 303/3735232. Employs: 500-
999.

Martin Marietta Astronautics
12999 W Deer Creek, Littleton CO
80127-5146. 303/9773000.
Employs: 500-999.

Additional small to medium sized employers: 50-249

AIRCRAFT

Boeing Co
Buckley Air National Guard Afb,
Aurora CO 80011. 303/3642411.
Employs: 50-99.

Fischer Agency Inc
9213 United States Air Force
Academy, USAF Academy CO
80840. 719/4720634. Employs: 50-
99.

Soar Black Forest
24566 David C Johnson Loop,
Elbert CO 80106-9521.
303/6483623. Employs: 50-99.

Alesat Corporation
1490 Rock Glen Cir, Monument
CO 80132-9532. 719/4889413.
Employs: 50-99.

Anser
1670 Newport Rd N, Colorado
Springs CO 80916-2750.
719/5704660. Employs: 50-99.

Customaire Interior Inc
8501 Montview Blvd, Denver CO
80220-2142. 303/3985623.
Employs: 50-99.

S K W Corporation
985 Space Center Dr Ste 310,
Colorado Springs CO 80915-3632.
719/5962325. Employs: 50-99.

Space Applications Corp
2900 Center Green Ct S, Boulder
CO 80301-5418. 303/4403544.
Employs: 50-99.

MISC. AIRCRAFT PARTS AND AUXILIARY EQUIPMENT

Sweeney Company
359 Inverness Dr S, Englewood CO
80112-5816. 303/7925240.
Employs: 50-99.

GUIDED MISSILES AND SPACE VEHICLES

Applied Technology Association Inc
1330 Inverness Dr Ste 335,
Colorado Springs CO 80910-3754.
719/5741976. Employs: 50-99.

Xon Tech Inc
1915 Aerotech Dr Ste 124,
Colorado Springs CO 80916-4222.
719/5962836. Employs: 50-99.

For more information on career opportunities in aerospace:

Associations

AIR TRANSPORT ASSOCIATION OF AMERICA
1301 Pennsylvania Avenue NW, Suite 1100, Washington DC 20004. 202/626-4000.

AMERICAN INSTITUTE OF AERONAUTICS AND ASTRONAUTICS
555 West 57th Street, New York NY 10019. 212/247-6500.

AVIATION MAINTENANCE FOUNDATION
P.O. Box 2826, Redmond WA 98073. 206/828-3917.

FUTURE AVIATION PROFESSIONALS OF AMERICA
4959 Massachusetts Boulevard, Atlanta GA 30337. 404/997-8097.

NATIONAL AERONAUTIC ASSOCIATION OF USA
1815 North Fort Meyer Drive, Suite 700, Arlington VA 22209. 703/527-0226.

PROFESSIONAL AVIATION MAINTENANCE ASSOCIATION
500 NW Plaza, Suite 809, St. Ann MO 63074. 314/739-2580.

AMUSEMENT, ARTS, AND RECREATION

During the past few years, the entertainment industry has been hit by a wave of major buy outs. For jobseekers, the competition is as fierce as in any other industry. The jobs are there but tough to get. Right now, the music industry is in a stronger position than the film industry.

CLOVERLEAF KENNEL CLUB
P.O. Box 88, Loveland CO 80539. 303/667-6211. **Contact:** Barbara Moore, Administrative Assistant. **Description:** Operates a dog racing and training facility, with associated pari-mutuel wagering operations. **Common positions:** Mutuel Teller. **Corporate headquarters:** This location. **Operations at this facility:** sales.

COPPER MOUNTAIN INC.
P.O. Box 3001, Copper Mountain CO 80443. 303/968-2882. **Contact:** Linda Willman, Human Resources. **Description:** Several area locations, including Dillon, Leadville, and Frisco. Operates a resort facility, with ski facilities in the winter, and a wide range of summer resort activities. **Corporate headquarters:** This location.

FIRST FILMS INC.
1380 Lawrence Street, Suite 1400, Denver CO 80204. 303/592-1715. **Contact:** Doug Olson, Hiring. **Description:** A motion picture production company.

VAIL ASSOCIATES INC.
P.O. Box 7, Vail CO 81658. 303/476-5601, ext. 3300. **Contact:** Personnel Department. **Description:** Owners and operators of Vail and Beaver Creek ski resorts. **Common positions:** Accountant; Computer Programmer; Hotel Manager/Assistant Manager; Front Line/Guest Service Positions (Food Service, Lift Operators, Ticket Sales, etc.). **Educational backgrounds sought:** Accounting; Business Administration; Computer Science; Finance. **Special programs:** Training programs and internships. **Benefits:** medical and life insurance; disability coverage; daycare; profit sharing; employee discounts; employee housing; free season ski pass; meal discounts. **Corporate headquarters:** This location. **Operations at this facility:** administration; service; sales.

Additional large employers: 250+

MOTION PICTURE AND VIDEO TAPE PRODUCTION

Office Of Cable Communications
300 La Porte Ave, Fort Collins CO 80521-2719. 303/2216510. Employs: 500-999.

THEATRICAL PRODUCERS (EXCEPT MOTION PICTURES) AND MISC. THEATRICAL SERVICES

Colorado Renaissance Festival
650 W Perry Park Rd, Larkspur CO 80118-8201. 303/6812500. Employs: 500-999.

RACING, INCLUDING TRACK OPERATION

Interstate Racing Association Inc
6200 Dahlia St, Commerce City CO 80022-3130. 303/2881591. Employs: 250-499.

Rocky Mountain Greyhound Park
3701 N Nevada Av, Colorado Springs CO 80907-5336. 7196321391. Employs: 500-999.

AMUSEMENT PARKS

Elitch Gardens Company
4620 W 38th Ave, Denver CO 80212-2001. 303/4554771. Employs: 500-999.

Additional small to medium sized employers: 50-249

MOTION PICTURES

Colorado Wildlife
6060 Broadway, Denver CO 80216-1029. 303/2971192. Employs: 100-249.

THEATRICAL PRODUCERS (EXCEPT MOTION PICTURES) AND MISCELLANEOUS THEATRICAL SERVICES

Country Dinner Playhouse
6875 S Clinton St, Englewood CO 80112-3625. 303/7991410. Employs: 100-249.

Denver Center Theatre Company
1050 13th St, Denver CO 80204-2157. 303/8934200. Employs: 50-99.

BOWLING CENTERS

Celebrity Sports Center
888 S Colorado Blvd, Denver CO
80222-2014.   303/7573321.
Employs: 50-99.

RACING, INCLUDING TRACK OPERATION

Cloverleaf Kennel Club
P O Box 88, Loveland CO 80539-
0088. 303/6676211. Employs: 100-
249.

PHYSICAL   FITNESS FACILITIES

Ballys US Swim & Fitness
2928 Straus Ln, Ste 210, Colorado
Springs   CO   80907-8805.
719/5931559. Employs: 50-99.

Denver Athletic Club
1325 Glenarm Pl, Denver CO
80204-2114.   303/5341211.
Employs: 100-249.

Denver Country Club
1700 E 1st Ave, Denver CO 80218-
4039. 303/7332441. Employs: 100-
249.

Point Athletic Club
2203 S Eldridge St, Lakewood CO
80228-4853.   303/9881300.
Employs: 50-99.

Ranch Country Club Inc
11887 Tejon St, Denver CO 80234-
2408. 303/4609700. Employs: 50-
99.

Sunset Beach Fitness & Racquet
2650 Alkire St, Golden CO 80401-
1621. 303/2792589. Employs: 50-
99.

The Point Athletic Club
2210 Academy Pl, # A168,
Colorado Springs CO 80909-1602.
719/5977775. Employs: 50-99.

Fort Collins Pulse
2555 S Shields St, Fort Collins CO
80526-1823.   303/4901300.
Employs: 50-99.

PUBLIC GOLF COURSES

Arrowhead Golf Club
10850 Sundown Trail, Littleton CO
80125-9213.   303/9739614.
Employs: 50-99.

AMUSEMENT PARKS

Lakeside Amusement Park
4601 Sheridan Blvd, Denver CO
80212-7406.   303/4771621.
Employs: 100-249.

MEMBERSHIP SPORTS AND RECREATION CLUBS

Broadmoor Golf Club
1 Lake Cir, Colorado Springs CO
80906-4254.   719/5775790.
Employs: 50-99.

Cherry Hills Country Club
4125   S   University   Blvd,
Englewood   CO   80110-4904.
303/7619900. Employs: 50-99.

Lakewood Country Club
6800 W 10th Ave, Lakewood CO
80215-5263.   303/2334614.
Employs: 100-249.

Mount Vernon Country Club
24933 Clubhouse Cir, Golden CO
80401-9615.   303/5260616.
Employs: 50-99.

Pinehurst Country Club
6255 W Quincy Ave, Denver CO
80235-3010.   303/9851551.
Employs: 100-249.

Pinery Country Club
6900 S Pinery Pky, Parker CO
80134-5427.   303/8412060.
Employs: 50-99.

Racquet World
374 Inverness Dr S, Englewood CO
80112-5810.   303/7907777.
Employs: 100-249.

MISC. AMUSEMENT AND RECREATION SERVICES

North Jeffco Metro Recreation
9101 Ralston Rd, Arvada CO
80002-2206.   303/4247733.
Employs: 100-249.

Northridge Recreation Center
8801 S Broadway, Littleton CO
80126-2301.   303/7912500.
Employs: 50-99.

Suburban Metro Recreation Park
6315 S University Blvd, Littleton
CO 80121-2914.   303/7982493.
Employs: 50-99.

Vail Ski Broadmoor
1 Lake Cir, Colorado Springs CO
80906-4254.   719/6353200.
Employs: 100-249.

Wheat Ridge City Government
4355 Field, Wheat Ridge CO
80033. 303/4210700. Employs:
100-249.

MUSEUMS AND ART GALLERIES

Denver Art Museum
100 W 14th Ave, Denver CO
80204-2713.   303/5752793.
Employs: 50-99.

Denver Museum Of Natural History
2001 Colorado Blvd, Denver CO
80205-5732.   303/3227009.
Employs: 100-249.

ARBORETA AND BOTANICAL OR ZOOLOGICAL GARDENS

Denver Botanic Gardens Inc
909 York St, Denver CO 80206-
3751. 303/3314000. Employs: 50-
99.

For more information on career opportunities in amusement, arts, and recreation:

Associations

ACTOR'S EQUITY ASSOCIATION
165 West 47th Street, New York
NY 10036. 212/869-8530.

AFFILIATE ARTISTS
37 West 65th Street, 6th Floor,
New York NY 10023. 212/580-
2000.

AMERICAN ALLIANCE FOR THEATRE AND EDUCATION
Division of Performing Arts,
Virginia Tech, Blacksburg VA
24061-0141. 703/231-5335.

AMERICAN ASSOCIATION OF MUSEUMS
1225 I Street NW, Washington DC
20005. 202/289-1818.

AMERICAN ASSOCIATION OF ZOOLOGICAL PARKS & AQUARIUMS
Oglebay Park, Wheeling WV
26003. 304/242-2160.

AMERICAN COUNCIL FOR THE ARTS
1 E. 53rd Street, New York NY
10022. 212/245-4510.

AMERICAN CRAFTS COUNCIL
72 Spring Street, New York NY 10012. 212/274-0630.

AMERICAN DANCE GUILD
33 West 21st Street, New York NY 10010. 212/627-3790.

AMERICAN FEDERATION OF MUSICIANS
1501 Broadway, Suite 600, New York NY 10036. 212/869-1330.

AMERICAN FEDERATION OF TELEVISION AND RADIO ARTISTS
260 Madison Avenue, New York NY 10016. 212/532-0800.

AMERICAN FILM INSTITUTE
John F. Kennedy Center for the Performing Arts, Washington DC 20566. 202/828-4000.

AMERICAN GUILD OF MUSICAL ARTISTS
1727 Broadway, New York NY 10019-5284. 212/265-3687.

AMERICAN MUSIC CENTER
30 West 26th Street, Suite 1001, New York NY 10010. 212/366-5260.

AMERICAN SOCIETY OF COMPOSERS, AUTHORS, AND PUBLISHERS
1 Lincoln Plaza, New York NY 10023. 212/595-3050.

AMERICAN SYMPHONY ORCHESTRA LEAGUE
777 14th Street NW, Suite 500, Washington DC 20005. 202/628-0099.

ASSOCIATION OF INDEPENDENT VIDEO AND FILMMAKERS
625 Broadway, 9th Floor, New York NY 10012. 212/473-3400.

BUSINESS COMMITTEE FOR THE ARTS
1775 Broadway, Suite 510, New York NY 10019-1942. 212/664-0600.

DANCE THEATER WORKSHOP
219 West 19th Street, New York NY 10011. 212/691-6500.

DANCE USA
777 14th Street NW, Suite 540, Washington DC 20005. 202/628-0144.

INTERNATIONAL SOCIETY OF PERFORMING ARTS ADMINISTRATORS
6065 Pickerel, Rockford MI 49341. 616/874-6200.

NATIONAL ARTISTS' EQUITY ASSOCIATION
P.O. Box 28068, Central Station, Washington DC 20038-8068. 202/628-9633.

NATIONAL DANCE ASSOCIATION
1900 Association Drive, Reston VA 22091. 703/476-3436.

NATIONAL ENDOWMENT FOR THE ARTS
1100 Pennsylvania Avenue NW, Washington DC 20506. 202/682-5400.

NATIONAL FOUNDATION FOR ADVANCEMENT IN THE ARTS
3915 Biscayne Boulevard, Miami FL 33137. 305/573-0490.

NATIONAL ORGANIZATION FOR HUMAN SERVICE EDUCATION
Fitchburg State College, 160 Pearl Street, Fitchburg MA 01420. 508/345-2151.

**NATIONAL RECREATION
AND PARK ASSOCIATION**
2775 S. Quincy Street, Suite 300,
Arlington VA 22206. 703/820-
4940.

**PROFESSIONAL ARTS
MANAGEMENT INSTITUTE**
408 West 57th Street, New York
NY 10019. 212/245-3850.

**PRODUCERS GUILD OF
AMERICA**
400 S. Beverly Drive, Suite 211,
Beverly Hills CA 90212. 310/557-
0807.

SCREEN ACTORS GUILD
7065 Hollywood Boulevard,
Hollywood CA 90028. 213/465-
4600.

**SOCIETY OF MOTION
PICTURE AND TELEVISION
ENGINEERS**
595 West Hartsdale Avenue, White
Plains NY 10607. 914/761-1100.

**THEATRE
COMMUNICATIONS GROUP**
355 Lexington Avenue, New York
NY 10017. 212/697-5230.

WOMEN'S CAUCUS FOR ART
Moore College of Art, 20th & The
Parkway, Philadelphia PA 19103.
215/854-0922.

Directories

**THE ACADEMY PLAYERS
DIRECTORIES**
The Academy of Motion Picture
Arts and Sciences, 8949 Wilshire
Boulevard, Beverly Hills CA
90211. 310/247-3000.

ARTIST'S MARKET
Writer's Digest Books, 1507 Dana
Avenue, Cincinnati OH 45207.
513/531-2222.

CREATIVE BLACK BOOK
115 5th Avenue, New York NY
10003. 212/254-1330.

PLAYERS GUIDE
165 West 46th Street, New York
NY 10036. 212/869-3570.

ROSS REPORTS TELEVISION
Television Index, Inc., 40-29 27th
Street, Long Island City NY 11101.
718/937-3990.

Magazines

AMERICAN ARTIST
One Astor Place, New York NY
10036. 212/764-7300.

**AMERICAN
CINEMATOGRAPHER**
American Society of
Cinematographers, 1782 North
Orange Drive, Los Angeles CA
90028. 213/876-7107.

ART BUSINESS NEWS
Myers Publishing Co., 777
Summer Street, Stamford CT
06901. 203/356-1745.

ART DIRECTION
10 East 39th Street, 6th Floor, New
York NY 10016. 212/889-6500.

ARTFORUM
65 Bleecker Street, New York NY
10012. 212/475-4000.

ARTWEEK
12 S. First Street, Suite 520, San
Jose CA 95113. 408/279-2293.

AVISO
American Association of
Museums, 1225 I Street NW,
Washington DC 20005. 202/289-
1818.

BACK STAGE
330 West 42nd Street, New York
NY 10036. 212/947-0020.

BILLBOARD
Billboard Publications, Inc., 1515
Broadway, New York NY 10036.
212/764-7300.

CASHBOX
157 West 57th Street, Suite 503,
New York NY 10019. 212/586-
2640.

CRAFTS REPORT
700 Orange Street, Wilmington DE
19801. 302/656-2209.

DRAMA-LOGUE
P.O. Box 38771, Los Angeles CA
90038. 213/464-5079.

HOLLYWOOD REPORTER
6715 Sunset Boulevard, Hollywood
CA 90028. 213/464-7411.

VARIETY
475 Park Avenue South, New York
NY 10016. 212/779-1100.

WOMEN ARTIST NEWS
300 Riverside Drive, New York
NY 10025. 212/666-6990.

APPAREL AND TEXTILES

After employment gains for four straight years in the late 80's, layoffs hit the apparel industry hard as the 90's opened. The worst now appears to be over and employment should rise. New jobs will not consist of old-style production line work; automation has changed the industry's make-up, and those with technical and computer backgrounds have a distinct advantage.

AD STORE COMPANY INCORPORATED
210 St. Paul Street, Denver CO 80206. 303/321-0404. **Contact:** Personnel Department. **Description:** A Denver women's retail apparel store.

GOLD BUG INC.
4999 Oakland, Denver CO 80239. 303/371-2535. **Contact:** Personnel. **Description:** A manufacturer of clothing for infants.

KARMAN, INC.
1513 Wazee Street, Denver CO 80202. 303/893-2320. **Contact:** Personnel Department. **Description:** An apparel manufacturer. **Corporate headquarters:** This location.

MILLER INTERNATIONAL, INC.
8500 Zuni Street, Federal Heights CO 80221. 303/428-5696. **Contact:** Frank Howe, Recruiting Manager. **Description:** Produces a wide range of women's and men's clothing and accessories. **Corporate headquarters:** This location. **Common positions:** Administrator; Advertising Worker; Blue-Collar Worker

Supervisor; Buyer; Credit Manager; Customer Service Representative; Instructor/Training/Teacher; Management Trainee; Operations/Production Manager; Marketing Specialist; Personnel and Labor Relations Specialist; Public Relations Specialist; Sales Representative. **Educational backgrounds sought:** Art/Design; Business Administration; Computer Science; Marketing. **Special programs:** Training programs and internships. **Benefits:** medical and life insurance; pension plan; tuition assistance; disability coverage; daycare assistance; profit sharing; employee discounts; stock options. **Operations at this facility:** research/development; administration; service; sales. **Revenues (1991):** $105 million. **Employees:** 900.

OCEAN PACIFIC/OP CHILDREN'S WEAR
4600 East 48th Avenue, Denver CO 80216. 303/399-2100. **Contact:** Donna Woodside, Personnel Director. **Description:** A distributor of Ocean Pacific children's wear.

WESCO FABRICS INC.
4001 Forest Street, Denver CO 80216. 303/388-4101. **Contact:** Richard Gentry, Chairman. **Description:** A wholesaler of drapery fabrics and a distributor of window coverings and bedspreads on a wholesale trade basis. Also manufactures bedspreads. Products are distributed nationally. **Corporate headquarters:** This location.

WESTERN ART MANUFACTURING COMPANY INC.
38 East Fifth Avenue, Denver CO 80203. 303/744-3627. **Contact:** Personnel. **Description:** Manufactures and distributes a wide range of apparel products, including men's and boys' shirts and sleepwear; girls' dresses and blouses; and men's neckwear. **Corporate headquarters:** This location.

WOOLRICH INC.
DOWN PRODUCTS DIVISION
P.O. Box 386, Broomfield CO 80038-0386. 303/469-3391. **Contact:** Personnel. **Description:** Produces and distributes a variety of down-insulated and synthetic fiber-insulated outerwear products, including coats, vests, hats, and other products. Nationally, company produces a broad range of natural and synthetic fabrics, and apparel products. **Corporate headquarters:** Woolrich, PA.

Additional large employers: 250+

MISC. WOMEN'S, MISSES', AND JUNIORS' OUTERWEAR

Temtex Corporation
1513 Wazee St, Denver CO 80202-1311. 303/8932325. Employs: 250-499.

HATS, CAPS, AND MILLINERY

Imperial Headwear
5200 E Evans Ave, Denver CO 80222-5222. 303/7571166. Employs: 250-499.

LUGGAGE

Samsonite Corp
11200 E 45th Ave, Denver CO 80239-3018. 303/3732000. Employs: 1,000+.

Additional small to medium sized employers: 50-249

MISC. FINISHERS OF TEXTILES

South Platte Tex-Style Corp
2690 W Barberry Pl, Denver CO 80204-3718. 303/5348422. Employs: 50-99.

CARPETS AND RUGS

Allegro Rug Weaving Company
7077 Winchester Cir, Boulder CO 80301-3505. 303/5819877. Employs: 50-99.

Mat Factory
237 Main St, Longmont CO 80501-5914. 303/6787848. Employs: 50-99.

MEN'S AND BOYS' SUITS, COATS, AND OVERCOATS

Bayly Corporation
5500 S Valentia Way, Englewood CO 80111-3105. 303/7733850. Employs: 100-249.

MEN'S AND BOYS' WORK CLOTHING

Valiant Products Corp
2727 W 5th Ave, Denver CO 80204-4804. 303/8921234. Employs: 50-99.

MISC. MEN'S AND BOY'S CLOTHING

Ferrell Reed Ltd
5571 Arapahoe, Boulder CO 80303. 303/4496610. Employs: 50-99.

Zohn Mfg Co -Gross Division
3950 Grape, Denver CO 80207-1144. 303/3216544. Employs: 100-249.

PLEATING, DECORATIVE, AND NOVELTY STITCHING, AND TUCKING FOR THE TRADE

Athalon Products Ltd
3333 E 52nd Ave, Denver CO 80216-2322. 303/2920400. Employs: 100-249.

AUTOMOTIVE TRIMMINGS, APPAREL FINDINGS, AND RELATED PRODUCTS

Good Decal
4650 S Garden St, Englewood CO 80110-5548. 303/7619217. Employs: 50-99.

Ocean Pacific Images
1990 S Broadway, Denver CO 80210-4005. 303/7781885. Employs: 50-99.

WOMEN'S FOOTWEAR, EXCEPT ATHLETIC

Rockmount Ranch Wear Mfg Co
1626 Wazee St, Denver CO 80202-1314. 303/6297777. Employs: 100-249.

MISC. LEATHER GOODS

Amar Inc
3305 N Cascade Ave, Colorado Springs CO 80907-5207. 719/6331266. Employs: 50-99.

Hunter Co
3300 W 71st, Westminster CO 80030. 303/4274626. Employs: 50-99.

For more information on career opportunities in the apparel and textile industries:

Associations

AFFILIATED DRESS MANUFACTURERS
1440 Broadway, New York NY 10018. 212/398-9797.

AMERICAN APPAREL MANUFACTURERS ASSOCIATION
2500 Wilson Boulevard, Suite 301, Arlington VA 22201. 703/524-1864.

AMERICAN CLOAK AND SUIT MANUFACTURERS ASSOCIATION
450 Seventh Avenue, New York NY 10123. 212/244-7300.

AMERICAN TEXTILE MANUFACTURERS INSTITUTE
1801 K Street NW, Suite 900, Washington DC 20006. 202/862-0500.

CLOTHING MANUFACTURERS ASSOCIATION OF THE USA
1290 Avenue of the Americas, New York NY 10104. 212/757-6664.

COUNCIL OF FASHION DESIGNERS OF AMERICA
1412 Broadway, Suite 1714, New York NY 10018. 212/302-1821.

THE FASHION GROUP
9 Rockefeller Plaza, Suite 1722, New York NY 10020. 212/247-3940.

INTERNATIONAL ASSOCIATION OF CLOTHING DESIGNERS
240 Madison Avenue, New York NY 10016. 212/685-6602.

MEN'S FASHION ASSOCIATION OF AMERICA
240 Madison Avenue, New York NY 10016. 212/683-5665.

NORTHERN TEXTILE ASSOCIATION
230 Congress Street, Boston MA 02110. 617/542-8220.

TEXTILE RESEARCH INSTITUTE
Box 625, Princeton NJ 08540. 609/924-3150.

Directories

AAMA DIRECTORY
American Apparel Manufacturers Association, 2500 Wilson Boulevard, Suite 301, Arlington VA 22201. 703/524-1864.

APPAREL TRADES BOOK
Dun & Bradstreet Inc., 1 Diamond Hill Road, Murray Hill NJ 07974. 908/665-5000.

FAIRCHILD'S MARKET DIRECTORY OF WOMEN'S AND CHILDREN'S APPAREL
Fairchild Publications, 7 West 34th Street, New York NY 10001. 212/630-4000.

Magazines

AMERICA'S TEXTILES
Billiam Publishing, 211 Century Drive, Suite 208-A, Greenville SC 29607. 803/242-5300.

APPAREL INDUSTRY MAGAZINE
Shore Communications Inc., 180 Allen Road NE, Suite 300-N, Atlanta GA 30328-4893. 404/252-8831.

BOBBIN
Bobbin Publications, P.O. Box 1986, 1110 Shop Road, Columbia SC 29202. 803/771-7500.

ACCESSORIES
Business Journals, 50 Day Street, P.O. Box 5550, Norwalk CT 06856. 203/853-6015.

WOMEN'S WEAR DAILY (WWD)
Fairchild Publications, 7 West 34th Street, New York NY 10001. 212/630-4000.

ARCHITECTURE, CONSTRUCTION, AND REAL ESTATE

In the construction industry, home building is expected to stabilize, but commercial real estate construction -- especially office buildings and hotels -- will continue to decline. Home improvement, hospitals, schools, water supply buildings, and public service buildings construction should offer the best opportunities.

BOB ANDERSON EXCAVATING & WRECKING
1930 East 40th Avenue, Denver CO 80205. 303/377-7115. **Contact:** Personnel Department. **Description:** An area wrecking and excavation firm.

ARAPAHOE ENTERPRISES, INC.
1750 South Holly Street, Denver CO 80222. 303/757-8008. **Contact:** Personnel Department. **Description:** A real estate development firm.

ARVADA HARDWOOD FLOOR COMPANY
11095 East 45th Avenue, Denver CO 80239. 303/373-0350. **Contact:** Personnel. **Description:** Engages in the installation and refinishing of hardwood. Also, installs carpet, vinyl, and ceramic tile, and related floor coverings. **Primary customers:** new home builders. **Common positions:** clerical; installers. **Special programs:** Training programs. **Employees:** 150. **Projected hires for the next 12 months:** 50.

BACON & SCHRAMM INCORPORATED
4020 Brighton Boulevard, Denver CO 80216. 303/295-2938. **Contact:** Personnel Department. **Description:** A Denver-area roofing contractor.

BEAUMONT PROPERTIES INCORPORATED
7700 East Iliff Avenue, Suite C, Denver CO 80231. 303/696-8806. **Contact:** Personnel Department. **Description:** Involved in real estate development.

BELL PLUMBING AND HEATING COMPANY
4201 East Evans, Denver CO 80222. 303/757-5661. **Contact:** Personnel. **Description:** A plumbing and heating contracting company.

BERNSTEIN REAL ESTATE DEVELOPERS
2170 South Parker Road, Suite 115, Denver CO 80231. 303/755-2546. **Contact:** Personnel Department. **Description:** Real estate developer.

BETAWEST, INC.
1999 Broadway, Suite 2000, Denver CO 80202. **Contact:** Human Resources Department. **Description:** Engages in real estate-asset management. **Common positions:** Accountant; Attorney; Financial Analyst; Property Manager. **Educational backgrounds sought:** Accounting; Business Administration; Finance; Real Estate. **Benefits:** medical, dental, and life insurance; disability coverage; savings plan. **Corporate headquarters:** This location. **Other U.S. locations:** Omaha, Honolulu, Phoenix, San Francisco, Albuquerque. **Operations at this facility:** Administration. **Employees:** 185.

BITUMINOUS ROADWAYS OF COLORADO
3609 South Wadsworth Boulevard, Suite 300, Lakewood CO 80235. 303/980-8300. **Contact:** Bill Lauer, Executive Vice President. **Description:** An asphalt road-paving company.

BOPA PARTNERSHIP
LOOP DEVELOPMENT CO.
10065 East Harvard Avenue, Suite 900, Denver CO 80231. 303/745-7000. **Contact:** Personnel Department. **Description:** Real estate investment firm.

BRANNAN SAND AND GRAVEL COMPANY
P.O. Box 16006, Denver CO 80216. 303/534-1231. **Contact:** Curt Marvel, Office Manager. **Description:** Produces asphalt products for construction; as well as other rock products. **Corporate headquarters:** This location.

CARDER CONCRETE PRODUCTS COMPANY
8311 West Carder Court, Littleton CO 80125. 303/791-1600. **Contact:** Mr. Tom Walters. **Description:** Produces concrete products, including culverts, storm and drainage pipes; box culverts; and roof tiles. Regional headquarters. **Operations at this facility:** manufacturing; administration; sales. **Corporate headquarters:** Los Angeles, CA. **Common positions:** Accountant; Administrator; Blue-Collar Worker Supervisor; Computer Programmer; Civil Engineer; Credit Manager; Mechanical Engineer; Department Manager; General Manager; Operations/Production Manager; Quality Control Supervisor; Sales Representative. **Educational backgrounds sought:** Accounting; Business Administration; Computer Science; Engineering; Marketing. **Benefits:** medical insurance; dental insurance; life insurance; tuition assistance; disability coverage; profit sharing; employee discounts.

CENTER RENTAL & SALES INCORPORATED
481 West 84th Avenue, Denver CO 80221. 303/428-7466. **Contact:** Personnel Department. **Description:** A general construction equipment rental company.

CHERRY CREEK REALTORS

7995 East Hampden Avenue, Suite 100, Denver CO 80231. 303/337-6446. **Contact:** Mike Hughes, Branch Manager. **Description:** A real estate company. Over 430 agents in five area offices. **Common positions:** Real Estate Sales-Experienced Agents. **Corporate headquarters:** Denver, CO. **Operations at this facility:** sales.

COLORADO CLARKLIFT, INC.

4105 Globeville Road, Denver CO 80216. 303/292-5438. **Contact:** Personnel Department. **Description:** A forklift rental and leasing operation.

CRAFTSMEN CONSTRUCTION COMPANY

1114 West 7th Avenue, Denver CO 80204. 303/770-4600. **Contact:** Carl Pearson, Vice President. **Description:** A Denver-area construction firm.

DONGARY INVESTMENTS LIMITED

P.O. Box 7240, Denver CO 80207. 303/320-3960. **Contact:** Personnel Department. **Description:** A Denver-based, nonresidential building operator.

FLANAGAN READY MIX

363 West Evans, Denver CO 80223. 303/777-3058. **Contact:** Connie Walborn, Personnel. **Description:** A privately owned construction products firm, primarily producing ready-mix concrete and other aggregate products. **Corporate headquarters:** This location.

THE GENESEE COMPANY

534 Commons Drive, Golden CO 80401. 303/526-0643. **Contact:** Nancy Sullivan, Director of Administration. **Description:** A Denver-area home builder and land development company. Also involved in commercial sales, leasing, and property management. **Benefits:** medical and dental insurance; profit sharing; 401K. **Corporate headquarters:** This location.

GREEN HOLDINGS, INC.

8055 East Tufts Avenue, Suite 700, Denver CO 80237. 303/779-5360. **Contact:** Debbie Leadbitter, Administrative Assistant. **Description:** A construction firm working on buildings, highways, bridges, dams, and heavy construction; also involved in mining. Established in 1929. **Classifications:** construction (primary), mining. **Employees:** 1,500 in the U.S., 1,650 worldwide.

HOME FREE VILLAGE RESORTS

1400 S. Colorado Boulevard., Suite 410, Denver CO 80222. 303/757-3002. **Contact:** Personnel. **Description:** A Denver real estate management company engaged in the operation of mobile home communities.

INTERMOUNTAIN ELECTRIC, INC.

602 South Lipan, Denver CO 80223. 303/733-7248. **Contact:** Personnel Department. **Description:** A company involved in the construction of electric utilities.

JORDON PERLMUTTER & COMPANY
1601 Blake, Suite 600, P.O. Box 5858, Denver CO 80217. 303/595-9919. **Contact:** Jack Hachen, Office Manager. **Description:** A commercial development company.

GLENN KAISER, INCORPORATED
1301 South Pierce, Lakewood CO 80232. 303/989-1670. **Contact:** Personnel Department. **Description:** Involved in landscaping and irrigation; also a contractor and provider of maintenance.

KALMAN FLOOR COMPANY
1202 State Highway 74, Suite 110, Evergreen CO 80439. 303/674-2290. **Contact:** Scott Vogler, Personnel Manager. **Description:** An installer of industrial concrete flooring.

GERALD F. KESSLER & ASSOC. INC.
5840 E. Evans Street, Suite 206, Denver CO 80222. 303/756-1536. **Contact:** Personnel Department. **Description:** A Denver-based landscape architect, project planner/ consultant, and a land and site designer doing business in the Rocky Mountain region and various other states. **Common positions:** Draftsperson and Civil Engineer. **Educational backgrounds sought:** Engineering and Architect/Landscape Architect. **Benefits:** partial medical, dental, and life insurance.

KIEWIT WESTERN COMPANY
7926 S. Platte Canyon Road, Littleton CO 80123. 303/979-9330. **Contact:** Del Grau, District Business Manager. **Description:** A Denver-area general contracting company. **Common positions:** Draftsperson; Construction Engineer. **Educational backgrounds sought:** Business Administration; Engineering. **Special programs:** Training programs. **Benefits:** medical, dental, and life insurance; tuition assistance; disability coverage; profit sharing; savings plan; stock options. **Corporate headquarters:** Omaha, Nebraska. **Parent company:** Peter Kiewit Sons' Inc. **Revenues (1991):** $75 million +. **Employees:** 115. **Projected hires for the next 12 months:** 5-10.

LINTON AND COMPANY INCORPORATED
6444 E Hampden Avenue, Denver CO 80222. 303/758-4412. **Contact:** Personnel Department. **Description:** Company provides sales and rental acquisitions.

MOBILE HOME COMMUNITIES
116 Inverness Drive, East, Suite 203, Englewood CO 80112. 303/792-2166. **Contact:** Wendy Chamberlain, Administration. **Description:** A real estate development company specializing in mobile home parks.

NATKIN GROUP
2700 South Zuni Street, Englewood CO 80110. 303/761-6603. **Contact:** Personnel Director. **Description:** A plumbing and heating contractor. **Corporate headquarters:** This location.

NYCO INCORPORATED

2880 S. Raritan, Englewood CO 80110. 303/783-0111. **Contact:** Tim Anderson, Owner. **Description:** A wholesaler of construction materials.

OWENS-CORNING FIBERGLAS CORPORATION

5201 Fox Street, Denver CO 80216. 303/295-1651. **Contact:** John Fuller, Office Manager. **Description:** Produces asphalt for use in roofing construction. Company is the world's leading manufacturer of glass fiber products, sold under the trade name `Fiberglas'. Also has manufacturing operations with related materials: wood fiberboard, urethane, calcium silicate, asphalt, and polyester resins. **Corporate headquarters:** Toledo, OH. **Listed on:** New York Stock Exchange.

GERALD H. PHIPPS, INC.

P.O. Box 4387, Denver CO 80204. 303/571-5377. **Contact:** Bruce Ferguson, President, or John Hendricks, Project Manager. **Description:** General construction contractors.

ROC PROPERTIES

6430 S. Quebec, Englewood CO 80111. 303/741-3707. **Contact:** Personnel. **Description:** Real estate management firm specializing in mobile home parks.

ROBINSON BRICK & TILE COMPANY

1845 W. Dartmouth, Denver CO 80217. 303/781-9002, ext. 217. **Contact:** Becky Gutierrez, Human Resources Manager. **Description:** Produces and markets a variety of brick and tile materials, including paving brick and clay brick. **Corporate headquarters:** This location. **Common positions:** Customer Service Representative; Ceramics and Mining Engineers; Sales Representative. **Educational backgrounds sought:** Engineering; Geology. **Special programs:** Training programs. **Operations at this facility:** manufacturing; research/development; administration; service; sales.

ROCKY MOUNTAIN PRESTRESS INC.

P.O. Box 21500, Denver CO 80221. 303/480-1111. **Contact:** Director of Employment Services, Personnel Department. **Description:** Manufactures and sells pre-stressed structural concrete building materials, primarily used in heavy construction projects. **Corporate headquarters:** This location. **Common positions:** Architect; Draftsperson; Engineer; Industrial Engineer; Mechanical Engineer; Quality Control Supervisor. **Educational backgrounds sought:** Business Administration; Engineering; Mathematics. **Benefits:** medical insurance; dental insurance; pension plan; life insurance; tuition assistance; disability coverage.

ROSENBERG INVESTMENT COMPANY

3400 East Bayaud Avenue, Suite 200, Denver CO 80209. 303/320-6067. **Contact:** Larry Rosenberg, President. **Description:** Investment company involved in operating apartment buildings.

STRESSCON CORPORATION

P.O. Box 15129, Colorado Springs CO 80935. 719/390-5041. **Contact:** Donald R. Logan, President. Two area locations. **Description:** Manufactures and distributes precast structural concrete, architectural concrete, and concrete used in other large-scale construction projects.

TRANSIT MIX CONCRETE

P.O. Box 1030, Colorado Springs CO 80901. **Contact:** Office Manager. **Description:** Produces a variety of construction and building products, including ready-mix concrete, sand, and gravel; and fabricated structural metal.

UNITED DRYWALL & PAINTING INCORPORATED

5300 North Broadway, Denver CO 80216. 303/295-0181. **Contact:** Doug Williams, Owner. **Description:** A dry wall and painting contractor.

VAN SCHAACK & COMPANY

4600 South Ulster Street, Suite 400, Denver CO 80237. 303/779-6000. **Contact:** Personnel Director. **Description:** A real estate sales company.

WESTERN MOBILE

P.O. Drawer 368, Glenwood Springs CO 81602. 303/945-8672. **Contact:** Office Secretary. **Description:** Nine area locations, including Avon, Steamboat, Glenwood Springs, and Aspen. Produces ready-mix concrete, with locations across the western slope of Colorado.

WESTERN MOBILE, INC.

1400 West 64th Avenue, Denver CO 80221. 303/426-1166. **Contact:** Human Resources. **Description:** Material supplier of ready-mix concrete aggregates and admixtures. General contractor for heavy construction industry. **Common positions:** Accountant; Blue-Collar Worker Supervisor; Chemist; Computer Programmer; Credit Manager; Customer Service Representative; Financial Analyst; Department Manager; General Manager; Management Trainee; Operations/Production Manager; Personnel and Labor Relations Specialist; Sales Representative; Systems Analyst. **Educational backgrounds sought:** Accounting; Business Administration; Computer Science; Engineering; Finance; Marketing. **Benefits:** medical, dental, and life insurance; pension plan; tuition assistance; disability coverage; daycare assistance; profit sharing; employee discounts; savings plan. **Corporate headquarters:** This location. **Operations at this facility:** regional headquarters; administration; service; sales.

WOODWINDS APARTMENTS

2079 Buchtel Boulevard, Denver CO 80210. 303/778-8023. **Contact:** Personnel Department. **Description:** Involved in the operation of apartment buildings.

Additional large employers: 250+

GENERAL CONTRACTORS-- RESIDENTIAL BUILDINGS, OTHER THAN SINGLE FAMILY

Orr Constr Co
4414 Vine St, Denver CO 80216-3822. 303/2949211. Employs: 250-499.

MISC. SPECIAL TRADE CONTRACTORS

Tmd Enterprises
Lowry Afb, Lowry Afb CO 80230.
303/3889708. Employs: 250-499.

OPERATORS OF NONRESIDENTIAL BUILDINGS

Ascot Centre
9116 W Bowles Ave, Littleton CO
80123-3440.   303/9330266.
Employs: 250-499.

ARCHITECTURAL SERVICES

Nobel/Sysco Food Services Co
1101 W 48th Ave, Denver CO
80221-1576.   303/4584000.
Employs: 250-499.

Additional small to medium sized employers: 50-249

GENERAL CONTRACTORS-- SINGLE-FAMILY HOUSES

Conner Construction Company
2670 S Delaware St, Denver CO
80223-4418.   303/7441096.
Employs: 50-99.

Flooring Dealers Inc
2050 W 9th Ave, Denver CO
80204-3846.   303/6234191.
Employs: 50-99.

Luna Construction Co Inc
4047 Tejon St, Denver CO 80211-
2214. 303/4332600. Employs: 50-
99.

RE Monks Construction Co
8355 Vollmer Rd, Colorado
Springs CO 80908-4721.
719/4953621. Employs: 100-249.

Modulaire Service
2400 W Union Ave, Englewood
CO 80110-5307. 303/7971600.
Employs: 100-249.

Everitt Homes
3000 S College Ave, Fort Collins
CO 80525-2558. 303/2261500.
Employs: 50-99.

GENERAL CONTRACTORS-- RESIDENTIAL BUILDINGS, OTHER THAN SINGLE FAMILIES

Integrity Construction
5895 E Evans Ave, Denver CO
80222-5306.   303/6920049.
Employs: 50-99.

Kambridge Building Co
6208 Lehman Dr, Ste 120,
Colorado Springs CO 80918-8400.
719/5939111. Employs: 50-99.

GENERAL CONTRACTORS-- INDUSTRIAL BUILDINGS AND WAREHOUSES

Lpr Construction Company
1171 Des Moines Ave, Loveland
CO 80537-5106. 303/6632233.
Employs: 100-249.

GENERAL CONTRACTORS-- NONRESIDENTIAL BUILDINGS, OTHER THAN INDUSTRIAL BUILDINGS AND WAREHOUSES

Ames Construction
25701 E 88th Ave, Commerce City
CO 80022-9529. 303/3735906.
Employs: 50-99.

Cedric Jones Constructors
5490 W 13th Ave, Denver CO
80214-2207.   303/2338440.
Employs: 100-249.

Craftsmen Construction Co Inc
5660 Greenwood Plaza Blvd, Englewood CO 80111-2416. 303/7704600. Employs: 50-99.

Crss Commercial Group Inc
216 16th St Suite 1700, Denver CO 80202-5131. 303/8205200. Employs: 100-249.

Elward Inc
680 Harlan St, Denver CO 80214-2340. 303/2396303. Employs: 50-99.

G E Johnson Cons Co Inc
310 S 14th St, Colorado Springs CO 80904-4009. 719/4735321. Employs: 100-249.

PCL Construction Services Inc
2000 S Colorado Blvd, Suite 400, Denver CO 80222-7907. 303/7536600. Employs: 50-99.

Pinkard Construction Company
1075 S Yukon St, Suite 301, Lakewood CO 80226-4333. 303/9864555. Employs: 100-249.

Robert Dougan Construction
2100 S Valentia St, Denver CO 80231-3325. 303/7521000. Employs: 50-99.

Roche Constructors Inc
3661 71st Ave, Greeley CO 80634. 303/3563611. Employs: 50-99.

Weitz Cohen Construction Co
899 Logan St, Suite 600, Denver CO 80203-3156. 303/8606600. Employs: 100-249.

Western States Construction Co
5400 N Garfield Ave, Loveland CO 80538-1825. 303/6675555. Employs: 50-99.

HIGHWAY AND STREET CONSTRUCTION, EXCEPT ELEVATED HIGHWAYS

Broderick & Gibbons
3390 Drennan Industrial Loop, Colorado Springs CO 80910. 719/3907200. Employs: 50-99.

Colorado Curb & Gutter Inc
5837 S Colorow Dr, Morrison CO 80465-2211. 303/2799785. Employs: 50-99.

County Public Works
2045 13th St, Boulder CO 80302-5201. 303/4413900. Employs: 100-249.

Dustrol Inc
3675 S Hwy 85 87, Colorado Springs CO 80906-5566. 719/5760777. Employs: 50-99.

Irving F Jensen Co
704 S Topeka Way, Castle Rock CO 80104-1568. 303/6886611. Employs: 100-249.

Mobil Premix
1400 W 67th Ave, Denver CO 80221. 303/4264419. Employs: 100-249.

Siegrist Construction Company
6999 York St, Denver CO 80229-7310. 303/2896441. Employs: 50-99.

BRIDGE, TUNNEL, AND ELEVATED HIGHWAY CONSTRUCTION

Flatiron Structures Company
10090 W I 25 Frontage Rd, Longmont CO 80504-9517. 303/4441760. Employs: 100-249.

Bridge Builders Construction
5439 N Foothills Hwy, Boulder CO 80302-9359. 303/4423209. Employs: 50-99.

WATER, SEWER, PIPELINE, COMMUNICATIONS, AND POWER CONSTRUCTION

C2 Utility Contractors
3213 Chelton Cir, Colorado Springs CO 80909-5216. 719/6325575. Employs: 50-99.

Insituform
8163 E Mineral Dr, Englewood CO 80112-3303. 303/7714991. Employs: 50-99.

Nelson Pipe Line Constructors Inc
6215 Colorado Blvd, Commerce City CO 80022-3004. 303/2895971. Employs: 50-99.

R A Waffensmith & Company Inc
6000 E Evans Ave, Denver CO 80222-5406. 303/7577411. Employs: 50-99.

Schmidt Construction Co
2635 Delta Dr, Colorado Springs CO 80910-1007. 719/3924207. Employs: 50-99.

Brown & Grimes Communications
PO Box 3609, Englewood CO 80155-3609. 303/6806846. Employs: 50-99.

MISC. HEAVY CONSTRUCTION

Jbk Landscape Inc
1250 S Chambers Rd, Aurora CO 80017-4046. 303/7510192. Employs: 100-249.

Stone & Webster Engineer Corp
7677 E Berry Ave, Englewood CO 80111-2102. 303/7417700. Employs: 100-249.

PLUMBING, HEATING, AND AIR-CONDITIONING

Robinson Mechanical Systems
5541 Central Ave, Boulder CO 80301-2846. 303/4432505. Employs: 50-99.

Trautman & Shreve Inc
4406 Race St, Denver CO 80216-3818. 303/2951414. Employs: 50-99.

U S Engineering Co
PO Box 905, Loveland CO 80539-0905. 303/4829492. Employs: 50-99.

MASONRY, STONE SETTING, AND OTHER STONE WORK

Soderberg Masonry Inc
239 S Summit View Dr, Fort Collins CO 80524-1419. 303/4823766. Employs: 100-249.

PLASTERING, DRYWALL, ACOUSTICAL, AND INSULATION WORK

Denver Dry Wall Company
3251 S Zuni St, Englewood CO 80110-1965. 303/7610515. Employs: 50-99.

South Valley Drywall Inc
12441 N Mead Way, Littleton CO 80125-9759. 303/7917212. Employs: 50-99.

Sunbelt Contractors Inc
2855 W Oxford Av, Englewood CO 80110-4368. 303/7819311. Employs: 50-99.

TERRAZZO, TILE, MARBLE, AND MOSAIC

Ace Tile & Terrazzo Inc
1485 S Lipan St, Denver CO 80223-3410. 303/7773091. Employs: 100-249.

ROOFING, SIDING, AND SHEET METAL WORK

Arapahoe Roofing & Sheet Metal
11936 Wadsworth Blvd, Broomfield CO 80020-2711. 303/4667386. Employs: 50-99.

Douglas Roofing Co
7281 E 54th Pl, Commerce City CO 80022-4809. 303/2882635. Employs: 100-249.

Douglass Roofing Company
110 14th Ave, Greeley CO 80631-2117. 303/3522040. Employs: 50-99.

Metaltech Industries Inc
20 Bowen St, Longmont CO 80501-5862. 303/7729374. Employs: 50-99.

Seamless Siding & Roofing
7000 W 117th Ave, Broomfield CO 80020-2958. 303/4608820. Employs: 50-99.

B & M Roofing Of Colorado Inc
3131 75th St, Boulder CO 80301-4635. 303/4435843. Employs: 100-249.

CONCRETE WORK

Por Mor Construction Company
3601 Nataches Ct, Englewood CO 80110-3320. 303/7891551. Employs: 50-99.

WATER WELL DRILLING

Slick Bore
1605 E Lincoln Ave, Fort Collins CO 80524-2740. 303/4842616. Employs: 50-99.

STRUCTURAL STEEL ERECTION

Prairie Tank & Construction Co
PO Box 189, Wellington CO 80549-0189. 303/5683433. Employs: 50-99.

EXCAVATING WORK

Arvada Excavating
7622 Reno Dr, Arvada CO 80002-3001. 303/4249557. Employs: 100-249.

Connell Resources Inc
1425 S Lincoln Ave, Loveland CO 80537-7146. 303/6671238. Employs: 50-99.

Quality Cable Underground Inc
6989 Jordan Rd, Englewood CO 80112-4217. 303/6930457. Employs: 50-99.

Tricon Kent Company
2931 N Hwy 85, Castle Rock CO 80104-9443. 303/6889568. Employs: 100-249.

WRECKING AND DEMOLITION WORK

Pro Sawing & Coring
1315 Clayton St, Denver CO 80206-2408. 303/3228025. Employs: 50-99.

Barnett Company
3800 Wynkoop St, Denver CO 80216-3637. 303/2932323. Employs: 100-249.

United Materials Inc
1777 W 13th Ave, Denver CO 80204-2405. 303/6234166. Employs: 50-99.

T C B Enterprises
PO Box 3160, Winter Park CO 80482-3160. 303/7265247. Employs: 50-99.

Asbestos Technology & Consulting
923 W Colorado Ave, Colorado Springs CO 80905-1517. 719/6322203. Employs: 50-99.

CERAMIC WALL AND FLOOR TILE

Robinson Brick Company
PO Box 5243, Denver CO 80217-5243. 303/7819002. Employs: 100-249.

CONCRETE PRODUCTS, EXCEPT BLOCK AND BRICK

Architectural Design Precast
6401 E 80th Ave, Commerce City CO 80022-1151. 303/2867339. Employs: 50-99.

Rocla Concrete Co
701 W 48th Ave, Denver CO 80216-1811. 303/2926323. Employs: 50-99.

Streisscon Corp
3210 Astrozon Blvd, Colorado Springs CO 80910-1032. 719/3905041. Employs: 50-99.

READY-MIXED CONCRETE

C&M Ready Mix
1859 US Highway 85, Brighton CO 80601-6647. 303/4431097. Employs: 50-99.

Flatiron Materials Company
1013 25th St, Greeley CO 80631-6941. 303/3563366. Employs: 50-99.

Holnam Ideal Division
4629 N Overland Trail, Laporte CO 80535. 303/4824065. Employs: 100-249.

Mobile Premix Concrete Inc
3390 Drennan Industrial Lo S, Colorado Springs CO 80910. 719/3906300. Employs: 50-99.

Mobile Premix Inc
E Walnut, Windsor CO 80550. 303/6867769. Employs: 50-99.

Ready Mixed Concrete Co
4395 Washington Blvd, Brighton CO 80601. 303/2921771. Employs: 50-99.

OPERATORS OF NONRESIDENTIAL BUILDINGS

Denver West Office Park
1546 Cole Blvd Suite 220, Golden CO 80401-3406. 303/2322006. Employs: 50-99.

Meridian International Business Ctr
4601 Dtc Blvd Suite 1000, Denver CO 80237-2553. 303/7923900. Employs: 50-99.

R & S Management Inc
7887 E Belleview Ave Suite 680, Englewood CO 80111-6021. 303/8509666. Employs: 100-249.

AT&T
1875 Lawrence St, Denver CO 80202-1847. 303/2967622. Employs: 50-99.

Thornton Town Center Mall
10001 Grant St, Denver CO 80229-2000. 303/2520007. Employs: 50-99.

OPERATORS OF APARTMENT BUILDINGS

Allied Housing Inc
22 S Adams St, Denver CO 80209-2908. 303/3991100. Employs: 50-99.

Colony Hills Apartments
3810 Patrick Dr, Colorado Springs
CO 80916-3460. 719/3905496.
Employs: 50-99.

Kenton Apts
1540 Grant St, Denver CO 80203-
1820. 303/8391381. Employs: 50-
99.

REAL ESTATE AGENTS AND MANAGERS

American Development Corp
6801 E Mississippi Av, Denver CO
80224-1872. 303/3771726.
Employs: 50-99.

Cherry Creek Ltd Realtors
2305 E Arapahoe Rd Suite 234,
Littleton CO 80122-1538.
303/7971901. Employs: 100-249.

Fuller & Company Realtors
1515 Arapahoe St Suite 1600,
Denver CO 80202-2132.
303/2923700. Employs: 100-249.

Realty Professionals America
274 Union Blvd Suite 310,
Lakewood CO 80228-1836.
303/9861230. Employs: 50-99.

Vision Real Estate Co
3886 Maizeland Rd, Colorado
Springs CO 80909-1606.
719/5746825. Employs: 50-99.

Visser Real Estate Investments
3643 S Elm Way, Denver CO
80237-1010. 303/7562401.
Employs: 50-99.

Wrench & Associate Inc
288 Clayton St, Denver CO 80206-
4815. 303/3210291. Employs: 50-
99.

Edelweiss Realty Co
9485 W Colfax Ave, Lakewood
CO 80215-3926. 303/2327458.
Employs: 50-99.

Denver Technological Center
4601 Dtc Blvd, Denver CO 80237-
2549. 303/7731700. Employs: 50-
99.

LAND SUBDIVIDERS AND DEVELOPERS, EXCEPT CEMETERIES

Highland Properties Inc
1837 S Nevada Ave # 266,
Colorado Springs CO 80906-2516.
719/6347722. Employs: 50-99.

Mission Viejo Company
8822 S Ridgeline Blvd, Littleton
CO 80126-2334. 303/7918180.
Employs: 100-249.

Trammell Crow
7995 E Prentice Ave Suite 300,
Englewood CO 80111-2749.
303/2200900. Employs: 50-99.

ARCHITECTURAL SERVICES

Arix Inc
800 8th Ave, Greeley CO 80631-
1100. 303/3563930. Employs: 50-
99.

Camp Dresser & McKee Inc
1331 17th St Suite 1200, Denver
CO 80202-1562. 303/2981311.
Employs: 50-99.

Rnl Facilities Corporation
1225 17, Denver CO 80202.
303/2951717. Employs: 50-99.

Wigand Corp
850 Elkton Dr, Colorado Springs
CO 80907-3521. 719/5998887.
Employs: 100-249.

SURVEYING SERVICES

Analytical Surveys Inc
1935 Jamboree Dr Suite 100,
Colorado Springs CO 80920-5398.
719/5930093. Employs: 50-99.

MANAGEMENT SERVICES

Colorado Transit Mgmt Inc
1210 Hancock Expy, Colorado
Springs CO 80903-4640.
719/4750635. Employs: 100-249.

Management Resource Technologies

125 Dorset Ct, Castle Rock CO
80104-9285. 303/6888883.
Employs: 50-99.

R D Roush Management Co
5650 Dtc Pky Suite 100,
Englewood CO 80111-3011.
303/6949467. Employs: 50-99.

For more information on career opportunities in architecture, construction, and real estate:

Associations

APARTMENT OWNERS AND MANAGERS ASSOCIATION
65 Cherry Plaza, Watertown CT
06795. 203/274-2589.

BUILDING OWNERS AND MANAGERS ASSOCIATION
1521 Ritchie Highway, P.O. Box
9709, Arnold MD 21012. 301/261-
2882.

INSTITUTE OF REAL ESTATE MANAGEMENT
430 North Michigan Avenue,
Chicago IL 60611. 312/661-1930.

INTERNATIONAL ASSOCIATION OF CORPORATE REAL ESTATE EXECUTIVES
440 Columbia Drive, Suite 100,
West Palm Beach FL 33409.
407/683-8111.

INTERNATIONAL REAL ESTATE INSTITUTE
8383 East Evans Road, Scottsdale
AZ 85260. 602/998-8267.

NATIONAL ASSOCIATION OF REAL ESTATE INVESTMENT TRUSTS
1129 20th Street NW, Suite 705,
Washington DC 20036. 202/785-
8717.

NATIONAL ASSOCIATION OF REALTORS
430 North Michigan Avenue,
Chicago IL 60611. 312/329-8200.

Magazines

JOURNAL OF PROPERTY MANAGEMENT
Institute of Real Estate
Management, 430 North Michigan
Avenue, Chicago IL 60611.
312/661-1930.

NATIONAL REAL ESTATE INVESTOR
6255 Barfield, Atlanta GA 30328.
404/256-9800.

REAL ESTATE FORUM
12 West 37th Street, New York NY
10018. 212/563-6460.

REAL ESTATE NEWS
2600 W. Peterson, Suite 100,
Chicago IL 60659. 312/465-5151.

AUTOMOTIVE

Industry insiders are counting on a healthier overall economy and the easing of regulatory burdens to revive the long-slumping auto industry. In the meantime, auto manufacturers are slashing costs by reducing production schedules, offering higher price-incentives to buyers, and laying off workers. On a brighter note, sales of American vans and trucks rose during the first half of 1992.

BEST CAR BUYS LTD
1200 West Alameda Avenue, Denver CO 80223. 303/777-3053. **Contact:** Jerry Mara, Manager. **Description:** A Denver retail car dealership. **Common positions:** Sales Representative.

BESTOP, INC.
P.O. Box 307, Broomfield CO 80038. 303/465-1755. **Contact:** Personnel Department. **Description:** An area manufacturer of four-wheel drive accessories. **Common positions:** Accountant; Blue-Collar Worker Supervisor; Buyer; Computer Programmer; Credit Manager; Customer Service Representative; Industrial Engineer; Mechanical Engineer; Operations/Production Specialist; Personnel and Labor Relations Specialist; Purchasing Agent; Quality Control Supervisor; Sales Representative; Transportation and Traffic Specialist. **Educational backgrounds sought:** Accounting; Business Administration; Communications; Computer Science; Engineering; Finance. **Benefits:** medical, dental, and life insurance; employee discounts. **Corporate headquarters:** This location. **Operations at this facility:** manufacturing; administration; service; sales.

CHRYSLER CORPORATION
12225 E. 39th Avenue, Denver CO 80239. 303/373-8840. **Contact:** Personnel Department. **Description:** A parts depot for the automobile and truck manufacturer.

JOHN CLARK INC./JCI
4955 Bannock Street, Denver CO 80216. 303/892-5800. **Contact:** Melanie Pora, Controller. **Description:** Produces specialized transportation equipment, primarily for the mining industry. Products include mining locomotives, carrier cars, and trucks used in mining. **Common positions:** Accountant; Blue-Collar Worker Supervisor; Computer Programmer; Draftsperson; Mechanical Engineer; Mining Engineer. **Educational backgrounds sought:** Accounting; Engineering. **Special programs:** Training programs. **Benefits:** medical and life insurance; tuition assistance; disability coverage. **Corporate headquarters:** This location. **Parent company:** INCO. **Operations at this facility:** manufacturing; administration; service; sales.

HATCH GRINDING COMPANY
320 South Lipan, Denver CO 80223. 303/778-1414. **Contact:** Personnel.

Description: A wholesaler of automotive equipment.

MERRITT EQUIPMENT COMPANY
9339 Highway 85, Henderson CO 80640. 303/287-7527. **Contact:** Personnel Department. **Description:** Manufactures specialty truck trailers (including farm trailers for carrying grain and other commodities), and livestock trailers. **Corporate headquarters:** This location.

MOUNTAIN STATES MOTORS
1260 South Colorado Boulevard, Denver CO 80222. 303/757-7751. **Contact:** Frank Murray, Office Manager. **Description:** An area car dealer specializing in, but not limited to, Volkswagon sales and service.

MURRAY MOTOR IMPORTS COMPANY
4300 East Kentucky Avenue, Denver CO 80222-2008. 303/759-3400. **Contact:** Garry McAuliffe, Personnel Director. **Description:** A foreign car and parts importer.

NEOPLAN USA CORPORATION
700 Gottlob Auwaerter Drive, Lamar CO 81052. 719/336-3256. **Contact:** Pat Robinette, Personnel Director. **Description:** Produces and markets buses; distributes internationally. **Common positions:** Accountant; Administration; Blue-Collar Worker Supervisor; Computer Programmer; Customer Service Representative; Draftsperson; Electrical Engineer; Industrial Engineer; Mechanical Engineer; Financial Analyst; Department Manager; General Manager; Management Trainee; Operations/Production Manager; Personnel and Labor Relations Specialist; Purchasing Agent; Quality Control Supervisor; Technical Writer/Editor. **Educational backgrounds sought:** Accounting; Business Administration; Communications; Computer Science; Economics; Engineering; Finance. **Benefits:** medical insurance; pension plan; life insurance; tuition assistance; disability coverage. **Corporate headquarters:** This location. **Operations at this facility:** manufacturing.

TIMPTE INC.
P.O. Box 5013, Commerce City CO 80037-5013. 303/289-6240. **Contact:** Linda Aho, Personnel Director. **Description:** Produces cab and trailer bodies for the trucking industry, including truck bodies, refrigerated trailers, tank trailers, dump trailers, and other specialty trailers.

Additional large employers: 250+

MOTOR VEHICLE PARTS AND ACCESSORIES

Bestop Inc
21241 Kimbark St, Longmont CO 80502. 303/4651755. Employs: 250-499.

Oea Inc

34501 E Quincy Ave, Denver CO 80210. 303/6931248. Employs: 500-999.

PASSENGER CAR RENTAL

Budget Rent A Car
7400 E 32nd Ave, Denver CO 80207-2402. 303/3990444. Employs: 250-499.

Additional small to medium sized employers: 50-249

MOTOR VEHICLE PARTS AND ACCESSORIES

Autotron Products
1290 Boston Ave, Longmont CO 80501-5810. 303/4431713. Employs: 50-99.

Dana Corp Clutch
1210 Garden Gods, Colorado Springs CO 80907. 719/5997240. Employs: 50-99.

Daniel Radiator Corp
5000 Clarkson St Suite C, Denver CO 80216-2062. 303/2950944. Employs: 50-99.

Drive Train Industries Inc
3301 Brighton Blvd, Denver CO 80216-5020. 303/2925176. Employs: 100-249.

Ford Microelectronics Inc
9965 Federal Dr, Colorado Springs CO 80921-3617. 719/5287600. Employs: 100-249.

Power Engr Co
2525 S Delaware St, Denver CO 80223-4415. 303/7778782. Employs: 50-99.

TRUCK TRAILERS

Intermountain Wholesale

5315 Vasquez Boulevard, Commerce City CO 80022-3712. 303/2961980. Employs: 50-99.

TRUCK RENTAL AND LEASING, WITHOUT DRIVERS

Service Systems Inc
26 W Dry Creek Cir # 650, Littleton CO 80120-4475. 303/7958414. Employs: 50-99.

PASSENGER CAR RENTAL

Dollar Rent A Car
7450 E 29th Ave, Denver CO 80207-2419. 303/3982323. Employs: 50-99.

Hertz Rent A Car
7600 Martin Lthr Kng Blvd, Denver CO 80207. 303/3552244. Employs: 100-249.

Professional Rent A Car
11000 W Colfax Ave, Lakewood CO 80215-3727. 303/2336438. Employs: 50-99.

AUTOMOBILE PARKING

Central Parking System
1625 Broadway, Denver CO 80202-4717. 303/8254948. Employs: 50-99.

TOP, BODY, AND UPHOLSTERY REPAIR SHOPS AND PAINT SHOPS

Deane Automotive Center Inc
1080 S Colorado Blvd, Denver CO
80222-2404.   303/7576161.
Employs: 100-249.

Maaco Auto Paint & Bodyworks
5791 Sheridan Blvd, Arvada CO
80002-2832.   303/4236626.
Employs: 50-99.

GENERAL AUTOMOTIVE REPAIR SHOPS

Colorado Chrysler Plymouth Inc
350 S Havana St, Aurora CO
80012-2001.   303/3436180.
Employs: 50-99.

Kar Go Service Center
7540 York St, Denver CO 80229-
6609. 303/2878633. Employs: 50-
99.

Emich Oldsmobile Gmc Truck
16400 W Colfax Ave, Golden CO
80401-3855.   303/2784433.
Employs: 50-99.

For more information on career opportunities in the automotive industry:

Associations

ASSOCIATION OF INTERNATIONAL AUTOMOBILE MANUFACTURERS
1001 19th Street North, Suite 1200,
Arlington VA 22209. 703/525-
7788.

AUTOMOTIVE AFFILIATED REPRESENTATIVES
25 Northwest Point Boulevard, Elk
Grove Village IL 60007. 708/228-
1310.

AUTOMOTIVE ELECTRIC ASSOCIATION
25 Northwest Point Boulevard,
Suite 425, Elk Grove Village IL
60007. 708/228-1310.

AUTOMOTIVE SERVICE ASSOCIATION
1901 Airport Freeway, Suite 100,
Bedford TX 76021-0929. 817/283-
6205.

AUTOMOTIVE SERVICE INDUSTRY ASSOCIATION
25 Northwest Point Boulevard, Elk
Grove Village IL 60007. 708/228-
1310.

MOTOR VEHICLE MANUFACTURERS ASSOCIATION
7430 2nd Avenue, Suite 300,
Detroit MI 48202. 313/872-4311.

NATIONAL AUTOMOTIVE PARTS ASSOCIATION
2999 Circle 75 Parkway, Atlanta
GA 30339. 404/956-2200.

NATIONAL INSTITUTE FOR AUTOMOTIVE SERVICE EXCELLENCE
13505 Dulles Technology Drive,
Herndon VA 22071. 703/713-3800.

SOCIETY OF AUTOMOTIVE ENGINEERS
400 Commonwealth Drive,
Warrendale PA 15096. 412/776-
4841.

Directories

AUTOMOTIVE NEWS MARKET DATA BOOK
Automotive News, 1400 Woodbridge Avenue, Detroit MI 48207. 313/446-6000.

WARD'S AUTOMOTIVE YEARBOOK
Ward's Communications, 28 West Adams Street, Detroit MI 48226. 313/962-4433.

Magazines

AUTOMOTIVE INDUSTRIES

Chilton Book Co., Chilton Way, Radnor PA 19089. 800/695-1214.

AUTOMOTIVE NEWS
1400 Woodbridge Avenue, Detroit MI 48207. 313/446-6000.

WARD'S AUTO WORLD
Ward's Communications, Inc., 28 West Adams Street, Detroit MI 48226. 313/962-4433.

WARD'S AUTOMOTIVE REPORTS
Ward's Communications, Inc., 28 West Adams Street, Detroit MI 48226. 313/962-4433.

BANKING/SAVINGS AND LOAN

Heading into 1993, the banking industry continues to evolve. The industry began the decade with a series of megamergers aimed at solidifying its strongest institutions, resulting in a series of major layoffs. Increasingly, banks are facing new competition from mutual funds and other financial services that are not faced with the same regulatory burdens. As a result, short-term job prospects in the banking industry are fairly weak, and the competition is heavy.

AFFILIATED BANKSHARES OF COLORADO
1125 17th Street, Suite 1500, Denver CO 80202. 303/297-4703. **Contact:** Human Resources. **Description:** Affiliated Bankshares is a state-wide bank-holding company with over $2 billion in assets, 28 banks, and four active non-banking subsidiaries serving the major markets of Colorado. **Common positions:** Accountant; Auditor; Bank Officer/Manager; Customer Service Representative; Financial Analyst; Branch Manager; Marketing Specialist; Teller; Secretary; Purchasing Agent; Systems Analyst; Lenders; Trust Administrators. **Educational backgrounds sought:** Accounting; Business Administration; Finance; Marketing. **Benefits:** medical and life insurance; pension plan; disability coverage; savings plan; flexible benefits program. **Corporate headquarters:** This location. **Operations at this facility:** administration. **Listed on:** NASDAQ National Market System.

BANK OF CHERRY CREEK
3033 East First Avenue, Denver CO 80206. 303/394-5100. **Contact:** Judy Martin, Personnel. **Description:** Operates a commercial bank with a complete range of banking services for private, commercial, and institutional customers. **Corporate headquarters:** This location. **Common positions:** Accountant; Administrator; Bank Officer/Manager; Credit Manager; Customer Service Representative; Branch Manager; Department Manager; General Manager; Management Trainee; Operations/Production Manager. **Educational backgrounds sought:** Accounting; Business Administration; Economics; Finance; Marketing. **Benefits:** medical, dental, and life insurance; pension plan; disability coverage; profit sharing; employee discounts. **Operations at this facility:** Administration; Service; Sales.

BANK OF DENVER
P.O. Box 5081, Denver CO 80217. 303/572-3600. **Contact:** Personnel Department. **Description:** An area bank.

BANK ONE
P.O. Box 59, Boulder CO 80306. 303/442-6770. **Contact:** Kathy Rasco, Personnel Officer. **Description:** A full-service commercial bank, offering traditional banking services to individuals, institutions, and businesses. **Corporate headquarters:** This location.

BANK ONE
2696 South Colorado Boulevard, Denver CO 80222. 303/757-7272. **Contact:** Laurie Klyne, Personnel Assistant. **Description:** A full-service community commercial bank. **Common positions:** Accountant; Bank Officer/Manager; Customer Service Representative; Department Manager; Marketing Specialist; Personnel and Labor Relations Specialist. **Educational backgrounds sought:** Accounting; Business Administration; Finance; Marketing. **Special programs:** Training programs. **Benefits:** medical and life insurance; pension plan; disability coverage; employee discounts; savings plan. **Corporate headquarters:** This location. **Parent company:** Affiliated Bankshares of Colorado, Inc. **Listed on:** NASDAQ.

BANK ONE ALAMEDA BANKING CENTER
P.O. Box 260669, Lakewood CO 80226. 303/922-1181. **Contact:** Personnel Department. **Description:** A Denver-area bank.

BANK ONE ENGLEWOOD BANKING CENTER
333 West Hampden Avenue, Englewood CO 80110. 303/761-1420. **Contact:** Human Resources Department. **Description:** A full-service bank.

BANK ONE LAKESIDE BANKING CENTER
P.O. Box 12000, Denver CO 80212. 303/455-2000. **Contact:** Linda Bjork, Personnel Director. **Description:** A full-service bank.

BANK ONE SERVICES CORPORATION
445 E 124th Avenue, Thornton CO 80241. 303/450-2272. **Contact:** Personnel Department. **Description:** An electronic data processing banking service.

BANK WESTERN FEDERAL SAVINGS BANK
200 University Boulevard, Denver CO 80206. 303/623-5100. **Contact:** Personnel Department. **Description:** A Denver savings and loan association.

COBANK
5500 South Quebec Street, Englewood CO 80111. 303/740-4163. **Contact:** Larry E. Williams, Senior Vice President/Corp. Development. **Description:** A banking institution.

COLORADO NATIONAL BANK
P.O. Box 5168, Denver CO 80217. 303/893-1862. **Contact:** Human Resources. **Description:** Serves customers throughout Colorado, primarily in Denver, Adams, Arapahoe, and Jefferson counties. Provides numerous banking services to retail, commercial, and corporate customers. **Corporate headquarters:** This location.

COMMERCIAL BANCORPORATION OF COLORADO
3300 East First Avenue, Denver CO 80206. 303/321-1234. **Contact:** Ann Brunger, Director of Personnel. **Description:** An area commercial bank. The holding company for Century Bank.

FIRST INTERSTATE BANK OF DENVER
633 17th Street, 8th Floor, P.O. Box 5808, Denver CO 80217. **Contact:** Call Jobline: 303/293-5777. Applicants need to know of a specific opening to apply for it. **Description:** A full-service bank. Offers savings, checking, loan, and trust services. Regional headquarters location. **Operations at this facility:** service, sales. **Corporate headquarters:** Los Angeles, CA. **Listed on:** New York Stock Exchange. **Common positions:** Accountant; Administrator; Bank Officer/Manager; Buyer; Commercial Lender; Customer Service Representative; Financial Analyst; Department Manager; Management Trainee; Operations/Production Manager; Marketing Specialist; Personnel and Labor Relations Specialist; Public Relations Worker; Sales Representative; Underwriter. **Educational backgrounds sought:** Accounting; Business Administration; Finance. **Benefits:** medical insurance; dental insurance; pension plan; life insurance; tuition assistance; disability coverage; profit sharing; employee discounts; savings plan; vision insurance.

NORTHWEST BANK OF BEAR VALLEY
5353 West Dartmouth Avenue, Denver CO 80227. 303/989-5353. **Contact:** Human Resources Department. **Description:** A full-service commercial bank. **Corporate headquarters:** This location. **Benefits:** medical insurance; dental insurance; pension plan; life insurance; disability coverage; profit sharing.

SOUTHWEST STATE BANK
1380 South Federal Boulevard, Denver CO 80219. 303/934-5511. **Contact:** JoAnn Brockway, Senior Vice President/Personnel. **Description:** A full-service commercial bank. **Corporate headquarters:** This location.

UNION BANK & TRUST COMPANY
SOUTH DENVER STATION
P.O. Box 9347, Denver CO 80209. 303/744-3221. **Contact:** Ulma Schaffer, Personnel Director. **Description:** Offers a wide range of banking, trust, and other financial services. **Corporate headquarters:** This location.

UNITED BANK OF DENVER
1740 Broadway Street, Denver CO 80274-8690. 303/863-6043. **Contact:** Joan Van Landingham, Human Resources Department. **Description:** Provides a full range of deposit and loan services, municipal bonds, and many other banking and financial services. **Corporate headquarters:** This location.

Additional large employers: 250+

BANKS, FEDERAL RESERVE

Federal Reserve Bank
1020 16th St, Denver CO 80202-2001. 303/5722300. Employs: 250-499.

BANKS, NATIONAL COMMERCIAL

Central Bank Denver
1515 Arapahoe St Box 5548 Ta, Denver CO 80202-2118. 303/8933456. Employs: 500-999.

Denver National Bank
1125 17th St Box 5586 Ta, Denver CO 80202-2016. 303/2924000. Employs: 1,000+.

First Bank Of Westland
10403 W Colfax Ave, Lakewood CO 80215-3809. 303/2322000. Employs: 250-499.

First National Bank
1800 Broadway, Boulder CO 80302-5246. 303/4426770. Employs: 250-499.

First National Bank Co Springs
Pikes Peak & Tejon Box 1699, Colorado Springs CO 80942-0002. 7194715000. Employs: 250-499.

Resources Trust Company
8051 E Maplewood Ave, Englewood CO 80111-4742. 303/6942917. Employs: 250-499.

United Bank Of Denver
1700 Broadway, Denver CO 80290. 303/8618811. Employs: 250-499.

BANKS, STATE COMMERCIAL

Empire Savings
1654 California St, Denver CO 80202-3702. 303/6231771. Employs: 250-499.

SAVINGS INSTITUTIONS, FEDERALLY CHARTERED

Columbia Savings & Loan
5850 S Ulster Cir E Suite 14, Englewood CO 80111-3208. 303/7733444. Employs: 250-499.

MISC. FUNCTIONS RELATED TO DEPOSITORY BANKING

American Express
181 Inverness Dr W, Englewood CO 80112-5201. 303/7992000. Employs: 250-499.

American Express Info Service
7401 W Mansfield Ave, Denver CO 80235-2220. 303/9803310. Employs: 250-499.

LOAN BROKERS

Colorado National Mortgage Co

950 17th St Suite 100, Denver CO 80202-2801.   303/8931913. Employs: 1,000+.

Additional small to medium sized employers: 50-249

BANKS, FEDERAL RESERVE

US Bureau Of The Mint
320 W Colfax Ave, Denver CO 80204-2605.   303/8443332. Employs: 100-249.

BANKS, NATIONAL COMMERCIAL

Affiliated First National Bank
200 E 7th St, Loveland CO 80537-4862. 303/6673443. Employs: 50-99.

Affiliated National Bank
333 W Hampden Ave, Englewood CO 80110-2330. 303/7611430. Employs: 50-99.

Alameda National Bank
5500 W Alameda Ave Box 26669, Lakewood CO 80226-3610. 303/9221181. Employs: 50-99.

Anco Production Co
2150 W 29th Ave, Denver CO 80211-3867.   303/4554584. Employs: 100-249.

Arapahoe National Bank
2500 Arapahoe Av, Boulder CO 80302-6711.   303/4434933. Employs: 50-99.

Bank Promotions Of Boulder Inc
3285 30th St, Boulder CO 80301-1451. 303/4447630. Employs: 50-99.

City Center Office
92nd Av & Sheridan, Westminster CO 80030. 303/4291551. Employs: 50-99.

Co Natl Bnk Denver Lowry Air
6th & Quebec, Lowry Afb CO 80230. 303/3441950. Employs: 100-249.

Colorado National Bank
2995 Pearl St, Boulder CO 80301-1130. 303/4407711. Employs: 50-99.

Colorado National Bank
1415 Carr St Box 15248, Lakewood CO 80215-4859. 303/2321331. Employs: 50-99.

Colorado National Bank
6 S Tejon St, Colorado Springs CO 80903-1511.   719/4731333. Employs: 100-249.

Colorado National Bank-Aurora
1411 E Alameda Ave, Denver CO 80209-2554.   303/3441330. Employs: 100-249.

Comerica Bank
999 18th St, Denver CO 80202-2440. 303/2949104. Employs: 100-249.

Croker National Bank
600 17, Denver CO 80202. 303/8938855. Employs: 100-249.

Financial Mgmt Task Force Inc
801 E 17th Ave, Denver CO 80218-1417.   303/8371050. Employs: 100-249.

First America Fed Svngs Bnk
400 S Lashley Ln, Boulder CO 80303-5446.   303/4479874. Employs: 50-99.

First Colorado Bank & Trust
2696 S Colorado Blvd Box 22355,
Denver   CO   80222-5938.
303/7577272. Employs: 100-249.

First Interstate Bank
1301 Jackson St, Golden CO
80401-1911.   303/2794563.
Employs: 100-249.

First Interstate Bank
205 W Oak St, Fort Collins CO
80521-2712.   303/4824861.
Employs: 100-249.

First Interstate Bnk Englewood
333 S Bannock St, Denver CO
80223-2112.   303/2969000.
Employs: 100-249.

First National Bank Englewood
333 W Hampden Ave, Englewood
CO   80110-2330.   303/7611420.
Employs: 50-99.

First National Longmont Bank
401 Main, Denver CO 80218.
303/6295592. Employs: 100-249.

First Natl Bk Uptown Facility
28 E Boulder St, Colorado Springs
CO   80903-1212.   719/4716075.
Employs: 50-99.

Firstbank
8800 Wadsworth Blvd, Broomfield
CO   80021-4586.   303/4671000.
Employs: 50-99.

Firstbank At Chambers
15250 E Mississippi Ave, Aurora
CO   80012-3731.   303/7551000.
Employs: 50-99.

Firstbank At Table Mesa
3600 Table Mesa Dr, Boulder CO
80303-5823.   303/2351080.
Employs: 50-99.

Firstbank At 30th & Arapahoe

1650 E 30th Ave, Denver CO
80205-4506.   303/2351070.
Employs: 100-249.

Firstbank At 30th/Arapahoe
1650 30th St Box 18568, Boulder
CO   80308-1568.   303/4428200.
Employs: 50-99.

Firstbank Of Cherry Creek
100 St Paul St Box 61038, Denver
CO   80206-5107.   303/3331000.
Employs: 100-249.

Firstbank Of Green Mountain
12043 W Alameda Pky Box
280217, Lakewood CO 80228-
2701. 303/9809900. Employs: 50-
99.

Firstbank Of Republic Plaza
370 17th T, Denver CO 80202.
303/6232000. Employs: 100-249.

Firstbank Of Wheatridge
44th & Wadworth Blvd, Wheat
Ridge CO 80033. 303/4241400.
Employs: 50-99.

First National Bank
7301 N Federal Blvd Bldg 10,
Westminster   CO   80030-4920.
303/4291551. Employs: 100-249.

Firstbank At Buckley/Quincy
4271 S Buckley Rd Box 460576,
Aurora   CO   80013-2952.
303/6931200. Employs: 50-99.

Fort Collins 1st Ind Bnk
2721 W College Ave, Denver CO
80219-6005.   303/5721611.
Employs: 100-249.

Lakeside National Bank
4704 Harlan St, Wheat Ridge CO
80033. 303/4552000. Employs: 50-
99.

Lakeside National Bank
4704 Harlan St, Denver CO 80212-7415. 303/4552000. Employs: 100-249.

Littleton National Bank
5734 S Prince St, Littleton CO 80120-1939. 303/7956611. Employs: 50-99.

Northern Co Springs Natl Bk
3100 N Nevada Av, Colorado Springs CO 80907. 719/4732000. Employs: 50-99.

Northwest Loan Office
1777 W 38th Ave, Denver CO 80211-2249. 303/4800402. Employs: 100-249.

Omnibancorp
3600 S Yosemite, Englewood CO 80111. 303/7736664. Employs: 50-99.

Rate Line
7590 W Colfax At Lakewood, Lakewood CO 80215. 303/2333555. Employs: 50-99.

Residential First Mrtg Loans
821 17, Denver CO 80202. 303/2932082. Employs: 100-249.

Santa Fe Loan Office
733 Santa Fe Dr, Denver CO 80204-4428. 303/8635955. Employs: 100-249.

Summit County Bank
1000 N Main, Denver CO 80218. 303/8931561. Employs: 100-249.

Tecnational Bank
7887 E Belleview Box 37545, Denver CO 80237-0545. 303/7739944. Employs: 100-249.

The Rawlins National Bank
1200 17, Denver CO 80202. 303/8931559. Employs: 100-249.

The Western Natl Bk Co Springs
1130 N Circle Dr, Colorado Springs CO 80909. 719/4730111. Employs: 50-99.

United Bank
90 S Cascade Ave, Colorado Springs CO 80903-1611. 719/6361361. Employs: 100-249.

United Bank
401 S College Ave, Fort Collins CO 80524-2901. 303/4821100. Employs: 100-249.

United Bank
1025 9th Ave, Greeley CO 80631-4000. 303/5340741. Employs: 100-249.

United Bank Of Academy Place
5360 N Academy Blvd, Colorado Springs CO 80918-4038. 719/5907740. Employs: 50-99.

United Bank Of Bear Valley
5353 W Dartmouth Ave Box 27015, Denver CO 80227-5515. 303/9895353. Employs: 50-99.

United Bank Of Broomfield
2 Garden Ctr, Broomfield CO 80020-1730. 303/4661801. Employs: 50-99.

United Bank Of Lakewood
7200 W Alameda Ave, Lakewood CO 80226-3290. 303/9367381. Employs: 50-99.

United Bank Of Northglenn
10701 Melody Dr, Denver CO 80234-4120. 303/4525111. Employs: 50-99.

Valley Bank
450 S Oak St, Lakewood CO 80226-2642. 303/6232002. Employs: 50-99.

Vectra Bank Of Denver
999 18th St Suite 111, Denver CO
80202-2441.   303/3911000.
Employs: 100-249.

**BANKS,   STATE
COMMERCIAL**

American Industrial Bank
3600 E Alameda Ave # 100,
Denver   CO   80209-3135.
303/3993400. Employs: 50-99.

Arapahoe Bank & Trust
7777 E Arapahoe Rd, Englewood
CO   80112-1253.   303/7705100.
Employs: 50-99.

Colorado National Bank
Bldg 444, Denver CO 80280.
303/3773011. Employs: 50-99.

Investment Trust Company
455 Sherman St Suite 180 Box
61338, Denver CO 80206-8338.
303/7229710. Employs: 50-99.

Jefferson Bank & Trust
7590 W Colfax Ave, Lakewood
CO   80215-4118.   303/2336561.
Employs: 100-249.

Lincoln Trust Company
6312 S Fiddlers Green Circle,
Englewood   CO   80111-4943.
303/7711000. Employs: 100-249.

Mellon Bank
1775 Sherman St Ste 2300, Denver
CO   80203-4395.   303/8372000.
Employs: 100-249.

Mountain States Bank
1635 E Colfax Ave, Denver CO
80218-2506.   303/3883641.
Employs: 50-99.

National Bank
5500 S Quebec St, Englewood CO
80111-1914.   303/7404000.
Employs: 100-249.

North Denver 1st Industrial
9555 Ralston Rd, Arvada CO
80002-2033.   303/4555600.
Employs: 50-99.

Professional Bank Of Colorado
717 17th St Box 5786, Denver CO
80217-5786.   303/2933000.
Employs: 50-99.

Sorbus
7000 E Belleview Ave, Littleton
CO 80121. 303/7794545. Employs:
50-99.

Union Colony Bank
1701 23rd Ave, Greeley CO 80631-
5050. 303/3567000. Employs: 50-
99.

Vectro Bank
1650 S Colorado Blvd Box 22296,
Denver   CO   80222-4029.
303/7827500. Employs: 50-99.

**SAVINGS   INSTITUTIONS,
FEDERALLY CHARTERED**

First Federal Savings & Loan
5225 N Academy Blvd, Colorado
Springs   CO   80918-4070.
719/5481515. Employs: 50-99.

**World   Savings   &   Loan
Association**
2420 W 26th Ave Suite 200,
Denver   CO   80211-5301.
303/9643200. Employs: 50-99.

1st Fed S & L Association Co
5225 N Academy Blvd, Colorado
Springs   CO   80918-4070.
719/5743500. Employs: 50-99.

**American   Federal   S   &   L
Association Co**
5475 Tech Center Dr, Colorado
Springs   CO   80919-2335.
719/5997400. Employs: 100-249.

Otero Savings
Box 9690, Colorado Springs CO
80932-0690.   719/5971011.
Employs: 50-99.

SAVINGS INSTITUTIONS, NOT FEDERALLY CHARTERED

Colorado State Bank Of Denver
1600 Broadway, Denver CO
80202-4928.   303/8612111.
Employs: 50-99.

CREDIT UNIONS, FEDERALLY CHARTERED

Air Academy Federal Cu
1355 Kelly Johnson Blvd,
Colorado Springs CO 80920-3907.
719/5938600. Employs: 50-99.

Pikes Peak Federal Credit Un
3655 E Fountain Blvd, Colorado
Springs CO 80910-3799.
719/5911524. Employs: 50-99.

School Dist 3 Federal Cr Union
108 Widefield Blvd, Colorado
Springs CO 80911-2235.
719/3928439. Employs: 50-99.

CREDIT UNIONS, NOT FEDERALLY CHARTERED

Bellco Credit Union
1111 S Colorado Blvd, Denver CO
80222-2905.   303/6927800.
Employs: 50-99.

Colorado State Employees C U
1390 Logan St, Denver CO 80203-
2344. 303/8324816. Employs: 50-
99.

Credit Union Of Denver
9305 W Alameda Pky, Lakewood
CO 80226-2830. 303/2341700.
Employs: 50-99.

MISC. FUNCTIONS RELATED TO DEPOSITORY BANKING

Checkright Ltd
7050 S Yosemite St, Englewood
CO 80112-2007. 303/7967220.
Employs: 50-99.

LOAN BROKERS

US West Financial Services Inc
6300 S Syracuse Way Suite 700,
Englewood CO 80111-6748.
303/7732363. Employs: 100-249.

For more information on career opportunities in the banking/savings and loan industry:

<u>Associations</u>

AMERICAN BANKERS ASSOCIATION
1120 Connecticut Avenue NW,
Washington DC 20036. 202/663-
5221.

BANK ADMINISTRATION INSTITUTE
1 North Franklin, Chicago IL
60606. 800/323-8552.

BANK MARKETING ASSOCIATION
309 West Washington Street,
Chicago IL 60606. 312/782-1442.

INDEPENDENT BANKERS ASSOCIATION OF AMERICA
One Thomas Circle NW, Suite 950,
Washington DC 20005. 202/659-
8111.

INSTITUTE OF FINANCIAL EDUCATION
111 East Wacker Drive, 9th Floor, Chicago IL 60601. 312/946-8800.

NATIONAL COUNCIL OF SAVINGS INSTITUTIONS
1101 15th Street NW, Suite 400, Washington DC 20005. 202/857-3100.

U.S. LEAGUE OF SAVINGS AND LOAN INSTITUTIONS
111 East Wacker Drive, Chicago IL 60601. 312/644-3100.

Directories

AMERICAN BANK DIRECTORY
McFadden Business Publications, 6195 Crooked Creek Road, Norcross GA 30092. 404/448-1011.

AMERICAN BANKER DIRECTORY OF U.S. BANKING EXECUTIVES
American Banker, Inc., 1 State Street Plaza, New York NY 10004. 212/943-6700.

AMERICAN BANKER YEARBOOK
American Banker, Inc., 1 State Street Plaza, New York NY 10004. 212/943-6700.

AMERICAN SAVINGS DIRECTORY
McFadden Business Publications, 6195 Crooked Creek Road, Norcross GA 30092. 404/448-1011.

BUSINESS WEEK/TOP 200 BANKING INSTITUTIONS ISSUE
McGraw-Hill, Inc., 1221 Avenue of the Americas, 39th Floor, New York NY 10020. 212/512-4776.

MOODY'S BANK AND FINANCE MANUAL
Moody's Investors Service, Inc., 99 Church Street, New York NY 10007. 212/553-0300.

POLK'S BANK DIRECTORY
R.L. Polk & Co., 2001 Elm Hill Pike, Nashville TN 37210. 615/889-3350.

Magazines

ABA BANKING JOURNAL
American Bankers Association, 1120 Connecticut Avenue NW, Washington DC 20036. 202/663-5221.

BANK ADMINISTRATION
1 North Franklin, Chicago IL 60606. 800/323-8552.

BANKERS MAGAZINE
Warren, Gorham & Lamont, 210 South Street, Boston MA 02111. 617/423-2020.

JOURNAL OF COMMERCIAL BANK LENDING
Robert Morris Associates, 1 Liberty Place, 1650 Market Street, Suite 2300, Philadelphia PA 19103. 215/851-9100.

BOOK AND MAGAZINE PUBLISHING

The continuing recession has hit the book and magazine industries hard. In fact, between 1989 and 1990 alone, over 2,600 book publishing workers lost their jobs. Despite cost containment efforts, most major houses have failed to prevent profits from shrinking further since that time. Higher postal rates and tighter school and library budgets have exacerbated the problem. Gradually, as the economy recovers and disposable income increases, sales in adult trade books should climb.

The expanding 5-14 year-old age group should prompt a rise in sales of juvenile books. These forces should help boost job prospects by about 2,000 new positions annually. In the magazine sector, where much of the revenues are derived from advertising sales, the recession has severely affected bottom lines, and ad pages have declined. An ongoing trend is specialty and niche magazines aimed at increasingly specific audiences.

CARDIFF PUBLISHING COMPANY
6300 South Syracuse Way, Suite 650, Englewood CO 80111. 303/220-0600. **Contact:** Personnel Department. **Description:** A magazine publishing company. **Corporate headquarters:** This location.

DUKE COMMUNICATIONS INTERNATIONAL
P.O. Box 3438, Loveland CO 80538. 303/663-4700. **Contact:** Kristi Brubaker, Human Resources Coordinator. **Description:** Publisher of technical information for IBM Computer Systems 34/36/38 and AS/400; three magazines; seminars; an electronic bulletin board; and books. **Employees:** 85.

JEPPESEN SANDERSON INC.
55 Inverness Drive East, Englewood CO 80112. 303/799-9090. **Contact:** Robert Muller, Director of Personnel. **Description:** Publishes and distributes flight information manuals, as well as flight training supplies and informational products. Part of the Times-Mirror Company's Information Services segment. **Corporate headquarters:** Los Angeles, CA.

JOHNSON PUBLISHING COMPANY
1880 South 57th Court, Boulder CO 80301. 303/443-1576. **Contact:** Alan Andrews, Personnel Director. **Description:** A publisher of both magazines and books.

PRC REALTY SYSTEMS
165 South Union Boulevard, Lakewood CO 80228. 303/980-3060. **Contact:** Personnel Department. **Description:** Publishing corporation; publishes a real estate multi-listing directory.

Additional large employers: 250+

PERIODICALS: PUBLISHING, OR PUBLISHING AND PRINTING

Cahners Publishing Company
44 Cook St, Denver CO 80206-5822. 303/3884511. Employs: 250-499.

BOOKS: PUBLISHING, OR PUBLISHING AND PRINTING

Scott Fetzer Company
6059 S Quebec St Suite 103, Englewood CO 80111-4522. 303/2900806. Employs: 250-499.

Shepards McGraw Hill Inc
420 N Cascade Ave, Colorado Springs CO 80903-3325. 7194757230. Employs: 500-999.

MISC. PUBLISHING

McDonnell Douglas
2450 S Peoria St, Aurora CO 80014-5418. 303/6714800. Employs: 250-499.

Additional small to medium sized employers: 50-249

PERIODICALS: PUBLISHING, OR PUBLISHING AND PRINTING

Group Publishing
2890 Monroe Ave, Loveland CO 80538-3274. 303/6693836. Employs: 50-99.

Shepards McGraw Hill Inc
1225 Aeroplaza Dr, Colorado Springs CO 80916-2245. 719/5747901. Employs: 100-249.

Wiesner Publishing
5951 Middlefield Rd Suite 204, Littleton CO 80123-2877. 303/7981274. Employs: 50-99.

BOOKS: PUBLISHING, OR PUBLISHING AND PRINTING

Dharma Bookstore
1837 Pearl St, Boulder CO 80302-5518. 303/4404343. Employs: 50-99.

Equimedia Corporation
PO Box 62295, Colorado Springs CO 80962-2295. 719/5999258. Employs: 50-99.

Piccadilly Books
4841 Ranch Dr, Colorado Springs CO 80918-4149. 719/5481844. Employs: 50-99.

Seventh-Wing Publications
310 W Platte Ave, Colorado Springs CO 80905-1330. 719/4712932. Employs: 50-99.

Shepard's Mcgraw Hill Inc
555 Middle Creek Pkwy, Monument CO 80132. 719/4883000. Employs: 50-99.

Touch Math
6760 Corporate Dr, Colorado Springs CO 80919-1985. 719/5932448. Employs: 50-99.

MISC. PUBLISHING

Centennial Media Corporation
5446 N Academy Blvd Suite 103, Colorado Springs CO 80918-3600. 719/5316000. Employs: 100-249.

Denver Directory Co
6061 S Willow, Englewood CO
80111. 303/2209500. Employs:
100-249.

Desktop Designs
7730 E Belleview Ave, Englewood
CO 80111-2616. 303/7718695.
Employs: 50-99.

Eastwood Printing & Publishing
2901 Blake St, Denver CO 80205-
2303. 303/2961905. Employs: 50-
99.

Media Image Corp
5299 Dtc Blvd, Englewood CO
80111-3321. 303/7707300.
Employs: 50-99.

Micromedex Inc
600 Grant St Suite 350, Denver CO
80203-3525. 303/8311400.
Employs: 100-249.

Personal Business Center
8801 Yosemite, Englewood CO
80111. 303/3377770. Employs: 50-
99.

Rocky Mtn Food Processors

6635 S Dayton St, Englewood CO
80111-6101. 303/7904349.
Employs: 50-99.

US West Inc
380 W 37th St, Loveland CO
80538-2260. 303/8929779.
Employs: 100-249.

Data Business Publishing
15 Inverness Way E, Englewood
CO 80112-5704. 303/7990381.
Employs: 50-99.

First Financial Publishing
2600 S Parker Rd, Aurora CO
80014-1613. 303/3374900.
Employs: 50-99.

R & K Productions
3340 S Richfield Way, Aurora CO
80013-2079. 303/6939886.
Employs: 50-99.

Desktop Concepts
7108 S Alton Way, Englewood CO
80112-2106. 303/2205333.
Employs: 50-99.

Icon Graphics
1930 S Havana St, Aurora CO
80014-1063. 303/7457233.
Employs: 50-99.

For more information on career opportunities in book and magazine publishing:

<u>Special Programs</u>

**THE NEW YORK
UNIVERSITY SUMMER
PUBLISHING PROGRAM**
48 Cooper Square, Room 108, New
York NY 10003. 212/998-7219.

**THE RADCLIFFE
PUBLISHING COURSE**
77 Brattle Street, Cambridge MA
02138. 617/495-8678.

**RICE UNIVERSITY
PUBLISHING PROGRAM**

Office of Continuing Studies, P.O.
Box 1892, Houston TX 77001.
713/520-6022.

**UNIVERSITY OF DENVER
PUBLISHING PROGRAM**
2199 South University Boulevard,
Denver CO 80208. 303/871-2570.

Associations

AMERICAN BOOKSELLERS ASSOCIATION
560 White Plains Road, Tarrytown NY 10591. 914/631-7800.

ASSOCIATION OF AMERICAN PUBLISHERS
220 East 23rd Street, New York NY 10010. 212/689-8920.

MAGAZINE PUBLISHERS ASSOCIATION
575 Lexington Avenue, Suite 540, New York NY 10022. 212/752-0055.

WRITERS GUILD OF AMERICA EAST
555 West 57th Street, Suite 1230, New York NY 10019. 212/767-7800.

WRITERS GUILD OF AMERICA WEST
8955 Beverly Boulevard, Los Angeles CA 90048. 310/550-1000.

BROADCASTING

Across the board, a very tough field to break into -- whether it's TV, radio, or cable. Many analysts look to local broadcast outlets for the most job opportunities, and local all-news cable stations are the newest trend on the dial.

HOME BOX OFFICE
5445 DTC Parkway, Suite 700, Englewood CO 80111. 303/220-2900. **Contact:** Terri L. Tuggle, Personnel. **Description:** Regional headquarters for the well-known pay television cable network. A subsidiary of Time/Warner, Inc. **Common positions:** Marketing Specialist. **Educational backgrounds sought:** Business Administration; Communications; Economics; Finance; Liberal Arts; Marketing. **Benefits:** medical insurance; dental insurance; pension plan; life insurance; tuition assistance; disability coverage; profit sharing; employee discounts; savings plan. **Corporate headquarters:** New York, NY. **Operations at this facility:** regional headquarters; administration; sales.

JONES INTERCABLE, INC.
9697 East Mineral Avenue, Englewood CO 80112. 303/792-3111. **Contact:** Bob Schultz, Personnel Director. **Description:** A cable television company.

SPACELINK, LTD.
9697 East Mineral Avenue, Englewood CO 80112. 303/792-9191. **Contact:** Bob Schultz, Personnel Director. **Description:** A Denver-area cable television company.

TELE-COMMUNICATIONS, INC.
P.O. Box 5630, Denver CO 80217. 303/721-5500. **Contact:** department of applicant's interest. **Description:** Owns and operates CATV systems, TV stations, and broadcast networks.

TELEMATION INC.
8745 East Orchard Road, Suite 500, Englewood CO 80111. 303/290-8000. **Contact:** department of applicant's interest. **Description:** Designs, produces, and markets goods and services to the television industry. Goods and services include TV origination equipment and other components used by television stations, CATV operators, and video production houses. Also produces TV commercials on a contract basis, as well as training materials, video products, and other TV program materials used in a broad range of television transmitting applications. **Corporate headquarters:** This location.

TELEVISION TECHNOLOGY CORPORATION
650 S. Taylor Avenue, Louisville CO 80027. **Contact:** Personnel. **Description:** An international company serving radio and television. Designers and manufacturers of low-and high-power transmitters/translators.

UNITED ARTIST ENTERTAINMENT
9110 Nichols Avenue, Englewood CO 80112. 303/779-5999. **Contact:** Francis Nutting, Personnel Director. **Description:** A CATV services organization. Services offered include multiple-channel basic television, including radio and television broadcasts received both over-the-air and via satellite. Offers single-channel premium services at an additional cost. Serves areas in California, Colorado, Connecticut, Idaho, Indiana, and Michigan. **Corporate headquarters:** This location.

Additional large employers: 250+

TELEVISION BROADCASTING STATIONS

Kusa Television Station
1089 Bannock St, Denver CO 80204-4036. 303/8939000. Employs: 250-499.

CABLE AND OTHER MESSAGE COMMUNICATIONS

United Cable Of Colorado
6850 S Tucson Way, Englewood CO 80112-3923. 303/7900386. Employs: 250-499.

Additional small to medium sized employers: 50-249

RADIO AND TELEVISION BROADCASTING AND COMMUNICATIONS EQUIPMENT

Ehrhorn Tech Inc

4975 N 30th St, Colorado Springs CO 80919-4101. 719/2600395. Employs: 50-99.

Houston Tracker System
90 Inverness Cir E, Englewood CO 80112-5317. 303/7904445. Employs: 100-249.

RADIO BROADCASTING STATIONS

KRDO Radio & Tv
399 S 8th St, Colorado Springs CO 80905-1803. 719/6321515. Employs: 100-249.

KYGO Radio Station
1095 S Monaco Pky, Denver CO 80224-1602. 303/3210950. Employs: 50-99.

TELEVISION BROADCASTING STATIONS

Channel 3-Tv
1200 S Sunset St, Longmont CO 80501-6527. 303/7761424. Employs: 50-99.

Full Gospel Outreach Tv-43
5050 Edison Av Ste 111, Colorado Springs CO 80915-3544. 719/5747777. Employs: 50-99.

KMGH Tv
3100 N Nevada Av, Colorado Springs CO 80907. 719/6337777. Employs: 50-99.

KUSA 9 News Boulder Bureau
1800 30th St Ste 218A, Boulder CO 80301-1026. 303/4420495. Employs: 50-99.

KCNC Tv Station
1044 Lincoln St, Denver CO 80203-2714. 303/8614444. Employs: 100-249.

KKTV Television Station
3100 N Nevada Ave, Colorado Springs CO 80907-5325. 719/6342844. Employs: 50-99.

American Technology Info Inc
10020 E Girard Ave, Denver CO 80231-5065. 303/7516100. Employs: 50-99.

Fort Collins Evening News
1201 University Ave, Fort Collins CO 80521-4554. 303/4931600. Employs: 50-99.

KBDI Channel 12
2246 Federal Blvd, Denver CO 80211-4642. 303/4581200. Employs: 50-99.

KCEC Channel 43
1111 W 8th Ave, Denver CO 80204-4346. 303/2374300. Employs: 50-99.

KMGH-Tv Channel 7
123 E Speer Blvd, Denver CO 80203-3417. 303/8327777. Employs: 100-249.

KSHP Channel 50
11111 W 8th Ave, Lakewood CO 80215-5516. 303/2380050. Employs: 50-99.

News 4 Mountain Bureau
619 Main, Frisco CO 80443. 303/6680444. Employs: 50-99.

Rbi/Remote Broadcast Inc
12439 N Mead Way, Littleton CO 80125-9759. 303/7911867. Employs: 50-99.

Sunbelt Media Inc
3800 Arapahoe Ave, Boulder CO 80303-1070. 303/7869111. Employs: 50-99.

Universal Broadcasting
2851 S Parker Rd, Aurora CO 80014-2736. 303/6710938. Employs: 50-99.

CABLE AND OTHER PAY TELEVISION SERVICES

American Tv & Communications
160 Inverness Dr W, Englewood CO 80112-5001. 303/7991200. Employs: 100-249.

Colorado Springs Cablevision
213 N Union Blvd, Colorado
Springs CO 80909-5705.
719/6336616. Employs: 50-99.

Daniels & Associates Inc
2930 E Third Ave, Denver CO
80206-5002. 303/3214242.
Employs: 100-249.

Kelly Cable Corporation
2626 Durango Dr, Colorado
Springs CO 80910-1021.
719/3900901. Employs: 50-99.

Mile High Cablevision
1617 S Acoma St, Denver CO
80223-3624. 303/7782978.
Employs: 100-249.

Netlink
7951 E Maplewood Ave Suite 200,
Englewood CO 80111-4725.
303/8433700. Employs: 50-99.

C V Cablevision
5961 S Middlefield Rd, Littleton
CO 80123-2877. 303/7302404.
Employs: 50-99.

Colorado State Office Of TCI
13701 W Jewell Ave, Lakewood
CO 80228-4172. 303/9690411.
Employs: 50-99.

International Cable
15000 W 6 Av, Golden CO 80401.
303/2784116. Employs: 50-99.

Mountain Valley Commctns Inc
26267 Conifer Rd, Conifer CO
80433-9138. 303/6747088.
Employs: 50-99.

Red Rox Cable Inc
16075 W Belleview Ave, Morrison
CO 80465-9607. 303/6970744.
Employs: 50-99.

Telcon Communications Inc
350 Indiana St, Golden CO 80401-
5050. 303/2790678. Employs: 50-
99.

The Mountain Channel
480 Sioux Trail, Pine CO 80470-
7809. 303/8389815. Employs: 50-
99.

For more information on career opportunities in broadcasting:

Associations

**ACADEMY OF TELEVISION
ARTS & SCIENCES**
5220 Lankershim Boulevard, North
Hollywood CA 91601. 818/754-
2800.

**BROADCAST EDUCATION
ASSOCIATION**
1771 N Street NW, Washington
DC 20036. 202/429-5355.

**BROADCAST PROMOTION
AND MARKETING
EXECUTIVES**
6225 Sunset Boulevard, Suite 624,
Los Angeles CA 90028. 213/465-
3777.

**INTERNATIONAL RADIO
AND TV SOCIETY**
420 Lexington Avenue, Suite 1714,
New York NY 10170. 212/867-
6650.

**INTERNATIONAL
TELEVISION ASSOCIATION**
6311 North O'Connor Road, LB51,
Irving TX 75039. 214/869-1112.

**NATIONAL ACADEMY OF
TELEVISION ARTS &
SCIENCES**
111 West 57th Street, Suite 1020,
New York NY 10019. 212/586-
8424.

**NATIONAL ASSOCIATION OF
BROADCASTERS**
1771 N Street NW, Washington
DC 20036. 202/429-5300.

**NATIONAL ASSOCIATION OF
BUSINESS AND
EDUCATIONAL RADIO**
1501 Duke Street, Suite 200,
Alexandria VA 22314. 703/739-
0300.

**NATIONAL ASSOCIATION OF
PUBLIC TELEVISION
STATIONS**
1350 Connecticut Avenue NW,
Suite 200
Washington DC 20036. 202/887-
1700.

**NATIONAL CABLE
TELEVISION ASSOCIATION**
1724 Massachusetts Avenue NW,
Washington DC 20036. 202/775-
3550.

**TELEVISION BUREAU OF
ADVERTISING**
477 Madison Avenue, New York
NY 10022-5892. 212/486-1111.

**WOMEN IN RADIO AND TV,
INC.**
1101 Connecticut Avenue NW,
Suite 700, Washington DC 20036.
202/429-5102.

Magazines

**BROADCAST MANAGEMENT/
ENGINEERING**
295 Madison Avenue, New York
NY 10017. 212/685-5320.

BROADCASTING
Broadcasting Publications Inc.,
1735 DeSales Street NW,
Washington DC 20036. 202/638-
1022.

ELECTRONIC MEDIA
Crain Communications, 220 East
42nd Street, New York NY 10017.
212/210-0100.

TELEVISION RADIO AGE
Television Editorial Corporation,
1270 Avenue of the Americas, New
York NY 10020. 212/757-8400.

CHARITABLE, NON-PROFIT, HUMANITARIAN

The outlook for social services workers is better than average. In fact, opportunities for qualified applicants are expected to be excellent, partly due to the rapid turnover in the industry, the growing number of older citizens, and an increased awareness of the needs of the mentally and physically handicapped.

Additional large employers: 250+

CHILD DAY CARE SERVICES

Child Opportunity Program Inc

3607 Martin Lthr Kng Blvd,
Denver CO 80205. 303/3990603.
Employs: 250-499.

Children's World Learning Centers
573 Park Point Dr, Golden CO 80401-9367. 303/5261600. Employs: 1,000+.

RESIDENTIAL CARE

Wheatridge Regional Center
10285 Ridge Rd, Wheat Ridge CO 80033-2301. 303/4247791. Employs: 250-499.

CIVIC, SOCIAL, AND FRATERNAL ASSOCIATIONS

Elks Lodge Westminster 2227
5860 Elk Dr, Westminster CO 80030. 303/4296696. Employs: 250-499.

Fraternal Order Of Eagles 3461

8160 Rosemary St, Commerce City CO 80022-4909. 303/2880861. Employs: 250-499.

Veterans Of Foreign Wars Post
3100 S Sheridan Blvd Suite P-7, Denver CO 80227-5528. 303/9361965. Employs: 250-499.

Ymca Of The Rockies
2515 Tunnel Rd, Estes Park CO 80511. 303/6239215. Employs: 250-499.

MISC. MEMBERSHIP ORGANIZATIONS

United Services Auto Association
1855 Telstar Dr, Colorado Springs CO 80920-1005. 7195988661. Employs: 250-499.

Additional small to medium sized employers: 50-249

LIBRARIES

Auraria Libraries
11th & Lawrence, Denver CO 80204. 303/5562775. Employs: 50-99.

Aurora Public Library
14949 E Alameda Dr, Aurora CO 80012-1544. 303/3402290. Employs: 50-99.

Boulder Public Library
1000 Canyon Blvd, Boulder CO 80302-5120. 303/4413100. Employs: 50-99.

Denver Public Library
1357 Broadway, Denver CO 80203-2103. 303/6408840. Employs: 50-99.

East Library Information Ctr
5550 N Union Blvd, Colorado Springs CO 80918-1950. 719/5316333. Employs: 50-99.

El Paso County Jail Library
15 E Cucharras St, Colorado Springs CO 80903-2269. 719/4715466. Employs: 100-249.

Penrose Public Library
20 N Cascade Ave, Colorado Springs CO 80903-1617. 719/4732080. Employs: 50-99.

INDIVIDUAL AND FAMILY SOCIAL SERVICES

Centennial Development Service Inc
3819 St Vrain St, Evans CO 80620-2610. 303/8257300. Employs: 100-249.

Citizens Affairs Board
11701 Community Center Dr # 20, Denver CO 80233-1001. 303/4508757. Employs: 100-249.

Developmental Disabilities Ctr
1343 Iris Ave, Boulder CO 80304-2226. 303/4411090. Employs: 100-249.

Human Services Inc
899 Logan St Suite 500, Denver CO 80203-3156. 303/8325683. Employs: 50-99.

Set Of Colorado Inc
1516 Xavier St Suite 100, Denver CO 80204-1071. 303/5348002. Employs: 50-99.

Cherry Hills Therapy Center
3575 S Washington St, Englewood CO 80110-3807. 303/7816005. Employs: 50-99.

Johnstone Development Center
5361 West 26th Ave, Wheat Ridge CO 80033. 303/2338518. Employs: 50-99.

JOB TRAINING AND VOCATIONAL REHABILITATION SERVICES

Boulder County Enterprises
735 S Lincoln St, Longmont CO 80501-6314. 303/4432028. Employs: 50-99.

Cheyenne Village
183 Crystal Park Rd, Manitou Springs CO 80829-2633. 719/6851801. Employs: 50-99.

CHILD DAYCARE SERVICES

Rent A Mom
1873 S Bellaire St Suite 1215, Denver CO 80222-4347. 303/6915099. Employs: 100-249.

Southwest Denver Headstart
979 Dela Pago St, Denver CO 80204. 303/5348573. Employs: 50-99.

Auraria Child Care Center

PO Box 173361, Denver CO 80217-3361. 303/5563188. Employs: 50-99.

Children's Ctr At Red Rocks
12600 W 6th Ave Box # 29, Golden CO 80401-5398. 303/9986160. Employs: 50-99.

Mile High Child Care Association
1510 High St, Denver CO 80218-1705. 303/3885700. Employs: 100-249.

The Learning Tree Childrns Ctr
3206 Norwood Court, Fort Collins CO 80525-2919. 303/2423980. Employs: 50-99.

RESIDENTIAL CARE

Bethphage Mission West
113 Cameron Dr, Fort Collins CO 80525-3802. 303/2233818. Employs: 50-99.

Colorado Christian Home
4325 W 29th Ave, Denver CO 80212-3032. 303/4332541. Employs: 100-249.

Excelsior Youth Center
15001 E Oxford Ave, Aurora CO 80014-4186. 303/6931550. Employs: 100-249.

Gardens At St Elizabeths
2825 W 32nd Ave, Denver CO 80211-3265. 303/4774442. Employs: 100-249.

Martin Luther Homes
404 Diamond Dr, Fort Collins CO 80525-4223. 303/2290311. Employs: 100-249.

Medalion Retirement Residence
1719 E Bijou St, Colorado Springs CO 80909-5728. 719/4714800. Employs: 100-249.

Villa At Greeley
1750 6th Ave, Greeley CO 80631-5814. 303/3539263. Employs: 50-99.

Kenton Manor Health Care Ctr
850 27th Ave, Greeley CO 80631-2807. 303/3531017. Employs: 50-99.

MISC. SOCIAL SERVICES

Acts Nineteen Eleven
6325 Sorpressa Ln, Colorado Springs CO 80920-5219. 719/4953908. Employs: 50-99.

Mile High United Way
2505 18th St, Denver CO 80211-3907. 303/4338383. Employs: 50-99.

Special Education
312 Cantril St, Castle Rock CO 80104-2508. 303/6889510. Employs: 100-249.

Volunteers Of America
1865 Larimer St, Denver CO 80202-1422. 303/2970408. Employs: 100-249.

BUSINESS ASSOCIATIONS

Denver Chamber Of Commerce
1445 Market St, Denver CO 80202-1727. 303/8948500. Employs: 50-99.

Denver Regl Council Of Govts
2480 W 26th Ave, Denver CO 80211-5503. 303/4551000. Employs: 50-99.

Mountain States Employment Council
1790 Logan St, Denver CO 80203-1248. 303/8395177. Employs: 50-99.

Natl Council On Compensation

7535 E Hampden Ave Suite 613, Denver CO 80231-4866. 303/6958888. Employs: 100-249.

Western Dairymen's Cooperative
12450 Washington St, Denver CO 80241-2405. 303/4510422. Employs: 50-99.

CIVIC, SOCIAL, AND FRATERNAL ASSOCIATIONS

Arvada Knights Of Columbus
5701 Independence St, Arvada CO 80002-2140. 303/4234603. Employs: 50-99.

Boulder Ymca
2850 Mapleton Ave, Boulder CO 80301-1122. 303/4422778. Employs: 50-99.

Longmont Ymca
950 Lashley St, Longmont CO 80501-3516. 303/7760370. Employs: 50-99.

Young Life
720 W Monument St, Colorado Springs CO 80904-3624. 719/4734262. Employs: 50-99.

RELIGIOUS ORGANIZATIONS

Calvary Temple Church
200 S University Blvd, Denver CO 80209-3220. 303/7447213. Employs: 50-99.

Catholic Archdiocese Of Denver
200 Josephine St, Denver CO 80206-4710. 303/3884411. Employs: 100-249.

Christian Missionary Alliance
8595 Explorer Dr, Colorado Springs CO 80920-1012. 719/5995999. Employs: 100-249.

Compassion International Inc
3955 Cragwood Dr, Colorado Springs CO 80918-7859. 719/5949900. Employs: 100-249.

Faith Mission House Of Prayer
611 E Espanola St, Colorado Springs CO 80907-7651. 719/6331233. Employs: 100-249.

Front Range Alliance Church
1015 Garden Of The Gods Rd, Colorado Springs CO 80907. 719/2600333. Employs: 100-249.

Ministry To The Handicapped
1050 S Birch St, Denver CO 80222-2601. 303/7595150. Employs: 100-249.

MISC. MEMBERSHIP ORGANIZATIONS

Jefferson County Community Ctr
5685 Gray St, Arvada CO 80002-2821. 303/4221305. Employs: 100-249.

CHEMICAL AND ENVIRONMENTAL

Historically, the chemicals industry has been a cyclical one and is currently on the low end of its cycle. As a result, the industry has diversified, imposed tight cost controls, and streamlined operations. Jobseekers with chemical engineering experience will benefit from the current shortage of workers in the industry. Look for a growing number of firms to move into the environmental field.

AMERICAN PRIDE
P.O. Box 98, Henderson CO 80640. 303/659-3640. **Contact:** Anthony Duran, Office Manager. **Description:** Markets bulk and bagged fertilizer, agricultural chemicals, seeds, feed, and veterinary supplies. **Operations at this facility:** administration; sales. **Corporate headquarters:** This location. **Common positions:** Agronomics Specialist. **Educational backgrounds sought:** Business Administration; Marketing. **Benefits:** medical insurance; dental insurance; pension plan; life insurance; tuition assistance; disability coverage; savings plan.

DOW CHEMICAL COMPANY
EXTRUSION PLANT
3555 Moline Street, Aurora CO 80010. 303/343-8667. **Contact:** Betty Allen, Personnel Director. **Description:** A chemical company production facility. **Corporate headquarters:** Midland, MI.

SCOTT'S LIQUID GOLD-INC.

4880 Havana Street, Denver CO 80239. 303/373-4860. **Contact:** Connie Miller, Director of Personnel. **Description:** Engaged in the manufacture and distribution of household chemical products, as well as disposable cigarette filters. Principal products include Scott's Liquid Gold Wood Cleaner and Preservative, Scott's Liquid Gold Glass Cleaner, Touch of Scent Air Freshener, and Touch of Scent Too Air Freshener. **Common positions:** Accountant; Chemist; Computer Programmer; Credit Manager; Consumer Relations Representative; Electrical Engineer; Mechanical Engineer; Food Technologist; Department Manager; Operations/Production Manager; Marketing Specialist; Quality Control Supervisor; Sales Representative. **Educational backgrounds sought:** Accounting; Business Administration; Chemistry; Computer Science; Engineering; Liberal Arts; Marketing. **Benefits:** medical, dental, and life insurance; pension plan; profit sharing; employee discounts; savings plan. **Corporate headquarters:** This location. **Operations at this facility:** regional headquarters; manufacturing; research/development; administration; service; sales.

Additional large employers: 250+

MISC. INDUSTRIAL INORGANIC CHEMICALS

Hach Co

5600 Lindburgh Dr, Loveland CO 80538-8902. 303/6693050. Employs: 250-499.

Additional small to medium sized employers: 50-249

INDUSTRIAL GASES

Union Carbide Corp
950 Des Moines Ave, Loveland CO 80537-5105. 303/6697800. Employs: 50-99.

MISC. INDUSTRIAL INORGANIC CHEMICALS

Bandgap Tech Corp
325 Interlocken, Broomfield CO 80021. 303/5460070. Employs: 50-99.

Molycorp Inc
9481 Hc 85, Louviers CO 80131. 303/7917600. Employs: 50-99.

PHOSPHATIC FERTILIZERS

Nu West Industries Inc

8400 E Prentice Ave, Englewood CO 80111-2912. 303/7211396. Employs: 100-249.

ADHESIVES AND SEALANTS

American Variseal Corp
510 Burbank St, Broomfield CO 80020-1604. 303/4651727. Employs: 50-99.

Central Products
1095 S 4th, Brighton CO 80601. 303/6540500. Employs: 100-249.

Sw Portland Cement
Hc 66, Frederick CO 80530. 303/8236685. Employs: 50-99.

MISC. CHEMICALS AND CHEMICAL PREPARATION

Computer Prods Tecnetics
6287 Araphoe, Boulder CO 80303.
303/4423837. Employs: 100-249.

Somatogen Inc
5979 Central, Boulder CO 80301.
303/4409988. Employs: 50-99.

For more information on career opportunities in the chemical and environmental industries:

Associations

AMERICAN CHEMICAL SOCIETY
Career Services, 1155 16th Street NW, Washington DC 20036.
202/872-4600.

AMERICAN INSTITUTE OF CHEMICAL ENGINEERING
345 East 47th Street, New York NY 10017. 212/705-7338.

AMERICAN INSTITUTE OF CHEMISTS
7315 Wisconsin Avenue, Bethesda MD 20814. 301/652-2447.

ASSOCIATION OF STATE & INTERSTATE WATER POLLUTION CONTROL ADMINISTRATORS
750 First Street NE, Suite 910, Washington DC 20002. 202/898-0905.

CHEMICAL MANUFACTURERS ASSOCIATION
2501 M Street, Washington DC 20037. 202/887-1100.

CHEMICAL MARKETING RESEARCH ASSOCIATION
60 Bay Street, Staten Island NY 10301. 718/876-8800.

WATER POLLUTION CONTROL FEDERATION
601 Wythe Street, Alexandria VA 22314. 703/684-2400.

Directories

CHEMICAL INDUSTRY DIRECTORY
State Mutual Book and Periodical Service, 521 Fifth Avenue, New York NY 10175. 212/682-5844.

CHEMICAL INDUSTRY DIRECTORY AND WHO'S WHO
Taylor & Francis, 1900 Frost Road, Suite 101, Bristol PA 19007.
800/821-8312.

CHEMICALS DIRECTORY
Cahners Publishing, 275 Washington Street, Newton MA 02158. 617/964-3030.

DIRECTORY OF CHEMICAL ENGINEERING CONSULTANTS
American Institute of Chemical Engineering, 345 East 47th Street, New York NY 10017. 212/705-7338.

DIRECTORY OF CHEMICAL PRODUCERS
SRI, 333 Ravenswood Avenue, Menlo Park CA 94025. 415/326-6200.

Magazines

CHEMICAL & ENGINEERING NEWS
1155 16th Street NW, Washington DC 20036. 202/872-4600.

CHEMICAL MARKETING REPORTER
Schnell Publishing Co., 80 Brot Street, 23rd Floor, New York NY 10004. 212/248-4177.

CHEMICAL PROCESSING

Putnam Publishing Co., 301 East Erie Street, Chicago IL 60611. 312/644-2020.

CHEMICAL WEEK
888 7th Avenue, 26th Floor, New York NY 10106. 212/621-4900.

COLLEGES AND UNIVERSITIES/EDUCATION

Job prospects for college faculty will increase at average speed during the 90's. Most openings will result from retirements. The best prospects are in business, engineering, health sciences, physical sciences, and mathematics. Among kindergarten and elementary school teachers, the best opportunities await those with training in special education. Among high school teachers, opportunities will increase rapidly. Increased teacher involvement and higher salaries will attract new applicants.

COLORADO STATE UNIVERSITY
Human Resource Services, Room 120, Student Service Building, Fort Collins CO 80523. 303/491-1794. **Contact:** Personnel Services. **Description:** A state university.

METROPOLITAN STATE COLLEGE
Campus Box C, P.O. Box 1773361, Denver CO 80217-3361. 303/556-3383. **Contact:** Human Resources Department. **Description:** A state college.

**UNIVERSITY OF COLORADO
AT BOULDER**
Staff Personnel, 1511 University Avenue, Campus Box 475, Boulder CO 80309. 303/492-6475. **Contact:** Personnel Department. **Description:** Boulder location of the large university.

**UNIVERSITY OF COLORADO
AT DENVER**
Campus Box 130, P.O. Box 173364, Denver CO 80217-3364. **Contact:** Personnel Department. **Description:** Denver location of the large university.

UNIVERSITY OF DENVER
2020 E. Evans, Suite 104, Denver CO 80208. 303/871-3460. **Contact:** Employment Coordinator, Human Resources. **Description:** A university. **Common positions:** Accountant; Blue-Collar Worker Supervisor; Financial Analyst; Department Manager; Management Trainee; Public Relations

Specialist. **Educational backgrounds sought:** Accounting; Business Administration; Communications; Finance; Liberal Arts; Marketing. **Special programs:** Training programs; internships. **Benefits:** medical insurance; dental insurance; pension plan; life insurance; tuition assistance; disability coverage; employee discounts; savings plan. **Corporate headquarters:** This location. **Operations at this facility:** research/development; administration; service.

UNIVERSITY OF NORTHERN COLORADO
9th Avenue 17th Street, Greeley CO 80639. **Contact:** Personnel Department. **Description:** A university.

Additional large employers: 250+

ELEMENTARY AND SECONDARY SCHOOLS

Douglas County Schools
620 S Wilcox St, Castle Rock CO 80104-1739. 303/6883195. Employs: 500-999.

Littleton School District 6
5776 S Crocker St, Littleton CO 80120-2012. 303/7957007. Employs: 500-999.

COLLEGES, UNIVERSITIES, AND PROFESSIONAL SCHOOLS

Aurora Higher Education Center
1027 9th St, Denver CO 80217. 303/5563291. Employs: 250-499.

Colorado College
14 E Cache La Poudre St, Colorado Springs CO 80903-3243. 7194732233. Employs: 250-499.

Colorado School Of Mines
1500 Illinois St, Golden CO 80401-1887. 303/2733000. Employs: 250-499.

Regis College
3539 W 50th Ave, Denver CO 80221-1011. 303/4584100. Employs: 500-999.

JUNIOR COLLEGES AND TECHNICAL INSTITUTES

Aims Community College
5401 20th St, Greeley CO 80634-3002. 303/3308008. Employs: 250-499.

MISC. VOCATIONAL SCHOOLS

Colorado Technical College
4435 N Chestnut St, Colorado Springs CO 80907-3812. 7195980200. Employs: 250-499.

Additional small to medium sized employers: 50-249

ELEMENTARY AND SECONDARY SCHOOLS

Adams Arapahoe County Dist 28
1085 Peoria St, Aurora CO 80011-6203. 303/3448060. Employs: 50-99.

Adams City High School
4625 E 68th Ave, Commerce City
CO 80022-2367. 303/2893111.
Employs: 50-99.

Adams County School
11285 Highline Dr, Denver CO
80233-3076. 303/4511561.
Employs: 50-99.

Arapahoe Co Cherry Creek Schls
4700 S Yosemite St, Englewood
CO 80111-1307. 303/7731184.
Employs: 50-99.

Blevins Junior High School
2101 S Taft Hill Rd, Fort Collins
CO 80526-1438. 303/4848350.
Employs: 50-99.

Boltz Junior High School
720 Boltz Dr, Fort Collins CO
80525-2703. 303/2263333.
Employs: 50-99.

Boulder High School
1604 Arapahoe Av, Boulder CO
80302-6312. 303/4422430.
Employs: 50-99.

Centaurus High School
10300 S Boulder Rd, Lafayette CO
80026-1402. 303/6659211.
Employs: 50-99.

Challenger Middle School
10215 Lexington Dr, Colorado
Springs CO 80920-1410.
719/5981007. Employs: 50-99.

Colorado Academy
3800 S Pierce St, Denver CO
80235-2404. 303/9861501.
Employs: 50-99.

**Colorado School For Deaf &
Blind**
33 N Institute St, Colorado Springs
CO 80903-3508. 719/6365186.
Employs: 100-249.

**Colorado Springs Christian
School**
301 Austin Bluffs Pky, Colorado
Springs CO 80918-3922.
719/5993553. Employs: 50-99.

Eagleview Middle School
1325 Vindicator Dr, Colorado
Springs CO 80919-3616.
719/5480316. Employs: 50-99.

Fort Collins High School
1400 Remington St, Fort Collins
CO 80524-4142. 303/4933110.
Employs: 50-99.

Gilpin Extended Day Center
2949 California St, Denver CO
80205-3053. 303/2970315.
Employs: 50-99.

Graland Country Day School
30 Birch St, Denver CO 80220-
5634. 303/3990390. Employs: 100-
249.

Greeley Central High School
1515 14th Ave, Greeley CO 80631-
4737. 303/3529325. Employs: 50-
99.

Greeley Public School District
811 15th St, Greeley CO 80631-
4625. 303/3521543. Employs: 50-
99.

Greeley Schools Custodial Dept
2204 5th Ave, Greeley CO 80631-
7120. 303/3539100. Employs: 50-
99.

Harrison High School
2755 Janitell Rd, Colorado Springs
CO 80906-4102. 719/5768522.
Employs: 50-99.

Heath Junior High School
2223 16th St, Greeley CO 80631-
5118. 303/3531750. Employs: 50-
99.

Kent School
4000 E Quincy Ave, Englewood CO 80110-4916. 303/7707660. Employs: 50-99.

Longmont Senior High School
1040 Sunset St, Longmont CO 80501-4118. 303/7766014. Employs: 50-99.

Longs Peak Junior High School
1500 14th Av, Longmont CO 80501-3204. 303/7765611. Employs: 50-99.

Martinez Elementary School
6460 Vickers Dr, Colorado Springs CO 80918-5657. 719/5202695. Employs: 50-99.

McLaine Community High School
2001 Hoyt St, Lakewood CO 80215-1639. 303/2387847. Employs: 50-99.

Poudre Senior High School
201 S Impala Dr, Fort Collins CO 80521-2216. 303/4841701. Employs: 50-99.

Rampart High School
8250 Lexington Dr, Colorado Springs CO 80920-4301. 719/5949292. Employs: 50-99.

Sabin Junior High School
3605 N Carefree Cir, Colorado Springs CO 80917-2030. 719/5202470. Employs: 50-99.

Sierra High School
2250 Jet Wing Dr, Colorado Springs CO 80916-2427. 719/5919400. Employs: 50-99.

Skyline High School
600 E Mountain View Av, Longmont CO 80501-3044. 303/6510123. Employs: 50-99.

Bill Reed Junior High School

370 W 4th St, Loveland CO 80537-5416. 303/6675136. Employs: 50-99.

Broomfield Heights Middle Sch
1555 Daphne St, Broomfield CO 80020-1161. 303/4662387. Employs: 50-99.

Carmody Middle School
2050 S Kipling St, Denver CO 80227-2122. 303/9858766. Employs: 50-99.

Castle Rock Junior High School
2693 N High School Rd, Castle Rock CO 80104-1641. 303/6883169. Employs: 50-99.

Columbia Middle School
17600 E Columbia Ave, Aurora CO 80013-4401. 303/6906570. Employs: 50-99.

East Middle School
1275 Fraser St, Aurora CO 80011-7050. 303/3649235. Employs: 50-99.

Euclid Middle School
777 W Euclid Ave, Littleton CO 80120-3406. 303/7944237. Employs: 50-99.

Irving Junior High School
1702 N Murray Blvd, Colorado Springs CO 80915-1333. 719/5202430. Employs: 50-99.

Mrachek Middle School
1955 S Telluride St, Aurora CO 80013-1337. 303/7502836. Employs: 50-99.

Newton Middle School
4001 E Arapahoe Rd, Littleton CO 80122-2174. 303/7715540. Employs: 50-99.

North Middle School
12095 Montview Blvd, Aurora CO
80010-1608.   303/3647411.
Employs: 50-99.

Northeast Junior High School
11700 Irma Dr, Denver CO 80233-
2173. 303/4521043. Employs: 50-
99.

Pecos Junior High School
9450 Pecos St, Denver CO 80221-
5923. 303/4284666. Employs: 50-
99.

Powell Middle School
8000 S Corona Way, Littleton CO
80122-2926.   303/7958822.
Employs: 50-99.

Rishel Middle School
451 S Tejon St, Denver CO 80223-
1928. 303/7774436. Employs: 50-
99.

Skinner Middle School
3435 W 40th Ave, Denver CO
80211-1921.   303/4338851.
Employs: 50-99.

West Middle School
10100 E 13th Ave, Aurora CO
80010-3302.   303/3662671.
Employs: 50-99.

Westlake Village Jr High School
2800 W 135th Ave, Broomfield CO
80020-5129.   303/4691867.
Employs: 50-99.

Air Academy High School
A F Academy, USAF Academy CO
80840. 719/4721295. Employs: 50-
99.

Arvada West Senior High School
11325 Allendale Dr, Arvada CO
80004-4477.   303/4222326.
Employs: 50-99.

Aurora Central High School

11700 E 11th Ave, Aurora CO
80010-3758.   303/3401600.
Employs: 50-99.

Brighton High School
270 S 8th Ave, Brighton CO
80601-2132.   303/6594830.
Employs: 50-99.

Broomfield High School
1000 Daphne Street, Broomfield
CO   80020-1906.   303/4667344.
Employs: 50-99.

Chatfield Senior High School
7227 S Simms St, Littleton CO
80127-3245.   303/9720763.
Employs: 100-249.

Columbine High School
6201 S Pierce St, Littleton CO
80123-3636.   303/9794700.
Employs: 50-99.

Coronado High School
1590 W Fillmore St, Colorado
Springs   CO   80904-1104.
719/5202500. Employs: 50-99.

Eaglecrest School
5100 S Picadilly St, Aurora CO
80015-3300.   303/6990408.
Employs: 100-249.

Englewood High School
3800 S Logan St, Englewood CO
80110-3723.   303/7628630.
Employs: 50-99.

Evergreen High School
5301 S Olive Rd, Evergreen CO
80439-7306.   303/6743341.
Employs: 50-99.

Gateway High School
1300 S Sable Blvd, Aurora CO
80012-4631.   303/7557160.
Employs: 100-249.

George Washington High School
655 S Monaco Pky, Denver CO
80224-1228.   303/3992214.
Employs: 100-249.

Golden High School
701 24th St, Golden CO 80401-
2398. 303/2784494. Employs: 50-
99.

Greeley West High School
2401 N 35th Ave, Greeley CO
80631-9443.   303/3305303.
Employs: 50-99.

Green Mountain High School
13175 W Green Mountain Dr,
Lakewood   CO   80228-3512.
303/9851591. Employs: 50-99.

Heritage High School
1401 W Geddes Ave, Littleton CO
80120-4120.   303/7951353.
Employs: 50-99.

Lakewood High School
9700 W 8th Ave, Lakewood CO
80215-5807.   303/2380566.
Employs: 50-99.

Mitchell High School
1205 Potter Dr, Colorado Springs
CO   80909-6908.   719/5202700.
Employs: 50-99.

Montbello High School
5000 Crown Blvd, Denver CO
80239-4329.   303/3712050.
Employs: 50-99.

North High School
2960 N Speer Blvd, Denver CO
80211-3754.   303/4332511.
Employs: 100-249.

Overland High School
12400 E Jewell Ave, Aurora CO
80012-5324.   303/6963700.
Employs: 100-249.

Ponderosa High School
7007 E Bayou Gulch Rd, Parker
CO   80134-5459.   303/8412770.
Employs: 50-99.

Rangeview High School
17599 E Iliff Ave, Aurora CO
80013-4212.   303/6956848.
Employs: 100-249.

Ranum High School
2401 W 80th Ave, Denver CO
80221-3801.   303/4289577.
Employs: 50-99.

Skyview High School
8890 York St, Denver CO 80229-
7907. 303/2870285. Employs: 50-
99.

Smoky Hill High School
16100 Smoky Hill Rd, Aurora CO
80015-1751.   303/6931700.
Employs: 100-249.

South High School
1700 E Louisiana Ave, Denver CO
80210-1810.   303/7774421.
Employs: 50-99.

Standley Lake High School
9300 W 104th Ave, Broomfield CO
80021-3686.   303/4651144.
Employs: 50-99.

Thomas Jefferson High School
3950 S Holly St, Denver CO
80237-1117.   303/7582400.
Employs: 50-99.

Thompson Valley High School
1669 Eagle Dr, Loveland CO
80537-6225.   303/6690801.
Employs: 50-99.

Westminster High School
4276 W 68th Ave, Westminster CO
80030-5832.   303/4289541.
Employs: 50-99.

Laradon Hall
5100 Lincoln St, Denver CO 80216-2056.   303/2962400. Employs: 50-99.

Aurora Adult Ed & Comm Ctr
1085 Peoria St, Aurora CO 80011-6203. 303/3666019. Employs: 50-99.

Horace Mann Middle School
4130 Navajo St, Denver CO 80211-2534. 303/4332553. Employs: 50-99.

Lake Middle School
1820 Lowell Blvd, Denver CO 80204-1549.   303/6296902. Employs: 50-99.

South Middle School
12310 E Parkview Dr, Aurora CO 80011-8311.   303/3647623. Employs: 50-99.

Aurora Hills Middle School
1009 S Uvalda St, Aurora CO 80012-3407.   303/3417450. Employs: 50-99.

Henry Middle School
3005 S Golden Way, Denver CO 80227-3849.   303/9892330. Employs: 50-99.

Hill Middle School
451 Clermont St, Denver CO 80220-5019.   303/3990254. Employs: 50-99.

Horizon Middle School
3981 S Reservoir Rd, Aurora CO 80013-3804.   303/6934242. Employs: 50-99.

Kepner Middle School
911 S Hazel Ct, Denver CO 80219-3418. 303/9354601. Employs: 50-99.

Kunsmiller Middle School

2250 S Quitman Way, Denver CO 80219-5139.   303/9345476. Employs: 50-99.

Laredo Middle School
5000 S Laredo St, Aurora CO 80015-1749.   303/6931500. Employs: 50-99.

North Arvada Jr High School
7285 Pierce St, Arvada CO 80003-3064. 303/4212660. Employs: 50-99.

Campus Middle School
4785 S Dayton St, Englewood CO 80111-1302.   303/7701150. Employs: 50-99.

Deer Creek Middle School
9201 W Columbine Dr, Littleton CO 80123-4140.   303/9781662. Employs: 50-99.

Martin Luther King Mid School
19535 E 46th Ave, Denver CO 80249-6637.   303/3739870. Employs: 50-99.

Parker Junior High School
6651 E Pine Ln, Parker CO 80134-8715. 303/8412656. Employs: 50-99.

Prairie Middle School
12600 E Jewell Ave, Aurora CO 80012-5325.   303/6963750. Employs: 50-99.

Jefferson High School
2305 Pierce St Denver CO 80214-1031. 303/2381361. Employs: 50-99.

Douglas County High School
2842 N High School Rd, Castle Rock   CO   80104-9496. 303/6883166. Employs: 50-99.

Alameda Senior High School
1255 S Wadsworth Blvd,
Lakewood CO 80232-5406.
303/9854421. Employs: 50-99.

Arvada Senior High School
7951 W 65th Ave, Arvada CO
80004-3300. 303/4233830.
Employs: 50-99.

Hinkley High School
1250 Chambers Rd, Aurora CO
80011-7117. 303/3401500.
Employs: 50-99.

Kennedy High School
2855 S Lamar St, Denver CO
80227-3809. 303/7634300.
Employs: 50-99.

Littleton High School
199 E Littleton Blvd, Littleton CO
80121-1106. 303/7982584.
Employs: 50-99.

Loveland High School
920 W 29th St, Loveland CO
80538-2559. 303/6675374.
Employs: 50-99.

Manual High School
1700 E 28th Ave, Denver CO
80205-4502. 303/3916300.
Employs: 50-99.

Palmer High School
301 N Nevada Ave, Colorado
Springs CO 80903-1218.
719/5202800. Employs: 50-99.

Rocky Mountain High School
1300 W Swallow Rd, Fort Collins
CO 80526-2412. 303/2265626.
Employs: 50-99.

Thornton High School
9351 Washington St, Denver CO
80229-3520. 303/4524800.
Employs: 50-99.

Wasson High School

2115 Afton Way, Colorado Springs
CO 80909-1921. 719/5202900.
Employs: 50-99.

Wheat Ridge High School
9505 W 32nd Ave, Wheat Ridge
CO 80033-5772. 303/2381281.
Employs: 50-99.

Abraham Lincoln High School
2285 S Federal Blvd, Denver CO
80219-5433. 303/7275000.
Employs: 100-249.

Arapahoe High School
2201 E Dry Creek Rd, Littleton CO
80122-3101. 303/7942641.
Employs: 100-249.

Bear Creek High School
3490 S Kipling St, Denver CO
80227-4331. 303/9854444.
Employs: 50-99.

Cherry Creek High School
9300 E Union Ave, Englewood CO
80111-1306. 303/7738920.
Employs: 100-249.

Doherty High School
4515 Barnes Rd, Colorado Springs
CO 80917-1519. 719/5202600.
Employs: 50-99.

East High School
1545 Detroit St, Denver CO 80206-
1508. 303/3948300. Employs: 100-
249.

Fairview High School
1515 Greenbriar Blvd, Boulder CO
80303-7043. 303/4997600.
Employs: 50-99.

**Highlands Ranch Jr & Sr High
School**
9375 Cresthill Ln, Littleton CO
80126-4409. 303/4700700.
Employs: 50-99.

Horizon High School
5321 E 136th Ave, Brighton CO 80601-7714.   303/4505227.
Employs: 100-249.

Northglenn High School
601 W 100th Pl, Denver CO 80221-6003.   303/4511241.
Employs: 100-249.

Pomona High School
8101 N Pomona Dr, Arvada CO 80005-2581.   303/4239092.
Employs: 100-249.

West High School
951 Elati St, Denver CO 80204-3939. 303/6205300. Employs: 100-249.

Widefield High School
615 Widefield Dr, Colorado Springs CO 80911-1839.
719/3923427. Employs: 50-99.

T H Pickens Tech Center
500 Buckley Rd, Aurora CO 80011-9307.   303/3444910.
Employs: 50-99.

Weld County Boces
PO Box 578, La Salle CO 80645-0578. 303/2846975. Employs: 100-249.

Burlington School Dist R E 6 J
PO Box 369, Burlington CO 80807-0369.   719/3468737.
Employs: 50-99.

Fort Lupton School Dist Re 8
301 Reynolds St, Fort Lupton CO 80621-1329.   303/8576291.
Employs: 50-99.

Academy School District 20
7610 N Union Blvd, Colorado Springs CO 80920-3861.
719/5982566. Employs: 100-249.

Denver School District 1

900 Grant St, Denver CO 80203-2907. 303/8371000. Employs: 100-249.

COLLEGES, UNIVERSITIES, AND PROFESSIONAL SCHOOLS

Aims Community College S Campus
260 College Ave, Fort Lupton CO 80621. 303/3524664. Employs: 50-99.

Arapahoe Community College
5900 S Santa Fe Dr, Littleton CO 80120-1801.   303/7941550.
Employs: 100-249.

Barnes Business College
150 Sheridan Blvd, Lakewood CO 80226-8101.   303/9228454.
Employs: 50-99.

Central Texas College
Building 2419 Ste 2419, Colorado Springs CO 80913. 719/5767371.
Employs: 50-99.

Chapman College
4710 Flintridge Dr Suite 201, Colorado Springs CO 80918-4299.
719/5930970. Employs: 50-99.

Colorado Christian University
180 S Garrison St, Lakewood CO 80226-1053.   303/2385386.
Employs: 50-99.

Community College Of Denver
1111 W Colfax Ave, Denver CO 80204-2026.   303/5562413.
Employs: 100-249.

Marilyn Hickey Bible College
8081 E Orchard Rd, Englewood CO 80111-2535.   303/6981155.
Employs: 50-99.

Nazarene Bible College
1111 Chapman Dr, Colorado Springs CO 80916-1901. 719/5965110. Employs: 50-99.

Pikes Peak Community College
5675 S Academy Blvd, Colorado Springs CO 80906-5422. 719/5767711. Employs: 100-249.

Univ Of Colorado
University Of Colo, Boulder CO 80309. 303/4920111. Employs: 100-249.

University Of Colorado
1420 Austin Bluffs Pk, Colorado Springs CO 80918-3733. 719/5933000. Employs: 100-249.

University Of The Rockies
3525 S Tamarac Dr Suite 370, Denver CO 80237-1433. 303/7700555. Employs: 50-99.

Webster University
1485 Kelly Johnson Blvd # 300, Colorado Springs CO 80920-3911. 719/5907340. Employs: 50-99.

Beth El Col Of Nursing
10 No Farragut, Colorado Springs CO 80909-5626. 303/4755170. Employs: 100-249.

Metropolitan State College
1006 11th Street, Denver CO 80204-2025. 303/5563018. Employs: 100-249.

National Col-Colorado Springs
2577 N Chelton, Colorado Springs CO 80909-1362. 719/3944800. Employs: 100-249.

Rockmont College
8801 W Alameda Ave, Lakewood CO 80226-2822. 303/2385386. Employs: 50-99.

Rocky Mt Teacher Training

C/O Rention 2000 Floral Drive, Boulder CO 80302. 303/4943002. Employs: 100-249.

U S Air Force Acad
Hq USAF Academy, USAF Academy CO 80840. 719/4722520. Employs: 100-249.

Univ Of Colo-Colorado Springs
1420 A Bluffs Pky PO Box 7150, Colorado Springs CO 80933-7150. 303/5933000. Employs: 100-249.

Univ Of Colorado At Denver
PO 173364, Denver CO 80217-3364. 303/5562800. Employs: 100-249.

Univ Of Northern Colorado
Carter Hall 4000, Greeley CO 80639. 303/3512881. Employs: 50-99.

JUNIOR COLLEGES AND TECHNICAL INSTITUTES

Denver Technical College
925 S Niagara St, Denver CO 80224-1658. 303/3293000. Employs: 50-99.

Parks Junior College
9065 Grant St, Denver CO 80229-4339. 303/4572757. Employs: 50-99.

Technical Trades Institute
1955 N Union Blvd, Colorado Springs CO 80909-2229. 719/6328116. Employs: 50-99.

Blair Jr College
828 Wooten Road, Colorado Springs CO 80915-3520. 303/5741082. Employs: 100-249.

Cmmty College Of Denver-Admin
1391 N Speer Blvd Ste 600, Denver CO 80204-2554. 303/8393481. Employs: 100-249.

Colorado Mountain College-East
901 South US Highway 24, Leadville CO 80461-9724. 719/4862015. Employs: 100-249.

Comm Col Of Aurora
16000 Centre Tech Parkway, Aurora CO 80011-9036. 303/3604700. Employs: 100-249.

Tech Trades Inst
772 Horizon Dr Junction Co, Colorado Springs CO 80909. 303/2458101. Employs: 100-249.

DATA PROCESSING SCHOOLS

Pc Squared Inc
2043 S Balsam St, Denver CO 80227-2478. 303/9801003. Employs: 50-99.

MISC. VOCATIONAL SCHOOLS

Career Education Center

2650 Eliot St, Denver CO 80211-4711. 303/4555966. Employs: 50-99.

College For Financial Planning
4695 S Monaco St, Denver CO 80237-3403. 303/7557101. Employs: 100-249.

MISC. SCHOOLS AND EDUCATIONAL SERVICES

OOLSA T & T National Training Ctr
3190 S Vaughn Way, Aurora CO 80014-3506. 303/6955000. Employs: 100-249.

Contempo Fashions
3638 S Galapago St, Englewood CO 80110-3421. 303/7818573. Employs: 100-249.

Junior Achievement National
45 E Clubhouse Dr, Colorado Springs CO 80906-4473. 719/5408000. Employs: 50-99.

For more information on career opportunities in colleges and universities, and education:

Associations

AMERICAN ASSOCIATION OF SCHOOL ADMINISTRATORS
1801 North Moore Street, Arlington VA 22209. 703/528-0700.

AMERICAN FEDERATION OF TEACHERS
555 New Jersey Avenue NW, Washington DC 20001. 202/879-4400.

ASSOCIATION OF AMERICAN UNIVERSITIES
One Dupont Circle NW, Suite 730, Washington DC 20036. 202/466-5030.

COLLEGE AND UNIVERSITY PERSONNEL ASSOCIATION
1233 20th Street NW, Suite 503, Washington DC 20036. 202/429-0311.

NATIONAL ASSOCIATION OF BIOLOGY TEACHERS
11250 Roger Bacon Drive, #19, Reston VA 22090. 703/471-1134.

NATIONAL ASSOCIATION OF COLLEGE AND UNIVERSITY BUSINESS OFFICERS
1 DuPont Circle, Suite 500, Washington DC 20036. 202/861-2500.

NATIONAL ASSOCIATION OF COLLEGE ADMISSION COUNSELORS
1631 Prince Street, Alexandria VA 22314. 703/836-2222.

NATIONAL SCIENCE TEACHERS ASSOCIATION
1742 Connecticut Avenue NW, Washington DC 20009. 202/328-5800.

Directories

HIGHER EDUCATION DIRECTORY
Council for Advancement and Support of Education, 11 DuPont Circle, Suite 400, Washington DC 20036. 202/328-5900.

Books

ACADEMIC LABOR MARKETS AND CAREERS
Falmer Press, Taylor & Francis, Inc., 1900 Frost Road, Suite 101, Bristol PA 19007. 800/821-8312.

HOW TO GET A JOB IN EDUCATION
Bob Adams, Inc., 260 Center Street, Holbrook MA 02343. 617/787-8100.

COMMUNICATIONS

Revenues in the domestic communications industry are expected to increase as the economy improves. Over the next few years, the globalization of private networks, innovations in broadband and radio technologies, and a steady march toward liberalized regulations will improve the prospects for the industry greatly. The short-term outlook for telecommunications equipment makers is fairly stable, with small 2-3 percent increases expected through the middle of the decade.
Unfortunately, employment in the equipment industry continues to decline due to continued mergers, new technology, and improved productivity.

AT&T MANUFACTURING
1200 West 120th Avenue, Westminster CO 80234-2795. 303/538-1200. **Contact:** Personnel. **Description:** A manufacturer of PBX equipment.

ANIXTER-DENVER
14509 East 33rd Place, Aurora CO 80011. 303/373-9200. **Contact:** Personnel Manager. **Description:** Wire and cable distribution company. Distributors of voice, video, data and power equipment. Leaders in the marketing of voice and data communication products.

INTERWEST COMMUNICATION
1313 S. Clarkson Street, Denver CO 80210. 303/722-1500. **Contact:** Customer Service. **Description:** A telecommunications company providing both systems and service to its clients.

LITTON DATA SYSTEMS
425 East Fillmore Street, Colorado Springs CO 80907. 719/475-7220. **Contact:** Norm Schmidt, Personnel Director. **Description:** A manufacturer of communications systems.

MCI TELECOMMUNICATIONS
WESTERN DIVISION
707 17th Street, Suite 4200, Denver CO 80202. 303/294-0005. **Contact:** Fred Viarrial, Regional Human Resources Director. **Description:** Provides domestic inter-state, long-distance service throughout the continental U.S., plus Hawaii, Puerto Rico, the Virgin Islands, and all foreign countries.

MOTOROLA COMMUNICATIONS & ELECTRONICS
20 Inverness Place East, Englewood CO 80112. 303/799-6000. **Contact:** Personnel. **Description:** A manufacturer and distributor of communications equipment, specifically two-way radios.

RAM COMMUNICATIONS OF COLORADO
6810 S. Tucson Way, Englewood CO 80112. 303/694-2337. **Contact:** Personnel Department. **Description:** A communications firm which provides paging services.

TELECRAFTER SERVICES CORPORATION
P.O. Box 27960, Denver CO 80227. 303/278-3800. **Contact:** Personnel Manager. **Description:** Subcontractor for cable television companies. Involved in the installation and marketing of client company's product. **Common positions:** Accountant; Advertising Worker; Blue-Collar Worker Supervisor; Computer Programmer; Customer Service Representative; Financial Analyst; General Manager; Management Trainee; Operations/Production Manager; Marketing Specialist; Personnel Specialist; Public Relations Specialist; Quality Control Supervisor; Reporter/Editor; Sales Representative; Cable TV Installer. **Educational backgrounds sought:** Accounting; Art/Design; Business Administration; Communications; Computer Science; Finance; Marketing. **Special programs:** Training programs. **Benefits:** medical, dental, and life insurance; tuition assistance; disability coverage; profit sharing; savings plan. **Corporate headquarters:** This location. **Parent company:** Wegener Communications. **Operations at this facility:** divisional headquarters; administration. **Listed on:** New York Stock Exchange; American Stock Exchange.

US WEST, COMMUNICATIONS
188 Inverness Drive West, Suite 170, Englewood CO 80112. 303/792-4485. **Contact:** department of interest. **Description:** A telecommunications corporation.

WESTMARC COMMUNICATIONS INC.
5619 DTC Parkway, Englewood CO 80111. 303/267-5500. **Contact:** department of applicant's interest. **Description:** Provides communication services to long distance telephone companies.

Additional large employers: 250+

TELEPHONE COMMUNICATIONS, EXCEPT RADIOTELEPHONE

AT&T Information Systems
2551 E 40th Ave, Denver CO 80205-3601. 303/2914200. Employs: 250-499.

Contel Federal Systems
1050 Academy Park Loop Ste 138, Colorado Springs CO 80910. 7193901212. Employs: 250-499.

U S West Communications Inc
1801 California St, Denver CO 80202-2614. 303/8962200. Employs: 1,000+.

US Sprint
1099 18th St Suite 1400, Denver CO 80202-1935. 303/2975000. Employs: 500-999.

US West Service Link Inc
1801 California St, Denver CO 80202-2614. 303/2915000. Employs: 250-499.

Westmarc Communications Inc
4643 S Ulster St, Denver CO 80237-2862. 303/7969100. Employs: 250-499.

Additional small to medium sized employers: 50-249

RADIOTELEPHONE COMMUNICATIONS

US West Communications
1545 Walnut St, Boulder CO 80302-5419. 303/4416211. Employs: 50-99.

TELEPHONE COMMUNICATIONS, EXCEPT RADIOTELEPHONE

AT&T
10375 E Harvard Ave Suite 300, Denver CO 80231-5967. 303/6713034. Employs: 100-249.

Automated Communications Inc
4100 E Mississippi Ave Ste 130, Denver CO 80222-3051. 303/7564333. Employs: 50-99.

MCI Telecommunications Corp
102 S Tejon St Ste 620, Colorado Springs CO 80903-5107. 719/6365033. Employs: 100-249.

MCI Telecommunications
6312 S Fiddlers Green Cir # 60, Englewood CO 80111-4943. 303/7707474. Employs: 100-249.

MCI West
707 17th St Suite 4200, Denver CO 80202-3442. 303/2940005. Employs: 100-249.

Republic Telcom Systems Corp
6150 Lookout Rd, Boulder CO 80301-3341. 303/5308600. Employs: 100-249.

Agate Mutual Telephone Company
38619 Monroe St, Agate CO 80101-9749. 719/7642578. Employs: 50-99.

Airfone Inc
9650 E 25th Ave, Aurora CO 80010-1040. 303/3445251. Employs: 100-249.

American Bell Phonecenter
7049 W, Lakewood CO 80226. 303/2329398. Employs: 100-249.

American Teladvantage
26 W Dry Creek Cir Ste 540, Littleton CO 80120-4475. 303/7306003. Employs: 50-99.

Audiotex Leasing Inc
2323 S Troy St, Aurora CO 80014-1946. 303/7509650. Employs: 100-249.

Automation Electronics
12791 E Villanova Dr, Aurora CO 80014-1913. 303/6717162. Employs: 100-249.

Bijou Telephone Cooprtv Association
Front & Main Sts, Byers CO 80103. 303/8225400. Employs: 50-99.

Bijou Telephone Cooprtv Association
Front & Main, Deer Trail CO 80105. 303/7694700. Employs: 50-99.

Combined Network Inc-28
1900 Grant St, Denver CO 80203-4301. 303/8631507. Employs: 100-249.

D-Mark Communication Inc
2065 S Raritan St, Denver CO 80223-3828. 303/9365562. Employs: 100-249.

El Paso Cnty Phone Co Bus Ofc
480 Peyton Hwy, Colorado Springs CO 80930. 719/6832501. Employs: 100-249.

Global Wats
1205 S Platte River Dr, Denver CO 80223-3100. 303/7443961. Employs: 100-249.

Gold Systems Inc
4880 Riverbend Rd, Boulder CO 80301-2615. 303/4472837. Employs: 50-99.

Idealdial
910 15th St, Denver CO 80202-2912. 303/5340300. Employs: 100-249.

Info Marketing Inc
3445 Penrose Pl, Boulder CO 80301-1874. 303/4447166. Employs: 50-99.

Intelesys Inc
58 Inverness Dr E, Englewood CO 80112-5114. 303/8631400. Employs: 50-99.

Interactive Info Systems Inc
910 15th St, Denver CO 80202-2912. 303/5950888. Employs: 100-249.

Mci Sales
419 Canyon Ave, Fort Collins CO 80521-2670. 303/4937425. Employs: 50-99.

Minor Suma Corp
3942 S Palo Verde Rd, Evergreen CO 80439. 303/6747117. Employs: 50-99.

Nettel
4260 E Evans Ave, Denver CO 80222-4934. 303/7571628. Employs: 100-249.

New Century Communications
8933 E Union Ave, Englewood CO
80111-1354.   303/6946907.
Employs: 50-99.

On Time
6529 Lynn Dr, Fort Collins CO
80525-4119.   303/2262131.
Employs: 50-99.

Premier Datavision
1658 Cole Blvd, Golden CO
80401-3304.   303/2321901.
Employs: 100-249.

Realcom Office Commctns Inc
370 17, Denver CO 80202.
303/5925002. Employs: 100-249.

Systems Network Inc
2755 S Locust St Ste 115, Denver
CO 80222-7131. 303/7563444.
Employs: 100-249.

TCS Inc
2785 Lafayette Dr, Boulder CO
80303-7104.   303/4993800.
Employs: 50-99.

Telecom
10720 W 38th Pl, Wheat Ridge CO
80033-4022.   303/4251624.
Employs: 100-249.

Telesphere Communications Inc
999 18th St, Denver CO 80202-
2440. 303/2981800. Employs: 100-
249.

US Sprint
1099 18th St, Golden CO 80401-
1826. 303/2795000. Employs: 100-
249.

US Volume Network
9200 E Mineral Ave, Englewood
CO 80112-3412. 303/7994827.
Employs: 50-99.

Wiggins Telephone Association

414 Main St, Wiggins CO 80654-
1313. 303/4837343. Employs: 50-
99.

Williams Telecommunicatio
3801 E Florida Ave, Denver CO
80210-2538.   303/7536774.
Employs: 100-249.

BSN Telecom Co
133 S Van Gordon St, Lakewood
CO 80228-1706. 303/9805600.
Employs: 100-249.

MCI
4678 Alpine Meadows Ln,
Colorado Springs CO 80919-3159.
719/5921300. Employs: 100-249.

Mci Sales
1942 Broadway St, Boulder CO
80302-5213.   303/4437947.
Employs: 50-99.

**NTA-National   Technical
Association**
2755 S Locust St Ste 115, Denver
CO 80222-7131. 303/7599550.
Employs: 100-249.

National Network Corp
999 18th St, Denver CO 80202-
2440. 303/2989113. Employs: 100-
249.

Northwest Telecom
720 S Colorado Blvd, Denver CO
80222-1904.   303/7582805.
Employs: 100-249.

Telagents
19 Switzerland Trail Rd, Boulder
CO 80302-8705. 303/4406604.
Employs: 50-99.

Telephone Express
1155 Kelly Johnson Blvd # 400,
Colorado Springs CO 80920-9904.
719/5921200. Employs: 100-249.

Telespectrum Commctns Inc
3300 E 1st Ave, Denver CO 80206-5810. 303/3221698. Employs: 100-249.

US Business Communications
4502 Constitution Ave, Colorado Springs CO 80915-1003. 719/5962558. Employs: 100-249.

US Telechoice Inc
5555 South, Englewood CO 80111. 303/6949414. Employs: 50-99.

Wtci Warehouse
7808 Cherry Creek South Dr, Denver CO 80231-3218. 303/7512073. Employs: 100-249.

Circle J Communications Inc

7155 W Walden Pl, Littleton CO 80123-5471. 303/9332556. Employs: 100-249.

Colorado Voice Center
323 S College Ave # 6, Fort Collins CO 80524-2845. 303/4825542. Employs: 50-99.

Deluxe Voice Messaging
7145 Lowell Blvd, Westminster CO 80030-5324. 303/4287523. Employs: 100-249.

Front Range Voice Mail
1223 Kirkwood Dr, Fort Collins CO 80525-1968. 303/2210027. Employs: 50-99.

Koechlein Communications
1019 8 Golden, Golden CO 80401. 303/2782244. Employs: 100-249.

For more information on career opportunities in communications:

Associations

COMMUNICATIONS WORKERS OF AMERICA
501 3rd Street NW, Washington DC 20001-2797. 202/434-1100.

UNITED STATES TELEPHONE ASSOCIATION
900 19th Street NW, Suite 800, Washington DC 20006. 202/835-3100.

COMPUTERS

Computer Services: Industry revenues for computer services, systems integration, consulting, and training services have been on the rise. Mergers and acquisitions of computer services firms have been an ongoing trend, and should continue. In the long-term, look for computer services firms to expand overseas, especially into Western Europe. Equipment and Software: The continuing effects of the long national recession have put the equipment and software industries on a bumpy road over the past few years.

Layoffs at major players like IBM, Apple, and Compaq grabbed big headlines. The biggest growth areas for U.S. firms will be in systems design, systems integration, software, and after-sales service. Over the long-term, the computer industry promises to be one of the best bets for jobseekers.

AUTO-TROL TECHNOLOGY CORPORATION
12500 North Washington Street, Denver CO 80241-2400. 303/452-4919. **Contact:** Human Resources Department. **Corporate headquarters:** This location. **Description:** Engaged in the development of graphics software and turnkey systems for computer aided design, manufacturing, engineering, and documentation. **Common positions:** Accountant; Computer Programmer; Civil Engineer; Technical Writer. Especially interested in engineers with strong scientific programming skills. **Educational backgrounds sought:** Computer Science; Engineering; Mathematics. **Benefits:** credit union; HMO; dental insurance; life insurance; tuition assistance; disability coverage; employee discounts; savings plan; three weeks vacation, first year. **Operations at this facility:** product integration; research/development; customer service; sales and marketing; administration.

BALL CORPORATION
COMPUTER PRODUCTS DIVISION
P.O. Box 1062, Boulder CO 80306. 303/939-4000. **Contact:** Personnel Department. **Description:** A producer of computer products. Parent company manufactures and packages a diverse line of industrial and high technology products. **Corporate headquarters:** Muncie, IN.

CROSS COMMUNICATIONS COMPANY
1881 9th Street, Suite 302, Boulder CO 80302. 303/444-7799. **Contact:** Tom Cross, CEO. **Description:** A Denver-area consulting firm specializing in computers and computer applications in business and industry.

DIGITAL EQUIPMENT CORPORATION

305 Rockrimmon Boulevard South, Colorado Springs CO 80919. **Contact:** Employment. **Description:** Designs, manufactures, sells and services computers, associated peripheral equipment, and related software and supplies. Applications and programs include: scientific research, computation, communications, education, data analysis, industrial control, time sharing, commercial data processing, graphic arts, word processing, health care, instrumentation, engineering, and simulation. **Employees:** 126,000 people in the United States and 37 foreign countries. Colorado Springs facility produces peripheral equipment. **Corporate headquarters:** Maynard, MA. **Listed on:** New York Stock Exchange. **Common positions:** System Manager. **Educational backgrounds sought:** Computer Science; Engineering; Mathematics. **Operations at this facility:** sales.

DIGITAL EQUIPMENT CORPORATION/ENGLEWOOD

8085 South Chester Street, Englewood CO 80112-1478. 303/649-3000. **Contact:** Personnel. **Description:** Regional headquarters for the computer firm.

EG & G ROCKY FLATS

P.O. Box 464, Golden CO 80402-0464. 303/966-7000. **Contact:** Professional Staffing. **Description:** A diversified FORTUNE 300 company of some 35,000 people worldwide. The corporation supplies advanced technical products and services to commercial, industrial, and governmental customers. **Common positions:** Buyer; Chemist; Computer Programmer; Civil Engineer; Electrical Engineer; Draftsperson; Ceramics Engineer; Industrial Engineer; Mechanical Engineer; Environmental Engineer; Metallurgical Engineer; Geophysicist; Operations/Production Manager; Physicist; Public Relations Specialist; Purchasing Agent; Quality Control Supervisor; Statistician; Systems Analyst; Technical Writer/Editor. **Educational backgrounds sought:** Chemistry; Communications; Computer Science; Engineering; Geology; Mathematics; Physics. **Special programs:** Internships. **Benefits:** medical, dental, and life insurance; pension plan; tuition assistance; disability coverage; employee discounts; savings plan. **Corporate headquarters:** Wellesley, MA. **Operations at this facility:** manufacturing; research/development; administration. **Listed on:** New York Stock Exchange.

HEWLETT PACKARD
TECHNICAL SOFTWARE CENTER

3404 East Harmony Road, Fort Collins CO 80525. **Contact:** Personnel. **Description:** Coordinates development of engineering design and technical software by outside vendors for HP workstations, desktop computers and personal computers. Parent company, Hewlett Packard, is engaged in the design and manufacture of measurement and computation products and systems used in business, industry, engineering, science, health care, and education. Principal products are integrated instrument and computer systems (including hardware & software), computer systems and peripheral products, and medical electronic equipment and systems.

IBM CORPORATION
INFORMATION PRODUCTS DIVISION
P.O. Box 1900, Department 402, Building 001-E, Boulder CO 80301-9200. 303/924-6300. **Contact:** Personnel Manager. **Description:** A manufacturer of magnetic discs and tapes.

INFORMATION SOLUTIONS
6486 South Quebec Street, Englewood CO 80111. 303/694-9180. **Contact:** Appropriate department. **Description:** A retailer of computers and related components.

INTERPRETER, INC.
11455 West I-70, N. Frontage Road, Wheat Ridge CO 80033. 303/431-8991. **Contact:** Kathleen Ortega, Manager of Administration. **Description:** A manufacturer of devices that allow dissimilar word processing systems to communicate with each other.

MTX INTERNATIONAL, INC.
98 Inverness Drive East, Suite 110, Englewood CO 80112. 303/790-1400. **Contact:** Personnel. **Description:** A retailer of computer hardware and software.

MAXTOR COLORADO
2190 Miller Drive, Longmont CO 80501. 303/678-2417. **Contact:** Kathy Powell, Manager, Human Resources. **Description:** Manufacturer of computer disk drives. **Employees:** 8,000.

MITCHELL & SONS INC.
5961 East 64th Avenue, Commerce City CO 80022. 303/287-0233. **Contact:** Mick Mitchell, General Manager. **Description:** Produces prefabricated housing. **Corporate headquarters:** This location.

MONOLITHIC SYSTEMS CORPORATION
7050 South Tucson Way, Englewood CO 80112. 303/790-7400. **Contact:** Joan Oakes, Personnel Manager. **Description:** A manufacturer of macro-computer systems.

NBI
P.O. Box 9001, Boulder CO 80301. 303/444-5710. **Contact:** Marla Hall, Manager, Human Resources. **Description:** Designs, develops, produces, and markets PC-based desktop publishing, word processing, and graphics software applications. Provides systems integration consulting and maintenance services to its worldwide user base. **Common positions:** Accountant; Computer Programmer; Customer Service Representative; Technical Writer/Editor. **Educational backgrounds sought:** Business Administration; Computer Science; Engineering Software. **Benefits:** medical insurance; dental insurance; life insurance; tuition assistance; disability coverage; profit sharing; savings plan. **Corporate headquarters:** This location. **Listed on:** New York Stock Exchange.

NCR/MICROELECTRONICS DIVISION
COLORADO SPRINGS

1635 Aero Plaza Drive, Colorado Springs CO 80916. 719/596-5795. **Contact:** John Beckert, Personnel Manager. **Description:** Develops, manufactures, markets, and supports complete business information systems for retail, financial, commercial, industrial, medical, educational, and government industries. Also manufactures and markets business forms and supplies.

NCR/MICROELECTRONICS DIVISION
FT. COLLINS

2001 Danfield Court, Ft. Collins CO 80525. 303/223-5100. **Contact:** Human Resources. **Description:** Develops, manufactures, markets, and supports complete business information systems for retail, financial. commercial, industrial, medical, educational, and government industries. Also manufactures and markets business forms and supplies.

NEODATA SERVICES

833 West South Boulder Road, Louisville CO 80027. 303/666-7000. **Contact:** Mary Ann Peterson, Human Resources Representative. **Description:** A division of the A.C. Neilsen Company.

QUARK, INC.

1800 Grant Street, Denver CO 80203. 303/894-8888. **Contact:** Liz McGrory, Personnel Administrator. **Description:** A software engineering firm.

SCIENTIFIC SOFTWARE CORPORATION

1801 California Street, Suite 295, Denver CO 80202. 303/292-1111. **Contact:** Personnel Department. **Description:** Engaged in the business of developing and marketing proprietary computer software, of furnishing management services in the petroleum and mining industries, and of furnishing other electronic data processing services. **Corporate headquarters:** This location.

STORAGE TECHNOLOGY CORPORATION

2270 South 88th Street, Louisville CO 80028. 303/673-5151. **Contact:** David Armstead, Manager of Employment. **Description:** Designs, develops, and manufactures information storage and retrieval equipment. **Common positions:** Accountant; Buyer; Electrical Engineer; Mechanical Engineer; Financial Analyst; Personnel and Labor Relations Specialist; Systems Analyst; Manufacturing Engineer; Software Engineer. **Educational backgrounds sought:** Accounting; Computer Science; Engineering; Finance. **Benefits:** medical, dental, and life insurance; tuition assistance; disability coverage; profit sharing; employee discounts; savings plan. **Corporate headquarters:** This location. **Operations at this facility:** divisional headquarters; manufacturing; research/development; administration. **Listed on:** New York Stock Exchange.

TEXAS INSTRUMENTS, INC.

1400 South Potomac, Suite 101, Aurora CO 80012. 303/368-8000. **Contact:** Personnel Department. **Description:** Regional office of the well-known electronics and computer systems corporation. This location serves three separate divisions: Semiconductors, Digital Systems/Sales and Digital Systems/Service.

UCS SYSTEMS
9600 East Arapaho Road, Suite 220, Englewood CO 80112. 303/790-9090. **Contact:** Ken Kurcab, President. **Description:** A producer of computerized accounting systems.

Z-AXIS CORPORATION
116 Inverness Drive East, Suite 110, Englewood CO 80112. 303/792-2400. **Contact:** Office Manager. **Description:** A Denver-area computer graphics firm. **Common positions:** Commercial Artist; Computer Programmer; Electrical Engineer; Operations/Production Manager; Sales Representative; Animators; Video Editors. **Educational backgrounds sought:** Art/Design; Computer Science. **Benefits:** medical insurance; dental insurance; life insurance; disability coverage; profit sharing. **Corporate headquarters:** This location. **Operations at this facility:** administration; service; sales.

Additional large employers: 250+

ELECTRONIC COMPUTERS

Hewlett Packard
700 71st Av, Greeley CO 80634-9776. 303/3504000. Employs: 500-999.

Solbourne Computer Inc
1900 Pike Rd, Longmont CO 80501-6700. 303/7723400. Employs: 250-499.

MISC. COMPUTER PERIPHERAL EQUIPMENT

Hewlett Packard Company
8245 N Union Blvd, Colorado Springs CO 80920-4456. 7195907788. Employs: 250-499.

Laser Magnetic Storage
4425 Arrows W, Colorado Springs CO 80907. 7195937900. Employs: 250-499.

Prairietec Corp
1830 Lefthand Cir, Longmont CO 80501-6720. 303/5433378. Employs: 250-499.

COMPUTERS AND COMPUTER PERIPHERAL

EQUIPMENT AND SOFTWARE

Cadnetic Corp
5775 Flatiron Pky, Boulder CO 80301-5730. 303/4448075. Employs: 250-499.

Exabyte Corporation
1745 38th St, Boulder CO 80301-2630. 303/4424333. Employs: 500-999.

Hewlett Packard Company
24 Inverness Pl E, Englewood CO 80112-5619. 303/6495000. Employs: 250-499.

COMPUTER PROGRAMMING SERVICES

Hathaway Corp
350 Interlocken Blvd, Broomfield CO 80021-3462. 303/4601500. Employs: 250-499.

Martin Marietta Data Systems
116 Inverness Dr E Suite 400, Englewood CO 80112-5125. 303/7903093. Employs: 250-499.

Trw Systems

1555 Newport Rd N, Colorado Springs CO 80916-2727. 7195708000. Employs: 250-499.

Additional small to medium sized employers: 50-249

ELECTRONIC COMPUTERS

Accutronics Design & Mfg Co
3200 S Zuni St, Englewood CO 80110-2142. 303/7628522. Employs: 100-249.

Clinicom Inc
4720 Walnut St Suite 106, Boulder CO 80301-2513. 303/4439660. Employs: 50-99.

Cray Computer Corp
1110 Bayfield Dr, Colorado Springs CO 80906-4634. 719/5796464. Employs: 100-249.

Outbound Systems Inc
4840 Pearl East Cir, Boulder CO 80301-2408. 303/4444606. Employs: 50-99.

MISC. COMPUTER PERIPHERAL EQUIPMENT

Accutool Division
4399 Delaware St, Denver CO 80216-2628. 303/4336667. Employs: 50-99.

Intellistore Inc
2402 Clover Basin Dr, Longmont CO 80503-7609. 303/6826400. Employs: 100-249.

Nti
980 Technology Ct, Colorado Springs CO 80915-3630. 719/5744900. Employs: 100-249.

Safetran Traffic Sys Inc
1485 Garden Rods Rd, Colorado Springs CO 80907. 719/5995600. Employs: 50-99.

COMPUTERS AND COMPUTER PERIPHERAL EQUIPMENT AND SOFTWARE

Array Technology
4775 Walnut St, Boulder CO 80301-2579. 303/4449300. Employs: 50-99.

Codar Technology Inc
2405 Trade Center Ave, Longmont CO 80503-7602. 303/7760472. Employs: 50-99.

Connecting Point
2370 S Trenton Way Ste G, Denver CO 80231-3844. 303/7457776. Employs: 50-99.

Harris & Paulson Inc
6251 Greenwood Plaza Blvd, Englewood CO 80111-4908. 303/7738283. Employs: 50-99.

IBM Corporation
685 Citadel Dr E Suite 400, Colorado Springs CO 80909-5368. 719/5702900. Employs: 100-249.

McDonnell Douglas Info Sys Grp
5299 Dtc Blvd, Englewood CO 80111-3321. 303/2206000. Employs: 100-249.

Spectranetics
96 Talamine Ct, Colorado Springs CO 80907-5160. 719/6338333. Employs: 50-99.

Sun Microsystems Inc
5251 Dtc Pky Suite 500, Englewood CO 80111-2700. 303/7967100. Employs: 50-99.

Unisys Corp
7222 Commerce Center Dr, Colorado Springs CO 80919-2630. 719/5938800. Employs: 50-99.

Western Automation Lab Inc
1700 55th St, Boulder CO 80301-2725. 303/4496400. Employs: 50-99.

COMPUTER PROGRAMMING SERVICES

American Management Systems
66 S Van Gordon St Suite 220, Lakewood CO 80228-1711. 303/9897065. Employs: 100-249.

Berg Engr Co
621 17th St Ste 1515, Denver CO 80293-1501. 303/6982873. Employs: 50-99.

Comms Computer Concepts
1960 Quebec St, Denver CO 80220-1926. 303/3335151. Employs: 50-99.

Conner Peripherals
2400 Trade Center Ave, Longmont CO 80503-7600. 303/6512881. Employs: 50-99.

Coral Group Inc
1050 17th St Suite 1800, Denver CO 80265-1801. 303/8203000. Employs: 50-99.

Data Storage Marketing
5718 Central Ave, Boulder CO 80301-2832. 303/4424747. Employs: 50-99.

Digital Equipment Corporation
1175 Chapel Hills Dr, Colorado Springs CO 80920-3952. 719/2602700. Employs: 100-249.

Gemisys

3605 S Teller St, Denver CO 80235-2115. 303/9696000. Employs: 50-99.

Genisys Inc
7175 W Jefferson Av, Denver CO 80235-2318. 303/3996666. Employs: 50-99.

Geodynamics Corporation
304 Inverness Way S Suite 300, Englewood CO 80112-5826. 303/7900101. Employs: 50-99.

Media Packaging Inc
2635 S Santa Fe Dr, Denver CO 80223-4429. 303/6981560. Employs: 100-249.

Mentor Software Inc
3907 E 120th Ave # 200, Denver CO 80233-1600. 303/2529090. Employs: 100-249.

Netwise
2477 55th St, Boulder CO 80301-5703. 303/4428280. Employs: 50-99.

Rela Inc
6175 Longbow Dr, Boulder CO 80301-5388. 303/5302626. Employs: 50-99.

Ro Mar Limited
2268 Executive Cir, Colorado Springs CO 80906-4136. 719/5400600. Employs: 50-99.

Scientific Software Intercomp
1801 California St Suite 295, Denver CO 80202-2699. 303/2921111. Employs: 100-249.

Sis Corporation
928 Quail St, Lakewood CO 80215-5510. 303/2356600. Employs: 100-249.

Spectrum Systems
1625 Broadway, Denver CO
80202-4717. 303/5348813.
Employs: 50-99.

Trw Development Division
16201 E Centre Tech Pky, Aurora
CO 80011-9041. 303/3604400.
Employs: 100-249.

Cta Inc
7150 Campus Dr, Colorado Springs
CO 80920-3177. 719/5908890.
Employs: 100-249.

**COMPUTER PROGRAMMING
SERVICES**

National Systems & Research Co
5475 Mark Dabling Blvd, Colorado
Springs CO 80918-3846.
719/5908880. Employs: 50-99.

**COMPUTER PROCESSING
AND DATA PREPARATION
AND PROCESSING SERVICES**

Affiliated Bank Service
445 E 124th Ave, Denver CO
80241-2402. 303/4502272.
Employs: 50-99.

Automatic Data Processing
12250 E Iliff Ave Suite 2nd Fl,
Aurora CO 80014-1252.
303/3687000. Employs: 100-249.

Basis Information Technologies

5850 Dtc Pky, Englewood CO
80111-3208. 303/7719000.
Employs: 100-249.

Cigna Systems
12396 Grant St, Denver CO 80241-
3120. 303/4501800. Employs: 100-
249.

Electronic Data System
12600 W Colfax Ave, Lakewood
CO 80215-3733. 303/2350101.
Employs: 100-249.

Emery Data Graphic Inc
6767 S Spruce St, Englewood CO
80112-1283. 303/7730484.
Employs: 50-99.

Item Processing Center Inc
7000 E 47th Avenue Dr Ste 1500,
Denver CO 80216-3450.
303/3936464. Employs: 50-99.

Columbine Systems Inc
1707 Cole Blvd, Golden CO
80401-3214. 303/2387600.
Employs: 100-249.

**COMPUTER MAINTENANCE
AND REPAIR**

Dsi Incorporated
1440 S Lipan St, Denver CO
80223-3411. 303/7778211.
Employs: 50-99.

Datacomm Services
8150 S Akron St, Englewood CO
80112-3507. 303/7904149.
Employs: 50-99.

For more information on career opportunities in the computer industry:

Associations

**INFORMATION AND
TECHNOLOGY
ASSOCIATION OF AMERICA**
1300 North 17th Street, Suite 300,
Arlington VA 22209. 703/522-
5055.

**ASSOCIATION FOR
COMPUTER SCIENCE**
P.O. Box 19027, Sacramento CA
95819. 916/421-9149.

ASSOCIATION FOR COMPUTING MACHINERY
1515 Broadway, 17th Floor, New York NY 10036. 212/869-7440.

COMPUTER AND BUSINESS EQUIPMENT MANUFACTURERS ASSOCIATION
1250 Eye Street NW, Suite 200, Washington DC 20005. 202/737-8888.

COMPUTER AND COMMUNICATIONS INDUSTRY ASSOCIATION
666 11th Street NW, Suite 600, Washington DC 20001. 202/783-0070.

COMPUTER SOCIETY OF THE INSTITUTE OF ELECTRICAL & ELECTRONICS ENGINEERS
1730 Massachusetts Avenue NW, Washington DC 20036. 202/371-0101.

COMPUTER-AIDED MANUFACTURING INTERNATIONAL
1250 E. Copeland Road, Suite 500, Arlington TX 76011. 817/860-1654.

IEEE COMPUTER SOCIETY
1730 Massachusetts Avenue NW, Washington DC 20036-1903. 202/371-0101.

INFORMATION INDUSTRY ASSOCIATION
555 New Jersey Avenue NW, Washington DC 20001. 202/639-8260.

SEMICONDUCTOR INDUSTRY ASSOCIATION
4300 Stevens Creek Boulevard, Suite 271, San Jose CA 95129. 408/973-9973.

Directories

INFORMATION INDUSTRY DIRECTORY
Gale Research Inc., 835 Penobscot Building, Detroit MI 48226. 313/961-2242.

Magazines

COMPUTER-AIDED ENGINEERING
Penton Publishing, 1100 Superior Avenue, Cleveland OH 44114. 216/696-7000.

COMPUTERWORLD
CW Communications, P.O. Box 9171, Framingham MA 01701. 508/879-0700.

DATA COMMUNICATIONS
McGraw-Hill, 1221 Avenue of the Americas, New York NY 10020. 212/512-2000.

DATAMATION
275 Washington Street, Newton MA 02158. 617/964-3030.

DESIGN COMPUTING
John Wiley & Sons, 605 Third Avenue, New York NY 10158. 212/850-6645.

IDC REPORT
International Data Corporation, Five Speen Street, Framingham MA 01701. 508/872-8200.

DEFENSE

The collapse of the Soviet Union could not have happened at a worse time -- at least for the defense industry, which was already reeling due to the decreasing number of contracts. In fact, the Pentagon's $65 billion procurement budget for 1992 was just half of its 1985 level. Since 1985, the defense industry has slashed 250,000 jobs, and 250,000 more should be cut between 1993 and 1995 alone.

McDONNELL DOUGLAS COMMUNICATIONS INDUSTRY SYSTEMS COMPANY
2450 S. Peoria Street, Suite 400, Aurora CO 80114. 303/671-4800. **Contact:** Administrative Manager. **Description:** A division of the well-known defense and electronics corporation.

OEA, INC.
P.O. 100488, Denver CO 80250. 303/693-1248. **Contact:** James H. Welsh, Director of Personnel. **Description:** A Denver manufacturer of aircraft crew escape systems. **Common positions:** Draftsperson; Aerospace Engineer; Electrical Engineer; Mechanical Engineer; General Manager; Operations/Production Manager; Quality Control Supervisor. **Educational backgrounds sought:** Engineering. **Benefits:** medical, dental, and life insurance; pension plan; tuition assistance; disability coverage; profit sharing; savings plan. **Corporate headquarters:** This location. **Operations at this facility:** divisional headquarters; manufacturing.

Additional large employers: 250+

ARMY, AIR FORCE, NAVY

Air National Guard
Buckley ANG Base, Aurora CO 80011. 303/3665363. Employs: 250-499.

GUIDED MISSLES AND SPACE VEHICLES

Ultrasystems Defense Inc
2864 S Circle Dr, Colorado Springs CO 80906-4114. 7195271400. Employs: 500-999.

Additional small to medium sized employers: 50-249

ARMY, AIR FORCE, NAVY

Colorado National Guard
2123 2nd Ave, Greeley CO 80631-7202. 303/3564629. Employs: 50-99.

US Government Army Reserves
1788 Helena St, Aurora CO 80011-4625. 303/3600963. Employs: 100-249.

ELECTRICAL AND ELECTRONIC

Electrical component industry shipments are expected to grow at an annual rate of 5-7 percent through the mid-90's. Suppliers will face a constant demand for higher performance products. The increased complexity of packaging and the interconnection of high-performance systems places a premium on compatibility among components. Jobseekers should search out companies that can anticipate which technologies and product variants will be among industry standards.

ALL PHASE ROCKY MOUNTAIN
DISTRICT OFFICES
500 Quivis Street, Denver CO 80204. 303/893-2111. **Contact:** John Michelch, Branch Manager. **Description:** A supplier of wholesale electric goods.

ASSOCIATED BUSINESS PRODUCTS, INC.
5285 Fox, Denver CO 80216. 303/295-0757. **Contact:** Jane M. Lemmon, Director, Human Resources. **Description:** Sales and service of Canon office equipment and supplies. **Common positions:** Sales Representative; Electronic Service Technician (copier repairs).

BI, INC.
6400 Lookout Road, Boulder CO 80301. 303/530-2911. **Contact:** Human Resources. **Description:** Consultants in the electronics industry, specializing in market identification.

BIGGS-KURTZ COMPANY
DBA: CASHWAY SUPPLY
275 Mariposa Street, Denver CO 80223-1319. 303/623-0151. **Contact:** Dick Allard, President. **Description:** A Denver wholesaler of electric supplies.

C.W. ELECTRONICS SALES COMPANY
800 Lincoln Street, Denver CO 80203. 303/832-1111. **Contact:** Personnel Department. **Description:** A wholesaler and retailer of electronic parts.

COLLIER ELECTRIC COMPANY
1025 West 7th Avenue, Denver CO 80204. 303/571-5030. **Contact:** Hal Engle, Division Manager. **Description:** An electric contractor.

DENVER DISTRIBUTORS INC.
P.O. Box 11368, Denver CO 80211. 303/433-7463. **Contact:** Personnel Department. **Description:** A wholesaler of electrical supplies and equipment.

GORDON SIGN COMPANY
2930 West 9th Avenue, Denver CO 80204. 303/629-6121. **Contact:** Mike Corrigan, Controller. **Description:** Manufactures electric signs.

HATHAWAY SYSTEMS CORPORATION
8228 Park Meadows Drive, Littleton CO 80124. 303/799-8200. **Contact:** Tracy Koenig, Supervisor, Administration and Payroll. **Description:** Designs, manufactures, and markets electric power recording equipment and systems, medical and other recording instruments, and precision motors. **Common positions:** Software Engineer. **Educational backgrounds sought:** Engineering. **Benefits:** medical, dental, and life insurance; pension plan; tuition assistance; disability coverage; profit sharing. **Corporate headquarters:** Broomfield, CO. **Parent company:** Hathaway Corporation. **Operations at this facility:** divisional headquarters.

HENSLEY BATTERY
2031 Bryant Street, Denver CO 80211. 303/455-3643. **Contact:** Personnel Department. **Description:** Corporation dealing in the remanufacture of automotive and electrical equipment.

ITT FEDERAL SERVICES CORPORATION
1 Gateway Plaza, 1330 Inverness Drive, Colorado Springs CO 80910. 719/574-5850. **Contact:** Employment Manager. **Description:** The worldwide service subsidiary of ITT Corporation. Company provides totally integrated information transfer systems on a turnkey basis for government, industrial, commercial, and military users. Systems include voice, data, video, and command and control capabilities. Company has a permanent staff of engineers to perform evaluation, design, implementation, and training services. Company systems are used by communications common carriers, industrial firms, military networks, and public and business clients throughout the world. **Corporate headquarters:** This location.

INTEGRATED ELECTRONICS CORPORATION
5750 North Logan Street, Denver CO 80216. 303/292-6121. **Contact:** Personnel Department. **Description:** A distributor of electronic goods.

JWP DYNALECTRIC COMPANY
P.O. Box 26233, Lakewood CO 80226-2448. 303/233-4488. **Contact:** Howard Gueck, Controller. **Description:** Contractors specializing in electrical work.

MARTIN MARIETTA CORPORATION
1101 W. Mineral Avenue, Englewood CO 80120. 303/971-2828. **Contact:** Aaron T. Brown, Staffing Representative. **Description:** Provides facilities management and professional services solutions to the federal government and the private sector. Encompasses all phases of the information management and data processing environment, including operations and maintenance, systems integration, life cycle operations, computing resources, and communications. **Common positions:** Computer Programmer; Technical Writer/Editor; System Programmer; Computer Operations. **Educational backgrounds sought:** Computer Science; Engineering. **Special programs:** Training programs. **Benefits:** medical, dental, and life insurance; pension plan; tuition assistance; disability coverage; savings plan; vision care. **Corporate headquarters:**

Bethesda, MD. **Parent company:** Martin Marietta Corporation. **Operations at this facility:** service.

METRUM INFORMATION STORAGE

P.O. Box 5227, MS 103, Denver CO 80217. 303/773-4457. **Contact:** Sue Wells, Manager of Employment. **Description:** A supplier of instrumentation, magnetic tape/information storage products and systems, graphic recorders, and a high-quality supplier of repair, calibration, and testing services. **Common positions:** Accountant; Computer Programmer; Draftsperson; Electrical Engineer; Mechanical Engineer; Software Engineer; Operations/Production Manager; Personnel and Labor Relations Specialist; Purchasing Agent. **Educational backgrounds sought:** Accounting; Business Administration; Computer Science; Engineering; Finance; Marketing; Mathematics. **Special programs:** Summer engineering internships. **Benefits:** medical insurance; dental insurance; pension plan; life insurance; tuition assistance; disability coverage; employee discounts; savings plan. **Corporate headquarters:** Minneapolis, MN. **Parent company:** Alliant Techsystems. **Operations at this facility:** divisional headquarters; manufacturing; research/development; administration; service; sales. **Listed on:** New York Stock Exchange.

MICROSEMI CORPORATION/COLORADO

800 Hoyt Street, Broomfield CO 80020. 303/469-2161. **Contact:** Lynne Willis, Personnel Director. **Description:** Produces a wide range of electronic component products, including thyristors, and silicon-based diode products. Subsidiary of Adolph Coors Company.

MINOLTA OFFICE EQUIPMENT COMPANY

5195 Marshall Street, Arvada CO 80002. 303/444-5582. **Contact:** Personnel Department. **Description:** A Denver dealer of Minolta copying machines.

SHERWOOD ENTERPRISES, INC.

120 9th Avenue, Longmont CO 80501. 303/772-9081. **Contact:** Personnel Department. **Description:** Produces a variety of electronics cable products, including cable and wire, and cable harnesses. Also engaged in electrical mechanical assembly work. **Common positions:** Accountant; Blue-Collar Worker Supervisor; Department Manager; Purchasing Agent; Quality Control Supervisor. **Corporate headquarters:** This location.

SPITZER ELECTRICAL COMPANY, INC.

43 West Ninth Avenue, Denver CO 80204. 303/629-6951. **Contact:** Personnel Department. **Description:** An area dealer of electronic car parts.

STEWART & STEVENSON POWER INC.

5840 Dahlia, P.O. Box 220, Commerce City CO 80022. 303/287-7441. **Contact:** General Manager. **Description:** Manufactures power units and power generators. Nationally, company provides a broad line of products, most of which are diesel or gas-turbine powered, serving a multitude of industries and markets. Principal divisions are: Engine Operations, which engineers and builds power systems utilizing diesel or gas turbine engines for such uses as irrigation systems, oil well drilling rigs, and generators; Electric Operations, which produces a line of switchgear and control systems for numerous industries; and Other Operations, which includes the production of materials handling equipment, and refrigeration equipment for the transportation industry. **Corporate headquarters:** Houston, TX.

STURGEON ELECTRIC COMPANY
12150 East 112th Avenue, Henderson CO 80640. Mailed inquiries only. **Contact:** Personnel. **Description:** An electric contractor. **Common positions:** Electrical Engineer. **Educational backgrounds sought:** Engineering.

SYNERGETICS INTERNATIONAL, INC.
1831 Left Hand Circle, Longmont CO 80501. 303/678-5200. **Contact:** Human Resources. **Description:** A manufacturer of sensory warning systems for use in geological, earthquake, and flood surveys.

TRW ELECTRONIC PRODUCTS INC.
3650 North Nevada Avenue, Colorado Springs CO 80907. 719/475-0660. **Contact:** Human Resources. **Description:** Produces a variety of electronics signal processing equipment and systems, including encoders and decoders, as a part of TRW Electronic Systems group (Redondo Beach, CA). Nationally, TRW operates in three industry segments: Car and Truck Components; Electronics and Space Systems (includes this facility); and Industrial and Energy (products include fasteners, tools, and bearings for industrial users, pumps and valves used by petroleum companies, and aircraft components for commercial and military aircraft). **Common positions:** Accountant; Administrator; Blue-Collar Worker Supervisor; Computer Programmer; Draftsperson; Electrical Engineer; Industrial Engineer; Mechanical Engineer; Financial Analyst; Department Manager; Operations/Production Manager; Personnel and Labor Relations Specialist; Purchasing Agent; Quality Control Supervisor; Systems Analyst; Technical Writer/Editor. **Educational backgrounds sought:** Accounting; Business Administration; Engineering; Mathematics; Physics. **Benefits:** medical insurance; dental insurance; pension plan; life insurance; tuition assistance; disability coverage; savings plan. **Corporate headquarters:** Cleveland, OH. **Parent company:** TRW Inc. **Operations at this facility:** Manufacturing. **Listed on:** New York Stock Exchange.

ULTRONIX INC.
P.O. Box 1090, Grand Junction CO 81502. **Contact:** Personnel Director. **Description:** Manufactures and distributes a wide range of electrical and electronic components, including power switching products for industrial OEM's.

XEROX CORPORATION
4600 S. Ulster Street, Suite 1000, Denver CO 80237. 303/796-6200. **Contact:** Personnel Administrator. **Description:** Regional sales and service office of the well-known office equipment company.

YOUNG ELECTRIC & MANUFACTURING COMPANY
1505 W. 3rd Avenue, Denver CO 80223-2811. 303/292-4841. **Contact:** Jim Sinclair, Personnel Department. **Description:** A Denver-based manufacturer of electrical switching gear and switchboard equipment.

Additional large employers: 250+

Electrical and Electronics

RELAYS AND INDUSTRIAL CONTROLS

Woodward Gov Co
1000 E Drake Rd, Fort Collins CO 80525-1824.   303/4825811.
Employs: 250-499.

MISC.   HOUSEHOLD APPLIANCES

Teledyne Water Pik
1730 E Prospect Rd, Fort Collins CO 80525-1310. 303/6695670.
Employs: 250-499.

HOUSEHOLD AUDIO AND VIDEO EQUIPMENT

Ampex Corporation
600 Wooten Rd, Colorado Springs CO 80915-3516. 7195962000.
Employs: 500-999.

TELEPHONE   AND TELEGRAPH APPARATUS

AT&T
1200 W 120th Ave, Denver CO 80234-2701.   303/5381200.
Employs: 500-999.

Rolm Corp
4678 Alpine Meadows Ln, Colorado Springs CO 80919-3159.
7195984678. Employs: 250-499.

ELECTRICAL WORK

Sturgeon Electric Company Inc
12150 E 112th Ave, Henderson CO 80640-9116.   303/2868000.
Employs: 250-499.

ELECTRON TUBES

Electronic Fab Technology Corp

7251 4th St, Greeley CO 80634-9763. 303/3533100. Employs: 250-499.

Hewlett Packard Tech
3404 E Harmony Rd, Fort Collins CO 80525-9544. 303/2263800.
Employs: 1,000+.

Sci Manufacturing Inc
4835 Centennial Blvd, Colorado Springs CO 80919-3308.
7195986888. Employs: 250-499.

SEMICONDUCTORS   AND RELATED DEVICES

NCR Corp Micro
1635 Aeroplaza Dr, Colorado Springs CO 80916-3804.
7195965795. Employs: 250-499.

United Tech Micro Electronic Ctr
1575 Garden Of The Gods Rd, Colorado Springs CO 80907.
7195948000. Employs: 250-499.

MISC.   ELECTRONIC COMPONENTS

Ford Aerospace Communications
9970 Federal Dr, Colorado Springs CO 80921-3616. 7195941000.
Employs: 500-999.

Hewlett Packard Company
5070 Centennial Blvd, Colorado Springs CO 80919-2402.
7195314000. Employs: 250-499.

Mc Data Corp
310 Interlochen Hwy, Broomfield CO 80021. 303/4609200. Employs: 250-499.

MAGNETIC AND OPTICAL RECORDING MEDIA

Nbi Inc

3375 Mitchell Lane Box 9001, Boulder CO 80301-2244.

303/4445710. Employs: 250-499.

Additional small to medium sized employers: 50-249

SWITCHGEAR AND SWITCHBOARD APPARATUS

Young Electric & Manufacturing
1505 W 3rd Ave, Denver CO 80223-1440. 303/2924841. Employs: 50-99.

MOTORS AND GENERATORS

Stewart & Stevenson Power
5840 Dahlia St, Commerce City CO 80022-3707. 303/2877441. Employs: 100-249.

MISC. ELECTRICAL INDUSTRIAL APPARATUS

Homespun Imports Inc
4824 Sterling Dr, Boulder CO 80301-2350. 303/4496771. Employs: 50-99.

CURRENT-CARRYING WIRING DEVICES

K B-Denver Inc
451 Oak St, Frederick CO 80530. 303/8333500. Employs: 50-99.

TELEPHONE AND TELEGRAPH APPARATUS

AT & T
7979 E Tufts Av, Denver CO 80237-2843. 303/3630110. Employs: 100-249.

Confertech International
2801 Youngfield St Suite 240, Golden CO 80401-2265. 303/2375151. Employs: 100-249.

Telwatch Inc

885 Arapahoe Ave, Boulder CO 80302-6029. 303/4404756. Employs: 50-99.

Xel Communications Inc
17600 E Exposition Dr, Aurora CO 80017-3233. 303/3697000. Employs: 100-249.

MISC. COMMUNICATIONS EQUIPMENT

Alpine Research Inc
1803 S Foothills Hwy, Boulder CO 80303-7366. 303/6427844. Employs: 50-99.

ELECTRON TUBES

Advanced Energy Industries Inc
1600 Prospect Pky, Fort Collins CO 80525-1283. 303/2214670. Employs: 100-249.

Center Line Circuits Inc
1820 Industrial Cir, Longmont CO 80501-6524. 303/4427598. Employs: 50-99.

Data Ray Nippon
12300 Pecos St, Denver CO 80234-3426. 303/4511300. Employs: 50-99.

Millenium Industries Inc
12421 Washington St, Denver CO 80241-2441. 303/2524035. Employs: 50-99.

Sae Circuits Colorado Inc
4820 63rd St, Boulder CO 80301-3272. 303/5301900. Employs: 50-99.

Sas Circuits Inc
10570 W Bradford Rd, Littleton CO 80127-4211. 303/9724105. Employs: 50-99.

Velie Circuits Of Colorado Inc
555 Alter St Suite 19, Broomfield CO 80020-7112. 303/4652786. Employs: 50-99.

SEMICONDUCTORS AND RELATED DEVICES

Ramtron Corp
1850 Ramtron Dr, Colorado Springs CO 80921-3620. 719/5944455. Employs: 50-99.

Technistar
2040 Miller Dr, Longmont CO 80501-6748. 303/6510188. Employs: 50-99.

ELECTRONIC COILS, TRANSFORMERS, AND OTHER INDUCTORS

Carefree Of Colorado
2145 W 6th Ave, Broomfield CO 80020-1656. 303/4653324. Employs: 100-249.

Tranex Inc
2350 Executive Circle, Colorado Springs CO 80906-4138. 719/5767994. Employs: 50-99.

MISC. ELECTRONIC COMPONENTS

Cencorp
1198 Boston Ave, Longmont CO 80501-5856. 303/7725933. Employs: 100-249.

Colorado Crystal Corp
2303 W 8th St, Loveland CO 80537-5268. 303/6679248. Employs: 100-249.

Sherwood Enterprises

120 9th Ave, Longmont CO 80501-4515. 303/4445499. Employs: 100-249.

Translogic Corporation
10825 E 47th Ave, Denver CO 80239-2913. 303/3717770. Employs: 100-249.

STORAGE BATTERIES

Eagle Picher Industries
3820 Hancock Expy, Colorado Springs CO 80911. 719/3924266. Employs: 100-249.

PRIMARY BATTERIES, DRY AND WET

Whittaker Tech Prods Inc
3850 Olive St, Denver CO 80207-1528. 303/3884836. Employs: 50-99.

ELECTRICAL WORK

Cupertino Electric Inc
1965 33rd St, Boulder CO 80301-2506. 303/4471000. Employs: 50-99.

Easter Owens Electric Company
6522 Fig St, Lakewood CO 80228. 303/4310111. Employs: 50-99.

Howard Electrical & Mechanical
6701 W Alameda Ave, Lakewood CO 80226-3462. 303/2321456. Employs: 100-249.

Icg Electric Inc
1220 Valley St, Colorado Springs CO 80915-2806. 719/5966262. Employs: 100-249.

Northern Electrical Contractor
2775 S Vallejo St, Englewood CO 80110-1219. 303/7610403. Employs: 50-99.

ELECTRICAL EQUIPMENT FOR INTERNAL COMBUSTION ENGINES

Cybermedic Inc
1500 Cherry St, Louisville CO 80027-3036. 303/6669253. Employs: 50-99.

MISC. ELECTRICAL MACHINERY, EQUIPMENT, AND SUPPLIES

Abb
333 W Hampden Ave, Englewood CO 80110-2330. 303/7892273. Employs: 50-99.

Accutech
PO Box 18418, Boulder CO 80308-1418. 303/6659229. Employs: 50-99.

B I Inc
6175 Longbow Dr, Boulder CO 80301-5388. 303/5302911. Employs: 50-99.

Crouse-Hinds Ecm Division
3000 S Jamaica Ct, Aurora CO 80014-4601. 303/3371166. Employs: 50-99.

Eagle Electric Manufacturing

10562 Quail Ct, Broomfield CO 80021-3528. 303/4607705. Employs: 50-99.

Hi Tech Mfg Inc
204 S Bowen St, Longmont CO 80501-5868. 303/6780153. Employs: 100-249.

I T Siemens E Electrical Prod
333 W Drake Rd, Fort Collins CO 80526-2883. 303/2232712. Employs: 50-99.

Lapp Insulator Co
7300 S Alton Way, Englewood CO 80112-2312. 303/7930066. Employs: 50-99.

O Z Gedney Co
1113 Spruce St, Boulder CO 80302-4049. 303/4406950. Employs: 50-99.

Power Distribution Sales Inc
7332 S Alton Way, Englewood CO 80112-2319. 303/7703431. Employs: 50-99.

Sigma Seven Products Inc
2888 Bluff St, Boulder CO 80301-1200. 303/4449319. Employs: 50-99.

For more information on career opportunities in the electrical and electronic industry:

Associations

AMERICAN ELECTROPLATERS AND SURFACE FINISHERS SOCIETY
12644 Research Parkway, Orlando FL 32826. 407/281-6441.

AMERICAN CERAMIC SOCIETY
735 Ceramic Place, Westerville OH 43081. 614/890-4700.

ELECTROCHEMICAL SOCIETY
10 South Main Street, Pennington NJ 08534-2896. 609/737-1902.

ELECTRONIC INDUSTRIES ASSOCIATION
2001 Pennsylvania Avenue NW, Washington DC 20006. 202/457-4900.

**ELECTRONICS
TECHNICIANS ASSOCIATION**
602 N. Jackson Street, Greencastle
IN 46135. 317/653-8262.

**INSTITUTE OF ELECTRICAL
AND ELECTRONICS
ENGINEERS**
345 East 47th Street, New York
NY 10017. 212/705-7900.

**INTERNATIONAL
BROTHERHOOD OF
ELECTRICAL WORKERS**
1125 15th Street NW, Washington
DC 20005. 202/833-7000.

**INTERNATIONAL SOCIETY
OF CERTIFIED
ELECTRONICS
TECHNICIANS**
2708 West Berry, Fort Worth TX
76109. 817/921-9101.

**INTERNATIONAL SOCIETY
FOR HYBRID
MICROELECTRONICS**
1861 Wiehle Avenue, Suite 340,
Reston VA 22090. 703/471-0066.

**NATIONAL ELECTRICAL
MANUFACTURERS
ASSOCIATION**
2101 L Street NW, Suite 300,
Washington DC 20037. 202/457-8400.

**NATIONAL ELECTRONICS
SALES AND SERVICES
ASSOCIATION**
2708 West Berry, Fort Worth TX
76109. 817/921-9061.

**ROBOTICS INTERNATIONAL
OF THE SOCIETY OF
MANUFACTURING
ENGINEERS**
P.O. Box 930, One SME Drive,
Dearborn MI 48121. 313/271-1500.

ENERGY, MINING, AND PETROLEUM

The short-term future for the petroleum industry depends upon the world economy, OPEC production, and world oil prices. U.S. crude and natural gas production is expected to remain flat, while energy use is forecasted to rise 2-3 percent annually for oil and natural gas respectively. Environmental concerns will have a greater effect on the industry.

Jobseekers, especially those with engineering backgrounds, should keep an eye out for the growing emphasis on the development of alternative fuels like methanol, and for growth in hydroelectric, geothermal, and other environmentally sound energy sources.

AMAX MINERAL RESOURCES CO.
1626 Cole Boulevard, Golden CO 80401-3293. 303/231-0549. **Contact:** Kelly Trimmer, Director, Human Resources. **Description:** A mining company, primarily for gold. **Common positions:** Draftsperson; Chemical Engineer; Metallurgical Engineer; Mining Engineer; Financial Analyst; Geologist. **Educational backgrounds sought:** Business Administration; Engineering;

Geology. **Benefits:** medical, dental, and life insurance; pension plan; tuition assistance; disability coverage; profit sharing; savings plan. **Corporate headquarters:** Greenwich, CT. **Parent company:** Amax Inc. **Operations at this facility:** divisional headquarters. **Listed on:** New York Stock Exchange.

AMAX/EXTRACTIVE R & D CENTER
5950 McIntyre, Golden CO 80403. 303/273-7200. **Contact:** Personnel Director. **Description:** A coal mining and production facility.

AMBER RESOURCES COMPANY
535 17th Street, Suite 3310, Denver CO 80202. 303/298-7425. **Contact:** Personnel. **Description:** An area oil and gas exploration company.

AMPOL EXPLORATION (USA)
1225 17th Street, Suite 3000, Denver CO 80202. 303/297-1000. **Contact:** Personnel Department. **Description:** An oil and gas exploration and production company.

ANDERSON OIL COMPANY
1200 17th Street, Suite 1150, Denver CO 80202. 303/820-3100. **Contact:** Personnel Department. **Description:** An oil and gas drilling company.

APACHE CORPORATION
1700 Lincoln, Suite 2000, Suite 1900, Denver CO 80203. 303/837-5000. **Contact:** Manager of Human Resources. **Description:** An exploration and production company that manages oil and gas investment-related products. **Corporate headquarters:** This location. **Operations at this facility:** research/development; administration; service; sales. **Listed on:** New York Stock Exchange. **Common positions:** Accountant; Computer Programmer; Executive Secretary. **Educational backgrounds sought:** Accounting; Computer Science. **Benefits:** medical insurance; pension plan; life insurance; tuition assistance; disability coverage; profit sharing.

ASPEN EXPLORATION CORPORATION
5031 South Ulster Street, Suite 310, Denver CO 80237. 303/337-3600. **Contact:** Personnel. **Description:** Engaged in oil and gas and other mineral exploration and development.

AXEM RESOURCES INCORPORATED
7800 East Union Avenue, Suite 1100, Denver CO 80237-2757. 303/740-9000. **Contact:** Personnel Department. **Description:** Oil and gas exploration and production.

BARRETT RESOURCES
1125 17th Street, Suite 2400, Denver CO 80202. 303/297-3900. **Contact:** Personnel Department. **Description:** A Denver corporation involved in oil and gas exploration.

CAMBIOR USA
8101 E. Prentice Avenue, Suite 800, Englewood CO 80111. 303/694-4936. **Contact:** Personnel Department. **Description:** A mining corporation specializing in talc gold, silica, and titanium.

CARD EQUIPMENT CO.
NATIONAL ENGINEERING AND CONSULTING CORPORATION
1705 East 39th Avenue, Denver CO 80205. 303/295-3385. **Contact:** Moris Martinez, President. **Description:** Produces a broad range of equipment and components for the mining industry, including mine cars, shaft conveyance equipment, and related components (wheels, axles, bodies). A subsidiary of Mentor Corporation. **Corporate headquarters:** This location.

COLORADO INTERSTATE GAS CO.
SUBSIDIARY OF THE COASTAL CORP.
P.O. Box 1087, Colorado Springs CO 80944. 719/520-4227. **Contact:** William D. Davis, Manager, Employee Relations/Employment. **Description:** Company gathers, processes, and transports natural gas by pipeline in a six-state Rocky Mountain area to customer utility companies along the Eastern front range of Colorado and Southern Wyoming. **Employees:** 1,200.

CONOCO, INC./DISTRIBUTION
5601 Brighton Boulevard, Commerce City CO 80022. 303/288-6821. **Contact:** Don Medaris, Supervisor. **Description:** The distribution center of a refinery for gasoline, jet fuel, diesel, and asphalt. **Corporate Headquarters:** Houston, TX.

CONSOLIDATED OIL & GAS, INC.
410 17th Street, Suite 2300, Denver CO 80202. 303/893-1225. **Contact:** Shery Dawson, Controller. **Description:** An oil and gas exploration, production, and development company. **Common positions:** Petroleum Engineer; Geologist. **Corporate headquarters:** This location.

CREDO PETROLEUM CORPORATION
1801 Broadway, Suite 900, Denver CO 80202. 303/297-2200. **Contact:** Personnel. **Description:** A petroleum and natural gas company.

CROWN RESOURCES CORPORATION
1225 17th Street, Suite 1500, Denver CO 80202. 303/295-2171. **Contact:** Paula Porter, Manager of Administration. **Description:** A Denver gold-mining and exploration company.

CYPRESS MINERALS COMPANY
9100 East Minerals Circle, Englewood CO 80112. 303/643-5000. **Contact:** Thomas LeBlanc, Human Resources Manager. **Description:** A Colorado mining company.

DEKALB ENERGY COMPANY
1625 Broadway, Suite 1300, Denver CO 80202. 303/595-0707. **Contact:** Personnel Department. **Description:** An oil and gas exploration and production company.

EAGLE EXPLORATION COMPANY
1775 Sherman Street, Suite 2995, Denver CO 80203. 303/863-0800. **Contact:** Raymond Joeckel, President. **Description:** An oil and gas exploration company.

ENERGY FUELS CORPORATION

1200 17th Street, Suite 2500, Denver CO 80202. 303/623-8317. **Contact:** Ron Nuzman, Personnel Director. **Description:** A minerals exploration and mining company. **Common positions:** Accountant; Attorney; Computer Programmer; Mining Engineer; Geologist; Department Manager; Marketing Specialist; Personnel and Labor Relations Specialist; Public Relations Specialist; Purchasing Agent. **Benefits:** medical, dental, and life insurance; pension plan; tuition assistance; disability coverage; profit sharing. **Corporate headquarters:** This location.

EXETER COMPANY

P.O. Box 17349, Denver CO 80217. 303/861-0181. **Contact:** Ginny Stoll, Administrative Services. **Description:** A Denver drilling company.

GRYNBERG PETROLEUM

5000 South Quebec, Suite 500, Denver CO 80237. 303/850-7490. **Contact:** Personnel Department. **Description:** Petroleum company involved in oil and gas exploration and production and petroleum engineering.

HALLADOR PETROLEUM COMPANY

1660 Lincoln Street, Suite 2700, Denver CO 80264. **Contact:** Personnel Department. **Description:** Company involved in oil and gas exploration and development.

HALLWOOD PETROLEUM/QUINOCO

P.O. Box 378111, Denver CO 80237. 303/850-7373. **Contact:** Human Resources Department. **Description:** A Denver petroleum company.

HAMILTON OIL COMPANY, INC.

1560 Broadway, Suite 2100, Denver CO 80202. 303/863-3000. **Contact:** Pam Miller, Administrative Assistant. **Description:** A petroleum and natural gas company. **Corporate headquarters:** This location.

KN ENERGY, INC.

12055 West 2nd Place, P.O. Box 281304, Lakewood CO 80228-8304. 303/989-1740. **Contact:** Carrie Fiore, Personnel Assistant. **Description:** A natural gas transmission and distribution company headquartered in Lakewood, CO. **Common positions:** Accountant; Administrator; Attorney; Computer Programmer; Draftsperson; Petroleum Engineer; Financial Analyst; Personnel and Labor Relations Specialist; Public Relations Specialist; Systems Analyst. **Educational backgrounds sought:** Accounting; Business Administration; Computer Science; Engineering. **Special programs:** Training programs; internships(limited). **Benefits:** medical, dental and life insurance; pension plan; tuition assistance; disability coverage; daycare assistance; profit sharing; employee discounts. **Corporate headquarters:** This location. **Listed on:** New York Stock Exchange.

LASER OIL COMPANY

7800 East Union Avenue, #1100, Denver CO 80237. 303/740-9000. **Contact:** Personnel Department. **Description:** A producer of oil and gas.

NEWMONT MINING CO.
1700 Lincoln Street, Denver CO 80203. 303/837-5909. **Contact:** Donald Miller, Manager, Compensation and Benefits. **Description:** Gold mining, milling, and processing.

OXFORD CONSOLIDATED INCORPORATED
P.O. Box 37390, Denver CO 80237. 303/741-2888. **Contact:** Personnel Department. **Description:** Oil and gas production and exploration.

PETROLEUM INFORMATION
P.O. Box 2612, Denver CO 80201-2612. 303/740-7100. **Contact:** Kathy McMahon, Employment Coordinator. **Description:** Publishes oil activity information (reports, maps, well data, etc.). A subsidiary of the Dun & Bradstreet Corp.

THE PITTSBURGH & MIDWAY COAL MINING COMPANY
6400 South Fiddler's Green Circle, Englewood CO 80111. 303/930-3600. **Contact:** Lois Brethour, Personnel Director. **Description:** A Denver mining operation involved exclusively in coal and coke production.

POLARIS RESOURCES INCORPORATED
410 17th Street, Suite 2100, Denver CO 80202. 303/592-7077. **Contact:** Personnel Department. **Description:** An oil and gas production company, also engaged in the wholesale of pipes and supplies.

RAPAHOE PETROLEUM, INC.
P.O. Box 3438, Englewood CO 80155. 303/779-0996. **Contact:** Joe Mazzola. **Description:** A petroleum exploration company.

ROYAL GOLD
1660 Wynkoop Street, 10th Floor, Suite 1000, Denver CO 80202. 303/573-1660. **Contact:** Karen Gross, Office Manager. **Description:** An area gold exploration company.

SHARON RESOURCES, INC.
5995 Greenwood Plaza Blvd., Suite 220, Englewood CO 80111. 303/694-4920. **Contact:** JoBeth McFadden, Secretary/Treasurer. **Description:** Engages in oil and gas exploration and production. **Common positions:** Administrator; Petroleum Engineer; Geologist; Geophysicist; Public Relations Specialist. **Educational backgrounds sought:** Business Administration; Finance; Geology. **Benefits:** medical, dental, and life insurance; tuition assistance; disability coverage; stock options.

TEXACO TRADING & TRANSPORTATION
1670 Broadway, 26th Floor, P.O. Box 5568, Denver CO 80217. 303/861-4475. **Contact:** Human Resources Department. **Description:** A subsidiary of Texaco, Inc., the large petroleum company is active in all phases of the industry, including exploration, production, manufacturing, marketing, and research. This division is engaged in the buying, selling, and transport of oil products.

TOTAL PETROLEUM INC.
999 18th Street, Suite 2201, Denver CO 80202. **Contact:** Nick Bambach, Manager, Employment and Training. **Description:** Total Petroleum Inc. is a Denver-based, mid-sized petroleum company with refining, retail and wholesale marketing, transport, pipeline, and trading operations in 22 mid-continent states. There are no exploration and production operations in the U.S. The company operates three refineries and has over 600 company-operated gasoline service station/convenience stores under the brand names of Total, APCO, Roadrunner, and Vickers. The company also serves approximately 2,000 wholesale jobbers. **Common positions:** Accountant; Computer Programmer; Retail Marketing Specialist. **Educational backgrounds sought:** Accounting; Business Administration; Computer Science; Finance; Marketing. **Special programs:** Training programs. **Benefits:** medical insurance; dental insurance; pension plan; life insurance; tuition assistance; disability coverage; savings plan. **Corporate headquarters:** This location. **Operations at this facility:** administration; service. **Listed on:** American Stock Exchange.

URANERZ USA INCORPORATED
165 South Union Boulevard, Suite 280, Denver CO 80228. 303/985-1511. **Contact:** Personnel Director. **Description:** A corporation involved in the exploration of uranium.

USMX, INC.
141 Union Boulevard, Suite 100, Lakewood CO 80228. 303/985-4665. **Contact:** Personnel. **Description:** A gold and silver ores mining operation.

WESTERN GAS RESOURCES INC.
12200 North Pecos Street, Denver CO 80234. 303/452-5603. **Contact:** Lou Gilmer, Personnel Director. **Description:** Produces natural gas.

WESTERN GAS SUPPLY COMPANY
1050 17th Street, Suite 500, Denver CO 80265. 303/534-1261. **Contact:** department of applicant's interest. **Description:** Producers of natural gas. A subsidiary of the Public Service Company of Colorado.

WESTERN NUCLEAR, INC.
200 Union Boulevard, Suite 300, Lakewood CO 80228. 303/989-8675. **Contact:** Personnel. **Description:** A subsidiary of Phelps Dodge. Corporation which specializes in mining and refining copper and uranium. Parent company also manufactures brass and copper products, wire, and cable.

WHITING PETROLEUM CORPORATION
1700 Broadway, Suite 2300, Denver CO 80290. 303/837-1661. **Contact:** Personnel Department. **Description:** Involved in oil and gas production.

WICHITA RIVER OIL
555 17th Street, Suite 905, Denver CO 80202. 303/292-3300. **Contact:** Personnel Department. **Description:** A corporation involved in oil and gas exploration and extraction.

WINCO PETROLEUM CORPORATION
1645 Court Place, Suite 312, Denver CO 80202. 303/623-9095. **Contact:** Personnel Department. **Description:** Involved in oil exploration and production.

Additional large employers: 250+

BITUMINOUS COAL UNDERGROUND MINING

Cyprus Coal Company
9100 E Mineral Cir, Englewood CO 80112-3401. 303/6435100. Employs: 250-499.

CRUDE PETROLEUM AND NATURAL GAS

Amoco Production Company
1670 Broadway Suite 715, Denver CO 80202-4807. 303/8304040. Employs: 500-999.

Ladd Petroleum Corp
370 Seventeenth St, Denver CO 80202-5656. 303/6200100. Employs: 250-499.

Mobil Oil Corporation
1225 17th St Suite 120, Denver CO 80202-5501. 303/2982000. Employs: 250-499.

Texaco Inc
4601 Dtc Blvd, Denver CO 80237-2549. 303/7934000. Employs: 250-499.

DRILLING OIL AND GAS WELLS

J W Gibson Well Service Co
7400 E Orchard Rd, Englewood CO 80111-2528. 303/7715222. Employs: 250-499.

MISC. NONMETALLIC MINERALS, EXCEPT FUELS

Mobil Oil Corp
PO Box 5444, Denver CO 80217-5444. 303/2982610. Employs: 500-999.

PETROLEUM REFINING

Marathon Oil Company
7400 S Broadway, Littleton CO 80122-2609. 303/7942601. Employs: 250-499.

PORCELAIN ELECTRICAL SUPPLIES

Coors Ceramics Co
600 9th St, Golden CO 80401-1099. 303/2784000. Employs: 1,000+.

CONCRETE PRODUCTS, EXCEPT BLOCK AND BRICK

Rocky Mountain Prestress Inc
5801 Pecos, Denver CO 80221-6644. 303/4801111. Employs: 250-499.

CRUDE PETROLEUM PIPELINES

Total Pipeline Corp
P O Box 500, Denver CO 80201-0500. 303/2912000. Employs: 1,000+.

Additional small to medium sized employers: 50-249

BITUMINOUS COAL AND LIGNITE SURFACE MINING

Fremont Energy Corp
P O Box 1442, Denver CO 80201-1442. 303/7917407. Employs: 50-99.

Nerco
9137 E Mineral Cir, Englewood CO 80112-3421. 303/7902001. Employs: 50-99.

Twenty Mile Coal Company
29587 Hwy County Rd 27 Ste 27, Oak Creek CO 80467. 303/8798050. Employs: 100-249.

Western Coal Council
4747 Otis Wheat Ridge, Wheat Ridge CO 80033. 303/4226621. Employs: 50-99.

COAL MINING SERVICES

Anschutz Coal Corporation
555 17th St Suite 2400, Denver CO 80202-3987. 303/2981000. Employs: 50-99.

Union Pacific Resources Company
5800 S Quebec St, Englewood CO 80111-2007. 303/7212000. Employs: 100-249.

CRUDE PETROLEUM AND NATURAL GAS

Associated Natural Gas Inc
1324 7th Ave, Greeley CO 80631-4132. 303/3569700. Employs: 50-99.

Associated Natural Gas Inc
36469 Weld County Rd 33 Ste 33, Eaton CO 80615. 303/5728002. Employs: 50-99.

Hallwood Energy Partners L P
4582 S Ulster St Pkwy, Denver CO 80237-2632. 303/8507373. Employs: 100-249.

Meridian Minerals Co
5613 Dtc Pky, Englewood CO 80111-3028. 303/7968586. Employs: 50-99.

Plains Petroleum Co
12596 W Bayaud Ave, Lakewood CO 80228-2018. 303/9699325. Employs: 50-99.

Hamilton Oil Corporation
1560 Broadway, Denver CO 80202-5133. 303/8633000. Employs: 100-249.

DRILLING OIL AND GAS WELLS

Apollo Drilling
1625 Broadway Ste 2030, Denver CO 80202-4726. 303/6231555. Employs: 50-99.

Gear Drilling Company
518 17th St, Denver CO 80202-4102. 303/6234422. Employs: 50-99.

OIL AND GAS FIELD EXPLORATION SERVICES

Anr Production Company
600 17th St Suite 800-S, Denver CO 80202-5438. 303/5721121. Employs: 100-249.

Bond Gold Corporation
4600 S Ulster St Suite 300, Denver CO 80237-2871. 303/2209727. Employs: 50-99.

Chevron USA Inc
6400 S Fiddlers Green Cir, Englewood CO 80111-4950. 303/9303000. Employs: 100-249.

Diamond Shamrock Exploration
370 17th St, Denver CO 80202-5656. 303/6230522. Employs: 50-99.

Forest Oil Corp
999 18th St Suite 1700, Denver CO 80202-2417. 303/2930460. Employs: 50-99.

Mallon Resources Corporation
1099 18th St Suite 2750, Denver CO 80202-1941. 303/2932333. Employs: 50-99.

Nicor Oil & Gas Corporation
1050 17th St Suite 1100, Denver CO 80265-1101. 303/8931666. Employs: 100-249.

Persidio Oil Company
5613 D T C Pk Ste 750, Englewood CO 80111. 303/7730172. Employs: 50-99.

Tipperary Corp
633 17, Denver CO 80202. 303/2939379. Employs: 50-99.

MISC. OIL AND GAS FIELD SERVICES

Caza Drilling & Exploration Co
1801 Broadway Suite 360, Denver CO 80202-3831. 303/2921206. Employs: 50-99.

Wilkerson Corporation
1201 W Mansfield Ave, Englewood CO 80110-3453. 303/7617601. Employs: 100-249.

Flint Engineering & Constrctn Co
1391 Denver Ave, Fort Lupton CO 80621-2648. 303/8572791. Employs: 50-99.

Oil Well Perforators Inc
12500 E Control Tower Rd, Englewood CO 80112-4146. 303/7902411. Employs: 50-99.

NONMETALLIC MINERAL SERVICES, EXCEPT FUELS

Carroni Mineral Corp
1621 18th St, Denver CO 80202-1266. 303/2925235. Employs: 50-99.

Kestrel Resources Inc
445 Union Blvd, Lakewood CO 80228-1237. 303/9871629. Employs: 50-99.

Statistics & Solutions US Inc
410 S Lincoln Ave, Steamboat Spr CO 80487-8908. 303/8797775. Employs: 50-99.

MISC. NONMETALLIC MINERALS, EXCEPT FUELS

Asarco Incorporated
748 County Rd 2 A, Leadville CO 80461. 719/4861772. Employs: 100-249.

Climax Molybdenum Company
Climax, Leadville CO 80429. 719/4862150. Employs: 50-99.

Cyprus Yampa Valley Coal Corp
29587 Routt County Rd 27, Oak Creek CO 80467. 303/8793800. Employs: 50-99.

Gold Fields Mining Corp
1687 Cole Blvd, Golden CO 80401-3301. 303/2319700. Employs: 50-99.

Western Mining Corp
141 Union Blvd, Lakewood CO 80228-1837. 303/9898308. Employs: 50-99.

PETROLEUM REFINING

Asamera Inc
1001 E Hampden Av, Denver CO 80227. 303/8637300. Employs: 100-249.

Colorado Refining
5800 Brighton Blvd, Commerce City CO 80022-3613. 303/2912270. Employs: 100-249.

Conoco Refinery
5801 Brighton Blvd, Commerce City CO 80022-3612. 303/4305001. Employs: 100-249.

Western Mobile Inc
6405 Valmont, Boulder CO 80301. 303/4439400. Employs: 100-249.

ASPHALT PAVING AND MIXTURES AND BLOCKS

Asphalt Paving Co
14802 W 44th Ave, Golden CO 80403. 303/2796611. Employs: 100-249.

CLAY REFRACTORIES

Denver Brick Company Inc
401 Santa Fe Rd, Castle Rock CO 80104-1541. 303/6886951. Employs: 50-99.

MISC. STRUCTURAL CLAY PRODUCTS

Carder Concrete Prods Co
8311 W Carder Ct, Littleton CO 80125-9705. 303/7911600. Employs: 100-249.

MISC. POTTERY PRODUCTS

Hand Built Pottery
835 Deer Ln, Guffey CO 80820-9105. 719/4792222. Employs: 50-99.

CONCRETE BLOCK AND BRICK

Gates & Sons Inc
90 S Fox St, Denver CO 80223-1609. 303/7446185. Employs: 50-99.

LIME

Colorado Lien Co
PO Box 1961, Fort Collins CO 80522-1961. 303/3493701. Employs: 50-99.

GYPSUM PRODUCTS

Eagle Gypsum Products
4704 Harlan St, Denver CO 80212-7415. 303/4801415. Employs: 50-99.

MINERALS AND EARTHS, GROUND OR OTHERWISE TREATED

Brannan Sand & Gravel Co
4800 Brighton Blvd, Denver CO 80216-2217. 303/5341231. Employs: 100-249.

Colorado Lien Co
16230 N US Hwy 287, Livermore CO 80536. 303/4937017. Employs: 50-99.

CRUDE PETROLEUM PIPELINES

Amoco Corporation
600 S Cherry St, Denver CO 80222-1702. 303/3701770. Employs: 50-99.

Associated Ntrl Gas Inc Lucerne
31495 Weld County Rd 43, Greeley CO 80631. 303/3523104. Employs: 50-99.

Energy Pipeline Inc
1801 California St, Denver CO 80202-2614. 303/2953333. Employs: 50-99.

Transcolorado Gas Trans Co
12055 W 2nd Pl, Lakewood CO 80228-1506. 303/9892560. Employs: 50-99.

U S Gasnet

8101 E Dartmouth Ave, Denver CO 80231-4257. 303/3689964. Employs: 50-99.

For more information on career opportunities in the energy, mining, and petroleum industries:

Associations

AMERICAN ASSOCIATION OF PETROLEUM GEOLOGISTS
P.O. Box 979, Tulsa OK 74101. 918/584-2555.

AMERICAN GAS ASSOCIATION
1515 Wilson Boulevard, Arlington VA 22209. 703/841-8400.

AMERICAN GEOLOGICAL INSTITUTE
4220 King Street, Alexandria VA 22302. 703/379-2480.

AMERICAN INSTITUTE OF MINING, METALLURGICAL AND PETROLEUM
345 East 47th Street, New York NY 10017. 212/705-7695.

AMERICAN NUCLEAR SOCIETY
555 North Kensington Avenue, La Grange Park IL 60525. 708/352-6611.

AMERICAN PETROLEUM INSTITUTE
1220 L Street NW, Washington DC 20005. 202/682-8000.

AMERICAN SOCIETY OF TRIBOLOGISTS AND LUBRICATION ENGINEERS
840 Busse Highway, Park Ridge IL 60068. 708/825-5536.

CLEAN ENERGY RESEARCH INSTITUTE
P.O. Box 248294, Coral Gables FL 33124. 305/284-4666.

GEOLOGICAL SOCIETY OF AMERICA
3300 Penrose Place, P.O. Box 9140, Boulder CO 80301. 303/447-2020.

PETROLEUM EQUIPMENT INSTITUTE
P.O. Box 2380, Tulsa OK 74101. 918/494-9696.

PETROLEUM MARKETERS ASSOCIATION OF AMERICA
1120 Vermont Avenue NW, Washington DC 20005. 202/331-1198.

SOCIETY OF EXPLORATION GEOPHYSICISTS
P.O. Box 702740, Tulsa OK 74170-2740. 918/493-3516.

Directories

BROWN'S DIRECTORY OF NORTH AMERICAN AND INTERNATIONAL GAS COMPANIES
Advanstar Communications, 7500 Old Oak Boulevard, Cleveland OH 44130. 800/225-4569.

NATIONAL PETROLEUM NEWS FACT BOOK
Hunter Publishing Co., 950 Lee Street, Des Plaines IL 60016. 708/296-0770.

OIL AND GAS DIRECTORY
Geophysical Directory, Inc., P.O. Box 130508, Houston TX 77219. 713/529-8789.

Magazines

AMERICAN GAS MONTHLY
1515 Wilson Boulevard, Arlington
VA 22209. 703/841-8686.

**GAS INDUSTRIES AND
APPLIANCE MAGAZINES**
Gas Industries and Appliance
News, Inc., P.O. Box 558, Park
Ridge IL 60068. 312/693-3682.

**NATIONAL PETROLEUM
NEWS**
Hunter Publishing Co., 950 Lee
Street, Des Plaines IL 60016.
708/296-0770.

OIL AND GAS JOURNAL
PennWell Publishing Co., 1421
South Sheridan Road, Tulsa OK
74112. 918/835-3161.

ENGINEERING AND DESIGN

Job prospects for engineers have been good for a number of years, and will continue to improve into the next century. Employers will need more engineers as they increase investment in equipment in order to expand output. In addition, engineers will find work improving the nation's deteriorating infrastructure.

CH2M HILL
P.O. Box 22508, Denver CO 80222. 303/771-0900. **Contact:** Michelle Larson, Assistant Recruiter. **Description:** A design/consulting firm. **Common positions:** Architect; Chemist; Computer Programmer; Draftsperson; Economist; Agricultural Engineer; Chemical Engineer; Civil Engineer; Electrical Engineer; Mechanical Engineer; Geologist; Personnel; Systems Analyst; Technical Writer/Editor; Transportation and Traffic Specialist; Structural, Sanitary, Hazardous Waste Engineer; Water Resource Engineers; Construction Managers. **Educational backgrounds sought:** Business Administration; Chemistry; Computer Science; Engineering; Hydrogeology. **Benefits:** medical, dental, and life insurance; pension plan; tuition assistance; disability coverage; profit sharing; savings plan; employee stock ownership plan. **Corporate headquarters:** This location. **Operations at this facility:** regional headquarters; administration; service.

ECI/ENGINEERING CONSULTANTS INC.
5660 Greenwood Plaza Boulevard, Suite 500, Englewood CO 80111. 303/773-3788. **Contact:** Personnel. **Description:** A Denver-area engineering consulting firm.

GREINER ENGINEERING
570 West 44th Avenue, Denver CO 80216. 303/455-7321. **Contact:** Personnel. **Description:** An area engineering firm.

MERRICK AND COMPANY

10855 East Bethany Drive, Aurora CO 80014. 303/751-0741. **Contact:** Sue H. Latham, Personnel Manager. **Description:** A Denver-area engineering and architecture firm. **Common positions:** Engineer; Architect; Designer; Technician. **Educational backgrounds sought:** Engineering; Architecture.

UNITED ENGINEERING AND CONSTRUCTION INC.
WESTERN OPS.

P.O. Box 5888, Denver CO 80217. 303/843-2000. **Contact:** J.A. Emmanuelli, Human Resources Manager. **Description:** A diversified corporation engaged in the design, engineering, and construction of industrial plants' electric power; architectural and community services; heavy machinery design and construction; industrial facilities; and mining and metallurgy. **Common positions:** Administrator; Architect; Buyer; Computer Programmer; Draftsperson; Chemical Engineer; Civil Engineer; Electrical Engineer; Mechanical Engineer; Metallurgical Engineer; Mining Engineer; Petroleum Engineer; Purchasing Agent; Quality Controller; Systems Analyst. **Educational backgrounds sought:** Business Administration; Computer Science; Engineering. **Benefits:** medical, dental, and life insurance; pension plan; tuition assistance; disability coverage; employee discounts; savings plan. **Corporate headquarters:** Philadelphia, PA. **Parent company:** Raytheon. **Operations at this facility:** divisional headquarters; service. **Employees:** 6000. **Projected hires for the next 12 months:** 600.

WRIGHT WATER ENGINEERS INCORPORATED

2490 West 26th Avenue, Suite 100A, Denver CO 80211-4208. 303/480-1700. **Contact:** Kenneth Wright, President. **Description:** An engineering consulting firm.

Additional small to medium sized employers: 50-249

ENGINEERING SERVICES

Avedon Engineering Inc
711 S Lincoln, Longmont CO 80501-6314. 303/7722633. Employs: 50-99.

Centennial Engineering Inc
15000 W 64th Ave, Arvada CO 80001. 303/4200221. Employs: 100-249.

Centennial Engineering Inc
1515 Arapahoe St Suite 1335, Denver CO 80202-2113. 303/6231719. Employs: 50-99.

Ebasco Construction Inc
72nd & Quebec Street, Commerce City CO 80022. 303/2897000. Employs: 100-249.

Johnson Engineering Corp
3055 Center Green Dr, Boulder CO 80301-5406. 303/4498152. Employs: 100-249.

Kellogg Corporation
26 W Dry Creek Cir Suite 8th F, Littleton CO 80120-4475. 303/7941818. Employs: 50-99.

Morrison Knudsen Engineering
1700 Lincoln St Suite 4800, Denver CO 80203-4548. 303/8608621. Employs: 50-99.

The Mitre Corporation
1259 Lake Plaza Dr, Colorado Springs CO 80906-3568. 719/5762602. Employs: 50-99.

The Rmh Group Inc
12600 W Colfax Ave Suite A-400, Lakewood CO 80215-3792. 303/2390909. Employs: 50-99.

Jacobs Engineering Group Inc

600 17, Denver CO 80202. 303/5958855. Employs: 50-99.

ENSR Consulting & Engineering
1716 Heath Pky, Fort Collins CO 80524-2719. 303/4938878. Employs: 50-99.

RW Beck & Associates
1125 17, Denver CO 80202. 303/2995200. Employs: 50-99.

For more information on career opportunities in engineering and design:

Associations

AMERICAN ASSOCIATION OF COST ENGINEERS
209 Prairie Avenue, Suite 100, Morgantown WV 26507. 304/296-8444.

AMERICAN ASSOCIATION OF ENGINEERING SOCIETIES
1111 19th Street, Suite 608, Washington DC 20036. 202/296-2237.

AMERICAN CONSULTING ENGINEERS COUNCIL
1015 15th Street NW, Washington DC 20005. 202/347-7474.

AMERICAN INSTITUTE OF ARCHITECTS
1735 New York Ave NW, Washington DC 20006. 202/626-7300.

AMERICAN INSTITUTE OF PLANT ENGINEERS
3975 Erie Avenue, Cincinnati OH 45208. 513/561-6000.

AMERICAN SOCIETY FOR ENGINEERING EDUCATION
11 Dupont Circle NW, Suite 200, Washington DC 20036. 202/293-7080.

AMERICAN SOCIETY OF CIVIL ENGINEERS
345 East 47th Street, New York NY 10017. 212/705-7496.

AMERICAN SOCIETY OF HEATING, REFRIGERATING AND AIR CONDITIONING ENGINEERS
1791 Tullie Circle NE, Atlanta GA 30329. 404/636-8400.

AMERICAN SOCIETY OF LANDSCAPE ARCHITECTS
4401 Connecticut Avenue, Fifth Floor, Washington DC 20008. 202/686-2752.

AMERICAN SOCIETY OF MECHANICAL ENGINEERS
345 East 47th Street, New York NY 10017. 212/705-7722.

AMERICAN SOCIETY OF NAVAL ENGINEERS
1452 Duke Street, Alexandria VA 22314. 703/836-6727.

AMERICAN SOCIETY OF PLUMBING ENGINEERS
3617 Thousand Oaks Boulevard, Suite #210, Westlake CA 91362. 805/495-7120.

AMERICAN SOCIETY OF SAFETY ENGINEERS
1800 East Oakton Street, Des Plaines IL 60018-2187. 312/692-4121.

ILLUMINATING ENGINEERING SOCIETY OF NORTH AMERICA
345 East 47th Street, New York NY 10017. 212/705-7926.

INSTITUTE OF INDUSTRIAL ENGINEERS
25 Technology Park, Norcross GA 30092. 404/449-0460.

NATIONAL ACADEMY OF ENGINEERING
2101 Constitution Avenue NW, Washington DC 20418. 202/334-3200.

NATIONAL ACTION COUNCIL FOR MINORITIES IN ENGINEERING
3 West 35th Street, New York NY 10001. 212/279-2626.

NATIONAL ASSOCIATION OF MINORITY ENGINEERING
500 N. Michigan Avenue, Suite 1400, Chicago IL 60611. 312/661-1700.

NATIONAL ENGINEERING CONSORTIUM
303 E. Wacker Drive, Suite 740, Chicago IL 60601. 312/938-3500.

JUNIOR ENGINEERING TECHNICAL SOCIETY
1420 King Street, Suite 405, Alexandria VA 22314. 703/548-JETS.

NATIONAL INSTITUTE OF CERAMIC ENGINEERS
735 Ceramic Place, Westerville OH 43081. 614/890-4700.

NATIONAL SOCIETY OF BLACK ENGINEERS
1454 Duke Street, Alexandria VA 22314. 703/549-2207.

NATIONAL SOCIETY OF PROFESSIONAL ENGINEERS
1420 King Street, Alexandria VA 22314. 703/684-2800.

SOCIETY FOR THE ADVANCEMENT OF MATERIAL AND PROCESS ENGINEERS
1161 Parkview Drive, Covina CA 91724. 818/331-0616.

SOCIETY OF FIRE PROTECTION ENGINEERS
1 Liberty Square, Boston MA 02109. 617/482-0686.

SOCIETY OF MANUFACTURING ENGINEERS
P.O. Box 930, One SME Drive, Dearborn MI 48121. 313/271-1500.

UNITED ENGINEERING TRUSTEES
345 East 47th Street, New York NY 10017. 212/705-7000.

Directories

DIRECTORY OF ENGINEERING SOCIETIES
American Association of Engineering Societies, 1111 19th Street, Suite 608, Washington DC 20036. 202/296-2237.

DIRECTORY OF ENGINEERS IN PRIVATE PRACTICE
National Society of Professional Engineers, 1420 King Street, Alexandria VA 22314. 703/684-2800.

ENCYCLOPEDIA OF PHYSICAL SCIENCES & ENGINEERING INFORMATION SOURCES
Gale Research Inc., 835 Penobscot Building, Detroit MI 48226. 313/961-2242.

Magazines

CAREERS AND THE ENGINEER
Bob Adams, Inc., 260 Center Street, Holbrook MA 02343. 617/767-8100.

EDN CAREER NEWS
Cahners Publishing Co., 275 Washington Street, Newton MA 02158. 617/964-3030.

ENGINEERING TIMES
National Society of Professional Engineers, 1420 King Street, Alexandria VA 22314. 703/684-2800.

PROFESSIONAL ENGINEER
National Society of Professional Engineers, 1420 King Street, Alexandria VA 22314. 703/684-2800.

FABRICATED AND PRIMARY METALS

For steel manufacturers, the past few years have been a nightmare, with prices falling to ten-year lows. The industry should begin a modest recovery, however, if lower mortgage rates can spur the home construction industry. Foreign companies will become more and more important; look for more joint ventures between the U.S. and overseas firms. Big Steel's toughest competition is now the increasing number of minimills that have spun off from rivals.
Overall, employment prospects are weak, although metallurgical engineering is in demand.

ALFRED MANUFACTURING COMPANY
4398 Elati Street, Denver CO 80216. 303/433-6385. **Contact:** Doug Alfred, President. **Description:** Manufacturer of special dies and tools; die sets; jigs; fixtures; and industrial molds. Machine shop production, metal stamping, welding, and special machines.

ALLIED STEEL COMPANY
3800 Wynkoop Street, Denver CO 80216. 303/295-3434. **Contact:** Personnel. **Description:** Manufacturer of fabricated structural steel.

ATLAS METAL & IRON CORPORATION
318 Walnut, Denver CO 80204. 303/825-7166. **Contact:** Personnel Department. **Description:** Wholesaler of scrap iron and metal recycling.

BALL CORPORATION
METAL CONTAINER GROUP
P.O. Box 589, Broomfield CO 80038-0589. 303/460-5136. **Contact:** Personnel Department. **Description:** An area metal container manufacturer. Parent company manufacturers and packages a diverse line of industrial and high technology products. **Corporate headquarters:** Muncie, IN.

CF&I STEEL CORPORATION
P.O. Box 316, Pueblo CO 81002. 719/561-6000. **Contact:** Vivian Sagona, Supervisor of Personnel. **Description:** A manufacturer of steel products including railroad rails, seamless oil country tubular pipe, wire and bar products. **Common positions:** Accountant; Blue-Collar Worker Supervisor; Computer Programmer; Ceramics Engineer; Metallurgical Engineer; Quality Control Supervisor. **Corporate headquarters:** This location. **Listed on:** NASDAQ.

DENVER METAL FINISHING
3100 East 43rd Avenue, Denver CO 80216. 303/295-1380. **Contact:** Personnel Department. **Description:** Corporation involved in metal plating and polishing.

EATON METAL PRODUCTS COMPANY
4800 York Street, Denver CO 80216. 303/296-4800. **Contact:** Personnel Department. **Description:** Produces a broad range of fabricated metal products, including structural metals, structural plate, and oil field equipment. **Corporate headquarters:** This location.

ELECTRON CORPORATION
P.O. Box 318, Littleton CO 80160-0318. 303/794-4392. **Contact:** Mike Starr, Employee Relations Director. **Description:** A metals manufacturer; produces gray iron and ductile iron castings, as well as other specialty metal products. **Corporate headquarters:** This location.

EXPLOSIVE FABRICATORS, INC.
1301 Courtesy Road, Louisville CO 80027. 303/666-6551. **Contact:** Cheryl Muench, Human Resources Coordinator. **Description:** A manufacturing company specializing in the bonding and forming of metals by explosive means. **Common positions:** Accountant; Blue-Collar Worker Supervisor; Buyer; Customer Service Representative; Draftsperson; Aerospace Engineer; Mechanical Engineer; Metallurgical Engineer; Operations/Production Specialist; Department Manager; Personnel and Labor Relations Specialist; Purchasing Agent; Quality Controller; Sales Representative; Systems Analyst; Technical Writer/Editor. **Educational backgrounds sought:** Accounting; Engineering; Finance; Marketing. **Special programs:** Training programs. **Benefits:** medical, dental, and life insurance; tuition assistance; disability coverage; 401K. **Corporate headquarters:** This location. **Operations at this facility:** manufacturing; research/development; administration; service; sales. **Listed on:** New York Stock Exchange. **Revenues (1991):** $14.6 million. **Employees:** 124. **Projected hires for the next 12 months:** 15.

FAGAN IRON AND METAL INC.
4701 Ivy Street, Denver CO 80216. 303/377-6598. **Contact:** Personnel Department. **Description:** A wholesaler of scrap and waste materials.

GATES & SONS INC.

P.O. Box 9509, Denver CO 80209-0509. **Contact:** Employment Manager. **Description:** Engaged in metals fabrication, and the production of fabricated metal products. **Benefits:** medical insurance; life insurance. **Corporate headquarters:** This location. **Operations at this facility:** manufacturing; administration; sales.

GOLDBERG BROTHERS MANUFACTURING COMPANY

P.O. Box 38819, Denver CO 80238. 303/321-1099. **Contact:** Randy Urlik, Executive Vice President. **Description:** Manufactures aluminum and sheet metal products, including aluminum castings, sheet metal stampings, and products made from these metals, including film cannisters, cases, and reels. **Corporate headquarters:** This location.

NEXUS CORPORATION

10983 Leroy Drive, Northglenn CO 80233. 303/457-9199. **Contact:** Administrator. **Description:** A manufacturer of prefabricated metal greenhouses.

QUALITY METAL PRODUCTS

11500 West 13th Avenue, Lakewood CO 80215-4491. 303/232-4242. **Contact:** Personnel Department. **Description:** A manufacturer of metal products.

SPECIAL PRODUCTS COMPANY

15000 West 44th Avenue, Golden CO 80403-1824. 303/279-5544. **Contact:** Glenda Thompson, Personnel Director. **Description:** Engaged in a broad range of custom metals fabrication activities, including custom steel fabrication, the fabrication of screw machine products, the manufacture of agricultural equipment attachments (blades, hitches, tractor accessories, specialized digging equipment), and other fabricated metal products. **Corporate headquarters:** This location.

STERLING STAINLESS TUBE CORPORATION

1400 West Dartmouth, Englewood CO 80110. 303/789-0528. **Contact:** Barbara Weithtman, Human Resources Manager. **Description:** Manufactures small diameter stainless steel tubing for medical, industrial, and automotive uses. Division of ITT Higbie Baylock (Auburn Hills, MI). **Common positions:** Mechanical Engineer. **Educational backgrounds sought:** Engineering. **Benefits:** medical insurance; dental insurance; pension plan; life insurance; tuition assistance; disability coverage; savings plan. **Operations at this facility:** divisional headquarters location; manufacturing; research/development; administration; sales.

THOMPSON PIPE & STEEL COMPANY

P.O. Box 2852, Denver CO 80201. 303/289-4080. **Contact:** Debbie Howbach, Personnel Director. **Description:** Produces a variety of steel products, including steel pipe, pipe fittings, and other products. Also engaged in boiler plate work. **Corporate headquarters:** This location.

ZIMMERMAN METALS, INC.

201 East 58th Avenue, Denver CO 80216. 303/294-0180. **Contact:** Arla Zimmerman, Personnel Manager. **Description:** Fabricators of structural and miscellaneous steel, architectural metals, machining, aluminum finishing, painting, and welding; also CNC machining and boring mills. **Common positions:** Computer Programmer; Estimator; Project Manager; Mechanical Engineer; Sales Representative; Welder; Layout Specialist; Machine Operator; Purchasing Agent; Quality Control Supervisor. CNC/NC Estimating. **Benefits:** medical insurance; pension plan; life insurance; tuition assistance; disability coverage. **Operations at this facility:** manufacturing; research and development; administration; service; sales. **Corporate headquarters:** This location.

Additional large employers: 250+

GOLD ORES

Atlas Corp
370 17th St, Denver CO 80202-5656. 303/8251200. Employs: 250-499.

SILVER ORES

Amax Gold Inc
350 Indiana, Golden CO 80401-5050. 303/2730600. Employs: 250-499.

FERROALLOY ORES, EXCEPT VANADIUM

Amax Henderson
PO Box 68, Empire CO 80438-0068. 303/5693221. Employs: 250-499.

METAL CANS

Ball Packaging Products Group
9300 W 108th Cir, Broomfield CO 80021-3682. 303/4605133. Employs: 1,000+.

HAND AND EDGE TOOLS, EXCEPT MACHINE TOOLS AND HANDSAWS

Western Forge Corp
4607 Forge Rd, Colorado Springs CO 80907-3517. 7195985070. Employs: 500-999.

MISC. HARDWARE

Schlage Lock Co
3899 Hancock Expy, Colorado Springs CO 80911-1230. 7193905071. Employs: 500-999.

MISC. ORDNANCE AND ACCESSORIES

Oea Inc
34501 E Quincy, Aurora CO 80015. 303/6931248. Employs: 250-499.

Additional small to medium sized employers: 50-249

GOLD ORES

American Cnsldtd Gold Corp
4600 S Olster St, Denver CO 80237. 303/2209727. Employs: 50-99.

Cnsldtd Nv Goldfields Corp
1801 Broadway, Denver CO 80202-3828. 303/2963200. Employs: 50-99.

Double Eagle Resources Inc
2555 S Santa Fe Dr, Denver CO 80223-4456. 303/7778889. Employs: 50-99.

Echo Bay Management Corp
370 17th St Suite 4050, Denver CO 80202-5675. 303/5925450. Employs: 50-99.

Minven Gold Corporation
7596 W Jewell Ave, Lakewood CO 80232-6839. 303/9805615. Employs: 50-99.

Tenneco Minerals Co
12136 W Bayaud Ave Suite 200, Lakewood CO 80228-2115. 303/9876200. Employs: 100-249.

SILVER ORES

Moritz Energy Corp
4740 N Mesa Dr, Castle Rock CO 80104-9320. 303/6882810. Employs: 50-99.

Petro-Global Inc
1515 Arapahoe St, Denver CO 80202-2118. 303/5735038. Employs: 50-99.

U S Gold Corp
55 Madison, Denver CO 80206. 303/3228002. Employs: 50-99.

METAL MINING SERVICES

Barnett Roy Co Drill & Exploration
215 N 5, Victor CO 80860. 719/6893705. Employs: 50-99.

Coppermex Management
165 S Union Blvd, Lakewood CO 80228-2215. 303/9690594. Employs: 50-99.

Denver Mining Finance Co
1660 Wynkoop St, Denver CO 80202-1115. 303/5739221. Employs: 50-99.

URANIUM-RADIUM-VANADIUM ORES

Energy Fuels Nuclear Inc
One Tabor Ctr 1200 17th St, Denver CO 80202. 303/6238317. Employs: 100-249.

Urangesellschaft USA Inc
10040 Yarrow St, Broomfield CO 80021-4045. 303/4690890. Employs: 50-99.

MISC. METAL ORES

Caprock Corp
8101 E Prentice Ave, Englewood CO 80111-2909. 303/7217200. Employs: 50-99.

STEEL WORKS, BLAST FURNACES (INCLUDING COKE OVENS), AND ROLLING MILLS

Colorado Steel & Wire Company
165 Sw 2nd St, Loveland CO 80537-6301. 303/6679390. Employs: 50-99.

STEEL PIPES AND TUBES

Oakley Tube Corp Illinois
3211 W Bear Creek Dr, Englewood CO 80110-3210. 303/7611835. Employs: 50-99.

Sterling Stainless Tube Corp
1400 W Dartmouth Ave, Englewood CO 80110-1305. 303/7899528. Employs: 100-249.

GRAY AND DUCTILE IRON FOUNDRIES

United Foundry
2959 N Liggett Rd, Castle Rock CO 80104. 303/6608449. Employs: 50-99.

Firebaugh Pre-Cast Concrete
PO Box 5440, Colorado Springs CO 80931-5440. 719/3929036. Employs: 50-99.

MISC. STEEL FOUNDRIES

Teilhaber Manufacturing Corp
2360 Industrial Ln, Broomfield CO 80020-1612. 303/4662323. Employs: 50-99.

ROLLING, DRAWING, AND EXTRUDING OF COPPER

Brass Smith
2625 Walnut St, Denver CO 80205-2230. 303/2968520. Employs: 50-99.

NONFERROUS FOUNDRIES, EXCEPT ALUMINUM AND COPPER

Western Foundries Inc
100 Marion St, Denver CO 80218-3926. 303/8255277. Employs: 50-99.

MISC. PRIMARY METAL PRODUCTS

Advanced Forming Technology
2150 Miller Dr, Longmont CO 80501-6744. 303/6516557. Employs: 50-99.

METAL CANS

Metal Container Corporation
1201 18th Ave, Windsor CO 80550-3218. 303/8251064. Employs: 100-249.

Robertson Associates Ltd
11084 Leroy Dr, Denver CO 80233-3617. 303/4527007. Employs: 50-99.

MISC. HARDWARE

Band-It Idex Inc
4799 Dahlia St, Denver CO 80216-3222. 303/3204555. Employs: 100-249.

PLUMBING FIXTURE FITTINGS AND TRIM

Wcm Industries Inc
2121 Waynoka Rd, Colorado Springs CO 80915-1602. 719/5740600. Employs: 50-99.

FABRICATED STRUCTURAL METAL

Ripsam Mfg
5100 N Boyd, Loveland CO 80537. 303/6697481. Employs: 50-99.

Silver Engr Works
14800 E Moncrieff Pl, Aurora CO 80011-1211. 303/3732311. Employs: 100-249.

Zimkor Industries Inc
7011 W Titan Rd, Littleton CO 80125-9505. 303/7911333. Employs: 50-99.

FABRICATED PLATE WORK

Cryenco Inc
5995 Washington St, Denver CO 80216-1336. 303/2951161. Employs: 100-249.

Eaton Metal Products Co
4800 York St, Denver CO 80216-2237. 303/2964800. Employs: 100-249.

Pioneer Astro Industries Inc
3410 N Prospect St, Colorado Springs CO 80907-5453. 719/4734186. Employs: 100-249.

Thompson Pipe & Steel Company
6030 Washington St, Denver CO 80216-1120. 303/2894080. Employs: 100-249.

SHEET METAL WORK

Automotive Spray Booth Mfg
1252 W Radcliff Ave, Englewood CO 80110-5528. 303/7816802. Employs: 50-99.

Electronic Metal Prods Inc
21000 E 32nd Pky, Aurora CO 80011-8148. 303/3758000. Employs: 50-99.

Goldberg Bros Inc
8000 E 40th Ave, Denver CO 80207-1711. 303/3211099. Employs: 50-99.

Golden Aluminum
1405 14th St, Fort Lupton CO 80621-2718. 303/8576257. Employs: 100-249.

Majestic Metals Inc
1400 E 66th Ave, Denver CO 80229-7242. 303/2886855. Employs: 50-99.

Pike Tool & Grinding Inc
4205 High Country Rd, Colorado Springs CO 80907-4320. 719/5989611. Employs: 100-249.

Rbm Precision Metal Products
3755 Mark Dabling Blvd, Colorado Springs CO 80907-9018. 719/6335596. Employs: 100-249.

ARCHITECTURAL AND ORNAMENTAL METAL WORK

Baab Steel Inc
410 Tia Juana St, Colorado Springs CO 80909-6225. 719/6345511. Employs: 50-99.

PREFABRICATED METAL BUILDINGS AND COMPONENTS

Denpak Bldg Prods Inc
6777 Downing St, Denver CO 80229-7106. 303/2895461. Employs: 50-99.

The Scotsman Group
2419 1st Ave, Greeley CO 80631-7429. 303/3565950. Employs: 50-99.

Wedge Cor Steel
6800 E Hampden Ave, Denver CO 80224-3008. 303/7593200. Employs: 100-249.

IRON AND STEEL FORGING

Explosive Fabricators Inc
1301 Courtesy Rd, Louisville CO 80027-1416. 303/6666551. Employs: 100-249.

ELECTROPLATING, PLATING, POLISHING, ANODIZING, AND COLORING

Colorado Anodizers
777 Umatilla St, Denver CO 80204-4225. 303/5348161. Employs: 50-99.

MISC. FABRICATED WIRE PRODUCTS

Carts Of Colorado
5750 Holly St, Commerce City CO 80022-3904. 303/2881000. Employs: 50-99.

MISC. FABRICATED METAL PRODUCTS

Alpine Mfg Inc
2421 International Blvd, Fort Collins CO 80524-1433. 303/4933242. Employs: 50-99.

Ami Industries Inc
P O Box 370, Colorado Springs CO 80901-0370. 719/4710020. Employs: 100-249.

Hps
5330 Sterling Dr, Boulder CO 80301-2309. 303/4499861. Employs: 100-249.

Rose Mfg Co
2250 S Tejon, Englewood CO 80110-1041. 303/9226246. Employs: 50-99.

For more information on career opportunities in the fabricated and primary metals industries:

Associations

AMERICAN FOUNDRYMEN'S SOCIETY
505 State Street, Des Plaines IL 60016. 708/824-0181.

AMERICAN IRON & STEEL INSTITUTE
1101 17th Street NW, 13th Floor, Washington DC 20036. 202/452-7100.

AMERICAN POWDER METALLURGY INSTITUTE
105 College Road East, Princeton NJ 08540. 609/452-7700.

AMERICAN SOCIETY FOR METALS
9639 Kinsman Road, Materials Park OH 44073-0002. 216/338-5151.

AMERICAN WELDING SOCIETY
P.O. Box 35140, 550 LeJeune Road NW, Miami FL 33135. 305/443-9353.

ASSOCIATION OF IRON AND STEEL ENGINEERS
Three Gateway Center, Suite 2350, Pittsburgh PA 15222. 412/281-6323.

ASSOCIATION OF STEEL DISTRIBUTORS
401 N. Michigan Avenue, Chicago IL 60611. 312/664-6610.

NATIONAL ASSOCIATION OF METAL FINISHERS
401 N. Michigan Avenue, Chicago IL 60611. 312/644-6610.

Directories

DIRECTORY OF STEEL FOUNDRIES IN THE UNITED STATES, CANADA, AND MEXICO
Steel Founder's Society of America, 455 State Street, Des Plaines IL 60016. 708/299-9160.

Magazines

AMERICAN METAL MARKET
Capital Cities ABC, 825 7th Avenue, New York NY 10019. 212/887-8580.

IRON AGE
191 S. Gary, Carol Stream IL 60188. 708/462-2285.

IRON & STEEL ENGINEER
Association of Iron and Steel Engineers, Three Gateway Center, Suite 2350, Pittsburgh PA 15222. 412/281-6323.

MODERN METALS
400 N. Michigan Avenue, Chicago IL 60611. 312/222-2000.

FINANCIAL SERVICES AND MANAGEMENT CONSULTING

Since the 1987 crash, the financial services industry has been struggling to redefine itself. In response to the recession, companies have been cutting costs -- and jobs -- in order to become leaner and more efficient. Jobseekers should look to conservative firms for the most stable career tracks. Tip: Take a close look at mutual funds, one of the few current hot areas.

AMERICAN GROWTH FUND SPONSORS, INC.
410 17th Street, Suite 800, Denver CO 80202. 303/623-6137. **Contact:** Timothy Taggart, Controller/Personnel Manager. **Description:** A Denver security brokerage house.

BENEFICIAL COLORADO INCORPORATED
P.O. Box 27416, Lakewood CO 80227. 303/988-3550. **Contact:** Personnel Department. **Description:** A Denver financial services firm specializing in consumer loans.

BOETTCHER & COMPANY
828 17th Street, Denver CO 80201. 303/628-8000. **Contact:** Assistant Director of Personnel. **Description:** An investment and securities firm, including real estate investment. **Corporate headquarters:** This location.

BROWNE BORTZ & CODDINGTON INC.
155 South Madison Street, Suite 230, Denver CO 80209. 303/321-2547. **Contact:** Personnel Department. **Description:** A Denver-based economic research and management consulting firm. **Common positions:** Computer Programmer; Economist; Marketing Specialist; Statistician. **Educational backgrounds sought:** Business Administration; Economics. **Benefits:** medical insurance; dental insurance; pension plan; life insurance; disability coverage; profit sharing. **Corporate headquarters:** This location.

BURNS ENTERPRISES INC.

1625 Broadway, Penthouse Suite, Denver CO 80202. 303/629-1899. **Contact:** Personnel Department. **Description:** A Denver-based corporation engaged in real estate and investment as well as owning and operating apartments and nonresidential buildings.

CAPITAL ASSOCIATES, INC.

7175 W. Jefferson Avenue, Suite 3000, Lakewood CO 80235. 303/980-1000. **Contact:** David Fabian, Employment Representative. **Description:** Capital Associates, Inc. (CAI) provides independent high-technology and capital equipment leasing, financing, and equipment remarketing, both domestically and internationally. **Common positions:** Accountant; Credit Manager; Customer Service Representative; Marketing Specialist; Sales Representative. **Educational backgrounds sought:** Accounting; Business Administration; Computer Science; Finance; Marketing. **Benefits:** medical, dental, and life insurance; tuition assistance; disability coverage; profit sharing. **Corporate headquarters:** This location. **Operations at this facility:** administration; service; sales. **Listed on:** National Association of Securities Dealers.

THE CENTENNIAL FUND

1999 Broadway, Suite 2100, Denver CO 80202. 303/298-9066. **Contact:** Personnel. **Description:** A Denver investment company.

CENTRAL BANK OF COLORADO

P.O. Box 5548, Denver CO 80217. 303/820-4242. **Contact:** Mr. Dan Martinez, Human Resources Manager. **Description:** Provides financial services in the state of Colorado at over 40 state locations. Financial services include: banking, and mortgage and credit services for both consumer and commercial customers. **Common positions:** Bank Officer/Manager; Credit Manager; Customer Service Representative; Branch Manager; Sales Representative. **Educational backgrounds sought:** Accounting; Business Administration; Finance; Marketing. **Special programs:** Training programs. **Benefits:** medical, dental, and life insurance; pension plan; tuition assistance; disability coverage; employee discounts; savings plan. **Corporate headquarters:** Minneapolis, MN. **Parent company:** First Bank Systems. **Operations at this facility:** Service; Sales. **Listed on:** New York Stock Exchange.

COLORADO HOUSING & FINANCE AUTHORITY

1981 Blake Street, Denver CO 80202. 303/297-2432. **Contact:** Human Resources. **Description:** Quasi-governmental organization. Provides financing for housing (rental or home ownership) to both low and moderate income people. Also provides financing for small businesses. **Common positions:** Accountant; Administrator; Attorney; Bank Officer/Manager; Computer Programmer; Financial Analyst; Personnel and Labor Relations Specialist; Underwriter; Mortgage Lender/Services; Commercial Lenders Property Management. **Benefits:** medical insurance; dental insurance; pension plan; life insurance; tuition assistance; disability coverage; daycare assistance; savings plan. **Educational backgrounds sought:** Accounting; Commercial Banking; Mortgage Banking.

DAIN BOSWORTH, INC.
1225 17th Street, Suite 1800, Denver CO 80202. 303/294-7200. **Contact:** Personnel Department. **Description:** A regional investment banking firm.

FIRST DATA CORPORATION
AMERICAN EXPRESS INTEGRATED PAYMENT SYSTEMS
6200 S. Quebec, Englewood CO 80111. 303/488-8000. **Contact:** Employment Department. **Description:** This location is headquarters for American Express money orders, American Express MoneyGram, and official check and cash management. **Common positions:** Accountant, Administrator; Computer Programmer; Customer Service Representative; Financial Analyst; Marketing Specialist; Personnel and Labor Relations Specialist; Purchasing Agent; Sales Representative; Systems Analyst; Computer Technical Servicer. **Educational backgrounds sought:** Accounting; Business Administration; Communications; Computer Science; Finance; Marketing. **Benefits:** medical insurance; dental insurance; pension plan; life insurance; tuition assistance; disability coverage; savings plan. **Corporate headquarters:** New York, NY. **Parent company:** American Express Information Services Co. **Operations at this facility:** divisional headquarters. **Listed on:** New York Stock Exchange.

FIRST FINANCIAL MANAGEMENT CORPORATION
THRIFT SERVICES DIVISION
5850 DTC Parkway, Building #14, Englewood CO 80111. 303/771-9000. Personnel is located in Oklahoma City. **Description:** FFMC is one of the largest financial transaction data processors in the country, with major subsidiaries throughout the U.S. **Common positions:** Accountant; Computer Programmer; Customer Service Representative; Financial Analyst; General Manager; Management Trainee; Operations/Production Manager; Marketing Specialist; Personnel and Labor Relations Specialist; Systems Analyst; Technical Writer/Editor. **Educational backgrounds sought:** Finance. **Corporate headquarters:** Atlanta, GA. **Operations at this facility:** divisional headquarters.

GRUBB & ELLIS
COMMERCIAL BROKERAGE SERVICE
One Tabor Center, 1200 17th Street, Suite 2000, Denver CO 80202. 303/572-7700. **Contact:** Daisy Whitney, Administrative Manager. **Description:** A Denver brokerage firm. **Common positions:** Sales Representative. **Educational backgrounds sought:** Business Administration; Marketing; Real Estate. **Special programs:** Training programs and internships. **Corporate headquarters:** San Francisco, CA. **Operations at this facility:** research/development; sales. **Listed on:** New York Stock Exchange.

HANIFEN IMHOFF INC.
P.O. Box 5050, Denver CO 80217-5050. 303/296-2300. **Contact:** Personnel. **Description:** An area securities brokerage firm. **Corporate headquarters:** This location.

HETTLER INVESTMENTS INCORPORATED
5223 South Ironton Way, Denver CO 80111. 303/779-1894. **Description:** A Denver investment company.

INFORMATION PROFESSIONALS & CO.
INFOPAC
14221 East 4th Avenue, Suite 315, Aurora CO 80011. 303/341-7149. **Contact:** Mary Ann Chaffin, Business Manager. **Description:** An area information broker. **Common positions:** Librarian; Records Manager. **Educational backgrounds sought:** Graduate Library Science Degree. **Corporate headquarters:** This location. **Operations at this facility:** service.

INVESTMENT RESEARCH CORPORATION
410 17th Street, Suite 800, Denver CO 80202. 303/623-6137. **Contact:** Personnel Department. **Description:** Corporation providing investment counseling.

JANUS CAPITAL CORPORATION
100 Filmore Street, Suite 300, Denver CO 80206-4923. 303/333-3863. **Contact:** Recruiting Manager. **Description:** Investment firm dealing in mutual funds.

JOHNSON-ANDERSON MORTGAGE COMPANY
55 East Centennial Avenue, Englewood CO 80110. 303/762-9373. **Contact:** Personnel Department. **Description:** A Denver-based mortgage company.

KELLOGG CORPORATION
26 West Dry Creek Circle, Littleton CO 80120. 303/794-1818. **Contact:** Mrs. D.K. Lewis, Director of Human Resources. **Description:** An international management services and engineering consulting firm, serving as planner, advisor and, problem-solver for complex construction projects. **Common positions:** Civil Engineer and Engineering Management Services. **Educational backgrounds sought:** Engineering and Management.

LIVINGSTON CAPITAL
370 17th Street, Suite 3290, Denver CO 80202. 303/573-8866. **Contact:** Personnel Department. **Description:** A Denver venture capital firm.

NEWMAN FINANCIAL SERVICES INCORPORATED
1801 California Suite 3700, Denver CO 80202. 303/293-8500. **Contact:** Personnel Department. **Description:** An investment banking company.

101 INVESTMENT COMPANY
1380 Zuni, Denver CO 80204. 303/893-3211. **Contact:** Personnel Department. **Description:** A Denver holding company.

OPPENHEIMER MANAGEMENT CORP.
P.O. Box 5061, Denver CO 80217. 303/671-3200. **Contact:** Ms. Chris Wells, Personnel Director. **Description:** A Denver investment firm.

PAINE WEBBER
1600 Broadway, Suite 2200, Denver CO 80202. 303/861-2400. **Contact:** Linda Gravning, Operations Manager. **Description:** Denver office of the financial stock-brokerage firm.

PREFERRED FINANCIAL CORPORATION
5990 Greenwood Plaza Boulevard., Suite 325, Englewood CO 80111. 303/220-8500. **Contact:** Personnel Department. **Description:** A financial services institution.

FREDERICK R. ROSS INVESTMENT CO.
730 17th Street, Suite 500, Denver CO 80202. 303/892-1111. **Contact:** Steve Paniguchi, Personnel Director. **Description:** A Denver investment firm.

TRANSAMERICA COMMERCIAL FINANCE CORP.
P.O. Box 22295, Denver CO 80222. 303/779-5757. **Contact:** department of applicant's interest. **Description:** Business consultants specializing in floor-planning for client companies.

TRIPLE A TAX & BUSINESS
2225 Stout Street, Denver CO 80205. 303/292-4489. **Contact:** Personnel Department. **Description:** A Denver tax return service.

UNITED BANKS OF COLORADO, INC.
1700 Broadway, Denver CO 80274. 303/861-8811. **Contact:** Joan Van Landingham, Personnel Director. **Description:** A bank holding company.

UNITED MORTGAGE COMPANY
1015 17th Street, Denver CO 80265. 303/899-4633. **Contact:** Human Resources. Send resume to: Norwest Bank of Denver, 1740 Broadway Street, Denver CO 80274-8690. **Description:** A regional mortgage company.

WESTAMERICA MORTGAGE COMPANY
5655 South Yosemite Street, Englewood CO 80111. 303/771-2800. **Contact:** Assistant Vice President/Human Resources. **Description:** Corporate headquarters of a Denver mortgage company.

WESTERN CAPITAL INVESTMENT CORPORATION
1675 Broadway, Denver CO 80202. 303/623-5577. **Contact:** Human Resources Department. **Description:** A holding company, and a savings and loan association.

Additional large employers: 250+

SECURITY BROKERS, DEALERS, AND FLOTATION COMPANIES

Jones International Securities
9697 E Mineral Ave, Englewood CO 80112-3408. 303/7923131. Employs: 1,000+.

MISC. OFFICES OF HOLDING COMPANIES

ANR Freight System Inc
PO Box 5070, Denver CO 80217-5070. 303/2789900. Employs: 1,000+.

Manville Corporation
PO Box 5108, Denver CO 80217-5108. 303/9782000. Employs: 1,000+.

US West Inc

7800 E Orchard Rd, Englewood CO 80111-2533. 303/7936500. Employs: 1,000+.

Additional small to medium sized employers: 50-249

PERSONAL   CREDIT INSTITUTIONS

Firstbank At Arapahoe & Holly
5050 E Arapahoe Rd, Littleton CO 80122-2302.   303/2351020. Employs: 50-99.

General Electric Credit Corp
12050 Pecos St Suite 300, Denver CO 80234-2080. 303/4574646. Employs: 100-249.

General   Motors   Acceptance Corp
7951 E Maplewood Ave Suite 300, Englewood   CO   80111-4726. 303/9305600. Employs: 50-99.

Gmac
13772 Denver West Pk Ste 200, Golden   CO   80401-3139. 303/2737800. Employs: 100-249.

Margaretten & Co Inc
5373 N Union Bl, Colorado Springs   CO   80918-2073. 719/5481100. Employs: 50-99.

United Bank
1242 Pearl St, Boulder CO 80302-5209. 303/4420351. Employs: 100-249.

Household Finance Corporation
1888   W   Eisenhower   Blvd, Loveland   CO   80537-3107. 303/6696666. Employs: 50-99.

SHORT-TERM   BUSINESS CREDIT INSTITUTIONS

Circle Business Credit Inc

9275 W 1st Ave, Lakewood CO 80226-1001.   303/2337852. Employs: 100-249.

Credit Planning Associates Inc
1100 W Littleton Blvd Ste 202, Littleton   CO   80120-2239. 303/7958033. Employs: 50-99.

Fresh Start
1010 S Joliet St, Aurora CO 80012-3150. 303/3441414. Employs: 50-99.

MISC.   BUSINESS   CREDIT INSTITUTIONS

Dana Commercial Credit
3025 S Parker Rd, Aurora CO 80014-2911.   303/7523262. Employs: 50-99.

Industrial Leasing Corp
13791 E Rice Pl, Aurora CO 80015-1090.   303/6805610. Employs: 50-99.

Industry Financial Corporation
1520 E Girard Av Suite 2050, Aurora CO 80014. 303/6938300. Employs: 50-99.

Mica Technology Services
3025 S Parker Rd, Aurora CO 80014-2911.   303/6961778. Employs: 50-99.

SECURITY BROKERS, DEALERS, AND FLOTATION COMPANIES

AL Williams & Associates
5309 Fossil Ridge Dr, Fort Collins
CO 80525-3817. 303/2265504.
Employs: 50-99.

Boettcher & Company
828 17th St Suite 100, Denver CO
80202-3103. 303/6288545.
Employs: 100-249.

Chatfield Bean Co Inc
7935 E Prentice Ave Suite 300,
Englewood CO 80111-2717.
303/7407707. Employs: 100-249.

JW Gant & Associates Inc
7600 E Orchard Rd Suite 160,
Englewood CO 80111-2518.
303/8507799. Employs: 50-99.

Marshall Davis Inc
630 E 17th Av Ste 200, Denver CO
80203-1433. 303/8894900.
Employs: 50-99.

Merrill Lynch Pierce Inc
3900 S Teller St, Denver CO
80235-2213. 303/9875700.
Employs: 100-249.

Prudential Bache Securities
370 17th St Suite 3900, Denver CO
80202-5688. 303/5925800.
Employs: 100-249.

RAF Financial Corporation
717 17th St Suite 2900, Denver CO
80202-3329. 303/2921400.
Employs: 100-249.

INVESTMENT ADVICE

AL Williams Company
2170 S Parker Rd Suite 120,
Denver CO 80231-5709.
303/3698300. Employs: 50-99.

Financial Programs Inc

7800 E Union Ave Suite 800P,
Denver CO 80237-2752.
303/7790731. Employs: 100-249.

MISC. SERVICES ALLIED WITH THE EXCHANGE OF SECURITIES OR COMMODITIES

Bnk Amer Stck Trnsfr
1776 Lincoln St, Denver CO
80203-1022. 303/8949155.
Employs: 50-99.

MISC. OFFICES OF HOLDING COMPANIES

Coaxial Capital Associates Inc
4582 S Ulster St Ste 1301, Denver
CO 80237-2639. 303/5954445.
Employs: 50-99.

Divisioners Management Acquisitions Inc
P O Box 18351, Denver CO 80218-
0351. 303/6940226. Employs: 100-
249.

Orion Broadcast Group
6061 S Willow Dr Suite 117,
Englewood CO 80111-5149.
303/7706369. Employs: 50-99.

RDS Inc
4380 E Alameda Ave, Denver CO
80222-1071. 303/3553549.
Employs: 100-249.

Universal Reserve Corporation
2630 Sunset Ln, Estes Park CO
80517. 303/5860980. Employs: 50-
99.

Western United Corp
5239 S Rio Grande, Denver CO
80223. 303/7949800. Employs:
100-249.

MORTGAGE BANKERS AND LOAN CORRESPONDENTS

Home American Mortgage Corp
3600 S Yosemite St Suite 600, Denver CO 80237-1887. 303/7731155. Employs: 250-499.

Citicorp Homeowners Inc
4643 S Ulster St, Denver CO 80237-2862. 303/7407104. Employs: 50-99.

Colorado Housing Fin Authority
1981 Blake St, Denver CO 80202-1272. 303/2972432. Employs: 100-249.

Home Federal Savings Bank
300 W Oak St, Fort Collins CO 80521-2737. 303/4823216. Employs: 50-99.

Icm Mortgage Corp
6061 S Willow Dr Suite 300, Englewood CO 80111-5151. 303/7403316. Employs: 100-249.

Moore Mortgage Co
PO Box 61429, Denver CO 80206-8429. 303/7781800. Employs: 100-249.

Platte Valley Mortgage Corp
13275 E Fremont Pl Ste 201, Englewood CO 80112-3910. 303/9698423. Employs: 50-99.

Shelter America Corp
718 17th St Suite 2400, Denver CO 80202-3535. 303/8927113. Employs: 100-249.

Universal Lending Corporation
6775 E Evans Ave, Denver CO 80224-2355. 303/7584969. Employs: 100-249.

UNIT INVESTMENT TRUSTS, FACE-AMOUNT CERTIFICATE OFFICES, AND

CLOSED-END MANAGEMENT INVESTMENT OFFICES

Colorado Venture Capital
4747 Ivy St, Denver CO 80216-6413. 303/4409018. Employs: 50-99.

PATENT OWNERS AND LESSORS

Colomex Inc
717 N Tejon St Ste 3, Colorado Springs CO 80903-1030. 719/6332500. Employs: 100-249.

Remax Headquarter Companies
5445 Dtc Pky Suite 1200, Englewood CO 80111-3057. 303/7705531. Employs: 50-99.

Cajun Joes Co Inc
PO Box 4023, Evergreen CO 80439-3432. 303/6749714. Employs: 50-99.

Fantastic Sams Regional Office
96 Inverness Dr E, Englewood CO 80112-5112. 303/7991334. Employs: 50-99.

Franchise Systems Internationall
8400 E Prentice Ave, Englewood CO 80111-2912. 303/2908561. Employs: 50-99.

Hospitality F Systems Inc
9200 E Mineral Ave, Englewood CO 80112-3412. 303/7990855. Employs: 50-99.

N Ctrl Food Systems Dba
318 Canyon Ave, Fort Collins CO 80521-2623. 303/2212636. Employs: 50-99.

Randall Enterprises Inc
721 Nichols Blvd, Colorado Springs CO 80907-5434. 719/4735582. Employs: 50-99.

The Aspen Group
200 W 48th Ave, Denver CO
80216-1802.   303/2988406.
Employs: 100-249.

Videomatic
1746 Cole Blvd, Golden CO
80401-3208.   303/2794449.
Employs: 50-99.

MISC. INVESTORS

Source Venture Capital Inc
6455 S Yosemite, Englewood CO
80111-5130.   303/6941171.
Employs: 50-99.

**MANAGEMENT
CONSULTING SERVICES**

Colorado Medical Consultants
501 S Cherry St Suite 700, Denver
CO   80222-1331.   303/7590400.
Employs: 100-249.

Group II Communications
7730 N Jilin Bl, Colorado Springs
CO 80920. 719/5997141. Employs:
50-99.

Information Resources Inc
1780 S Bellaire St Suite 520,
Denver   CO   80222-4326.
303/7536857. Employs: 50-99.

Olson Marketing Group
8400 E Prentice Ave Suite Ph,
Englewood   CO   80111-2912.
303/7933710. Employs: 50-99.

**Signature Hospitality Mgmt Co
Lease**
8690 Wolff Ct, Westminster CO
80030-3691.   303/6501450.
Employs: 100-249.

Trend Communications Inc
9250 E Costilla Ave Ste 620,
Englewood   CO   80112-3649.
303/6499910. Employs: 50-99.

Compu Serve Inc
1512 Larimer St, Denver CO
80202-1610.   303/6295514.
Employs: 100-249.

**MISC.   BUSINESS
CONSULTING SERVICES**

Rooney Operating Corporation
7670 S Vaughn Ct Suite 200,
Englewood   CO   80112-4120.
303/7922535. Employs: 50-99.

**NONDEPOSIT   TRUST
FACILITIES**

American Trust Company
4727 Hackamore Dr N, Colorado
Springs   CO   80918-2628.
719/5319203. Employs: 50-99.

Peak Brokerage
10395 W Colfax Ave, Lakewood
CO   80215-3925.   303/2388121.
Employs: 50-99.

**OFFICES OF BANK HOLDING
COMPANIES**

First Capitol Financial Corp
3300 S Parker Rd, Aurora CO
80014-3520.   303/6711000.
Employs: 100-249.

United Banks Of Colorado
1700 Lincoln St Suite 3200,
Denver   CO   80203-4532.
303/8614700. Employs: 100-249.

**For more information on career opportunities in financial services and
management consulting:**

Associations

**AMERICAN FINANCIAL
SERVICES ASSOCIATION**
919 18th Street, 3rd Floor,
Washington DC 20006. 202/296-
5544.

**AMERICAN MANAGEMENT
ASSOCIATION**
Management Information Service,
135 West 50th Street, New York
NY 10020. 212/586-8100.

**AMERICAN SOCIETY OF
APPRAISERS**
P.O. Box 17265, Washington DC
20041. 703/478-2228.

**ASSOCIATION OF
MANAGEMENT
CONSULTING FIRMS**
521 Fifth Avenue, 35th Floor, New
York NY 10175. 212/697-9693.

**COUNCIL OF CONSULTANT
ORGANIZATIONS**
521 Fifth Avenue, 35th Floor, New
York NY 10175. 212/697-8262.

**FEDERATION OF TAX
ADMINISTRATORS**
444 North Capital Street NW,
Washington DC 20001. 202/624-
5890.

**ASSOCIATION FOR
INVESTMENT
MANAGEMENT AND
RESEARCH**
200 Park Avenue, 18th Floor, New
York NY 10166. 212/957-2860.

**FINANCIAL EXECUTIVES
INSTITUTE**
10 Madison Avenue, P.O. Box
1938, Morristown NJ 07962-1938.
201/898-4600.

**INSTITUTE OF FINANCIAL
EDUCATION**
111 East Wacker Drive, Chicago IL
60601. 312/644-3100.

**INSTITUTE OF
INTERNATIONAL FINANCE**
2000 Pennsylvania Ave NW,
Washington DC 20006. 202/857-
3600.

**INSTITUTE OF
MANAGEMENT
CONSULTANTS**
521 Fifth Avenue, 35th Floor, New
York NY 10175. 212/697-8262.

**NATIONAL ASSOCIATION OF
BUSINESS ECONOMISTS**
28790 Chagrin Boulevard, Suite
300, Cleveland OH 44122.
216/464-7986.

**NATIONAL ASSOCIATION OF
CREDIT MANAGEMENT**
8815 Centre Park Drive, Suite 200,
Columbia MD 21045-2117.
301/740-5560.

**NATIONAL ASSOCIATION OF
REAL ESTATE INVESTMENT
TRUSTS**
1129 20th Street NW, Suite 705,
Washington DC 20036. 202/785-
8717.

**NATIONAL COMMERCIAL
FINANCE ASSOCIATION**
225 West 34th Street, New York
NY 10122. 212/594-3490.

**TREASURY MANAGEMENT
ASSOCIATION**
7315 Wisconsin Avenue, Suite
1250-W, Bethesda MD 20814.
301/907-2862.

**SECURITIES INDUSTRY
ASSOCIATION**
120 Broadway, New York NY
10271. 212/608-1500.

PUBLIC SECURITIES ASSOCIATION
40 Broad Street, New York NY 10004. 212/809-7000.

Directories

DIRECTORY OF AMERICAN FINANCIAL INSTITUTIONS
McFadden Business Publications, 6195 Crooked Creek Road, Norcross GA 30092. 404/448-1011.

MOODY'S BANK AND FINANCE MANUAL
Moody's Investor Service, 99 Church Street, New York NY 10007. 212/553-0300.

Magazines

BARRON'S: NATIONAL BUSINESS AND FINANCIAL WEEKLY
Dow Jones & Co., 200 Liberty Street, New York NY 10281. 212/416-2700.

FINANCIAL PLANNING
40 W. 57th Street, 8th Floor, New York NY 10019. 212/765-5311.

INSURANCE TIMES
M & S Communications, 437 Newtonville Avenue, Newton MA 02160. 617/924-8161.

FINANCIAL WORLD
Financial World Partners, 1450 Broadway, New York NY 10001. 212/594-5030.

FUTURES: THE MAGAZINE OF COMMODITIES AND OPTIONS
250 South Wacker Drive, Suite 1150, Chicago IL 60606. 312/977-0999.

INSTITUTIONAL INVESTOR
488 Madison Avenue, New York NY 10022. 212/303-3300.

FOOD AND BEVERAGES: PRODUCTION AND DISTRIBUTION

The best bets in the food industry are meats and poultry; processed fruits and vegetables; and soft drinks. One of the worst areas in the food industry is liquor and spirits.

ALBERTSON'S, INC.
2750 North Tower Road, Aurora CO 80011. 303/360-7424. **Contact:** Sharon Cleverley, Training Coordinator. **Description:** Divisional office of the consumer grocery store chain.

ANDRE'S CONTISERIE SUISSE
370 South Garfield, Denver CO 80209. 303/322-8871. **Contact:** Personnel Department. **Description:** A retail candy and pastry company.

BARBER POULTRY INC.

P.O. Box 363, Broomfield CO 80038. 303/466-7338. **Contact:** David Barber, General Manager. **Description:** Processes and distributes poultry products, especially processed turkey items. **Corporate headquarters:** This location.

BAR-S FOODS

P.O. Box 5448 TA, Denver CO 80217. 303/292-2277. **Contact:** Greg Nelson, Industrial Relations Manager. **Description:** Produces and distributes smoked meat products, including bacon and ham. **Corporate headquarters:** This location.

CELESTIAL SEASONINGS INC.

4600 Sleepytime Drive, Boulder CO 80301-3292. 303/530-5300. **Contact:** Mike Biery, Human Resources Manager. **Description:** A producer of a large line of herbal teas and beverages; also involved in the processing of herbs used to make the company's products. **Corporate headquarters:** This location.

CHAMPION BOXED BEEF

P.O. Box 16303, Denver CO 80216. 303/288-0766. **Contact:** Dick Sheldon, Vice President. **Description:** Produces and packages beef and beef by-products. **Corporate headquarters:** This location.

COCA-COLA/DENVER

P.O. Box 17100, T.A., Denver CO 80217. 303/292-2653. **Contact:** Tony Rodriguez, Director of Personnel. **Description:** Regional facility of the international soft drink company. **Corporate headquarters:** Atlanta, GA.

CONAGRA FLOUR MILLING COMPANY

4545 East 64th Avenue, Commerce City CO 80022. 303/289-6141. **Contact:** Personnel. **Description:** Engaged in the production of flour, wheat germ, and feed; all agricultural products made from wheat. **Corporate headquarters:** Omaha, NE. **Listed on:** New York Stock Exchange. **Common positions:** Chemist; Customer Service Representative; Manager; Department Manager; Quality Control Supervisor; Sales Representative. **Educational backgrounds sought:** Business Administration; Milling Science. **Benefits:** medical insurance; dental insurance; pension plan; life insurance; tuition assistance; disability coverage; profit sharing; savings plan.

CONTINENTAL BAKING COMPANY

80 East 62nd Ave, Denver CO 80216. 303/428-7431. **Contact:** Mr. W.L. White, Human Resources Manager. **Description:** Produces a wide variety of bread and bakery products as a division of the international manufacturing and consumer goods firm. Hiring for entry-level jobs in the areas of manufacturing, sales, and office work only.

ENTENMANN'S/ORWEAT

5050 East Evans Avenue, P.O. Box 22505, Denver CO 80222. 303/691-6398. **Contact:** Personnel Department. **Description:** Produces a variety of breads and rolls; distributes cake and pastry products. **Common positions:** Accountant; Customer Service Representative; Mechanical Engineer; Branch Manager; Department Manager; General Manager; Operations/Production Manager; Marketing Specialist; Purchasing Agent; Sales Representative; Systems Analyst;

Product Workers; Route Sales. **Educational backgrounds sought:** Accounting; Business Administration; Finance. **Benefits:** medical insurance; dental insurance; pension plan; life insurance; tuition assistance; disability coverage; profit sharing; employee discounts; savings plan. **Corporate headquarters:** White Plains, NY. Subsidiary of General Foods. **Operations at this facility:** manufacturing; administration; sales.

EXCEL
C.S. 4100, Fort Morgan CO 80701. 303/867-8223. **Contact:** Personnel Manager. **Description:** An area beef-packing plant and distribution center. **Common positions:** Accountant; Blue-Collar Worker Supervisor; Mechanical Engineer; Department Manager; Operations/Production Manager; Marketing Specialist; Personnel and Labor Relations Specialist; Purchasing Agent; Sales Representative. **Benefits:** medical insurance; dental insurance; life insurance; disability coverage.

EXCEL CORPORATION
1500 Right of Way Road, P.O. Box 1728, Sterling CO 80751. 303/522-1784. **Contact:** Mark Sheldon, Personnel Director. **Description:** An area branch of the beef packing company. **Corporate headquarters:** Denver.

FBC FOODS INTERNATIONAL
900 East 11th Avenue, Denver CO 80218. 303/832-6800. **Contact:** Jane Dorsey, Personnel Director. **Description:** A gourmet/specialty food retail market. **Common positions:** Department Manager; General Manager; Management Trainee. **Special programs:** Training programs. **Corporate headquarters:** This location.

FULL SERVICE BEVERAGE COMPANY
OF DENVER
2840 South Zuni, Englewood CO 80110. 303/761-7777. **Contact:** Mike May, Personnel Manager. **Description:** A bottling facility for a number of national brands. **Corporate headquarters:** Wichita, Kansas.

GENERAL FOODS CORPORATION
P.O. Box 38129, Denver CO 80238. 303/780-5440. **Contact:** Personnel Manager. **Description:** Regional office of the consumer foods company. **Corporate headquarters:** White Plains, NY.

THE JOLLY RANCHER
5060 Ward Road, Wheat Ridge CO 80033. 303/422-1456. **Contact:** Human Resources Department. **Description:** Produces a variety of confectionery products as a subsidiary of Beatrice Foods Company (Chicago, IL). **Corporate headquarters:** This location.

KEEBLER COMPANY
DENVER BAKERY
5000 Osage Street, Denver CO 80221. 303/433-6221. **Contact:** Barbara Bronson, Employment Manager. **Description:** Produces and distributes a wide range of cookies, crackers, and similar snack products. **Common positions:** Accountant; Blue-Collar Worker Supervisor; Buyer; Draftsperson; Electrical Engineer; Industrial Engineer; Mechanical Engineer; Food Technologist;

Department Manager; General Manager; Management Trainee; Operations/Production Manager; Marketing Specialist; Personnel and Labor Relations Specialist; Purchasing Agent; Quality Control Supervisor; Sales Representative. **Educational backgrounds sought:** Accounting; Business Administration; Chemistry; Food Science. **Benefits:** medical insurance; dental insurance; pension plan; life insurance; tuition assistance; disability coverage; employee discounts; savings plan. **Operations at this facility:** manufacturing. **Parent company:** United Biscuits (Elmhurst, IL).

KENTUCKY FRIED CHICKEN
3120 South Broadway, Englewood CO 80110. 303/781-1180. **Contact:** Personnel Department. **Description:** Area office of the chain of fast-food fried chicken restaurants.

KRAFT WESTMAN FOOD SERVICE
11955 East Peakview Avenue, Englewood CO 80111. 303/792-9230. **Contact:** Rick Fuelling, Manager. **Description:** Produces canned and frozen goods as well as fresh produce and meats. A subsidiary of Kraft Inc.

LONGMONT FOODS
P.O. Box 1479, Longmont CO 80502-1479. 303/776-6611. **Contact:** Personnel Director. **Description:** Engaged in poultry dressing operations. **Corporate headquarters:** This location.

LOVELAND FOODS
P.O. Box 178, Loveland CO 80539. 303/667-3476. **Contact:** Cindy Russell, Personnel Department. **Description:** Processes and distributes fresh pork and pork products, such as sausage and smoked meats. **Corporate headquarters:** This location.

MOUNTAIN STATES BEAN COMPANY
P.O. Box 16488, 4401 East 46th Avenue, Denver CO 80216. 303/355-3545. **Contact:** Controller. **Description:** A packaging and storage company dealing in coffee, rice, and other staples.

NESTLE FOOD COMPANY
2216 South Xanadu Way, Suite 3390, Aurora CO 80014. 303/743-3750. **Contact:** Sales Manager. **Description:** A sales division and office of the large canned milk and confectionery food products manufacturer. **Corporate headquarters:** Glendale, CA.

NOBEL/SYSCO FOOD SERVICE COMPANY
1101 West 48th Avenue, Denver CO 80221. 303/480-3475, Jobline. **Contact:** Cindy Trost, Personnel Director. **Description:** A Denver food distributor. **Common positions:** Accountant; Buyer; Computer Programmer; Credit Manager; Customer Service Representative; Draftsperson; Sales Representative. **Educational backgrounds sought:** Accounting; Business Administration. **Special programs:** Training programs. **Benefits:** medical, dental, and life insurance; pension plan; disability coverage; daycare assistance; profit sharing; employee discounts; savings plan; 401K; stock options. **Corporate headquarters:** Houston, TX. **Parent company:** Sysco Corp. **Operations at**

this facility: administration; service; sales. **Revenues (1991):** $8 billion. **Employees:** 880. **Projected hires for the next 12 months:** 60.

OSCAR MAYER & COMPANY
P.O. Box 6623, Englewood CO 80155. 303/740-8895. **Contact:** Personnel Department. **Description:** Regional sales office of the consumer food processing company. **Corporate headquarters:** Madison, WI.

RAINBOW BREAD COMPANY/DENVER
P.O. Box 268, Denver CO 80201. 303/288-2675. **Contact:** Dale Neilsen, Personnel. **Description:** A Colorado bakery.

RALSTON PURINA COMPANY
4555 York Street, Denver CO 80216. 303/295-0818. **Contact:** Office Manager. **Description:** Produces a nationally-advertised line of dog foods, cat foods, and feed for other domestic animals. Overall, company is a large producer of dog and cat foods, commercial livestock feeds, cereals, canned goods (tuna and mushrooms), soybean meal, and soybean oil. Also involved in various diversified businesses. **Employees:** More than 63,000 people worldwide at 250 facilities. **Corporate headquarters:** St. Louis, MO. **Listed on:** New York Stock Exchange.

RED SEAL POTATO CHIP COMPANY
4300 Oneida Street, Denver CO 80216. 303/399-0533. **Contact:** Sharon King, Personnel Manager. **Description:** Produces and distributes a variety of snack products, including potato chips, corn chips, tortilla chips, and others. **Corporate headquarters:** This location.

ROBINSON DAIRY INC.
P.O. Box 5774, Denver CO 80217. 303/825-2990. **Contact:** Paul Christensen, Personnel Office. **Description:** Produces a complete range of dairy products, including milk, ice cream, and others; also produces fruit-flavored drinks. **Corporate headquarters:** This location.

ROYAL CREST DAIRY, INC.
350 South Pearl, Denver CO 80209-2098. 303/777-3055. **Contact:** Keith Gaertner, Personnel Director. **Description:** A dairy-products processing company.

RUSTCO PRODUCTS COMPANY
1485 East 61st Avenue, Denver CO 80216. 303/287-3203. **Contact:** Personnel Director. **Description:** A manufacturer of bakery mixes, jams, jellies, food, oils; also sells wholesale bakery supplies and performs some chemical testing.

THE SIGMAN MEAT COMPANY INC.
6000 West 54th Avenue, Arvada CO 80002. 303/424-5531. **Contact:** Marcella Gendill, Personnel. **Description:** A regional meat packer, distributing processed meat products in 13 western states. **Corporate headquarters:** This location.

SINTON DAIRY FOODS COMPANY, INC.
3720 North Sinton Road, Colorado Springs CO 80907. 719/633-3821. **Contact:** Beatrice Steahlin, Personnel Director. **Description:** A Colorado dairy-products processing company.

SOUTHLAND STORES
7-ELEVEN STORES
7167 S. Alton Way, Englewood CO 80112. 303/740-9333. **Contact:** Debby Magruder, Human Resources Manager. **Description:** Divisional headquarters for 7-Eleven stores in Colorado and Utah. **Common positions:** Administrator; Blue-Collar Worker Supervisor; Buyer; Management Trainee; Personnel and Labor Relations Specialist; Loss Prevention; Merchandising. **Educational backgrounds sought:** Accounting; Business Administration; Finance; Marketing. **Special programs:** Training programs. **Benefits:** medical insurance; dental insurance; life insurance; daycare assistance; profit sharing; credit union. **Corporate headquarters:** Dallas, TX. **Parent company:** Southland Corporation. **Operations at this facility:** divisional headquarters.

STOKES/ELLIS FOODS
P.O. Box 16787, Denver CO 80216. 303/292-4018. **Contact:** Pat Bayhouse, Administrative Assistant. **Description:** A food processing company.

TRINIDAD-BENHAM CORPORATION
P.O. Box 22139, Denver CO 80222. 303/220-1400. **Contact:** Human Resources. **Description:** A Denver grain company.

VSA INCORPORATED
4582 South Ulster Street Parkway, Suite 800, Denver CO 80237. 303/779-4900. **Contact:** Lisa Burnham, Human Resources Department. **Description:** A wholesaler of vendable merchandise; an office coffee service. Also involved in theater and fund raising distribution. **Common positions:** Accountant; Administrator; Advertising Worker; Blue-Collar Worker Supervisor; Buyer; Claim Representative; Computer Programmer; Credit Manager; Customer Service Representative; Financial Analyst; Food Technologist; Branch Manager; Department Manager; General Manager; Management Trainee; Operations/Production Manager; Marketing Specialist; Personnel and Labor Relations Specialist; Purchasing Agent; Quality Control Supervisor; Reporter/Editor; Sales Representative; Statistician; Systems Analyst; Technical Writer/Editor. **Educational backgrounds sought:** Accounting; Business Administration; Communications; Computer Science; Finance; Marketing. **Benefits:** medical insurance; dental insurance; pension plan; life insurance; tuition assistance; disability coverage; employee discounts. **Corporate headquarters:** This location. **Operations at this facility:** research/development; administration; service; sales. **Listed on:** New York Stock Exchange.

Additional large employers: 250+

BEEF CATTLE AND MEAT PACKING PLANTS

Monfort Inc
1930 AA St Box G, Greeley CO
80632-0350.   303/3532311.
Employs: 1,000+.

FROZEN   BAKERY PRODUCTS, EXCEPT BREAD

Stouffer Foods Corp
3333 Quebec St Ste 2900, Denver
CO   80207-2324.   2162483600.
Employs: 1,000+.

MALT BEVERAGES

Adolph Coors Bio-Tech
8714 Highway 60, Johnstown CO
80534-9122.   303/5874711.
Employs: 500-999.

Adolph Coors Brewing Company
311 10th St, Golden CO 80401-
1087.   303/2796565.   Employs:
1,000+.

Anheuser Busch Inc
2351 Busch Dr, Fort Collins CO
80524-9400.   303/4904500.
Employs: 500-999.

New Belgium Brewing Co
129 Frey Ave, Fort Collins CO
80521-2331.   303/2210524.
Employs: 500-999.

Odell Brewing Co
119 E Lincoln Ave, Fort Collins
CO   80524-2419.   303/4989070.
Employs: 500-999.

Old Colorado Brewing Co Inc
123 N College Ave, Fort Collins
CO   80524-2443.   303/4932739.
Employs: 500-999.

BOTTLED   AND   CANNED SOFT   DRINKS   AND CARBONATED WATERS

Pepsi Cola Bottling Co
3801 Brighton Blvd, Denver CO
80216-3625.   303/2929220.
Employs: 250-499.

GROCERY STORES

Biggs
10001 Grant St, Denver CO 80229-
2000. 303/2524447. Employs: 250-
499.

Cub Foods
8055 Sheridan Blvd, Arvada CO
80003-1910.   303/4274441.
Employs: 250-499.

Cub Foods
2751 S Parker Rd, Aurora CO
80014-2701.   303/6951236.
Employs: 250-499.

King Soopers
1555 Quail St, Lakewood CO
80215-2743.   303/2331511.
Employs: 250-499.

King Soopers
1750 W Uintah St, Colorado
Springs   CO   80904-2958.
7196365043. Employs: 250-499.

King Soopers Pharmacy
1155 E 9th Ave, Denver CO
80218-3438.   303/8325298.
Employs: 250-499.

Safeway Stores Inc
2888 E Mexico Ave, Denver CO
80219-4833.   303/7597600.
Employs: 250-499.

Safeway Stores Inc
2798 Arapahoe Ave, Boulder CO 80302-6714.   303/4435888.
Employs: 250-499.

RETAIL BAKERIES

King Soopers Bakery
60 Yuma St, Denver CO 80223-1204.   303/7783128.   Employs: 1,000+.

MISC. FOOD STORES

Alfalfa Market Inc
5910 S University Blvd, Littleton CO   80121-2836.   303/7989699.
Employs: 250-499.

Additional small to medium sized employers: 50-249

VEGETABLES AND MELONS

Tanaka Brothers Farms Inc
5640 N 115th St, Longmont CO 80501-8434.   303/8921864.
Employs: 100-249.

ORNAMENTAL FLORICULTURE AND NURSERY PRODUCTS

Chipsea Inc
10420 Isabelle Rd, Lafayette CO 80026-9106.   303/6657130.
Employs: 50-99.

GENERAL FARMS, PRIMARILY CROPS

MJ Farms
8356 Syracuse St, Commerce City CO   80022-5049.   303/2897126.
Employs: 50-99.

BEEF CATTLE FEEDLOTS

Monfort Of Colorado Inc
28625 Hwy 34, Kersey CO 80644-9525. 303/3562323. Employs: 100-249.

HOGS

National Hog Farms Inc
25000 Weld County Rd, Kersey CO 80644. 303/3539960. Employs: 100-249.

DAIRY FARMS

Colorado Dairy Farms
7388 Hwy 66, Longmont CO 80504-9617.   303/5354626.
Employs: 50-99.

MEAT PACKING PLANTS

Gold Star Sausage Company
2800 Walnut St, Denver CO 80205-2236.   303/2956400.
Employs: 50-99.

King Soopers Meat Plant
65 Yuma St, Denver CO 80223-1203. 303/7783010. Employs: 100-249.

Litvak Meat Company
5900 York St, Denver CO 80216-1230. 303/2880766. Employs: 100-249.

Monfort Feed Lot
22777 Weld County Rd 31, Gilcrest CO 80623. 303/7372444. Employs: 50-99.

Nutra Beef Inc
7300 S Alton Way Ste H, Englewood CO 80112-2312. 303/2207273. Employs: 50-99.

SAUSAGES AND OTHER PREPARED MEAT PRODUCTS

Anderson Boneless Beef Co
909 E 75th Ave, Denver CO 80229-6401.   303/2895551.
Employs: 50-99.

Curtice Burns Meat Inc
208 S Kalamath St, Denver CO 80223-1813.   303/7225771.
Employs: 100-249.

NATURAL, PROCESSED, AND IMITATION CHEESE

Leprino Foods
1830 W 38th Ave, Denver CO 80211-2225.   303/4802600.
Employs: 100-249.

DRY, CONDENSED, AND EVAPORATED DAIRY PRODUCTS

Sinton Dairy Foods Company Inc
3801 Sinton Rd, Colorado Springs CO   80907-5036.   719/6333821.
Employs: 100-249.

FLUID MILK

Meadow Gold Inc
450 25th St, Greeley CO 80631-7140. 303/3527860. Employs: 100-249.

Mountain High Yogurt
1325 W Oxford St, Englewood CO 80110-4429.   303/7612210.
Employs: 100-249.

Safeway Milk Inc
4301 Forest St, Denver CO 80216-4540. 303/3207940. Employs: 50-99.

CANNED SPECIALTIES

Dale's Natural Products
780 N 9th Ave, Brighton CO 80601-9700.   303/6598796.
Employs: 50-99.

CANNED FRUITS, VEGETABLES, PRESERVES, JAMS, AND JELLIES

Bartell Distributing Inc
699 10th, Dillon CO 80435. 303/4685938. Employs: 50-99.

PICKLED FRUITS, AND VEGETABLES, VEGETABLE SAUCES AND SEASONINGS, AND SALAD FRUITS

Green Bay Food Co
502 1st Ave, La Salle CO 80645-5113. 303/2847859. Employs: 50-99.

WET CORN MILLING

Coors Biotech
12200 Pecos St, Denver CO 80234-3439. 303/2523000. Employs: 100-249.

PREPARED FEEDS AND FEED INGREDIENTS FOR ANIMALS AND FOWL, EXCEPT DOGS AND CATS

Coors Biotech Inc
Hc 60, Johnstown CO 80534. 303/5875131. Employs: 100-249.

BREAD AND OTHER BAKERY PRODUCTS, EXCEPT COOKIES AND CRACKERS

Kirchners Bakery Inc
180 Talamine Ct, Colorado Springs CO   80907-5177.   719/4759521.
Employs: 50-99.

Oroweat Foods Company
5050 E Evans Ave, Denver CO 80222-5218.   303/6916334.
Employs: 100-249.

Rainbo Bread Company
7300 Brighton Blvd, Commerce City CO 80022-1503. 303/2882675. Employs: 100-249.

CANE SUGAR, EXCEPT REFINING

Amalgamated Sugar Co
25 Walnut St, Windsor CO 80550-5135. 303/6867398. Employs: 50-99.

Great Western Salvage
11 & Factory Av, Loveland CO 80537. 303/6671125. Employs: 50-99.

The Western Sugar Co
25891 Weld County Rd 61, Kersey CO 80644. 303/3569003. Employs: 50-99.

The Western Sugar Co
1201 Ash Ave, Greeley CO 80631-9710. 303/3522732. Employs: 50-99.

The Western Sugar Co
590 Railroad Av, Ault CO 80610. 303/8341159. Employs: 50-99.

The Western Sugar Co
32501 Weld County Rd 16, Keenesburg CO 80643. 303/7324675. Employs: 50-99.

The Western Sugar Co
22484 Hwy 52, Hudson CO 80642. 303/5369258. Employs: 50-99.

The Western Sugar Co
14332 Weld County Rd 13, Mead CO 80542. 303/5354731. Employs: 50-99.

CANE SUGAR REFINING

The Western Sugar Co
11801 Sugarmill, Longmont CO 80501-9713. 303/7768738. Employs: 100-249.

BEET SUGAR

Holly Sugar Corporation
2 N Cascade Ave, Colorado Springs CO 80903-1614. 719/4710123. Employs: 50-99.

The Western Sugar Company
1302 1st Ave, Greeley CO 80631-4276. 303/3522756. Employs: 50-99.

CANDY AND OTHER CONFECTIONERY PRODUCTS

Stephany's Chocolates Inc
4969 Colorado Blvd, Denver CO 80216-3115. 303/3551522. Employs: 50-99.

MALT BEVERAGES

Anheuser Busch Inc
1455 E 62nd Ave, Denver CO 80216-1241. 303/2893421. Employs: 100-249.

BOTTLED AND CANNED SOFT DRINKS AND CARBONATED WATERS

Full Service Beverage Co
802 W Garden Of The Gods, Colorado Springs CO 80907. 719/5988146. Employs: 50-99.

Hires Royal Crown Bottling Company
1505 W 3rd Av Ste A, Denver CO 80223-1440. 303/5731812. Employs: 50-99.

Pepsi Cola Bottling Company
3605 N Stone Ave, Colorado Springs CO 80907-5315. 719/6345566. Employs: 100-249.

Seven Up & Canada Dry
2840 S Zuni St, Englewood CO
80110-1227.   303/7617777.
Employs: 100-249.

POTATO CHIPS, CORN CHIPS, AND SIMILAR SNACKS

Frito Lay Inc
11645 E 37th Ave, Denver CO
80239-3304.   303/3731425.
Employs: 50-99.

MISC. FOOD PREPARATIONS

Deep Rock Water Co
2640 California St, Denver CO
80205-2932.   303/2922020.
Employs: 50-99.

Pep Products Inc
3155 Commerce Ct, Castle Rock
CO   80104-9458.   303/6886633.
Employs: 50-99.

White Wave Inc
1990 57th Ct N, Boulder CO
80301-2854.   303/4433470.
Employs: 50-99.

GROCERY STORES

Albertson's Food Centers
1710 Dublin Blvd, Colorado
Springs   CO   80918-8348.
719/5287004. Employs: 100-249.

Albertson's Foods
1716 Main St, Longmont CO
80501-2036.   303/7769393.
Employs: 100-249.

Albertson's Food Centers
731 S Lemay Ave, Fort Collins CO
80524-3251.   303/2215845.
Employs: 100-249.

Albertson's Food Centers
2325 23rd Ave, Greeley CO 80631-
6633. 303/3304910. Employs: 100-
249.

Albertson's Food Centers
2900 Iris Ave, Boulder CO 80301-
1413. 303/4495220. Employs: 100-
249.

Albertson's Food Centers
455 E Cheyenne Mountain Blvd,
Colorado Springs CO 80906-4506.
719/5763310. Employs: 100-249.

Albertson's Food Centers
3970 Palmer Park Blvd, Colorado
Springs   CO   80909-3404.
719/5977601. Employs: 50-99.

Albertson's Food Centers
6600 W 120th Ave, Broomfield CO
80020-2967.   303/4652366.
Employs: 50-99.

Albertson's Inc
15220 E 6th Ave, Aurora CO
80011-8802.   303/3403160.
Employs: 50-99.

Albertson's Inc
12201 E Mississippi Ave, Aurora
CO   80012-3417.   303/3417310.
Employs: 50-99.

Albertson's Inc
4100 S Parker Rd, Aurora CO
80014-4132.   303/6908550.
Employs: 50-99.

Albertson's Inc
9052 W Ken Caryl Ave, Littleton
CO   80123-5250.   303/9736474.
Employs: 100-249.

Albertson's Inc
6575 W Colfax Ave, Denver CO
80214-1803.   303/2398954.
Employs: 50-99.

Albertson's Inc
225 S Sheridan Blvd, Lakewood
CO   80226-2400.   303/2399620.
Employs: 100-249.

Albertson's Inc
1339 S Federal Blvd, Denver CO 80219-4235.   303/9368229. Employs: 50-99.

Alfalfa's Market
1651 Broadway St, Boulder CO 80302-6218.   303/4420082. Employs: 100-249.

City Market
777 Gold Hill Pl S, Woodland Park CO 80863. 719/6873592. Employs: 50-99.

Cub Foods
1985 Sheridan Blvd, Denver CO 80214-1325.   303/2328972. Employs: 100-249.

Cub Foods
5400 S Wadsworth Blvd, Littleton CO 80123-2220. 303/9330221. Employs: 100-249.

Cub Foods
4304 Austin Bluffs Pky, Colorado Springs   CO   80918-2932. 719/5932400. Employs: 100-249.

Food Bonanza
7410 W 52nd Ave, Arvada CO 80002-3710.   303/4673666. Employs: 100-249.

Food Bonanza
400   W   South   Boulder   Rd, Lafayette   CO   80026-2776. 303/6664704. Employs: 50-99.

Greeley Sure Saver
3635 10th St, Greeley CO 80634-1820. 303/8934038. Employs: 100-249.

King Soopers
253 E 29th St, Loveland CO 80538-2721.   303/6696275. Employs: 100-249.

King Soopers

3600 Table Mesa Dr, Boulder CO 80303-5823.   303/4994004. Employs: 100-249.

King Soopers
2255 Main St, Longmont CO 80501-1417.   303/7727950. Employs: 100-249.

King Soopers
1015 S Taft Hill Rd, Fort Collins CO 80521-4240. 303/2214943. Employs: 100-249.

King Soopers
5125 W Florida Ave, Denver CO 80219-3605.   303/9367493. Employs: 50-99.

King Soopers
2727 W Evans Ave, Denver CO 80219-5507.   303/9362375. Employs: 50-99.

King Soopers
890 S Monaco Pky, Denver CO 80224-1574.   303/3331535. Employs: 50-99.

King Soopers
1927 S Wadsworth Blvd, Denver CO   80227-2434.   303/9858795. Employs: 50-99.

King Soopers
3125 S Sheridan Blvd, Denver CO 80227-5506.   303/9851509. Employs: 100-249.

King Soopers
12043 W Alameda Pky, Lakewood CO   80228-2701.   303/9888000. Employs: 100-249.

King Soopers
6470 E Hampden Ave, Denver CO 80222-7605.   303/7581210. Employs: 100-249.

King Soopers
825 S Colorado Blvd, Denver CO
80222-8006.   303/7225779.
Employs: 100-249.

King Soopers
10350 Federal Blvd, Denver CO
80221-6101.   303/4651747.
Employs: 100-249.

King Soopers
3801 E 120th Ave, Denver CO
80233-1659.   303/4516955.
Employs: 100-249.

King Soopers
750 E 104th Ave, Denver CO
80233-4301.   303/4528657.
Employs: 100-249.

King Soopers
9983 Wadsworth Pky, Broomfield
CO   80021-4249.   303/4240670.
Employs: 50-99.

King Soopers
6040 E 64th Ave, Commerce City
CO   80022-3319.   303/2873419.
Employs: 100-249.

King Soopers
9731 W 58th Ave, Arvada CO
80002-2009.   303/4210871.
Employs: 100-249.

King Soopers
64th & Ward Rd, Arvada CO
80004. 303/4310080. Employs:
100-249.

King Soopers
8031 Wadsworth Blvd, Arvada CO
80003-1639.   303/4204611.
Employs: 100-249.

King Soopers
15109 E Colfax Ave, Aurora CO
80011-5729.   303/3430064.
Employs: 50-99.

King Soopers

King Soopers
17000 E Iliff Ave, Aurora CO
80013-1520.   303/7524777.
Employs: 100-249.

King Soopers
1155 S Havana St, Aurora CO
80012-4017.   303/7551244.
Employs: 100-249.

King Soopers
15250 E Mississippi Ave, Aurora
CO   80012-3731.   303/6718697.
Employs: 100-249.

King Soopers
3190 S Parker Rd, Aurora CO
80014-3110.   303/7502450.
Employs: 100-249.

King Soopers
6760 S Pierce St, Littleton CO
80123-4574.   303/9792280.
Employs: 100-249.

King Soopers
9820 W Belleview Ave, Littleton
CO   80123-2101.   303/9789618.
Employs: 100-249.

King Soopers
5050 E Arapahoe Rd, Littleton CO
80122-2302.   303/7703400.
Employs: 50-99.

King Soopers
7575 S University Blvd, Littleton
CO   80122-3180.   303/7980530.
Employs: 100-249.

King Soopers
17761 Cottonwood Dr, Parker CO
80134-3925.   303/6934800.
Employs: 100-249.

King Soopers
5505 W 20th Ave, Denver CO
80214-1215.   303/2388269.
Employs: 100-249.

King Soopers
1331 N Speer Blvd, Denver CO
80204-2512.   303/5715566.
Employs: 100-249.

King Soopers
3325 Denargo St, Denver CO
80216-5036.   303/2950369.
Employs: 50-99.

King Soopers
100 W Littleton Blvd, Littleton CO
80120-2400.   303/7941583.
Employs: 100-249.

King Soopers
7301 Federal Blvd, Westminster
CO   80030-4938.   303/4291597.
Employs: 100-249.

King Soopers
3400 Youngfield St, Wheat Ridge
CO   80033-5245.   303/2386486.
Employs: 100-249.

King Soopers
3817 Sheridan Blvd, Wheat Ridge
CO 80033. 303/4257356. Employs:
100-249.

King Soopers
101 Englewood Pky, Englewood
CO   80110-2459.   303/7610013.
Employs: 100-249.

King Soopers
5050 S Federal Blvd, Englewood
CO   80110-6342.   303/7982521.
Employs: 100-249.

King Soopers
4910 S Yosemite St, Englewood
CO   80111-1309.   303/7733342.
Employs: 100-249.

King Soopers
3175 S Academy Blvd, Colorado
Springs   CO   80916-3203.
719/3909191. Employs: 100-249.

King Soopers

6930 N Academy Blvd, Colorado
Springs   CO   80918-1127.
719/5985177. Employs: 100-249.

King Soopers
2727 Palmer Park Blvd, Colorado
Springs   CO   80909-3032.
719/6361628. Employs: 100-249.

King Soopers
20 N Spruce St, Colorado Springs
CO   80905-1408.   719/6340231.
Employs: 100-249.

King Soopers
2833 E Fountain Blvd, Colorado
Springs   CO   80910-2312.
719/4712990. Employs: 100-249.

King Soopers
665 N Murray Blvd, Colorado
Springs   CO   80915-3405.
719/5740910. Employs: 100-249.

King Soopers Discount
6550 Lookout Rd, Boulder CO
80301-3303.   303/5301020.
Employs: 100-249.

King Soopers Mayfair
1370 Kearney St, Denver CO
80220-2726.   303/3991086.
Employs: 100-249.

Orchard Market
6000 S Holly St, Englewood CO
80111-4251.   303/2209000.
Employs: 100-249.

PDQ Food Stores Of Colorado
10890 E Dartmouth Ave, Aurora
CO   80014-4857.   303/6719533.
Employs: 100-249.

Safeway Store-Brighton
1605 Brg St, Brighton CO 80601.
303/6596461. Employs: 50-99.

Safeway Stores Inc
1122 11th Ave, Greeley CO 80631-
3826. 303/3529152. Employs: 50-
99.

Safeway Stores Inc
860 N Cleveland Ave, Loveland
CO 80537-4717. 303/6693440.
Employs: 50-99.

Safeway Stores Inc
2321 W Eisenhower Blvd,
Loveland CO 80537-3151.
303/6691342. Employs: 100-249.

Safeway Stores Inc
425 S College Av, Fort Collins CO
80524-2901. 303/4840222
Employs: 50-99.

Safeway Stores Inc
2160 W Drake Rd, Fort Collins CO
80526-1486. 303/4846048.
Employs: 100-249.

Safeway Stores Inc
1653 S Colorado Blvd, Denver CO
80222-4003. 303/6912960.
Employs: 100-249.

Safeway Stores Inc
4950 E Hampden Ave, Denver CO
80222-7328. 303/6910051.
Employs: 100-249.

Safeway Stores Inc
4600 E 46th Ave, Denver CO
80216-4304. 303/3889385.
Employs: 100-249.

Safeway Stores Inc
4500 Dahlia St, Denver CO 80216-
4410. 303/3207920. Employs: 100-
249.

Safeway Stores Inc
3904 E 120th Ave, Denver CO
80233-1606. 303/4572995.
Employs: 50-99.

Safeway Stores Inc
451 E Wonderview Dr, Estes Park
CO 80517. 303/5864447. Employs:
50-99.

Safeway Stores Inc

700 Florida Ave, Longmont CO
80501-6452. 303/7729660.
Employs: 50-99.

Safeway Stores Inc
1632 Hover Rd, Longmont CO
80501-2441. 303/7760506.
Employs: 100-249.

Safeway Stores Inc
4700 Baseline Rd, Boulder CO
80303-2603. 303/4942783.
Employs: 50-99.

Safeway Stores Inc
16921 E Quincy Ave, Aurora CO
80015-1901. 303/6902991.
Employs: 100-249.

Safeway Stores Inc
100 Retail Ctr, Broomfield CO
80020-2099. 303/4667374.
Employs: 50-99.

Safeway Stores Inc
201 E Jefferson Ave, Englewood
CO 80110-3726. 303/7810463.
Employs: 50-99.

Safeway Stores Inc
100 S Wilcox St, Castle Rock CO
80104-1911. 303/6885028.
Employs: 100-249.

Safeway Stores Inc
8200 S Quebec St, Englewood CO
80112-3194. 303/7731467.
Employs: 100-249.

Safeway Stores Inc
3800 W 44th Ave, Denver CO
80211-1305. 303/4588418.
Employs: 100-249.

Safeway Stores Inc
5025 S Kipling St, Littleton CO
80127-1314. 303/9736770.
Employs: 50-99.

Safeway Stores Inc
6770 S University Blvd, Littleton
CO 80122-1513. 303/7714599.
Employs: 50-99.

Safeway Stores Inc
1920 S Nevada Ave, Colorado
Springs CO 80906-3407.
719/6365255. Employs: 100-249.

Safeway Stores Inc
5060 N Academy Blvd, Colorado
Springs CO 80918-4124.
719/5931343. Employs: 50-99.

Safeway Stores Inc Dist Ofc
2214 N Wahsatch Av, Colorado
Springs CO 80907-6940.
719/4737100. Employs: 50-99.

Steeles Market Inc
200 W Foothills Pky, Fort Collins
CO 80525-2626. 303/2263086.
Employs: 50-99.

Sysco Foods
10061 E Colfax Ave, Aurora CO
80010-2201. 303/3410455.
Employs: 50-99.

The Grocery Warehouse
7170 Federal Blvd, Westminster
CO 80030-5511. 303/4294401.
Employs: 50-99.

Three Thieves Market
560 14th St, Burlington CO 80807-
1612. 719/3468118. Employs: 50-
99.

Toddys Super Market
2601 S Lemay Ave, Fort Collins
CO 80525-2247. 303/2233456.
Employs: 50-99.

Albertson's Inc
161 W County Line Rd, Littleton
CO 80126-1901. 303/7951414.
Employs: 50-99.

Safeway Stores Inc

High Country Sq-Hwy 74,
Evergreen CO 80439.
303/6746625. Employs: 50-99.

MEAT AND FISH MARKETS, INCLUDING FREEZER PROVISIONERS

W & W Meat
1501 Lakeside Ave, Fort Collins
CO 80521-3346. 303/2243336.
Employs: 50-99.

CANDY, NUT, AND CONFECTIONERY STORES

Planters-Life Savers Inc
1873 S Bellaire St, Denver CO
80222-4341. 303/7564142.
Employs: 50-99.

RETAIL BAKERIES

Harvest Restaurant & Bakery
1738 Pearl St, Boulder CO 80302-
5525. 303/4496223. Employs: 100-
249.

Harvest Restaurant & Bakery
7730 E Belleview Ave Suite G,
Englewood CO 80111-2616.
303/7794111. Employs: 50-99.

Word Of Mouth Catering Inc
5741 Arapahoe Av Rm 3, Boulder
CO 80303-1341. 303/4430839.
Employs: 50-99.

Marie Callender's Rest & Bakeries
15500 E Centretech Pky, Aurora
CO 80011-9032. 303/3671610.
Employs: 50-99.

MISC. FOOD STORES

FBC Foods International
900 E 11th Ave, Denver CO
80218-2804. 303/8326800.
Employs: 100-249.

For more information on career opportunities in food and beverage production and distribution:

Associations

ALLIED TRADES OF THE BAKING INDUSTRY
P.O. Box 398, Memphis TN 38101. 800/238-5765.

AMERICAN ASSOCIATION OF CEREAL CHEMISTS
3340 Pilot Knob Road, St. Paul MN 55121. 612/454-7250.

AMERICAN FROZEN FOOD INSTITUTE
1764 Old Meadow Lane, McLean VA 22102. 703/821-0770.

AMERICAN SOCIETY OF AGRICULTURAL ENGINEERS
2950 Niles Road, St. Joseph MI 49085. 616/429-0300.

AMERICAN SOCIETY OF BREWING CHEMISTS
3340 Pilot Knob Road, St. Paul MN 55121. 612/454-7250.

DAIRY AND FOOD INDUSTRIES SUPPLY ASSOCIATION
6245 Executive Boulevard, Rockville MD 20852. 301/984-1444.

DISTILLED SPIRITS COUNCIL OF THE UNITED STATES
1250 I Street NW, Suite 900, Washington DC 20005. 202/628-3544.

MASTER BREWERS ASSOCIATION OF THE AMERICAS
4513 Vernon Boulevard, Madison, WI 53705. 608/231-3446.

NATIONAL AGRICULTURAL CHEMICALS ASSOCIATION
1155 15th Street NW, Suite 900, Washington DC 20005. 202/296-1585.

NATIONAL BEER WHOLESALERS' ASSOCIATION
5205 Leesburg Pike, Suite 1600, Falls Church VA 22041. 703/578-4300.

NATIONAL DAIRY COUNCIL
10255 W. Higgins Road, Suite 900, Rosemont IL 60018. 708/803-2000.

NATIONAL FOOD PROCESSORS ASSOCIATION
1401 New York Avenue NW, Suite 400, Washington DC 20005. 202/639-5900.

NATIONAL SOFT DRINK ASSOCIATION
1101 16th Street NW, Washington DC 20036. 202/463-6732.

UNITED FOOD AND COMMERCIAL WORKERS INTERNATIONAL UNION
1775 K Street NW, Washington DC 20006. 202/223-3111.

Directories

FOOD ENGINEERING'S DIRECTORY OF U.S. FOOD PLANTS
Chilton Book Co., Chilton Way, Radnor PA 19089. 800/695-1214.

THOMAS FOOD INDUSTRY REGISTER
Thomas Publishing Co., One Penn Plaza, New York NY 10019. 212/695-0500.

Magazines

BEVERAGE INDUSTRY
Advanstar Communications, 7500
Old Oak Boulevard, Cleveland OH
44130. 216/243-8100.

BEVERAGE WORLD
150 Great Neck Road, Great Neck
NY 11021. 516/829-9210.

FOOD MANAGEMENT
233 North Michigan, Chicago IL
60601. 312/938-2300.

FOOD PROCESSING
301 East Erie, Chicago IL 60611.
312/644-2020.

FROZEN FOOD AGE
Maclean Hunter Media, #4
Stamford Forum, Stamford CT
06901. 203/325-3500.

PREPARED FOODS
Gorman Publishing Co., 8750 West
Bryn Mawr, Chicago IL 60631.
312/693-3200.

GENERAL MERCHANDISE: RETAIL AND WHOLESALE

While much of the retail industry has been struggling against low consumer confidence, discount department stores have been booming. This trend holds true for both merchandise and apparel stores, as well as for other broad areas like health and beauty aides. Overall, retailing will continue to grow at a relatively slow pace. Unfortunately for professionals, most new jobs will be entry-level, where there is currently a major labor shortage.

ABC BOOKS AND POSTERS
2550 S. Colorado Boulevard, Denver CO 80222. 303/759-0250. **Contact:**
Personnel Department. **Description:** Wholesale frames, prints, and moldings.

AIR PURIFICATION COMPANY
4755 Fox Street, Denver CO 80216. 303/297-0388. **Contact:** Personnel
Department. **Description:** Wholesale air-conditioning, heating, and ventilating
equipment.

AMPLE DUDS
2121 S. Oneida, Suite 248, Denver CO 80224. 303/753-1885. **Contact:**
Personnel Department. **Description:** A Denver-area clothing store specializing
in the retail of large-sized women's clothing.

BIG SUR WATERBEDS INCORPORATED
13300 East 38th Avenue, Denver CO 80239. 303/371-8560. **Contact:** Personnel
Department. **Description:** Retail furniture dealer.

BOYD DISTRIBUTING COMPANY, INC.
1400 West Third Avenue, Denver CO 80223. 303/534-7701. **Contact:** Personnel Department. **Description:** A distributor of appliances, electronic goods, turf equipment, and other products.

BULRICH CORPORATION
875 Parfet, Lakewood CO 80215. 303/237-6321. **Contact:** Personnel Department. **Description:** A sporting goods retailer.

BURT CHEVROLET, INC.
5200 South Broadway, Englewood CO 80110. 303/761-0333. **Contact:** Mr. Mel Nordentoft, Office Manager. **Description:** A new and used automobile dealership.

COAST-TO-COAST STORES, INC.
P.O. Box 5820, Denver CO 80217. 303/377-8400. **Contact:** Terrie Westlake, Manager of Human Resources. **Description:** Retailer of hardware, auto supplies, and electrical appliances.

COLORADO JEEP EAGLE
505 South Havana Street, Denver CO 80012. 303/341-4050. **Contact:** Personnel Department. **Description:** A new and used automobile dealer.

COLORADO NATIONAL LEASING, INC.
950 17th Street, Suite 2400, Denver CO 80202. 303/629-7750. **Contact:** Human Resources. **Description:** A leasing company.

DENVER WHOLESALE FLORISTS COMPANY
P.O. Box 173354, Denver CO 80217-3354. 303/399-0970. **Contact:** Debbie Barber, Personnel Director. **Description:** An area wholesale florist.

ECONOMY LUMBER & HARDWARE COMPANY
975 West Mississippi Avenue, Denver CO 80223-3124. 303/744-6161. **Contact:** Steve Stokesberry, General Manager. **Description:** A local retailer of lumber and hardware.

ELDER COMPANIES
4800 Race Street, Box 16159, Denver CO 80216. 303/292-4800. **Contact:** Personnel Department. **Description:** A leasing agent offering trucks, trailers, and other heavy equipment.

EMPIRE OLDSMOBILE, INC.
6160 East Colfax Avenue, Denver CO 80220. 303/399-1950. **Contact:** Judy Grinestaff, Payroll Supervisor. **Description:** A Denver auto dealership.

FOSS COMPANY
1224 Washington Avenue, Golden CO 80401. 303/279-3373. **Contact:** Donna Owen, Personnel Manager. **Description:** Retail drug and sundry operation with a full liquor store. Also headquarters for: Ski Country Ceramic Decanters, and H.J. Foss Inc., men's and women's clothing. **Common positions:** Accountant; Buyer; Credit Manager; Department Manager; Management Trainee. **Benefits:**

medical insurance; dental insurance; life insurance; employee discounts. **Corporate headquarters:** This location. **Operations at this facility:** administration; service; sales.

GART BROS. SPORTING GOODS

1000 Broadway, Denver CO 80203. 303/861-1122. **Contact:** Arden Merckel, Personnel Director. **Description:** A Denver sporting-goods retail store. **Common positions:** Administrator; Buyer; General Manager; Management Trainee; Sales Representative. **Educational backgrounds sought:** Business Administration; Liberal Arts; Marketing. **Special programs:** Training programs. **Benefits:** medical and life insurance; pension plan; employee discounts. **Corporate headquarters:** This location. Other U.S. locations: Utah, Wyoming, Idaho. **Parent company:** Thrifty Corp. **Operations at this facility:** administration; service. **Employees:** 1,500. **Projected hires for the next 12 months:** 1,200.

HIT OR MISS, INC.

Village West Plaza, 8555 Bellview Sp. D-26, Denver CO 80123. 303/973-9598. **Contact:** Jeff Burton, Regional Manager. **Description:** A chain of women's fashion stores.

HOMESTEAD HOUSE INC.

P.O. Box 499, Broomfield CO 80038. 303/425-6544. **Contact:** Personnel Director. **Description:** Operates an area chain of retail appliance stores. **Corporate headquarters:** This location.

JHB IMPORTS INCORPORATED

1955 South Quince Street, Denver CO 80231. 303/751-8100. **Contact:** Personnel Department. **Description:** Wholesale dealer and exporter of buttons and thimbles.

THE KEY PEOPLE

777 S. Wadsworth, Building 3, Suite 102, Lakewood CO 80226. 303/988-6644. **Contact:** Personnel Department. **Description:** A services firm engaged in contracted office cleaning.

LAKEWOOD FORD, INC.

11000 West Colfax, Lakewood CO 80215-3795. 303/232-2200. **Contact:** Shelley Burnhans, Personnel Director. **Description:** A used and new car dealership.

LEWAN & ASSOCIATES, INC.

1400 South Colorado Boulevard, P.O. Box 22855, Denver CO 80222. 303/759-5440. **Contact:** Nancy J. Stenberg, Human Resources Coordinator. **Description:** A retail office-products dealer. **Common positions:** Administrator; Advertising Worker; Buyer; Credit Manager; Customer Service Representative; Electrical Engineer; Branch Manager; Marketing Specialist; Public Relations Specialist; Purchasing Agent; Sales Representative. **Educational backgrounds sought:** Business Administration; Computer Science; Engineering; Marketing. **Special programs:** Training programs. **Benefits:** medical insurance; dental insurance; pension plan; life insurance;

tuition assistance; disability coverage; profit sharing; employee discounts; savings plan 401K. **Corporate headquarters:** This location.

LLOYDS FURS INCORPORATED
E. 2nd Avenue, North Cherry Creek, Denver CO 80206. 303/393-8600. **Contact:** Fred Serhelm. **Description:** Involved in the retail selling and servicing of furs.

LEN LYALL CHEVROLET COMPANY
14500 East Colfax, Aurora CO 80011. 303/344-3100. **Contact:** Marge Lyall, Office Manager. **Description:** A regional sales office of Chevrolet, the national car dealership.

MAY DEPARTMENT STORES COMPANY
16th At Tremont Place, Denver CO 80202. 303/620-7500. **Contact:** Joe Bornhorst, Senior Vice President, Human Resources. **Description:** A Denver department store.

McGEE COMPANY/JASON ENTERPRISES INC.
1140 South Jason Street, Denver CO 80223. 303/777-2615. **Contact:** Personnel Department. **Description:** Company dealing in wholesale tire service and retread equipment and supplies.

PATTLEN ENTERPRISES INCORPORATED
4700 Holly, Denver CO 80216. 303/320-1270. **Contact:** Greg Lamont, Personnel Department. **Description:** Corporation involved in the selling of wholesale snowblowers, power mowers, and irrigation equipment.

SAFEWAY STORES, INC.
1355 South Sheridan Boulevard, Denver CO 80232. 303/937-0278. **Contact:** Personnel Department. **Description:** Employment office for local Safeway Stores operations.

GEORGE T. SANDERS COMPANY
10201 West 49th Avenue, Wheat Ridge CO 80033-2211. 303/423-9660. **Contact:** Tom Tooley, Personnel Manager. **Description:** A plumbing and heating hardware wholesaler.

FRED SCHMID APPLIANCE & TELEVISION CO.
2405 West Fifth Avenue, Denver CO 80204. 303/623-6135. **Contact:** Personnel Director. **Description:** A local retailer of various household appliances.

SILL-TERHAR MOTORS, INC.
P.O. Box 344, Broomfield CO 80038. 303/469-1801. **Contact:** Beverly Neal, Office Manager. **Description:** A local car dealership.

SILO WAREHOUSE
12775 East 38th Avenue, Denver CO 80239. 303/373-4330. **Contact:** Personnel. **Description:** One of the largest specialty retailers of electronics and appliances. **Common positions:** Accountant; Customer Service Representative; Sales Representative; General Bookkeeper; Warehouse Worker. **Special programs:** Training programs. **Benefits:** medical, dental, and life insurance;

pension plan; tuition assistance; disability coverage; profit sharing; employee discounts. **Corporate headquarters:** Philadelphia, PA. **Parent company:** Dixon's of Great Britain. **Operations at this facility:** regional headquarters; sales. **Listed on:** American Stock Exchange.

SUN ENTERPRISES INCORPORATED
8877 North Washington, Thornton CO 80229. 303/287-7566. **Contact:** Personnel Department. **Description:** A Denver retailer of motorcycles and automotive supplies.

TUXALL UNIFORM MANUFACTURER
5700 North Washington Street, Denver CO 80216. 303/295-0216. **Contact:** Personnel. **Description:** A retail store for uniforms and public safety equipment.

VETERANS INTERIORS
280 West Mississippi Avenue, Denver CO 80223. 303/744-6341. **Contact:** Personnel Department. **Description:** Dealer in the retail carpet industry.

YOUNG SQUIRE SHOP INCORPORATED
2770 East Second Avenue, Denver CO 80206. 303/388-4249. **Contact:** Personnel Department. **Description:** A Denver-area retailer of men's and boys' apparel.

Additional large employers: 250+

OFFICE EQUIPMENT

Digital Equipment Corp
8085 S Chester St, Englewood CO 80112-3509. 303/6493000. Employs: 250-499.

MEDICAL, DENTAL, AND HOSPITAL EQUIPMENT AND SUPPLIES

Electromedics Inc
7337 S Revere Pky, Englewood CO 80112-3931. 303/7908700. Employs: 250-499.

METALS SERVICE CENTERS AND OFFICES

Amsco Amalloy Corp
10554 W Ontario Pl, Littleton CO 80127-2893. 303/9729503. Employs: 250-499.

COAL AND OTHER MINERALS AND ORES

Pittsburg & Midway Coal Mining
1720 S Bellaire St, Denver CO 80222-4304. 303/7581700. Employs: 1,000+.

MISC. ELECTRONIC PARTS AND EQUIPMENT

AT&T Communications
11900 E Cornell Ave, Aurora CO 80014-3194. 303/3682000. Employs: 250-499.

Hewlett Packard Company
1900 Garden Of The Gods Rd, Colorado Springs CO 80907. 7195901900. Employs: 500-999.

Maxtor Colorado Corp
2190 Miller Dr, Longmont CO 80501-6744. 303/6516000. Employs: 1,000+.

NCR Corp Prod
2001 Danfield Ct, Fort Collins CO 80525-2905.   303/2235100.
Employs: 500-999.

Rolm Company
4700 S Syracuse Pky Suite 3-F4, Denver   CO   80237-2710. 303/7737500. Employs: 500-999.

HARDWARE

Amdura Corporation
501 S Cherry St Box 5820, Denver CO   80222-1325.   303/3778400. Employs: 1,000+.

INDUSTRIAL MACHINERY AND EQUIPMENT

Norgren Corporation
5400 S Delaware St, Littleton CO 80120-1663.   303/7942611.
Employs: 500-999.

SERVICE ESTABLISHMENT EQUIPMENT AND SUPPLIES

Hobart Corporation
1325 E 58th Ave, Denver CO 80216-1511.   303/2940784.
Employs: 500-999.

Melco Industries Inc
1575 W 124th Ave, Denver CO 80234-1707.   303/4571234.
Employs: 250-499.

PRINTING AND WRITING PAPER

Dixon Paper Co
55 Madison St Suite 800, Denver CO   80206-5423.   303/3296644.
Employs: 250-499.

Howard Fort Corporation
1906 13th St, Boulder CO 80302-5205. 303/9389589. Employs: 500-999.

DRUGS, DRUG PROPRIETARIES, AND DRUGGISTS' SUNDRIES

Pharmacy Corp Of America
1800 38th St Suite 200, Boulder CO   80301-2622.   303/4400888.
Employs: 500-999.

GROCERIES, GENERAL LINE

Shamrock Foods Company
5199 Ivy St, Commerce City CO 80022-4404.   303/2893581.
Employs: 250-499.

DAIRY PRODUCTS, EXCEPT CANNED OR DRIED

Kraft Westman Foods
11955   E   Peakview   Ave, Englewood   CO   80111-6819. 303/7929230. Employs: 250-499.

MEATS AND MEAT PRODUCTS

Horton Foods
443   4,   Kersey   CO   80644. 303/3562333. Employs: 250-499.

PETROLEUM BULK STATIONS AND TERMINALS

Texaco Trading & Transportation
1670 Broadway Suite 2600, Denver CO   80202-4826.   303/8614475.
Employs: 250-499.

PETROLEUM AND PETROLEUM PRODUCTS WHOLESALERS, EXCEPT BULK STATIONS AND TERMINALS

Denver #2
899 Decatur St, Denver CO 80204-3724. 303/8258117. Employs: 250-499.

BEER AND ALE

Coors Distributing Company
14062 Denver West Pky # 52-325, Golden CO 80401-3121. 303/2784866. Employs: 250-499.

Western Davis Limited
5270 Fox St, Denver CO 80216-1604. 303/2921711. Employs: 250-499.

DEPARTMENT STORES

JC Penney Co Inc
5453 W 88th Ave, Westminster CO 80030-3002. 303/4278912. Employs: 250-499.

JC Penney Company Inc
680 Citadel Dr E, Colorado Springs CO 80909-5301. 7195970050. Employs: 250-499.

JC Penney Company Inc
14200 E Alameda Ave Suite 200, Aurora CO 80012-2511. 303/3449901. Employs: 250-499.

Joslins Department Store
595 W Hampden Ave, Englewood CO 80110-2109. 303/7811111. Employs: 250-499.

Joslins Department Store
7200 W Alameda Ave, Lakewood CO 80226-3206. 303/9227575. Employs: 250-499.

May D & F
350 16th St, Denver CO 80202-5023. 303/6207575. Employs: 1,000+.

May D & F
2700 S Colorado Blvd, Denver CO 80222-6619. 303/7588533. Employs: 250-499.

Sears Roebuck & Co
8501 W Bowles Ave Suite 1271, Littleton CO 80123-7201. 303/9726000. Employs: 250-499.

Sears Roebuck & Co
14200 E Alameda Ave, Aurora CO 80012-2511. 303/3604535. Employs: 250-499.

Sears Roebuck & Co
205 E Foothills Pky, Fort Collins CO 80525-2612. 303/2265500. Employs: 250-499.

Sears Roebuck & Co Inc
Southwest Plaza, Littleton CO 80123. 303/9726150. Employs: 250-499.

Sears Roebuck & Co Inc
10686 Melody Dr, Denver CO 80234-4114. 303/4578990. Employs: 250-499.

Sears Roebuck & Company
240 Josephine St # 203, Denver CO 80206-4700. 303/3987770. Employs: 250-499.

Wal-Mart Discount Cities
3600 Youngfield St, Wheat Ridge CO 80033-5247. 303/4200640. Employs: 250-499.

Joslins
W 88 & Sheridan, Westminster CO 80030. 303/4274278. Employs: 250-499.

Target Stores
7899 Wadsworth Blvd, Arvada CO 80003-2107. 303/4250124. Employs: 250-499.

MOTOR VEHICLE DEALERS

Stevinson Lexus
801 Indiana St, Golden CO 80401-4007. 303/2779339. Employs: 500-999.

AUTO AND HOME SUPPLY STORES

Big O Tires Inc
11755 E Peakview Ave, Englewood CO 80111-6819. 303/7902800. Employs: 250-499.

Montgomery Ward & Co
1400 S Havana St, Aurora CO 80012-4014. 303/6963064. Employs: 250-499.

Montgomery Ward & Co
5801 W 44th Ave, Denver CO 80212-7414. 303/4806661. Employs: 250-499.

MEN'S AND BOYS' CLOTHING AND ACCESSORY STORES

K-G Retail Stores Inc
10065 E Harvard, Denver CO 80231-5940. 303/6714600. Employs: 500-999.

FAMILY CLOTHING STORES

Fashion Bar
401 S Buckley Rd, Aurora CO 80017-2122. 303/6957979. Employs: 500-999.

Miller International Inc
8500 Zuni St, Denver CO 80221-5007. 303/4285696. Employs: 250-499.

HOUSEHOLD APPLIANCE STORES

Carpet Magnet Co

114 Kalamath St, Denver CO 80223-1437. 303/8920907. Employs: 250-499.

DRUG STORES AND PROPRIETARY STORES

King Soopers Pharmacy
1575 W 84th Ave, Denver CO 80221-4722. 303/4279295. Employs: 250-499.

GIFT, NOVELTY, AND SOUVENIR SHOPS

Coach House Gifts
420 E 58th Ave, Denver CO 80216-1400. 303/2925537. Employs: 500-999.

CATALOG AND MAIL-ORDER HOUSES

Current Inc
1005 E Woodmen Rd, Colorado Springs CO 80920-3181. 7195944100. Employs: 500-999.

AUTOMATIC MERCHANDISING MACHINE OPERATORS

Canteen Food & Vending
123 Yuma St, Denver CO 80223-1205. 303/7222861. Employs: 250-499.

OPTICAL GOODS STORES

Montgomery Ward
Lakeside Shopping Center, Denver CO 80212. 303/4806644. Employs: 250-499.

Additional small to medium sized employers: 50-249

AUTOMOBILES AND OTHER MOTOR VEHICLES

Denver Auto Auction

17500 E 31st Ave, Aurora CO 80011-3316. 303/3433443. Employs: 100-249.

Rocky Mountain International
3280 Brighton Blvd, Denver CO
80216-5019.   303/2951452.
Employs: 50-99.

MOTOR VEHICLE SUPPLIES AND NEW PARTS

APS Incorporated
500 W 53rd Pl, Denver CO 80216-
1614. 303/2925262. Employs: 50-
99.

Northern Automotive
3155 S Platte River Dr, Englewood
CO   80110-2138.   303/7611370.
Employs: 50-99.

TIRES AND TUBES

Brad Ragan Inc
14900 E 39th Ave, Aurora CO
80011-1203.   303/3711010.
Employs: 50-99.

FURNITURE

Scott Rice Company
5353 Bannock St, Denver CO
80216-1623.   303/2971122.
Employs: 100-249.

Alumicolor Division Of Matrix
1118 Ne Frontage Rd, Fort Collins
CO   80524-9218.   303/4934312.
Employs: 50-99.

HOME FURNISHING

Shalomar Inc
4001 Forest St, Denver CO 80216-
4501. 303/3881641. Employs: 50-
99.

LUMBER, PLYWOOD, MILLWORK, AND WOOD PANELS

Pella Products Of Colorado Inc
2401 S Colorado Blvd, Denver CO
80222-5942.   · 303/7820222.
Employs: 50-99.

BRICK, STONE, AND RELATED CONSTRUCTION MATERIALS

Frontier Materials Inc
3600 Hwy 52, Erie CO 80516-
9406: 303/4478951. Employs: 50-
99.

Ideal Basic Industries Inc
950   17,   Denver   CO   80202.
303/6235661. Employs: 50-99.

ROOFING, SIDING, AND INSULATION MATERIALS

Walt Flanagan & Co Inc
363 W Evans Ave, Denver CO
80223-4102.   303/7773058.
Employs: 100-249.

MISC. CONSTRUCTION MATERIALS

Oldach Stained Glass
2815 N Prospect St, Colorado
Springs   CO   80907-6324.
719/6365181. Employs: 100-249.

PHOTOGRAPHIC EQUIPMENT AND SUPPLIES

Eastman Kodak Co
1 Inverness Dr E, Englewood CO
80112-5510.   303/7993339.
Employs: 100-249.

Robert Waxman Inc
1514 Curtis St, Denver CO 80202-
2343. 303/6231200. Employs: 50-
99.

OFFICE EQUIPMENT

AM International
7075 S Alton Way, Englewood CO
80112-2017.   303/7733500.
Employs: 50-99.

Associated Business Products
5285 Fox St, Denver CO 80216-1603. 303/2950757. Employs: 100-249.

Colorado Copier Systems Inc
637 S Pierce Av, Louisville CO 80027-3021. 303/6657700. Employs: 50-99.

Copy Duplicating Products
4665 Paris St, Denver CO 80239-3117. 303/3730505. Employs: 50-99.

Duplication Equipment Brokerage
1501 W Tufts Ave Suite 102, Englewood CO 80110-5574. 303/7811132. Employs: 50-99.

Finzer Business Systems
11001 E 51st Ave, Denver CO 80239-2511. 303/3734711. Employs: 50-99.

Frontier Business Products
13800 E 39th Ave, Aurora CO 80011-1608. 303/3732900. Employs: 50-99.

Minolta Business Systems Inc
5195 Marshall St, Arvada CO 80002-4628. 303/4234231. Employs: 100-249.

Pitney Bowes Inc
780 Grant St, Denver CO 80203-3509. 303/8329141. Employs: 50-99.

Ricoh Corporation
10200 E Girard Ave Suite 102, Denver CO 80231-5500. 303/6951167. Employs: 100-249.

Xerox Service Center
4600 S Ulster St Ste 1000, Denver CO 80237-2874. 303/6968966. Employs: 100-249.

MISC. PROFESSIONAL EQUIPMENT AND SUPPLIES

Cryogenic Energy Co
5995 Washington St, Denver CO 80216-1336. 303/2873372. Employs: 50-99.

BNZ Materials Inc
6901 S Pierce, Littleton CO 80123. 303/9781199. Employs: 100-249.

Rocky Mountain Instrument Co
1501 S Sunset St, Longmont CO 80501-6750. 303/6512211. Employs: 100-249.

METALS SERVICE CENTERS AND OFFICES

Joseph T Ryerson & Son Inc
6600 US Hwy 85, Commerce City CO 80022-2404. 303/2870101. Employs: 50-99.

RJ Gallagher Co
5530 Joliet St, Denver CO 80239-2006. 303/3719560. Employs: 50-99.

MISC. ELECTRICAL APPARATUS AND EQUIPMENT, WIRING SUPPLIES, AND CONSTRUCTION EQUIPMENT

Allphase Electric Supply Co
500 Quivas St, Denver CO 80204-4916. 303/8932111. Employs: 50-99.

Denver Burglar Alarm Inc
1955 Sherman St, Denver CO 80203-1115. 303/2922222. Employs: 100-249.

Front Range Cable Corporation
630 S Sunset St, Longmont CO 80501-6338. 303/4492177. Employs: 50-99.

Ryall Electric Supply Co
2625 Redwing Rd, Fort Collins CO
80526-2878.   303/6297721.
Employs: 100-249.

Ryall Electric Supply Co
2627 W 6th Ave, Denver CO
80204-4105.   303/6297721.
Employs: 100-249.

Techna-Quip Inc
679 W Littleton Blvd, Littleton CO
80120-2355.   303/7944799.
Employs: 50-99.

MISC. ELECTRONIC PARTS AND EQUIPMENT

AVX Corp
2435 Executive Cir, Colorado
Springs   CO   80906-4182.
719/5763510. Employs: 50-99.

Capstone Electronics Corp
3254 Fraser St, Aurora CO 80011-
1238. 303/3751300. Employs: 50-
99.

Comlinear Corporation
4800 Wheaton Dr, Fort Collins CO
80525-9483.   303/2260500.
Employs: 100-249.

Echosphere Corp
90 Inverness Cir E, Englewood CO
80112-5317.   303/7998222.
Employs: 100-249.

Executone Of Southern Colorado Inc
6001 S Willow Dr, Englewood CO
80111-5104.   719/5288211.
Employs: 50-99.

Motorola Commnctn & Electrncs
20 Inverness Pl E, Englewood CO
80112-5616.   303/7996000.
Employs: 100-249.

NCR Comten

2000 S Colorado Blvd, Denver CO
80222-7900.   303/7561600.
Employs: 100-249.

Telectronics Pacing Systems
7400 S Tucson Way, Englewood
CO 80112-3938. 303/7908000.
Employs: 100-249.

US West Cellular
2000 S Colorado Blvd, Denver CO
80222-7900.   303/7821800.
Employs: 100-249.

Vari-L Co Inc
11101 E 51st Ave, Denver CO
80239-2601.   303/3711560.
Employs: 50-99.

Microsemi Corp Colorado
800 Hoyt St, Broomfield CO
80020-1008.   303/4692161.
Employs: 50-99.

HARDWARE

Cotter & Co
10875 E 40th Ave, Denver CO
80239-3210.   303/3730966.
Employs: 100-249.

PLUMBING AND HEATING EQUIPMENT AND SUPPLIES

Honeywell Inc
304 Inverness Way S Suite 100,
Englewood   CO   80112-5897.
303/7921500. Employs: 100-249.

United States Water Company
10065 E Harvard Ave Suite 311,
Denver   CO   80231-5942.
303/6714777. Employs: 50-99.

CONSTRUCTION AND MINING (EXCEPT PETROLEUM) MACHINERY AND EQUIPMENT

Barton Bros Inc
2245 S Raritan St, Englewood CO
80110-1035.   303/9354673.
Employs: 100-249.

Caterpillar Tractor Company
4705 E 48th Ave, Denver CO
80216-3213.   303/3884061.
Employs: 100-249.

Power Equipment Co
500 E 62nd Ave, Denver CO
80216-1133.   303/2886801.
Employs: 50-99.

Power Motive Corporation
5000 Vasquez Blvd, Denver CO
80216-3029.   303/3555900.
Employs: 50-99.

INDUSTRIAL MACHINERY AND EQUIPMENT

Forney Industries Inc
1830 La Porte Ave, Fort Collins
CO   80521-2341.   303/4827271.
Employs: 100-249.

Great Northern Warehouse Co
1227A Lake Plaza Dr, Colorado
Springs   CO   80906-7402.
719/5767000. Employs: 50-99.

Hia Inc
560 S Lipan St, Denver CO 80223-
2333. 303/7446371. Employs: 50-
99.

Materials Handling Equipment
1740 W 13th Ave, Denver CO
80204-2406.   303/5735333.
Employs: 50-99.

Packaging Systems Intl
4990 Acoma St, Denver CO 80216-
2030. 303/2964445. Employs: 50-
99.

Packers Engineering & Equipment
300 E 16th St Suite 307, Greeley
CO   80631-6065.   303/3569339.
Employs: 100-249.

Pamco Inc
10777 E 45th Ave, Denver CO
80239-2905.   303/3710330.
Employs: 50-99.

United States Welding Inc
600 S Santa Fe Dr, Denver CO
80223-2403.   303/7776671.
Employs: 100-249.

INDUSTRIAL SUPPLIES

Advance Tank & Construction Co
3700   E   County   Road   64,
Wellington   CO   80549-1533.
303/5683444. Employs: 100-249.

SERVICE ESTABLISHMENT EQUIPMENT AND SUPPLIES

LSC Distributors
8080 S Holly St, Littleton CO
80122-4001.   303/7798822.
Employs: 50-99.

SPORTING AND RECREATIONAL GOODS AND SUPPLIES

The Allen Company Inc
525 Burbank St, Broomfield CO
80020-1647.   303/4691857.
Employs: 50-99.

TOYS AND HOBBY GOODS AND SUPPLIES

Matrix Investment Corporation
1118 Ne Frontage Rd, Fort Collins
CO   80524-9218.   303/4934284.
Employs: 50-99.

SCRAP AND WASTE MATERIALS

Atlas Metal & Iron Inc
318 Walnut St, Denver CO 80204-1809. 303/8257166. Employs: 100-249.

Golden Aluminum Company
3000 Youngfield St, Lakewood CO 80215-6545. 303/2355000. Employs: 50-99.

Tri-R Systems Corp
4930 Dahlia St, Denver CO 80216-3122. 303/3996351. Employs: 50-99.

PRINTING AND WRITING PAPER

Butler Paper Company
23 Inverness Way E Suite 200, Englewood CO 80112-5708. 303/7908343. Employs: 100-249

STATIONERY AND OFFICE SUPPLIES

Commercial Office Products
13800 E 39th Ave, Aurora CO 80011-1608. 303/3732800. Employs: 100-249.

Eastman Inc
5280 Joliet St, Denver CO 80239-2103. 303/3717100. Employs: 100-249.

Hilb & Co Inc
4600 E 48th Ave, Denver CO 80216-3212. 303/3992100. Employs: 100-249.

Mile High Office Supply Co
60 Tejon St, Denver CO 80223-1222. 303/7446467. Employs: 100-249.

INDUSTRIAL AND PERSONAL SERVICE PAPER

Dixon Paper Company
3900 Lima St, Denver CO 80239-3309. 303/3717510. Employs: 100-249.

Harry H Post Company
1881 Bassett St, Denver CO 80202-1019. 303/2967678. Employs: 50-99.

Nationwide Papers
4800 E 48th Ave, Denver CO 80216-3214. 303/3886211. Employs: 100-249.

DRUGS, DRUG PROPRIETARIES, AND DRUGGISTS' SUNDRIES

Bergen Brunswig
501 W 44th Ave, Denver CO 80216-2612. 303/4336644. Employs: 50-99.

Fox Meyer Drug Company
1100 W 47th Ave, Denver CO 80211-2315. 303/4557094. Employs: 100-249.

McKesson Drug Company
14500 E 39th Ave, Aurora CO 80011-1210. 303/3710770. Employs: 50-99.

PIECE GOODS, NOTIONS, AND OTHER DRY GOODS

JHB International Incorporated
1955 S Quince St, Denver CO 80231-3206. 303/7518100. Employs: 100-249.

MEN'S AND BOYS' CLOTHING AND FURNISHING

Ocean Pacific Children's Wear
4600 E 48th Ave, Denver CO 80216-3212. 303/3889696. Employs: 100-249.

WOMEN'S, CHILDREN'S AND INFANTS' CLOTHING AND ACCESSORIES

Gold Inc
4999 Oakland, Denver CO 80239-2719. 303/3712535. Employs: 50-99.

Rocky Mountain Clothing Co
8500 Zuni St, Denver CO 80221-5007. 303/4293133. Employs: 50-99.

GROCERIES, GENERAL LINE

Associated Marketing Services Inc
3045 S Parker Rd Suite 255, Aurora CO 80014-2905. 303/7520030. Employs: 50-99.

Clover Club Food
4300 Oneida St, Denver CO 80216. 303/4336411. Employs: 100-249.

Food Products Company
4303 Brighton Blvd, Denver CO 80216-3709. 303/2950812. Employs: 100-249.

Frontier Foods Inc
12770 E 39th Ave, Denver CO 80239-3425. 303/3750258. Employs: 100-249.

Highland Sales Inc
4845 Oakland St, Denver CO 80239-2721. 303/3711112. Employs: 50-99.

Hyundai Training Co
6100 E 49th Ave, Commerce City CO 80022-4503. 303/2867251. Employs: 50-99.

Super Valu Stores Inc
1983 Tower Rd, Aurora CO 80011-5109. 303/3636505. Employs: 100-249.

Yancey Food Service Inc
3900 Canal Dr, Fort Collins CO 80524-8500. 303/4843123. Employs: 50-99.

L & Z Tortilla Factory
227 N Main St, Brighton CO 80601-1628. 303/6596714. Employs: 50-99.

Five Star Brokerage Co
14707 E 2nd Ave, Aurora CO 80011-8907. 303/3600811. Employs: 50-99.

PACKAGED FROZEN FOODS

Mile Hi Frozen Foods
4701 E 50th Ave, Denver CO 80216-3106. 303/3996066. Employs: 100-249.

POULTRY AND POULTRY PRODUCTS

Hudson Pullett Farm
19166 Hwy 52, Hudson CO 80642. 303/5364298. Employs: 50-99.

MEATS AND MEAT PRODUCTS

Sigman Meat Co Inc
6000 W 54th Ave, Arvada CO 80002-4021. 303/4245531. Employs: 50-99.

FRESH FRUITS AND VEGETABLES

Ralph Nix Produce
19480 U S Hwy 85, Gilcrest CO 80623. 303/7372461. Employs: 50-99.

MISC. GROCERIES AND RELATED PRODUCTS

All American Seasonings Inc
1540 Wazee St, Denver CO 80202-1312. 303/6232320. Employs: 50-99.

Stokes Canning Co
5590 High St, Denver CO 80216-1523. 303/2924018. Employs: 50-99.

Boyer Gourmet Products
5095 Paris St, Denver CO 80239-2808. 303/3750828. Employs: 50-99.

GRAIN AND FIELD BEANS

Agland Inc
260 Factory Rd, Eaton CO 80615. 303/3524562. Employs: 100-249.

Mountain States Bean Company
4401 E 46th Ave, Denver CO 80216-3231. 303/3553543. Employs: 50-99.

Trinidad Bean & Elevator Co
P O Box 22139, Denver CO 80222-0139. 303/2201400. Employs: 100-249.

MISC. CHEMICALS AND ALLIED PRODUCTS

United Agri- Products
4687 18th St, Greeley CO 80634-3216. 303/3308801. Employs: 100-249.

United Agri-Products
419 18th St, Greeley CO 80631-5852. 303/3564400. Employs: 50-99.

PETROLEUM BULK STATIONS AND TERMINALS

Arco Coal Company
555 17th St, Denver CO 80202-3941. 303/2934900. Employs: 100-249.

PETROLEUM AND PETROLEUM PRODUCTS WHOLESALERS, EXCEPT BULK STATIONS AND TERMINALS

Amsoil Synthetic Lubricants
11387 Kendall St, Broomfield CO 80020-3082. 303/4669345. Employs: 50-99.

Cities Service Oil Co
1600 Broadway, Denver CO 80202-4928. 303/8612464. Employs: 100-249.

G & S Oil Products Inc
6800 S Dawson Cir Suite 201, Englewood CO 80112-4210. 303/6934474. Employs: 50-99.

Merchants Oil Inc
105 S Cherokee St, Denver CO 80223-1834. 303/7334627. Employs: 50-99.

Phillips Petroleum Company
8055 E Tufts Ave, Denver CO 80237-2835. 303/8503000. Employs: 100-249.

Presidio Oil Company
5613 Dtc Pkwy, Englewood CO 80111-3028. 303/7730100. Employs: 100-249.

Conoco Inc
6855 S Havana St, Englewood CO 80112-3837. 303/6494000. Employs: 50-99.

BEER AND ALE

Miller Brands Inc
4500 E 51st Ave, Denver CO 80216-3110. 303/3885755. Employs: 100-249.

Murray Distributing
1505 W 3rd Ave, Denver CO 80223-1440. 303/5731155. Employs: 50-99.

Rocky Mountain Wine & Spirits
14200 E Moncrieff Pl Suite C, Aurora CO 80011-1623. 303/3713662. Employs: 100-249.

WINE AND DISTILLED ALCOHOLIC BEVERAGES

National Distributing Company
1800 Bassett St Suite B, Denver CO 80202-1020. 303/2929977. Employs: 50-99.

FARM SUPPLIES

Seedex Inc
1254 Sherman Dr Unit 1, Longmont CO 80501-6134. 303/6787333. Employs: 50-99.

BOOKS, PERIODICALS, AND NEWSPAPERS

Gordons Books Inc
2323 Delgany St, Denver CO 80216-5129. 303/2961830. Employs: 100-249.

Anderson News Inc
3601 E 46th Ave, Denver CO 80216-6513. 303/3211111. Employs: 50-99.

PAINTS, VARNISHES, AND SUPPLIES

Komac Paint Inc
1201 Osage St, Denver CO 80204-3435. 303/5345191. Employs: 100-249.

Kwal-Howells Inc
3900 Joliet St Box 39-R, Denver CO 80239-3231. 303/3715600. Employs: 100-249.

LUMBER AND OTHER BUILDING MATERIALS DEALERS

Alpine Lumber Co
5800 N Pecos St Box 21470, Denver CO 80221-6645. 303/4584740. Employs: 50-99.

Builders Square
1725 Sheridan Blvd, Denver CO 80214-1323. 303/2320237. Employs: 100-249.

Builders Square
13600 E Mississippi Ave, Aurora CO 80012-3572. 303/7453500. Employs: 100-249.

Builders Square
7325 W 88th Ave, Broomfield CO 80021-6443. 303/4673353. Employs: 100-249.

C & M Companies
7916 Niwot Rd, Niwot CO 80544. 303/6522334. Employs: 50-99.

Elcar Fence & Supply Company
2155 S Valentia St, Denver CO 80231-3324. 303/7555211. Employs: 50-99.

Hugh M Woods Building Matl
2390 W 104th Ave, Denver CO 80234-3618. 303/4691776. Employs: 50-99.

Hugh M Woods Co
4995 S Santa Fe Dr, Littleton CO 80120-1036. 303/7982463. Employs: 50-99.

Hugh M Woods Company
9330 Wadsworth Blvd, Broomfield CO 80021-4704. 303/4258939. Employs: 50-99.

Hugh M Woods Company
5855 N Academy Blvd, Colorado Springs CO 80918-3414. 719/5995400. Employs: 50-99.

Hugh M Woods Company
625 N Murray Blvd, Colorado Springs CO 80915-3405. 719/5916700. Employs: 50-99.

Hugh M Woods Company Inc
1420 Oak St, Lakewood CO 80215-4413. 303/2388291. Employs: 50-99.

Payless Cashways Inc
1565 E 66th Ave, Denver CO
80229-7223.   303/2893531.
Employs: 50-99.

Pioneer Sand Company Inc
5000 Northpark Dr, Colorado
Springs   CO   80918-3822.
719/5998100. Employs: 50-99.

Builders Square
4887 S Wadsworth Blvd, Littleton
CO   80123-1362.   303/9334466.
Employs: 100-249.

Home Club Retail Warehouse
14000 E Jewell Ave, Aurora CO
80012-5651.   303/7501803.
Employs: 50-99.

**PAINT,   GLASS,   AND
WALLPAPER STORES**

Gump Glass Company
1265 S Broadway, Denver CO
80210-1503.   303/7781155.
Employs: 50-99.

HARDWARE STORES

Bis Toolbox
2000 S Havana St, Aurora CO
80014-1014.   303/7553522.
Employs: 50-99.

**Economy Lumber & Hardware
Co Inc**
975 W Mississippi Ave, Denver
CO   80223-3124.   303/7446161.
Employs: 50-99.

Home Club
2855 S Academy Blvd, Colorado
Springs   CO   80916-3001.
719/3903000. Employs: 50-99.

Hugh Woods Building Materials
2085 S Sheridan Blvd, Denver CO
80227-3717.   303/9883475.
Employs: 50-99.

Hugh Woods Building Materials
2150 S Abilene St, Aurora CO
80014-1401.   303/7518987.
Employs: 50-99.

**McGuckin Hardware & Sporting
Goods**
2525 Arapahoe Ave, Longmont CO
80501. 303/6513573. Employs:
100-249.

Snap On Tools
6632 Fig St, Arvada CO 80004-
1044. 303/4254602. Employs: 50-
99.

Hugh M Woods Building Matl
2450 W 29, Greeley CO 80631.
303/3300660. Employs: 50-99.

Sears Roebuck and Co
100   Southgate   Ctr,   Colorado
Springs   CO   80906-2651.
719/5796242. Employs: 50-99.

**RETAIL NURSERIES, LAWN
AND   GARDEN   SUPPLY
STORES**

American Garden Center
840 S Havana St, Aurora CO
80012-3016.   303/3419713.
Employs: 50-99.

Stratton Equity Co-Op Co
98   Colorado   Av,   Stratton   CO
80836. 719/3485396. Employs: 50-
99.

DEPARTMENT STORES

Best Products Company Inc
7450 S University Blvd, Littleton
CO   80122-1688.   303/7718900.
Employs: 100-249.

JC Penney Company Inc
7200 W Alameda Ave, Lakewood
CO   80226-3206.   303/9227890.
Employs: 100-249.

JC Penney Company Inc
701 W Hampden Ave, Englewood
CO 80154-1006. 303/7619606.
Employs: 100-249.

JC Penney Company Inc
8140 S Holly St, Littleton CO
80122-4004. 303/6947600.
Employs: 100-249.

JC Penney Company Inc
245 E Foothills Pky, Fort Collins
CO 80525-2612. 303/2238100.
Employs: 100-249.

JC Penney Company Inc
6920 N Academy Blvd, Colorado
Springs CO 80918-1127.
719/5980989. Employs: 50-99.

Joslins
1750 Briargate Blvd, Colorado
Springs CO 80920-3443.
719/5281500. Employs: 100-249.

Joslins
1840 Greeley Mall, Greeley CO
80631-8518. 303/3563330.
Employs: 100-249.

Joslins
1250 S Hover Rd, Longmont CO
80501-7905. 303/7769300.
Employs: 100-249.

Joslins
934 16th St, Denver CO 80202-
2902. 303/5340441. Employs: 100-
249.

Joslins Department Store
1122 S Havana St, Aurora CO
80012-4008. 303/6961400.
Employs: 100-249.

K Mart Corporation
5005 W 120th Ave, Broomfield CO
80020-5606. 303/4691702.
Employs: 100-249.

K Mart Corporation

9505 E County Line Rd Ste R,
Englewood CO 80112-3501.
303/7908769. Employs: 50-99.

K Mart Discount Stores
200 W Belleview Ave, Englewood
CO 80110-6610. 303/7941200.
Employs: 50-99.

K Mart Discount Stores
2151 Main St, Longmont CO
80501-1406. 303/7721213.
Employs: 100-249.

K Mart Discount Stores
2829 10th St, Greeley CO 80631-
3424. 303/3538100. Employs: 100-
249.

K Mart Discount Stores
2535 S College Ave, Fort Collins
CO 80525-1725. 303/4933232.
Employs: 50-99.

K Mart Discount Stores
6460 S Hwy 85 87, Fountain CO
80817-1008. 719/3924215.
Employs: 100-249.

K Mart Discount Stores
2665 W Eisenhower Blvd,
Loveland CO 80537-3156.
303/6632440. Employs: 100-249.

K Mart Discount Stores
3325 28th St, Boulder CO 80301-
1410. 303/4437850. Employs: 50-
99.

K Mart Discount Stores
3020 N Nevada Ave, Colorado
Springs CO 80907-5323.
719/4713555. Employs: 50-99.

K Mart Discount Stores
2520 Airport Rd, Colorado Springs
CO 80910-3120. 719/4733961.
Employs: 50-99.

K Mart Stores
2150 S Monaco Pky, Denver CO
80222-5812.   303/7571243.
Employs: 100-249.

May D & F
235 Foothill Pkwy, Fort Collins CO
80525. 303/2262111. Employs:
100-249.

May D & F
6801 S University Blvd, Littleton
CO   80122-1514.   303/7973990.
Employs: 100-249.

May D & F
8501 W Bowles Ave, Littleton CO
80123-7201.   303/9736211.
Employs: 50-99.

Mervyn's
1700 28th St Ste 142, Boulder CO
80301-1007.   303/4428802.
Employs: 50-99.

Mervyn's
820 E Citadel Dr, Colorado Springs
CO   80909-5305.   719/5968484.
Employs: 100-249.

Mervyn's
1730 Briargate Blvd, Colorado
Springs   CO   80920-3443.
719/5319000. Employs: 100-249.

Mervyn's Department Store
10602 Melody Dr, Denver CO
80234-4114.   303/4507755.
Employs: 100-249.

Mervyn's Department Store
8055 W Bowles Ave, Littleton CO
80123-3049.   303/9797779.
Employs: 50-99.

Mervyn's Department Store
1980 E County Line Rd, Littleton
CO   80126-2403.   303/7988848.
Employs: 50-99.

Mervyn's Department Store

5483 W 88th Ave, Westminster CO
80030-3002.   303/4278800.
Employs: 100-249.

Mervyn's Department Store
1301 S Kenton Way, Aurora CO
80012-4161.   303/7458800.
Employs: 50-99.

Mervyn's Department Stores
235 E Foothills Pky, Fort Collins
CO 80525-2612.   303/2299888.
Employs: 100-249.

Montgomery Ward
1600 28th St Ste 279, Boulder CO
80301-1017.   303/9383500.
Employs: 50-99.

Montgomery Ward & Co
7200 W Alameda Ave, Lakewood
CO   80226-3206.   303/9376413.
Employs: 100-249.

Montgomery Ward & Co Inc
S Wadsworth & W Alam Av,
Lakewood   CO   80226.
303/5732000. Employs: 50-99.

Montgomery Ward & Company
550 E 84th Ave, Denver CO
80229-5328.   303/2866813.
Employs: 100-249.

Montgomery Ward & Company
Greeley Mall Suite 2160, Greeley
CO 80631-8516.   303/3562000.
Employs: 100-249.

Montgomery Ward & Company
8501 W Bowles Ave, Littleton CO
80123-7201.   303/9725250.
Employs: 100-249.

Montgomery Ward & Company
2420 E Pikes Peak Ave, Colorado
Springs   CO   80909-6005.
719/6306504. Employs: 100-249.

Neiman Marcus
3030 E 1st Ave, Denver CO 80206-5612. 303/3292600. Employs: 100-249.

Sears
1600 28th St Ste 244, Boulder CO 80301-1017.		303/4402840. Employs: 50-99.

Sears Roebuck & Co
1250 S Hover Rd, Longmont CO 80501-7905.		303/8513100. Employs: 50-99.

Sears Roebuck & Co
1701 W 6th Ave, Denver CO 80204-4902.		303/8928680. Employs: 100-249.

Sears Roebuck & Co
10785 W Colfax Ave, Lakewood CO 80215-3807. 303/2356170. Employs: 100-249.

Sears Roebuck & Co
7001 S University Blvd, Littleton CO 80122-1518. 303/7305560. Employs: 100-249.

Sears Roebuck & Company
2800 Greeley Mall, Greeley CO 80631-8517.		303/3518500. Employs: 100-249.

Sears Roebuck & Company
1650 Briargate Blvd, Colorado Springs	CO	80920-3442. 719/5934870. Employs: 100-249.

Target Stores Inc
335 N Academy Blvd, Colorado Springs	CO	80909-6605. 719/5966220. Employs: 100-249.

Target Stores Inc
5240 N Academy Blvd, Colorado Springs	CO	80918-4004. 719/5949600. Employs: 100-249.

Target Stores Inc

2800 Pearl St, Boulder CO 80301-1123. 303/4493400. Employs: 100-249.

Target Stores Inc
10301 Washington St, Denver CO 80229-2003.		303/4524500. Employs: 100-249.

Target Stores Inc
2155 S Sheridan Blvd, Denver CO 80227-3719.		303/9862261. Employs: 100-249.

Target Stores Inc
9390 W Cross Dr, Littleton CO 80123-2202.		303/9734944. Employs: 100-249.

Target Stores Inc
1625 Owens St, Lakewood CO 80215-2751.		303/2387551. Employs: 100-249.

Target Stores Inc
5801 W 44th Ave, Denver CO 80212-7414.		303/4800512. Employs: 100-249.

Target Stores Inc
1200 S Abilene St, Aurora CO 80012-4629.		303/7517900. Employs: 100-249.

Target Stores Inc
6767 S Clinton St, Englewood CO 80112-3617.		303/7902583. Employs: 100-249.

Wal-Mart Discount Cities
880 S Briscoe St, Castle Rock CO 80104-1936.		303/6888200. Employs: 100-249.

Wal-Mart Discount Cities
3133 N Garfield Ave, Loveland CO 80538-2298.		303/6693640. Employs: 100-249.

Wal-Mart
800 S Hover Rd, Longmont CO
80501-7906.   303/6780931.
Employs: 50-99.

Sears Authorized Catalog Sales
255 E Agate Av, Granby CO
80446. 303/8873763. Employs: 50-
99.

Anne Klein Outlet
227 Blue River Pkwy, Silverthorne
CO 80498. 303/2621266. Employs:
50-99.

Bass Shoe Factory Outlet
135 Stephens Wy, Silverthorne CO
80498. 303/4682025. Employs: 50-
99.

Cash Card
1949 Wadsworth Blvd, Lakewood
CO   80215-3349.   303/2338334.
Employs: 50-99.

Gitano Factory Store
125 Stephens Wy, Silverthorne CO
80498. 303/4682354. Employs: 50-
99.

Great Outdoor Clothing Co
227 Blue River Pkwy, Silverthorne
CO 80498. 303/2620807. Employs:
50-99.

Hanes Activewear Factory Outlet
145 Stephens Wy, Silverthorne CO
80498. 303/4689462. Employs: 50-
99.

J Crew Factory Store
167 Wildernest Rd, Silverthorne
CO 80498. 303/2621612. Employs:
50-99.

JH Collectibles
237 Blue River Pkwy, Silverthorne
CO 80498. 303/4689023. Employs:
50-99.

Jackie's Factory Outlet

3869 Hwy 74-Safeway Center,
Evergreen   CO   80439.
303/6746220. Employs: 50-99.

Leggs Hanes Bali Factory Outlet
145 Stephens Wy, Silverthorne CO
80498. 303/4689563. Employs: 50-
99.

Silverthorne Factory Stores
145 Stephens Wy, Silverthorne CO
80498. 303/4689440. Employs: 50-
99.

The Wallet Works
135 Stephens Wy, Silverthorne CO
80498. 303/4689599. Employs: 50-
99.

Van Heusen Factory Store #195
135 Stephens Wy, Silverthorne CO
80498. 303/4680793. Employs: 50-
99.

Windsor Shirt Company
227 Blur River Pkwy, Silverthorne
CO 80498. 303/2620815. Employs:
50-99.

Alco Discount Store
233 Lincoln St, Burlington CO
80807-1407.   719/3467774.
Employs: 50-99.

Branlins Ltd Of Steamboat Spr
745 Lincoln Ave, Steamboat Spr
CO   80487-5026.   303/8792970.
Employs: 50-99.

Buyer's Club
5295 Dtc Pky, Englewood CO
80111-2702.   303/6942500.
Employs: 50-99.

May D & F
5613 W 88th Ave, Westminster CO
80030-3004.   303/4271300.
Employs: 100-249.

May D & F
225 E Foothills Pky, Fort Collins
CO 80525-2612. 303/2265300.
Employs: 50-99.

May D & F
7200 W Alameda Ave, Lakewood
CO 80226-3206. 303/9361232.
Employs: 50-99.

May D & F
The Citadel Mall, Colorado Springs
CO 80909. 719/5977246. Employs:
50-99.

Gaskill's Dept Store
219 E Av, Limon CO 80828.
719/7752231. Employs: 50-99.

Joslin's Telephone Shopping
701 W Hampden Ave, Englewood
CO 80154-1006. 303/7622900.
Employs: 50-99.

K Mart Discount Store
8500 W Crestline Ave, Littleton
CO 80123-2222. 303/9710817.
Employs: 50-99.

Lord & Taylor Department Store
2810 E 1st Ave, Denver CO 80206-
5608. 303/3993500. Employs: 50-
99.

Mark Wal Disc Cities Str Info
840 N Summit Blvd, Frisco CO
80443. 303/6683959. Employs: 50-
99.

Smart Shoppers Mart
2700 S Colorado Blvd, Denver CO
80222-6619. 303/7563121.
Employs: 50-99.

Sputies Fashion
9724 E Colfax Ave, Aurora CO
80010-5011. 303/3647015.
Employs: 50-99.

TJ Maxx

3949 Palmer Park Blvd, Colorado
Springs CO 80909-2695.
719/5747103. Employs: 50-99.

Target Stores
16910 E Quincy Ave, Aurora CO
80015-2745. 303/6991020.
Employs: 100-249.

Target Stores
2626 11th Ave, Greeley CO 80631-
8441. 303/3518511. Employs: 100-
249.

Wal-Mart Discount Cities
8181 S Quebec St, Englewood CO
80112-3187. 303/8507125.
Employs: 100-249.

VARIETY STORES

Big R Stores Of Greeley
310 8th Ave, Greeley CO 80631-
2334. 303/3520544. Employs: 100-
249.

FW Woolworth Co
820 16th St, Denver CO 80202-
3218. 303/5927415. Employs: 100-
249.

Target Stores
4301 E Virginia Ave, Denver CO
80222-1510. 303/3990890.
Employs: 100-249.

Target Stores Inc
1950 E County Line Rd, Littleton
CO 80126-2403. 303/7971911.
Employs: 100-249.

Wal-Mart Discount Stores
525 S 8th St, Colorado Springs CO
80905-1807. 719/6337474.
Employs: 100-249.

MISC. GENERAL MERCHANDISE STORES

Best Products
8601 Sheridan Blvd, Arvada CO 80003-1439. 303/4282000. Employs: 50-99.

Best Products Inc
110 W Troutman Pky, Fort Collins CO 80525-3037. 303/2238200. Employs: 50-99.

Joslin Dry Goods Co
S Wadsworth & W Bowl, Littleton CO 80123. 303/9796111. Employs: 100-249.

Pace Membership Warehouse
7370 W 52nd Ave, Arvada CO 80002-3708. 303/4208401. Employs: 100-249.

Pace Membership Warehouse
1801 S Academy Blvd, Colorado Springs CO 80916-4511. 719/5974613. Employs: 100-249.

Sams Wholesale Club
715 S Academy Blvd, Colorado Springs CO 80910-2677. 719/5972311. Employs: 100-249.

Wal-Mart Discount Stores
701 N Academy Blvd, Colorado Springs CO 80909-8305. 719/3800800. Employs: 100-249.

Wal-Mart
6510 South Highway 85-87, Fountain CO 80817-1010. 719/3911700. Employs: 50-99.

MOTOR VEHICLE DEALERS

Academy Ford Subaru Inc
175 N Academy Blvd, Colorado Springs CO 80909-6553. 719/5972200. Employs: 100-249.

Burt Chevrolet Inc
5200 S Broadway, Englewood CO 80110-6708. 303/7610333. Employs: 100-249.

Carlin Dodge Inc
3204 E Platte Ave, Colorado Springs CO 80909-6409. 719/4758550. Employs: 50-99.

Chesrone Chevrolet Inc
7300 Broadway, Denver CO 80221-3610. 303/4285656. Employs: 100-249.

Classic Honda
15601 W Colfax Ave, Golden CO 80401-3937. 303/2977707. Employs: 50-99.

Colorado Kenworth Inc
4901 York St, Denver CO 80216-2245. 303/2920833. Employs: 100-249.

Courtesy Ford Inc
8252 S Broadway, Littleton CO 80122-2708. 303/7944343. Employs: 100-249.

Daniels Motors Inc
105 N Weber St, Colorado Springs CO 80903-1307. 719/6325591. Employs: 100-249.

Douglas Toyota Inc
1650 W 104th Ave, Denver CO 80234-3713. 303/4661921. Employs: 50-99.

Ed Bozarth Chevrolet
2001 S Havana St, Aurora CO 80014-1013. 303/7517500. Employs: 100-249.

Emich Amc Jeep
5701 W Colfax Ave, Denver CO 80214-1819. 303/2319646. Employs: 50-99.

Empire Lakewood Nissan
10345 W Colfax Ave, Lakewood CO 80215-3913. 303/2328881. Employs: 50-99.

Gateway Mazda
90 Havana St, Aurora CO 80010-4313. 303/3445800. Employs: 50-99.

Jerry Roth Chevrolet Inc
8303 W Colfax Ave, Lakewood CO 80215-4006. 303/2371311. Employs: 50-99.

Johnny Haas Motors Inc
9200 W Colfax Ave, Lakewood CO 80215-3916. 303/2380551. Employs: 50-99.

Lakewood Chrysler Plymouth Inc
7200 W Colfax Ave, Lakewood CO 80215-4113. 303/2375403. Employs: 50-99.

Leo Payne Pontiac Inc
300 Wadsworth Blvd, Lakewood CO 80226-1508. 303/2388111. Employs: 100-249.

Lincoln Mercury Dealership
945 Motor City Dr, Colorado Springs CO 80906-1308. 719/5779007. Employs: 50-99.

Luby Chevrolet Company
2033 S Wadsworth Blvd, Denver CO 80227-2435. 303/9862233. Employs: 50-99.

Mark Chevrolet Inc
9301 E Arapahoe Rd, Englewood CO 80112-3606. 303/7900443. Employs: 50-99.

Mark Toyota Volvo
444 S Havana St, Aurora CO 80012-2002. 303/3402170. Employs: 100-249.

Medved Chevrolet Company

11001 I 70 Frontage Rd N, Wheat Ridge CO 80033-2102. 303/4210100. Employs: 50-99.

Metro Auto Inc
2999 W 104th Ave, Denver CO 80234-3506. 303/4695551. Employs: 100-249.

Mike Naughton Ford Acres
150 S Havana St, Aurora CO 80012-1025. 303/3431900. Employs: 100-249.

Mile High Honda
2777 S Havana St, Aurora CO 80014-2803. 303/3697800. Employs: 50-99.

Monarch Motors Ltd
6120 S Broadway, Littleton CO 80121-8015. 303/7942626. Employs: 100-249.

Novak Ford Auto Company Inc
3625 E Colfax Ave, Denver CO 80206-1844. 303/3214401. Employs: 50-99.

Phil Long Ford Co
3535 S Kipling St, Denver CO 80235-1201. 303/9883673. Employs: 100-249.

Phil Long Nissan Inc
1115 Motor City Dr, Colorado Springs CO 80906-1312. 719/4718460. Employs: 50-99.

Pro Jeep Eagle Inc
1800 W 104th Ave, Denver CO 80234-3602. 303/4691931. Employs: 50-99.

Reilly Buick Gmc Truck
1313 Motor City Dr, Colorado Springs CO 80906-1316. 719/6363881. Employs: 50-99.

Rickenbaugh Cadillac Volvo
777 Broadway, Denver CO 80203-3409. 303/5737773. Employs: 50-99.

Rosen Novak Ford Inc
3625 E Colfax Ave, Denver CO 80206-1844.   303/3213673. Employs: 50-99.

Spradley Barr Company
2601 S College Ave, Fort Collins CO   80525-2137.   303/2263673. Employs: 50-99.

Suss Pontiac Gmc Inc
1301 S Havana St, Aurora CO 80012-4011.   303/7513400. Employs: 50-99.

Team Chevrolet Inc
230 N Academy Blvd, Colorado Springs   CO   80909-6604. 719/5963040. Employs: 50-99.

Tynans Volkswagen Inc
700 S Havana St, Aurora CO 80012-3014.   303/3438180. Employs: 50-99.

Weld County Garage
810 10th St, Greeley CO 80631-1116. 303/5715717. Employs: 50-99.

MOTOR VEHICLE DEALERS

Red Barn Motor Co
555   Hathaway   Dr,   Colorado Springs   CO   80915-3818. 719/5960011. Employs: 50-99.

AUTO AND HOME SUPPLY STORES

Discount Tire Company
6300 S Syracuse Way Suite 440, Englewood   CO   80111-6724. 303/7738084. Employs: 50-99.

Napa Auto Parts

2101 E Highway 224, Denver CO 80229-6910.   303/2896711. Employs: 100-249.

Montgomery Ward & Co
2201 S College Ave, Fort Collins CO   80525-1418.   303/2218461. Employs: 100-249.

Peerless Tyre Co
4705 Paris St, Denver CO 80239-2841. 303/3714300. Employs: 100-249.

GASOLINE   SERVICE STATIONS

Automatic Gas Distributors Inc
7670 S Vaughn Ct, Englewood CO 80112-4120.   303/7902900. Employs: 50-99.

Conoco Cono-Marts
11515 N Highway 83, Parker CO 80134-9014.   303/8412413. Employs: 50-99.

Top Hat Car Wash
215 E Drake Rd, Fort Collins CO 80525-1764.   303/2263640. Employs: 50-99.

MISC.   AUTOMOTIVE DEALERS

Denver Jet Center
7625 S Peoria St, Englewood CO 80112-4103.   303/7904321. Employs: 50-99.

Turbo West Inc
10656 W 120th Ave, Broomfield CO   80021-2511.   303/4696671. Employs: 50-99.

WOMEN'S CLOTHING STORES

Aspen Leaf Inc
222 Detroit St, Denver CO 80206-4807. 303/3226935. Employs: 100-249.

Montaldos
100 Fillmore St Ste 120, Denver CO 80206-4921. 303/6291111. Employs: 50-99.

WOMEN'S ACCESSORY AND SPECIALTY STORES

I B Diffusion
135 Stephens Wy, Silverthorne CO 80498. 303/4682288. Employs: 50-99.

FAMILY CLOTHING STORES

County Seat
1700 28th St Ste 172, Boulder CO 80301-1007. 303/4409001. Employs: 50-99.

Sador's
605 Harrison Av, Leadville CO 80461-3559. 719/4863552. Employs: 50-99.

Saks Fifth Avenue
2900 E 1st Ave, Denver CO 80206-5610. 303/3936333. Employs: 100-249.

Wheelers
1515 Main St, Longmont CO 80501-2843. 303/7763110. Employs: 50-99.

FURNITURE STORES

American Furniture Wholesale Co
5445 N Bannock, Denver CO 80216-1624. 303/2961651. Employs: 50-99.

MISC. HOMEFURNISHINGS STORES

Burlington Coat Factory
12455 E Mississippi Ave, Aurora CO 80012-3463. 303/3670111. Employs: 50-99.

Pfaltzgraff Collector's Center
Interstate 70 Exit 205, Silverthorne CO 80498. 303/4689694. Employs: 50-99.

RADIO, TELEVISION, AND CONSUMER ELECTRONICS STORES

Quarterdeck Systems Inc
4665 S Nautilus Ct, Boulder CO 80301-5303. 303/5303677. Employs: 50-99.

COMPUTER AND COMPUTER SOFTWARE STORES

Monolithic Systems Corp
7050 S Tucson Way, Englewood CO 80112-3921. 303/7907400. Employs: 50-99.

Random Access Connecting Point
2370 S Trenton Way, Denver CO 80231-3844. 303/7459600. Employs: 50-99.

Soft Warehouse
15660 E 6th Ave, Aurora CO 80011-9048. 303/7413777. Employs: 100-249.

DRUG STORES AND PROPRIETARY STORES

K Mart Pharmacy
9881 W 58th Ave, Arvada CO 80002-2011. 303/4228008. Employs: 50-99.

K Mart Pharmacy
15200 E Colfax Ave, Aurora CO
80011-6965.   303/3417420.
Employs: 50-99.

King Soopers
8200 S Holly St, Littleton CO
80122-4004.   303/7794242.
Employs: 100-249.

Safeway Stores Pharmacy
8430 Federal Blvd, Westminster
CO 80030-3818. 303/4287681.
Employs: 100-249.

Wal-Mart Discount Cities
7900 W Quincy Ave, Littleton CO
80123-1350.   303/9710337.
Employs: 50-99.

Wal-Mart Discount Cities
14000 E Exposition Ave, Aurora
CO 80012-2538. 303/3681116.
Employs: 50-99.

King Soopers
1173 Colorado Hwy 74, Evergreen
CO 80439. 303/6748246. Employs:
100-249.

Safeway Stores Inc
7561 W 80th Ave, Arvada CO
80003-2113.   303/4250371.
Employs: 50-99.

Wal-Mart Discount Cities
550 E 102nd Ave, Denver CO
80229-2014.   303/4516404.
Employs: 100-249.

USED   MERCHANDISE STORES

Goodwill Industries
6850 Federal Blvd, Denver CO
80221-2628.   303/6507724.
Employs: 100-249.

Tattered Cover Bookstore
1536 Wynkoop St, Denver CO
80202-1162.   303/3227112.
Employs: 100-249.

St Luke's Thrift Shop
143 Remington St, Fort Collins CO
80524-2833.   303/4848922.
Employs: 50-99.

SPORTING GOODS STORES AND BICYCLES SHOPS

Bulrich Corporation
938 Quail St, Lakewood CO
80215-5513.   303/2376321.
Employs: 50-99.

D Cook Sporting Goods Center
1350 16th St, Denver CO 80202-
1506. 303/8921929. Employs: 100-
249.

Hight Enterprises Ltd
2525 Arapahoe Ave, Boulder CO
80302-6720.   303/4472161.
Employs: 100-249.

Winter Park Ski Shop Ltd
Box 55, Winter Park CO 80482-
0055. 303/7265554. Employs: 50-
99.

STATIONERY STORES

Commercial Office Products
1636 Champa St, Denver CO
80202-2706.   303/8931881.
Employs: 100-249.

GIFT,   NOVELTY,   AND SOUVENIR SHOPS

Blue Mountain Arts
1942 Broadway St Ste 403,
Boulder   CO   80302-5239.
303/4490536. Employs: 50-99.

Flying W Ranch
3330 Chuckwagon Rd, Colorado
Springs   CO   80919-3501.
719/5984000. Employs: 50-99.

Host International
Stapleton Airport Suite 3143A, Denver CO 80207. 303/3986070. Employs: 100-249.

Red Rooster Country Str
225 Elkhorn Dr, Estes Park CO 80517. 303/5866758. Employs: 50-99.

Wiland Services Inc
6707 Winchester Ct, Boulder CO 80301-3513. 303/5300606. Employs: 50-99.

AUTOMATIC MERCHANDISING MACHINE OPERATORS

ARA Leisure Services
4600 Humboldt St, Denver CO 80216-2819. 303/2952457. Employs: 100-249.

DIRECT SELLING ESTABLISHMENTS

Mary Kay Cosmetics
8167 S Yukon Way, Littleton CO 80123-5524. 303/9795191. Employs: 50-99.

FUEL OIL DEALERS

Cox Oil Co

103 S Railroad Ave, Loveland CO 80537-6304. 303/6671411. Employs: 50-99.

FLORISTS

Flowers A La Karte Airport
Stapleton International Airprt, Denver CO 80238. 303/3982287. Employs: 50-99.

OPTICAL GOODS STORES

Accurate Plastics & Eng Inc
1921 Miller Dr, Longmont CO 80501-6736. 303/7724722. Employs: 100-249.

Boulder Arts & Crafts Co Op
1421 Pearl St, Boulder CO 80302-5306. 303/4433683. Employs: 50-99.

Starkey Labs
3020 N El Paso St, Colorado Springs CO 80907-5454. 719/6329331. Employs: 50-99.

Communications World
419 Canyon Blvd, Boulder CO 80302-4923. 303/4471331. Employs: 50-99.

Breckenridge Hilton
550 Village Rd, Breckenridge CO 80424. 303/4534500. Employs: 50-99.

For more information on career opportunities in general merchandise - retail and wholesale:

Associations

AMERICAN INTERNATIONAL AUTOMOTIVE DEALERS ASSOCIATION
99 Canal Center Plaza, Suite 500, Alexandria VA 22314-1538. 703/519-7800.

INTERNATIONAL ASSOCIATION OF CHAIN STORES
38100 Moor Place, Alexandria VA 22305. 703/549-4525.

INTERNATIONAL COUNCIL OF SHOPPING CENTERS
665 Fifth Avenue, New York NY 10022. 212/421-8181.

MENSWEAR RETAILERS OF AMERICA
2011 I Street NW, Suite 300, Washington DC 20006. 202/347-1932.

NATIONAL AUTOMOTIVE DEALERS ASSOCIATION
8400 Westpark Drive, McLean VA 22102. 703/821-7000.

NATIONAL INDEPENDENT AUTOMOTIVE DEALERS ASSOCIATION
2521 Brown Boulevard, Suite 100, Arlington TX 76006. 817/640-3838.

NATIONAL RETAIL MERCHANTS ASSOCIATION
100 West 31st Street, New York NY 10001. 212/244-8780.

Directories

AUTOMOTIVE NEWS MARKET DATA BOOK
Automotive News, 1400 Woodbridge Avenue, Detroit MI 48207. 313/446-6000.

GOVERNMENT

Additional large employers: 250+

EXECUTIVE, LEGISLATIVE, AND GENERAL GOVERNMENT

Colorado Springs City Manager
30 S Nevada Av Rm 401, Colorado Springs CO 80903-1825. 7195786600. Employs: 1,000+.

US Dept Comm Admn Servs Genl
325 Broadway St, Boulder CO 80303-3328. 303/4975414. Employs: 500-999.

US Trans Dept F A A Denver
2211 17th Av, Longmont CO 80501-9763. 303/7764100. Employs: 500-999.

GOVERNMENT OFFICES

Greeley City Hall
1000 10th St, Greeley CO 80631-3808. 303/3509723. Employs: 250-499.

Longmont City Hall
Civic Center, Longmont CO 80501. 303/7766050. Employs: 250-499.

US Environmental Protection
999 18th St, Denver CO 80202-2440. 303/2931603. Employs: 500-999.

US National Park Service
12795 W Alameda, Lakewood CO 80228. 303/9692000. Employs: 500-999.

US Veterans Affairs
44 Union Blvd, Lakewood CO 80228-1808. 303/9801300. Employs: 250-499.

Westminster City Hall
4800 W 92nd Ave, Westminster CO 80030-6387. 303/4302400. Employs: 500-999.

Arapahoe County Sheriff's Dept
5686 S Court Pl, Littleton CO 80120-1205. 303/7954932. Employs: 250-499.

Colorado Health Department
4210 E 11th Ave, Denver CO 80220-3716. 303/3208333. Employs: 250-499.

Colorado Regulatory Reform Office
1525 Sherman St, Denver CO 80203-1712. 303/8662802. Employs: 500-999.

Additional small to medium sized employers: 50-249

UNITED STATES POSTAL SERVICE

Contract Station 5
2699 47th Ave, Greeley CO 80634. 303/3302942. Employs: 50-99.

Golden Post Office
619 12th St, Golden CO 80401-9998. 303/2788537. Employs: 50-99.

United States Post Office
1905 15th St, Boulder CO 80302-9998. 303/9381100. Employs: 50-99.

United States Post Office
1860 38th St, Boulder CO 80301-9998. 303/9383725. Employs: 50-99.

United States Post Office
925 11th Ave, Greeley CO 80631-9998. 303/3530398. Employs: 100-249.

United States Post Office
466 E 29th St, Loveland CO 80538-2743. 303/6670344. Employs: 100-249.

United States Postal Service
1550 Dayton St, Aurora CO 80010-9998. 303/3649215. Employs: 100-249.

United States Postal Service
1745 Stout St Suite 700, Denver CO 80202-3034. 303/2976097. Employs: 50-99.

EXECUTIVE LEGISLATIVE AND GENERAL GOVERNMENT

Lafayette City Fire Department
110 N Harrison Av, Lafayette CO 80026-2336. 303/6659661. Employs: 50-99.

GOVERNMENT OFFICES

Castle Rock Town Hall
680 Wilcox St, Castle Rock CO 80104-1739. 303/6601015. Employs: 50-99.

Wheat Ridge City Hall
7500 W 29th Ave, Littleton CO 80125. 303/2376944. Employs: 100-249.

Federal Bureau-Investigation
Federal Bldg, Denver CO 80294. 303/6297171. Employs: 50-99.

US Defense Contract Mgmt
2006 N Academy Blvd, Colorado Springs CO 80909-1506. 719/5912170. Employs: 50-99.

US Fish & Wildlife Service
134 Union Blvd, Lakewood CO 80228-1807. 303/2367920. Employs: 100-249.

US Government National Forest
29587 W US 40, Steamboat Spr CO 80487-9500. 303/8791722. Employs: 50-99.

US Government Printing Office
Denver Federal Ctr, Denver CO 80225. 303/2365292. Employs: 50-99.

Boulder Police Dept Adm
Justice Center, Boulder CO 80302. 303/4413320. Employs: 100-249.

Lakewood City Clerk
445 S Allison Pky, Lakewood CO 80226-3106. 303/9877080. Employs: 100-249.

Adams Sheriff's Dept
1901 E Bridge St, Brighton CO 80601-1937. 303/6541850. Employs: 100-249.

CO State Wildlife Division
317 W Prospect Rd, Fort Collins CO 80526-2003. 303/4842836. Employs: 100-249.

Colorado Highway Department
4201 E Arkansas Ave, Denver CO 80222-3406. 303/2394501. Employs: 100-249.

MISC. GOVERNMENT OFFICES

Census Bureau Regional Office
7655 W Mississippi Ave, Lakewood CO 80226-4332. 303/9696750. Employs: 50-99.

Colorado Springs Facilities
545 E Pikes Peak Ave Suite 200, Colorado Springs CO 80903-3653. 719/5786037. Employs: 50-99.

County Administrative Services
2040 14th St, Boulder CO 80302-5312. 303/4414548. Employs: 50-99.

Natl Conf Of State Legislatures
1560 Broadway Ste 700, Denver CO 80202-5140. 303/6237800. Employs: 50-99.

El Paso County Clerk Recorder
200 S Cascade Ave, Colorado Springs CO 80903-2215. 719/5206430. Employs: 50-99.

Weld County Government Employment
1551 N 17th Ave, Greeley CO 80631. 303/3533800. Employs: 50-99.

COURTS

United States District Court
1929 Stout St, Denver CO 80294-2900. 303/8444208. Employs: 100-249.

POLICE DEPARTMENTS

City & County Of Denver Police
1331 Cherokee St Suite 402, Denver CO 80204-2720. 303/6403875. Employs: 50-99.

Colorado Bureau Investigation
690 Kipling St Suite 3000, Lakewood CO 80215-5844. 303/2394300. Employs: 100-249.

Greenwood Village Police Dept
6060 S Quebec St, Englewood CO 80111-471 . 303/7415960. Employs: 50-99.

DETENTION CENTERS

Larimer County Detention Ctr
2405 Midpoint Dr, Fort Collins CO 80525-4419. 303/2217120. Employs: 100-249.

GOVERNMENT FINANCIAL DEPARTMENT

US Government Financial Center
143 Union Blvd Suite 300, Lakewood CO 80228-1826. 303/9851814. Employs: 100-249.

GOVERNMENT EDUCATIONAL DEPARTMENT

Education Commission Of States
707 17th St Suite 2700, Denver CO 80202-3427. 303/2993600. Employs: 50-99.

GOVERNMENT HEALTH AND SOCIAL SERVICES DEPARTMENTS

Boulder County Dept Social Services
3400 Broadway, Boulder CO 80304-1824. 303/4411000. Employs: 100-249.

El Paso Department Of Health
501 N Foote Ave, Colorado Springs CO 80909-4501. 719/5783125. Employs: 100-249.

Tri County District Health Dept
15400 E 14th Pl Suite 309, Aurora CO 80011-5828. 303/3419370. Employs: 100-249.

ENVIRONMENTAL AND ECOLOGICAL SERVICES

USGS National Water Quality
5293 Ward Rd, Arvada CO 80002-1811. 303/2365345. Employs: 100-249.

FEDERAL CONSERVATION DEPARTMENTS

US Bureau Of Land Management
2850 Youngfield St, Lakewood CO 80215-7076. 303/2361700. Employs: 100-249.

US Forest Service
240 W Prospect Rd, Fort Collins CO 80526-2002. 303/4981100. Employs: 100-249.

Environmental Control Division
7060 E 54th Pl, Commerce City CO 80022-4806. 303/2860311. Employs: 50-99.

HEALTH CARE AND PHARMACEUTICALS

Employment in the health care industry has gone up steadily from 7 million in 1989, to over 9 million just three years later, with an average annual growth rate of 8 percent -- and that doesn't include medical equipment manufacturers or pharmaceutical companies, which are also booming. Health care expenditures are now rising to over $800 billion a year. Various approaches to controlling the cost of health care have been proposed, although Washington has yet to take any specific action. Reforms to the health care system should lead to more efficient and effective services. The hottest areas in this hot industry are health maintenance organizations (HMOs) and home health care.

COBE LABORATORIES INC.
1185 Oak Street, Lakewood CO 80215. 303/232-6800. **Contact:** Theresa Blandford, Corporate Director for Human Resources. **Description:** Develops, manufactures, sells, and services therapeutic systems and products for use in the treatment of irreversible end-stage kidney disease, heart surgery, and blood pressure monitoring; also a researcher of blood component technology in the United States and abroad. **Corporate headquarters:** This location.

COLORADO SERUM COMPANY
P.O. Box 16428, Denver CO 80216. 303/295-7527. **Contact:** Mr. Joe Huff, Human Resources. **Description:** Develops and produces veterinary serums and biologicals.

ELECTROMEDICS, INC.
P.O. Box 3315, Englewood CO 80155. 303/790-8700. **Contact:** Susie Perleman, Personnel Director. **Description:** A manufacturer of medical supplies and equipment.

GENEVA PHARMACEUTICALS
2555 West Midway Boulevard, Broomfield CO 80020. 303/469-2131. **Contact:** Barbee Hunsley, Human Resources Assistant. **Description:** A pharmaceutical manufacturer and distributor; primarily produces generic pharmaceutical products. A subsidiary of Geneva Generic, Inc. **Corporate headquarters:** This location.

HEALTHWATCH TECHNOLOGIES
3400 Industrial Lane, Suite A, Broomfield CO 80020. 303/465-2000. **Contact:** Personnel. **Description:** An ambulatory health care and family practice provider. Also provides pharmacy, lab, and physical therapy services. Provides specialist physician services through their own group practice. **Benefits:** medical, dental, and life insurance; disability coverage; employee discounts. **Corporate headquarters:** This location. **Operations at this facility:** divisional headquarters; administration; sales.

HEMOTEC, INC.
7103 South Revere Parkway, Englewood CO 80112. 303/790-7900. **Contact:** Valerie Bonacci, Personnel Administrator. **Description:** Develops, manufactures, and markets computerized medical instruments which monitor human blood-clotting activity; also supplies disposable cartridges of reagent chemicals for use in those systems. **Common positions:** Accountant; Biologist; Chemist; Customer Service Representative; Draftsperson; Electrical Engineer; Industrial Engineer; Operations/ Production Manager; Purchasing Agent; Quality Control Supervisor; Sales Representative; Systems Analyst; Technical Writer/Editor. **Educational backgrounds sought:** Accounting; Art/Design; Biology; Business Administration; Chemistry; Computer Science; Economics; Engineering; Finance; Marketing. **Benefits:** medical insurance; dental insurance; life insurance; disability coverage. **Corporate headquarters:** This location.

IMEX MEDICAL SYSTEMS, INC.
6355 Joyce Drive, Golden CO 80403. 303/431-9400. **Contact:** Personnel. **Description:** A manufacturer and distributor of doppler equipment for primary care physicians.

IOTECH INCORPORATED
11080 Irma Drive, Northglen CO 80233. 303/450-6449. **Contact:** Personnel Department. **Description:** Company involved in the sterilization of medical equipment for medical products manufactured in Colorado.

MARQUEST MEDICAL PRODUCTS
11039 East Lansing Circle, Englewood CO 80112. 303/790-4835. **Contact:** Stacey Hill, Personnel Director. **Description:** A Denver-area manufacturer of medical equipment and supplies. **Corporate headquarters:** This location.

MESA MEDICAL, INC.
3904 Youngfield Street, Wheat Ridge CO 80033. 303/431-4474. **Contact:** Steve Peterson, Personnel. **Description:** A manufacturer of dialysis equipment and miniaturized temperature recording instrumentation.

OLSTEN HEALTHCARE SERVICES
1777 South Harrison, #303, Denver CO 80210. 303/759-2991. **Contact:** Gelnnys Lee, Administrator. **Description:** A home healthcare service. Provides temporary health care personnel in home care settings. Also provides supplemental staff to hospitals. **Common positions:** Registered Nurse; Home Health Aid. **Educational backgrounds sought:** Nursing. **Special programs:** Training programs. **Benefits:** medical, dental, and life insurance; tuition assistance; disability coverage. **Corporate headquarters:** Westbury, NY. **Parent company:** Olsten Corporation. **Operations at this facility:** administration; service; sales. **Listed on:** New York Stock Exchange.

ST. MARY'S HOSPTIAL
P.O. Box 1628, Grand Junction CO 81502-1628. 303/244-2540. **Contact:** Beth Costello, Employment Coordinator. **Description:** An area healthcare facility. **Employees:** 1,500.

SYNTEX CHEMICALS, INC.
2075 North 55th Street, Boulder CO 80301. 303/442-1926. **Contact:** Pat Vassallo, Personnel Director. **Description:** A Denver pharmaceutical products company.

VALLEYLAB INC.
5920 Longbow Drive, P.O. Box 9015, Boulder CO 80301. 303/530-2300. **Contact:** Personnel Department. **Description:** Develops, manufactures, markets, and services medical equipment and accessories used in the hospital and other medical environments. Principal products are electro-surgical, used to perform a variety of surgical and medical procedures. Valleylab is a division of Pfizer, Inc., 235 East 42nd Street, New York NY 10017. **Common positions:** Accountant; Administrator; Blue-Collar Worker Supervisor; Buyer; Computer Programmer; Chemist; Credit Manager; Customer Service Representative; Draftsperson; Biomedical Engineer; Electrical Engineer; Industrial Engineer; Mechanical Engineer; Financial Analyst; Personnel Specialist; Quality Control

Supervisor; Sales Representative. **Educational backgrounds sought:** Accounting; Business Administration; Computer Science; Engineering; Finance; Marketing. **Special programs:** Training programs; internships. **Benefits:** medical insurance; dental insurance; life insurance; pension plan; tuition assistance; disability coverage; profit sharing; employee discounts; savings plan; fitness center. **Corporate headquarters:** New York, NY. **Operations at this facility:** divisional headquarters; manufacturing; research and development; administration; service; sales. **Listed on:** New York Stock Exchange.

WILSA INCORPORATED
2172 South Jason, Denver CO 80223. 303/936-1137. **Contact:** Personnel Department. **Description:** A manufacturer of contact lens solutions and polymers.

Additional large employers: 250+

LABORATORY ANALYTICAL INSTRUMENTS

Perkin-Elmer
8301 E Prentice Av, Englewood CO 80111-2903. 2037624507. Employs: 1,000+.

MISC. MEASURING AND CONTROLLING DEVICES

Hewlett Packard Instrument
815 Sw 14th St, Loveland CO 80537-6330. 303/6695001. Employs: 1,000+.

SURGICAL AND MEDICAL INSTRUMENTS AND APPARATUS

Cobe Cardiovascular Inc
14401 W 65th Way, Arvada CO 80004-3524. 303/4256000. Employs: 500-999.

Marquest Medical Products Inc
11039 Lansing Cir, Englewood CO 80112-5910. 303/7904835. Employs: 500-999.

Valleylab Inc
5920 Longbow Dr, Boulder CO 80301-3202. 303/5302300. Employs: 500-999.

DENTAL EQUIPMENT AND SUPPLIES

Rocky Mountain Orthodonics
650 W Colfax Ave, Denver CO 80204-2611. 303/5348181. Employs: 250-499.

ELECTROMEDICAL AND ELECTROTHERAPEUTIC APPARATUS

Ball Electro Optics
PO Box 1062, Boulder CO 80306-1062. 303/9394000. Employs: 250-499.

Ohmeda
1315 W Century Dr, Louisville CO 80027-9560. 303/6667001. Employs: 250-499.

Colorado Medical Info Network
4815 List Dr, Colorado Springs CO 80919-3315. 7192601104. Employs: 250-499.

OFFICES AND CLINICS OF DOCTORS OF MEDICINE

Kaiser Foundation Health Plan
8383 W Alameda Ave, Lakewood
CO 80226-3007. 303/2321885.
Employs: 250-499.

Longmont Clinic Pc
1925 Mountain View Ave,
Longmont CO 80501-3128.
303/9398000. Employs: 250-499.

North Colorado Medical Center
1801 16, Greeley CO 80631.
303/3524121. Employs: 500-999.

Poudre Valley Emergency Phys
1024 S Lemay Ave, Fort Collins
CO 80524-3929. 303/4824111.
Employs: 500-999.

MISC. OFFICES AND CLINICS OF HEALTH PRACTITIONERS

Laradon Industries
5100 Lincoln St, Denver CO
80216-2056. 303/2963444.
Employs: 250-499.

SKILLED NURSING CARE FACILITIES

ARA Living Centers
2020 Clubhouse Dr, Greeley CO
80634-3654. 303/3307222.
Employs: 1,000+.

INTERMEDIATE CARE FACILITIES

Bonell Good Samaritan Center
708 22nd St, Greeley CO 80631-
7041. 303/3526082. Employs: 250-
499.

St Pavillion Hlth Care Ctr
1601 Lowell Blvd, Denver CO
80204-1545. 303/8252190.
Employs: 500-999.

GENERAL MEDICAL AND SURGICAL HOSPITALS

Avista Hosp
100 Health Pk Dr, Louisville CO
80027-9583. 303/6731000.
Employs: 250-499.

Avista Hospital
400 Mc Caslin Blvd, Louisville CO
80027-9701. 303/6658782.
Employs: 250-499.

Boulder Memorial Hospital
311 Mapleton Ave, Boulder CO
80304-3979. 303/4430230.
Employs: 250-499.

Craig Hosp
3425 S Clarkson, Englewood CO
80110-2811. 303/7898000.
Employs: 250-499.

Doctors Hospital
1920 High St, Denver CO 80218-
1213. 303/3205871. Employs: 250-
499.

Eisenhower Medical Center
2502 E Pikes Peak Ave, Colorado
Springs CO 80909-6023.
7194752111. Employs: 250-499.

Fitzsimmons Army Medical Cntr
Colfax & Peoria St, Aurora CO
80045. 303/3618223. Employs:
250-499.

Mercy Medical Center
1650 Fillmore St, Denver CO
80206-1550. 303/3933000.
Employs: 250-499.

Penrose Community Hospital
3205 N Academy Blvd, Colorado
Springs CO 80917. 7195913000.
Employs: 250-499.

Penrose Hospital
2215 N Cascade Ave, Colorado
Springs CO 80907-6736.
7196305000. Employs: 500-999.

Platte Valley Medical Center
1850 E Egbert St, Brighton CO
80601-2404.   303/6591531.
Employs: 250-499.

Porter Memorial Hospital
2525 S Downing St, Denver CO
80210-5817.   303/7781955.
Employs: 250-499.

Presbyterian Aurora Hospital
700 Potomac St, Aurora CO 80011-
6701. 303/3637200. Employs: 500-
999.

Presbyterian Denver Med Ctr
1719 E 19th Ave, Denver CO
80218-1235.   303/8396000.
Employs: 250-499.

Saint Lukes Medical Center
601 E 19th Ave, Denver CO
80203-1416.   303/8391000.
Employs: 500-999.

Swedish Medical Ctr
501 E Hampden Ave, Englewood
CO   80110-2702.   303/7885000.
Employs: 500-999.

Va Medical Center
1055 Clermont St, Denver CO
80220-3808.   303/3998020.
Employs: 500-999.

Humana Hosp Mountain View
9191 Grant St, Denver CO 80229-
4361. 303/4517800. Employs: 250-
499.

Natl Jewish Ctr
1400 Jackson St, Denver CO
80206-2761.   303/3884461.
Employs: 250-499.

Spalding Rehab Hosp
4500 E Iliff Ave, Denver CO
80222-6021.   303/8610504.
Employs: 250-499.

Penrose Hosp

3205 N Academy St, Colorado
Springs   CO   80917-5101.
7196303300. Employs: 250-499.

PSYCHIATRIC HOSPITALS

Cleo Wallace Center
8405 W 100th Ave, Broomfield CO
80021-3918.   303/4667391.
Employs: 250-499.

Fort Logan Mental Health Ctr
3520 W Oxford Ave, Denver CO
80236-3108.   303/7610220.
Employs: 500-999.

SPECIALTY HOSPITALS, EXCEPT PSYCHIATRIC

Childrens Hospital
1056 E 19th Ave, Denver CO
80218-1007.   303/8618888.
Employs: 1,000+.

Boulder Community Hosp
N Broadway & Balsam, Boulder
CO 80304. 303/4402273. Employs:
500-999.

Longmont United Hosp
1950 W Mountain View Ave,
Longmont   CO   80501-3129.
303/6515111. Employs: 500-999.

West Pines Psych Hosp
3400 Lutheran Pkwy, Wheat Ridge
CO   80033-6029.   303/2394000.
Employs: 250-499.

MEDICAL LABORATORIES

Met Path Laboratories
2131 N Tejon St, Colorado Springs
CO   80907-6957.   7196338460.
Employs: 250-499.

HOME HEALTH CARE SERVICES

Denver Visiting Nurse Asso
1391 N Speer Bl Ste 800, Denver CO 80204-2555. 303/5737575. Employs: 250-499.

Prn Inc
611 N Weber St Suite 104, Colorado Springs CO 80903-1071. 7196333897. Employs: 250-499.

Visiting Nurse Association Of Denver
3801 E Florida Ave Suite 800, Denver CO 80210-2545. 303/6885421. Employs: 500-999.

MISC. SPECIALTY OUTPATIENT FACILITIES

Mental Health Center
1333 Iris Ave, Boulder CO 80304-2226. 303/4438500. Employs: 250-499.

Pikes Peak Mental Health Ctr
875 W Moreno Ave, Colorado Springs CO 80905-1731. 7194718300. Employs: 250-499.

Charter Hospital Of Denver
421 Zang St, Lakewood CO 80228-1052. 303/9895000. Employs: 250-499.

Memorial Hosp
1400 E Boulder St, Colorado Springs CO 80909-5533. 7194755000. Employs: 500-999.

St Joseph Hosp
1835 Franklin St, Denver CO 80218-1126. 303/8377111. Employs: 500-999.

Luthern Medical Ctr
8300 W 38th Ave, Wheat Ridge CO 80033-6005. 303/4254500. Employs: 500-999.

Platte Valley Medical Ctr
1850 Egbert St, Brighton CO 80601-2404. 303/6591351. Employs: 250-499.

MISC. HEALTH AND ALLIED SERVICES

Lincoln Community Hosp
111 6th St, Hugo CO 80821. 303/7432421. Employs: 250-499.

Additional small to medium sized employers: 50-249

MEDICINAL CHEMICALS AND BOTANICAL PRODUCTS

Napro
2885 Wilderness Pl # B, Boulder CO 80301-2257. 303/4440952. Employs: 50-99.

PHARMACEUTICAL PREPARATIONS

Pharmaceutical Basics Inc
301 S Cherokee St, Denver CO 80223-2114. 303/7337207. Employs: 100-249.

IN CITRO AND IN VIVO DIAGNOSTIC SUBSTANCES

Immunotechnology Corp
7800 E Elati, Littleton CO 80120-4483. 303/7894751. Employs: 50-99.

BIOLOGICAL PRODUCTS, EXCEPT DIAGNOSTIC SUBSTANCES

Preferred Blood Prods Inc
3505 11th Ave, Evans CO 80620-2011. 303/3303558. Employs: 50-99.

OPTICAL INSTRUMENTS AND LENSES

Burris Company
331 E 8th St, Greeley CO 80631-9559. 303/3561670. Employs: 50-99.

MISC. MEASURING AND CONTROLLING DEVICES

Hauser Labs
5555 Airport Blvd, Boulder CO 80301-2339. 303/4434662. Employs: 50-99.

Redfield Inc
5800 E Jewell Ave, Denver CO 80224-2303. 303/7576411. Employs: 100-249.

SURGICAL AND MEDICAL INSTRUMENTS AND APPARATUS

Aspen Labs Inc
8136 S Grant Way, Littleton CO 80122-2702. 303/7985800. Employs: 100-249.

Baxa Corporation
13760 E Arapahoe Rd, Englewood CO 80112-3903. 303/7996660. Employs: 50-99.

Colorado Serum Company
4950 York St, Denver CO 80216-2246. 303/2957527. Employs: 50-99.

Fischer Imaging Corp

12300 Grant St, Denver CO 80241-3120. 303/4526800. Employs: 100-249.

Ohmeda-Bti
4765 Walnut St, Boulder CO 80301-2549. 303/4479842. Employs: 100-249.

Prism Imaging
650 S Taylor Ave, Louisville CO 80027-3032. 303/6669300. Employs: 100-249.

Staodynamics
1225 Florida Ave, Longmont CO 80501-6332. 303/4492061. Employs: 50-99.

ORTHOPEDIC, PROSTHETIC, AND SURGICAL APPLIANCES AND SUPPLIES

Life Products Inc
2445 Central Av, Boulder CO 80301-5725. 303/4447606. Employs: 50-99.

Lifecare
655 Aspen Ridge Dr, Lafayette CO 80026-9341. 303/6669234. Employs: 100-249.

Synthes USA
1051 Synthes Ave, Monument CO 80132-8174. 719/4813021. Employs: 100-249.

Teledyne Getz
3840 Forest St, Denver CO 80207-1121. 303/3990240. Employs: 50-99.

ELECTROMEDICAL AND ELECTROTHERAPEUTIC APPARATUS

Care Electronics Inc
2805 Wilderness Pl, Boulder CO 80301-5452. 303/4442273. Employs: 50-99.

MEDICAL, DENTAL, AND HOSPITAL EQUIPMENT SUPPLIES

Electric Wire Corp
2275 W Midway Blvd, Broomfield CO 80020-1627. 303/4600794. Employs: 100-249.

Intermountain Specialty Equipment
33 Inverness Dr E, Englewood CO 80112-5403. 303/7901444. Employs: 50-99.

Technology Management & Marketing Inc
P O Box 621453, Littleton CO 80162-1453. 303/9728771. Employs: 50-99.

Viapont Inc
1625 Sharp Point Dr, Fort Collins CO 80525-4423. 303/4823126. Employs: 50-99.

OFFICES AND CLINICS OF DOCTORS OF MEDICINE

Accord Medical Center
701 E Colfax Ave, Denver CO 80203-2005. 303/8317171. Employs: 100-249.

Colorado Foundation Med Care
1260 S Parker Rd, Denver CO 80231-2179. 303/6953300. Employs: 50-99.

East Side Health Center
501 28th St, Denver CO 80205-3003. 303/2971241. Employs: 100-249.

Kaiser Permanente
11245 Huron St, Denver CO 80234-2806. 303/4519494. Employs: 100-249.

Kaiser Permanente
10400 E Alameda Ave, Denver CO 80231-5104. 303/3601510. Employs: 100-249.

Student Health Center
Colorado St Univ, Fort Collins CO 80523. 303/4917121. Employs: 50-99.

Westside Health Center
1100 Federal Blvd, Denver CO 80204-3219. 303/5731300. Employs: 100-249.

Univ Colorado Sports Medicine Clinic
5250 Leetsdale Dr Ste 301, Denver CO 80222-1452. 303/3310055. Employs: 50-99.

Capron Rehabilitation
2215 N Cascade Ave, Colorado Springs CO 80907-6736. 719/6305789. Employs: 50-99.

Gates Medical & Dental Center
1000 S Broadway, Denver CO 80209-4012. 303/7771315. Employs: 100-249.

Greeley Medical Clinic PC
1900 16th St, Greeley CO 80631-5114. 303/3502427. Employs: 100-249.

Highlands Ranch Family Medcn
206 W County Line Rd, Littleton CO 80126-2318. 303/7910301. Employs: 50-99.

MISC. OFFICES AND CLINICS OF HEALTH PRACTITIONERS

Mount Evans Home Health Care
3709 Hwy 74, Evergreen CO 80439. 303/6746400. Employs: 50-99.

SKILLED NURSING CARE FACILITIES

Allison Health Care Center
1660 Allison St, Lakewood CO
80215-3223.   303/2327177.
Employs: 50-99.

Applewood Living Center
1800 Stroh Pl, Longmont CO
80501-3214.   303/7766081.
Employs: 50-99.

Aspen Living Center
1795 Monterey Rd, Colorado
Springs   CO   80910-1823.
719/4717850. Employs: 50-99.

Autumn Heights Health Care Ctr
3131 S Federal Blvd, Denver CO
80236-2799.   303/7610260.
Employs: 100-249.

Bethany Care Center
5301 W 1st Ave, Lakewood CO
80226-2431.   303/2388333.
Employs: 100-249.

Boulder Manor Nursing Home
4685 Baseline Rd, Boulder CO
80303. 303/4940535. Employs:
100-249.

Camellia Care Center
500 Geneva St, Aurora CO 80010-
4305. 303/3649311. Employs: 100-
249.

Castle Garden Nursing Home
401 Malley Dr, Denver CO 80233-
2095. 303/4524700. Employs: 100-
249.

Cedars Health Center
1599 Ingalls St, Denver CO 80214-
1500. 303/2323551. Employs: 100-
249.

Cherrelyn Manor Hlth Care Ctr
5555 S Elati St, Littleton CO
80120-1624.   303/7988686.
Employs: 100-249.

Cherry Creek Nursing Center
14699 E Hampden Ave, Aurora CO
80014-3903.   303/6930111.
Employs: 100-249.

Cheyenne Mountain Nursing Ctr
835 Tenderfoot Hill Rd, Colorado
Springs   CO   80906-3903.
719/5768380. Employs: 100-249.

Cinnamon Park
1335 Cinnamon St, Longmont CO
80501-2748.   303/7722882.
Employs: 50-99.

Colorado Lutheran Health Care
7991 W 71st Ave, Arvada CO
80004-1828.   303/4225088.
Employs: 100-249.

Fairacres Manor Inc
1700 18th Ave, Greeley CO 80631-
5134. 303/3533370. Employs: 50-
99.

Foothills Care Center Inc
1440 Coffman St, Longmont CO
80501-2726.   303/7762814.
Employs: 100-249.

Glen Ayr Health Center
1655 Eaton St, Denver CO 80214-
1600. 303/2385363. Employs: 50-
99.

Golden West Nursing Home
1005 E Elizabeth St, Fort Collins
CO   80524-3911.   303/4822525.
Employs: 50-99.

Good Samaritan Health Care Ctr
2525 Taft Dr, Boulder CO 80302-
6800. 303/4496157. Employs: 100-
249.

Grandview Manor Health Care
855 Franklin Ave, Berthoud CO
80513. 303/5322683. Employs: 50-
99.

Homestead Group Home For Elderly
1734 Cambridge Dr, Longmont CO 80503-1703.   303/7720115.
Employs: 50-99.

Iliff Care Center
6060 E Iliff Ave, Denver CO 80222-5793.   303/7594221.
Employs: 50-99.

Julia Temple Center
3401 S Lafayette St, Englewood CO   80110-2926.   303/7610075.
Employs: 100-249.

Loveland   Good   Samaritan Village
2101 S Garfield Ave, Loveland CO 80537-7377.   303/6693100.
Employs: 50-99.

Mullen Home For The Aged
3629 W 29th Ave, Denver CO 80211-3601.   303/4337221.
Employs: 100-249.

Myron Stratton Home
2525 S Hwy 115, Colorado Springs CO   80906-3807.   719/5790930.
Employs: 100-249

North Shore Manor
1365 W 29th St, Loveland CO 80538-2561.   303/6676111.
Employs: 100-249.

Pikes Peak Manor
2719 N Union Blvd, Colorado Springs   CO   80909-1145. 719/6361676. Employs: 100-249.

Saint Paul Health Center
1667 St Paul St, Denver CO 80206-1614. 303/3992040. Employs: 100-249.

Sierra Vista Health Care Ctr
821 Duffield Ct, Loveland CO 80537-5228.   303/6690345.
Employs: 50-99.

Sunny Acres Villa Inc
2501 E 104th Ave, Denver CO 80233-4412.   303/4524181.
Employs: 100-249.

Sunshine Health Care Center
7150 Poplar St, Commerce City CO 80022-2147. 303/2897110.
Employs: 50-99.

Terrace Heights Care Center
2121 Mesa Dr, Boulder CO 80304-3621. 303/4424037. Employs: 100-249.

Villa Manor Care Center
7950   W   Mississippi   Ave, Lakewood   CO   80226-4392.
303/9864511. Employs: 100-249.

Western Hills Nursing Home
1625 Carr St, Lakewood CO 80215-3187.   303/2326881.
Employs: 100-249.

Westland Manor Nursing Home
1150 Oak St, Lakewood CO 80215-4408.   303/2387505.
Employs: 100-249.

Windsor Health Care Center
710 3rd St, Windsor CO 80550-5420. 303/6867473. Employs: 50-99.

INTERMEDIATE   CARE FACILITIES

Briarwood Health Care Center
1440 Vine St, Denver CO 80206-2099. 303/3990350. Employs: 100-249.

Country View Care Center
5425   Weld   County   Rd   32, Longmont   CO   80504.
303/4440489. Employs: 100-249.

Treemont Of Denver
10200 E Harvard Ave, Denver CO 80231-3957.   303/6960622.
Employs: 50-99.

Univ Hills Christian Living Campus
2480 S Clermont St, Denver CO 80222-6598. 303/7584528. Employs: 100-249.

MISC. NURSING AND PERSONAL CARE FACILITIES

Alzheimers Well At Brookside
225 W Brookside St, Colorado Springs CO 80906-2105. 719/5781200. Employs: 50-99.

Assisted Living Centers Of Co
17601 Junegrass Pl, Parker CO 80134-8921. 303/6991788. Employs: 50-99.

Autumn Heights Health Care Ctr
3131 S Federal Blvd, Englewood CO 80110. 303/7610260. Employs: 50-99.

Avista Hospice
90 Health Park Dr # 140, Louisville CO 80027-9586. 303/6653019. Employs: 50-99.

Bear Creek Nursing Center
150 Spring, Morrison CO 80465. 303/6978181. Employs: 50-99.

Boulder County Hospice
1510 9th Ave, Longmont CO 80501-4228. 303/6513922. Employs: 50-99.

Brentwood Care Center
1825 S Federal Blvd, Denver CO 80219-4905. 303/9354600. Employs: 50-99.

Care Group Of Colorado
1398 Zephyr St, Lakewood CO 80215-5029. 303/2324331. Employs: 50-99.

Cent Hlth Care Ctr An ARA Lvng
1637 29th Avenue Pl, Greeley CO 80631-4822. 303/3568181. Employs: 50-99.

Center Care Center
2025 E Egbert St, Brighton CO 80601-2517. 303/6594580. Employs: 50-99.

Cheyenne Manor
561 W 1 N, Cheyenne Wls CO 80810. 719/7675602. Employs: 50-99.

Columbine Care Center West
940 Worthington Cir, Fort Collins CO 80526-1840. 303/2212273. Employs: 50-99.

Denver Health Group
1200 17, Denver CO 80202. 303/5723300. Employs: 50-99.

Garden Terrace Alzheimers Ctr
1600 S Potomac St, Aurora CO 80012-5406. 303/7508418. Employs: 50-99.

Gray Cara West
3705 Carson Ave, Evans CO 80620-2501. 303/3305133. Employs: 50-99.

Heritage Haus
208 19 S E, Loveland CO 80537. 303/6695616. Employs: 50-99.

Heritage Park Manor
6005 S Holly St, Littleton CO 80121-3400. 303/7731000. Employs: 50-99.

Johnson Center Nursing Home
5000 E Arapahoe Rd # A, Littleton CO 80122-2302. 303/7795000. Employs: 50-99.

Lambda House Office
512 W Colorado Ave, Colorado Springs CO 80905-1511. 719/6357671. Employs: 50-99.

Life Care Center Of Longmont
2451 Pratt St, Longmont CO
80501-1123.   303/7765000.
Employs: 50-99.

Linc Community Hospital &
Nurse Home
323 7th St, Hugo CO 80821.
719/7432426. Employs: 50-99.

Manor Care Nursing Center
2800 Palo Pky, Boulder CO 80301-
1540. 303/4409100. Employs: 50-
99.

Medcath Inc
1050 Walnut St, Boulder CO
80302-5144.   303/4406768.
Employs: 50-99.

New Life Center
1819 Birch Ave, Greeley CO
80631-6142.   303/3530535.
Employs: 50-99.

Nursing Home Network
1665 Logan St, Denver CO 80203-
1277. 303/8395451. Employs: 50-
99.

Porter Home & Residential
Hospice
2525 S Downing St, Denver CO
80210-5817.   303/7785672.
Employs: 50-99.

Rose Hill Care Center
5230 E 66th Way, Commerce City
CO   80022-2442.   303/2891848.
Employs: 50-99.

Sable Care Center
656 Dillon Way, Aurora CO
80011-6803.   303/3440636.
Employs: 100-249.

Sandalwood Manor
3835 Harlan St, Wheat Ridge CO
80033-5111.   303/4221533.
Employs: 50-99.

Split Rail Manor

1109 Greenbriar Dr, Fort Collins
CO   80524-8509.   303/4846421.
Employs: 50-99.

Spring Creek Health Care Ctr
1000 E Stuart St, Fort Collins CO
80525-1555.   303/4825712.
Employs: 100-249.

Temenos House Inc
3113 Teller, Wheat Ridge CO
80033. 303/2332808. Employs: 50-
99.

The Courtyard
605 California Ave, Loveland CO
80537-5378.   303/6673342.
Employs: 50-99.

Timberline Lodge
9198 Jotipa Dr, Longmont CO
80503-9246.   303/7767215.
Employs: 50-99.

Valley Manor Health Care Ctr
4601 E Asbury Cir, Denver CO
80222-4798.   303/7571228.
Employs: 50-99.

Wheatridge Manro Nurse Home
2920 Fenton, Wheat Ridge CO
80033. 303/2380481. Employs: 50-
99.

Women S Christian Temperance
426 Terry St, Longmont CO
80501-5442.   303/7765673.
Employs: 50-99.

4 Seasons Hlth Care Ctr An ARA
1020 Patton St, Fort Collins CO
80524-4018.   303/4846133.
Employs: 50-99.

Long Term Health Care Service
Inc
304 S 8th St, Colorado Springs CO
80905-1829.   719/5789498.
Employs: 50-99.

Castle Rock Care Center
4001 Home St, Castle Rock CO
80104-2802.   303/6883174.
Employs: 50-99.

GENERAL MEDICAL AND SURGICAL HOSPITALS

Centennial Peaks Hospital
2255 S 88th St, Louisville CO
80027-9716.   303/6739990.
Employs: 100-249.

Cheyenne County Hosp
602 N 6th St, Cheyenne Wls CO
80810. 303/7675661. Employs: 50-
99.

Namaste Penrose Hosp Alzheimer
2 Penrose Blvd, Colorado Springs
CO   80906-4214.   719/4752000.
Employs: 50-99.

Saint Anthony Hospital North
2551 W 84th Ave, Westminster CO
80030-3807.   303/4262151.
Employs: 100-249.

Estes Park Medical Ctr
555 Prospect, Estes Park CO
80517. 303/5862317. Employs: 50-
99.

Rose Medical Ctr
4567 E 9th Ave, Denver CO
80220-3908.   303/3202121.
Employs: 100-249.

PSYCHIATRIC HOSPITALS

Charter Hospital Of Ft Collins
4601 Corbett Dr, Fort Collins CO
80525-9579.   303/2210200.
Employs: 100-249.

Cheyenne Mesa
1301 S 8th St, Colorado Springs
CO   80906-1340.   719/5201400.
Employs: 50-99.

SPECIALTY HOSPITALS, EXCEPT PSYCHIATRIC

AMC Cancer Research Center
1600 Pierce St, Denver CO 80214-
1433. 303/2336501. Employs: 100-
249.

Rocky Mountain Rehabilitation
900 Potomac St, Aurora CO 80011-
6716. 303/3671166. Employs: 100-
249.

MEDICAL LABORATORIES

Metpath Laboratories Inc
6116 E Warren Ave, Denver CO
80222-5703.   303/7582655.
Employs: 100-249.

Roman Labs Inc
7325 S Revere Pky Suite 234,
Englewood   CO   80112-3931.
303/3200416. Employs: 100-249.

HOME HEALTH CARE SERVICES

AMI Expercare Homecare Inc
950 S Cherry St Suite 304, Denver
CO   80222-2663.   303/7531929.
Employs: 50-99.

Boulder Home Health Services
310 S McCaslin Blvd, Louisville
CO   80027-9749.   303/6653022.
Employs: 50-99.

Lutheran Home Care Inc
3974 Youngfield St, Wheat Ridge
CO   80033-3865.   303/4241300.
Employs: 50-99.

Nursing Services Inc
55 Madison St Suite 200, Denver
CO   80206-5420.   303/3332255.
Employs: 100-249.

Pro Care Inc
1242 N Cleveland Ave, Loveland
CO 80537. 303/6692398. Employs:
50-99.

Professional Home Health Care
2905 Center Green Ct, Boulder CO
80301-2274.   303/4441981.
Employs: 50-99.

Professional Nursing Service
2490 W 26th Ave Suite 19-A,
Denver   CO   80211-5601.
303/4770431. Employs: 50-99.

RVNA Home Care
1500 11th Ave, Greeley CO 80631-
4730. 303/3525655. Employs: 50-
99.

Western Home Health
5460 Ward Rd Suite 220, Arvada
CO   80002-1818.   303/4240688.
Employs: 100-249.

Community Health Services
950 S Cherry St Ste 310, Denver
CO   80222-2663.   303/7531922.
Employs: 50-99.

Normedco Home Care
1801   16,   Greeley   CO   80631.
303/3506222. Employs: 50-99.

**SPECIALTY   OUTPATIENT
FACILITIES**

**Addiction Research & Treatment
Service**
3738 W Princeton Cir, Denver CO
80236-3110.   303/7616703.
Employs: 50-99.

Arapahoe House
3530 W Lehigh Ave, Denver CO
80236-6123.   303/7621550.
Employs: 100-249.

Arapahoe Mental Health Center
6801 S Yosemite St, Englewood
CO   80112-1411.   303/7799666.
Employs: 100-249.

**Barbara Davis Ctr Childhood
Diab**
4200 E 9th Av, Denver CO 80220-
3706. 303/3948796. Employs: 50-
99.

Foothills Gateway Rehab
301 Skyway Dr, Fort Collins CO
80525-3911.   303/2262345.
Employs: 50-99.

**Franklin Kaiser Special Care
Clnc**
1835 Franklin St, Denver CO
80218-1126.   303/8316700.
Employs: 100-249.

Intracorp
9250 E Costilla Ave Suite 350,
Englewood   CO   80112-3659.
303/7990500. Employs: 100-249.

**Jefferson   County   Chem
Dependence**
260 S Kipling St, Lakewood CO
80226-1099.   303/2377763.
Employs: 50-99.

Weld Mental Health Center Inc
1306 11th Ave, Greeley CO 80631-
3835. 303/3533686. Employs: 50-
99.

Humana Hosp Aurora
1501 S Potomac, Aurora CO
80012-5411.   303/6952600.
Employs: 100-249.

**MISC. HEALTH AND ALLIED
SERVICES**

Belle Bonfils Blood Center
4200 E 9th Ave, Denver CO
80220-3706.   303/3557366.
Employs: 100-249.

Oneday
PO Box 1032, Denver CO 80201-
1032. 303/7225133. Employs: 50-
99.

For more information on career opportunities in health care and pharmaceuticals:

Associations

ACCREDITING BUREAU OF HEALTH EDUCATION SCHOOLS
Oak Manor Office, 29089 US 20 West, Elkhart IN 46514. 219/293-0124.

AMERICAN ACADEMY OF FAMILY PHYSICIANS
8880 Ward Parkway, Kansas City MO 64114. 816/333-9700.

AMERICAN ACADEMY OF PHYSICIAN ASSISTANTS
950 North Washington Street, Alexandria VA 22314. 703/836-2272.

AMERICAN ASSOCIATION FOR CLINICAL CHEMISTRY
2029 K Street NW, 7th Floor, Washington DC 20006. 202/857-0717.

AMERICAN ASSOCIATION OF BLOOD BANKS
8101 Glenbrook Road, Bethesda MD 20814. 301/907-6977.

AMERICAN ASSOCIATION OF COLLEGES OF OSTEOPATHIC MEDICINE
6110 Executive Boulevard, Suite 405, Rockville MD 20852. 301/468-2037.

AMERICAN ASSOCIATION OF COLLEGES OF PHARMACY
1426 Prince Street, Alexandria VA 22314. 703/739-2330.

AMERICAN ASSOCIATION OF COLLEGES OF PODIATRIC MEDICINE
1350 Piccard Drive, Suite 322, Rockville MD 20850. 301/990-7400.

AMERICAN ASSOCIATION OF DENTAL SCHOOLS
1625 Massachusetts Avenue NW, Washington DC 20036. 202/667-9433.

AMERICAN ASSOCIATION OF HOMES FOR THE AGED
901 E Street NW, Suite 500, Washington DC 20004. 202/783-2242.

AMERICAN ASSOCIATION OF MEDICAL ASSISTANTS
20 North Wacker Drive, Suite 1575, Chicago IL 60606. 312/899-1500.

AMERICAN ASSOCIATION OF NURSE ANESTHETISTS
216 Higgins Road, Park Ridge IL 60068. 708/692-7050.

AMERICAN ASSOCIATION OF RESPIRATORY CARE
11030 Ables Lane, Dallas TX 75229-4593. 214/243-2272.

AMERICAN CHIROPRACTIC ASSOCIATION
1701 Clarendon Boulevard, Arlington VA 22209. 703/276-8800.

AMERICAN COLLEGE OF HEALTHCARE ADMINISTRATORS
325 South Patrick Street, Alexandria VA 22314. 703/549-5822.

AMERICAN COLLEGE OF HEALTHCARE EXECUTIVES
840 North Lake Shore Drive, Chicago IL 60611. 312/943-0544.

AMERICAN COUNCIL ON PHARMACEUTICAL EDUCATION
311 West Superior Street, Chicago IL 60610. 312/664-3575.

AMERICAN DENTAL ASSOCIATION
211 East Chicago Avenue, Chicago IL 60611. 312/440-2500.

AMERICAN DENTAL HYGIENISTS ASSOCIATION
Division of Professional Development, 444 North Michigan Avenue, Suite 3400, Chicago IL 60611. 312/440-8900.

AMERICAN DIETETIC ASSOCIATION
216 West Jackson Street, Chicago IL 60606. 312/899-0040.

AMERICAN HEALTH CARE ASSOCIATION
1201 L Street NW, Washington DC 20005. 202/842-4444.

AMERICAN HOSPITAL ASSOCIATION
840 North Lake Shore Drive, Chicago IL 60611. 312/280-6000.

AMERICAN MEDICAL ASSOCIATION
515 North State Street, Chicago IL 60605. 312/464-5000.

AMERICAN HEALTH INFORMATION MANAGEMENT ASSOCIATION
919 North Michigan Avenue, Suite 1400, Chicago IL 60611. 312/787-2672.

AMERICAN MEDICAL TECHNOLOGISTS
Registered Medical Assistants, 710 Higgins Road, Park Ridge IL 60068. 708/823-5169.

AMERICAN NURSES ASSOCIATION
600 Maryland Avenue SW, Suite 100W, Washington DC 20024. 202/554-4444.

AMERICAN OCCUPATIONAL THERAPY ASSOCIATION
1383 Piccard Drive, P.O. Box 1725, Rockville MD 20849-1725. 301/948-9626.

AMERICAN OPTOMETRIC ASSOCIATION
243 North Lindbergh Boulevard, St. Louis MO 63141. 314/991-4100.

AMERICAN PHARMACEUTICAL ASSOCIATION
2215 Constitution Avenue NW, Washington DC 20037. 202/628-4410.

AMERICAN PHYSICAL THERAPY ASSOCIATION
1111 North Fairfax Street, Alexandria VA 22314. 703/684-2782.

AMERICAN SOCIETY FOR BIOCHEMISTRY AND MOLECULAR BIOLOGY
9650 Rockville Pike, Bethesda MD 20814. 301/530-7145.

AMERICAN SOCIETY OF HOSPITAL PHARMACISTS
4630 Montgomery Avenue, Bethesda MD 20814. 301/657-3000.

AMERICAN VETERINARY MEDICAL ASSOCIATION
1931 North Meacham Road, Suite 100, Schaumburg IL 60173-4360. 708/925-8070.

CARDIOVASCULAR CREDENTIALING INTERNATIONAL
P.O. Box 611, Dayton OH 45419.
513/294-5225.

MEDICAL GROUP MANAGEMENT ASSOCIATION
104 Invernes Terrace E, Englewood CO 80112. 303/799-1111.

NATIONAL ASSOCIATION OF PHARMACEUTICAL MANUFACTURERS
747 Third Avenue, New York NY 10017. 212/838-3720.

NATIONAL ASSOCIATION OF PRIVATE PSYCHIATRIC HOSPITALS
1319 F Street NW, Washington DC 20004. 202/393-6700.

NATIONAL HEALTH COUNCIL
1730 M Street NW, Suite 500, Washington DC 20036. 202/785-3910.

NATIONAL MEDICAL ASSOCIATION
1012 Tenth Street NW, Washington DC 20001. 202/347-1895.

NATIONAL PHARMACEUTICAL COUNCIL
1894 Preston White Drive, Reston VA 22091. 703/620-6390.

Directories

BLUE BOOK DIGEST OF HMOs
National Association of Employers on Health Care Alternatives, P.O. Box 220, Key Biscayne FL 33149. 305/361-2810.

DRUG TOPICS RED BOOK
Medical Economics Co., P.O. Box 1935, Marion OH 43306-4035. 201/358-7200.

ENCYCLOPEDIA OF MEDICAL ORGANIZATIONS AND AGENCIES
Gale Research Inc., 835 Penobscot Building, Detroit MI 48226. 313/961-2242.

HEALTH ORGANIZATIONS OF THE UNITED STATES, CANADA, AND THE WORLD
Gale Research Inc., 835 Penobscot Building, Detroit MI 48226. 313/961-2242.

MEDICAL AND HEALTH INFORMATION DIRECTORY
Gale Research Inc., 835 Penobscot Building, Detroit MI 48226. 313/961-2242.

NATIONAL DIRECTORY OF HEALTH MAINTENANCE ORGANIZATIONS
Group Health Association of America, 1129 20th Street NW, Washington DC 20036. 202/778-3200.

Magazines

AMERICAN MEDICAL NEWS
American Medical Association, 515 North State Street, Chicago IL 60605. 312/464-5000.

CHANGING MEDICAL MARKETS
Theta Corporation, Theta Building, Middlefield CT 06455. 203/349-1054.

DRUG TOPICS
Medical Economics Co., 5 Paragon Drive, Montvale NJ 07645. 201/358-7200.

HEALTH CARE EXECUTIVE
American College of Health Care Executives, 840 North Lake Shore Drive, Chicago IL 60611. 312/943-0544.

MODERN HEALTHCARE
Crain Communications, 740 North Rush Street, Chicago IL 60611. 312/649-5374.

PHARMACEUTICAL ENGINEERING
International Society of Pharmaceutical Engineers, 3816 W. Linebaugh Avenue, Suite 412, Tampa FL 33624. 813/960-2105.

HOSPITALITY: HOTELS AND RESTAURANTS

In the restaurant segment, the fastest-growing sector of the market continues to be fast-food-style establishments, although increased public concern has led industry leaders to develop new products and marketing strategies. McDonald's has released its lower-fat "McLean Deluxe", and Kentucky Fried Chicken has changed its name to "KFC" to de-emphasize the word "Fried". The take-out trend, spurred by changing demographics and eating habits, is changing the industry as a whole, not just at the fast-food end.

Managerial prospects are better than average, but the industry is hampered by a shortage of entry-level workers. The hotel industry is tied closely to other segments of the travel industry, which in turn relies on the U.S. economy as a whole. International arrivals are the fastest-growing segment of the travel industry, so hotels in major American international destinations are better positioned. Look for greater specialization within the industry, with specific companies advertising as "budget", "luxury", or "corporate/meeting", for example. Hotels will also need to respond to the growing number of working couples who take shorter vacations together.

AIRCOA HOLDINGS INCORPORATED
4600 S Ulster Street, Suite 1200, Denver CO 80237. 303/220-2000. **Contact:** Bill Clifford, Senior VP/Chief Administrative Officer. **Description:** A Denver company involved in hotel management and ownership.

BEST WESTERN COURTYARD PINES
4411 Peoria Street, Denver CO 80239. 303/373-5730. **Contact:** Ginna Schlender. **Description:** A Denver hotel, owned by the Hilton Hotels Corporation. **Corporate headquarters:** Beverly Hills, CA.

THE BROWN PALACE HOTEL
321 17th Street, Denver CO 80202. 303/297-3111. **Contact:** Katey June, Employment Specialist. **Description:** An historic hotel. **Common positions:** Hotel Manager/Assistant Manager; Pastry Cook; Maitre d'Hotel; Restaurant Manager; Rooms Manager; Hotel Sales Manager. All positions require experience in four-or-five-star property. **Educational backgrounds sought:** Hospitality. **Special programs:** Internships. **Benefits:** medical insurance; dental insurance; pension plan; life insurance; tuition assistance; disability coverage; employee discounts; meals. **Corporate headquarters:** Dallas, TX. **Parent company:** Rank Hotels of North America.

CLARION HARVEST HOUSE
1345 28th Street, Boulder CO 80302. 303/443-3850, ext. 569. **Contact:** Judy Malloy, Human Resources Director. **Description:** A Boulder hotel owned by the Hilton Hotels Corporation. **Common positions:** Accountant; Administrator; Hotel Manager/Assistant Manager; General Manager; Personnel and Labor Relations Specialist; Purchasing Agent; Sales Representative. **Educational backgrounds sought:** Accounting; Business Administration; Communications; Engineering; Finance; Marketing; Mathematics. **Special programs:** Training programs; internships. **Benefits:** medical, dental, and life insurance; disability coverage; employee discounts; retirement plan. **Corporate headquarters:** Denver, CO. **Parent company:** Aircoa. **Operations at this facility:** regional headquarters; divisional headquarters; administration; service; sales.

EMBASSY SUITES HOTEL
4444 North Havana, Denver CO 80239. 303/375-0400. **Contact:** Personnel Department. **Description:** A national chain of hotels.

EXECUTIVE TOWER INN
1405 Curtis Street, Denver CO 80202. 303/571-0300. **Contact:** John Mercill, Controller. **Description:** A Denver hotel.

HOLIDAY INN
DENVER NORTH
4849 Bannock, Denver CO 80216-1813. 303/292-9500. **Contact:** Stella L. Nau, Controller. **Description:** A Denver hotel.

HOLIDAY INN
3200 South Parker, Aurora CO 80014. 303/695-1700. **Contact:** Personnel Department. **Description:** A Denver-area hotel.

HOTEL DENVER DOWNTOWN
1450 Glenarm Place, Denver CO 80202. 303/573-1450, ext. 7443. **Contact:** Carlene Goldthwaite, Director of Human Resources. **Description:** A Denver hotel. **Common positions:** Blue-Collar Worker Supervisor; Customer Service Representative; Hotel Manager/Assistant Manager; Department Manager; General Manager; Marketing Specialist; Personnel and Labor Relations Specialist; Sales Representative. **Educational backgrounds sought:** Accounting; Communications; Finance; Liberal Arts; Marketing. **Special programs:** Training programs. **Benefits:** medical insurance; dental insurance; life insurance; disability coverage; employee discounts. **Corporate**

headquarters: Dallas, TX. **Operations at this facility:** service; administration; sales.

OMNIVEST INTERNATIONAL
1401 17th Street, Suite 2800, Denver CO 80202. 303/850-7231. **Contact:** Jim Russo, President. **Description:** A local franchise of the national chain of quick-steak restaurants.

RADISSON HOTEL/DENVER
1550 Court Place, Denver CO 80202. 303/893-3333, ext. 6800. **Contact:** Human Resources Department. **Description:** A convention hotel located in downtown Denver. Managed by Ash & Associates Inc. **Common positions:** Accountant; Blue-Collar Worker Supervisor; Credit Manager; Customer Service Representative; Electrical Engineer; Mechanical Engineer; Hotel Manager/Assistant Manager; Personnel and Labor Relations Specialist; Purchasing Agent; Sales Representative; Hotel and Food Service Workers. **Educational backgrounds sought:** Accounting; Business Administration; Communications; Liberal Arts; Hotel and Restaurant Management. **Benefits:** medical insurance; dental insurance; life insurance; pension plan, 401K; disability coverage; employee discounts; tuition assistance; daycare assistance; savings plan. **Corporate headquarters:** Minneapolis, MN. **Operations at this facility:** service. 275+ locations worldwide. **Employees:** 375. **Projected hires for the next 12 months:** 250.

RED LION HOTEL/DENVER
3203 Quebec Street, Denver CO 80207. 303/321-3333. **Contact:** Jeannie Pershin, Personnel Director. **Description:** An area hotel.

RICHFIELD HOTEL MANAGEMENT
4600 South Ulster Street, Suite 1200, Denver CO 80237. 303/220-2000. **Contact:** Bill Clifford, Vice President of Human Resources. **Description:** An owner and operator of hotel and resort facilities.

SHERATON DENVER AIRPORT HOTEL
3535 Quebec Street, Denver CO 80207. 303/333-7711. **Contact:** department of interest. **Description:** A Denver hotel. **Common positions:** Accountant; Industrial Engineer; Mechanical Engineer; General Manager; Personnel and Labor Relations Specialist; Sales Representative; Food/Beverage Management. **Educational backgrounds sought:** Accounting; Business Administration; Engineering; Hotel/Restaurant Management. **Benefits:** medical insurance; dental insurance; pension plan; life insurance; tuition assistance; disability coverage; employee discounts; savings plan. **Corporate headquarters:** Boston MA. A subsidiary of ITT. **Operations at this facility:** service. **Listed on:** New York Stock Exchange.

SHERATON DENVER TECH CENTER
4900 DTC Parkway, Denver CO 80237. 303/779-1100. **Contact:** Cindy Gruel, Personnel Director. **Description:** A Denver hotel. **Common positions:** Accountant; Administrator; Buyer; Credit Manager; Hotel Manager/Assistant Manager; Department Manager; Sales Representative; Entry Level Rooms Department positions; Food and beverage positions. **Educational backgrounds sought:** Accounting; Business Administration; Hotel/Motel; Food and

Beverage. **Benefits:** medical insurance; life insurance; tuition assistance; use of hotels at no charge. **Corporate headquarters:** Denver, CO. **Parent company:** AIRCOA. **Operations at this facility:** service

STAPLETON PLAZA HOTEL
3333 Quebec Street, Denver CO 80207. 303/321-3500, ext. 6601. **Contact:** Jeff Sullivan, Human Resources Manager. **Description:** An airport area hotel. **Common positions:** Credit Manager; Customer Service Representative; Hotel Manager/Assistant Manager; Department Manager; Sales Representative. **Benefits:** medical, dental, and life insurance; employee discounts. **Corporate headquarters:** Portland, OR. **Parent company:** Harsch Investment. **Operations at this facility:** administration; service; sale.

VENTURE MANAGEMENT INC.
1421 Oneida Street, Denver CO 80220. 303/320-0757. **Contact:** Ed Novak, President. **Description:** A restaurant management company. **Corporate headquarters:** This location.

VICORP RESTAURANTS INC.
400 West 48th Avenue, Denver CO 80216. 303/296-2121. **Contact:** Julie Cunningham, Personnel. **Description:** Corporate headquarters of Village Inn, a nationally known restaurant chain.

WENDY'S INTERNATIONAL
5250 Leetsdale Drive, Suite 110, Denver CO 80222. 303/393-0670. **Contact:** Human Resources. **Description:** Regional office of the well-known fast-food restaurant chain.

Additional large employers: 250+

EATING PLACES

Casa Bonita Restaurant
6715 W Colfax Ave, Denver CO 80214-1807. 303/2325115. Employs: 250-499.

Concession Air
Stapleton Airport Suite 3159, Denver CO 80207. 303/3983766. Employs: 250-499.

Jamco Ltd
5100 Race Ct, Denver CO 80216-2135. 303/2923070. Employs: 250-499.

Le Peep Restaurants Inc
4 W Dry Creek Circle, Littleton CO 80120-4413. 303/7306300. Employs: 250-499.

Stouffer Concourse Hotel
3801 Quebec St, Denver CO 80207. 303/3997500. Employs: 250-499.

Taco Bell
1607 S Havana St, Aurora CO 80012-5007. 303/7453978. Employs: 500-999.

HOTELS AND MOTELS

Cheyenne Mt Conference Resort
3225 Broadmoor Valley Rd, Colorado Springs CO 80906-4455. 7195764600. Employs: 500-999.

Denver Marriott Southeast
6363 E Hampden Ave, Denver CO
80222-7602.   303/7587000.
Employs: 250-499.

Denver West Marriott
1717 Denver West Blvd, Golden
CO   80401-3144.   303/2799100.
Employs: 250-499.

Executive Tower Inn
1405 Curtis St, Denver CO 80202-
2349. 303/5710300. Employs: 250-
499.

**Hyatt   Regency   Denver
Downtown**
1750 Welton St, Denver CO
80202-3940.   303/2951200.
Employs: 250-499.

Inn At Silver Creek
62927 US Hwy 40, Granby CO
80446-9322.   303/8872131.
Employs: 250-499.

Marriott City Center
1701 California St, Denver CO
80202-3402.   303/2971300.
Employs: 250-499.

Marriott Hotels & Resorts
5580 Tech Center Dr, Colorado
Springs   CO   80919-2308.
7192601800. Employs: 250-499.

Red Lion Inn
1775 E Cheyenne Mntn Blvdd,
Colorado Springs CO 80906-4030.
7195768900. Employs: 250-499.

Regency Hotel
3203 Quebec St, Denver CO
80207-2319.   303/3213333.
Employs: 250-499.

Sheraton Hotel
2886 S Circle Dr, Colorado Springs
CO   80906-4111.   7195765900.
Employs: 250-499.

The Broadmoor Hotel
1 Lake Ave, Colorado Springs CO
80906-3616.   7196347711.
Employs: 500-999.

Additional small to medium sized employers: 50-249

EATING PLACES

Applebees Neighborhood Grill
3301 S Tamarac Dr, Denver CO
80231-4305.   303/7553085.
Employs: 50-99.

ARA Food Service
4915 Pontiac St, Commerce City
CO   80022-4709.   303/2881521.
Employs: 50-99.

Armadillo Club
111 1st St, La Salle CO 80645.
303/2845565. Employs: 50-99.

Bennigan's
7425 W Alameda Ave, Lakewood
CO   80226-3204.   303/2335090.
Employs: 50-99.

Bennigan's
2710 S Havana St, Aurora CO
80014-2618.   303/7507822.
Employs: 50-99.

Bennigan's
9281 E Arapahoe Rd, Englewood
CO   80112-3620.   303/7920280.
Employs: 100-249.

Bennigan's
1699 S Colorado Blvd Suite 1,
Denver   CO   80222-4036.
303/7530272. Employs: 100-249.

Blue Parrot
640 Main St, Louisville CO 80027-1828. 303/6669994. Employs: 50-99.

Boulder's Dinner Theatre
5501 Arapahoe Ave, Boulder CO 80303-1334. 303/4496000. Employs: 50-99.

Burger King
2726 10th St, Greeley CO 80631-3423. 303/3531596. Employs: 50-99.

Burger King
6801 W 120th Ave, Broomfield CO 80020-2331. 303/4697744. Employs: 50-99.

Burger King
1717 W 38th Ave, Denver CO 80211-2222. 303/4551545. Employs: 50-99.

Burger King
2934 E Fountain Blvd Suite B, Colorado Springs CO 80910-2315. 719/4750555. Employs: 100-249.

Caliente
7293 E Hampden Av, Denver CO 80224-3015. 303/3370937. Employs: 50-99.

Chi Chis Mexican Restaurant
2155 Academy Pl, Colorado Springs CO 80909-1685. 719/5978806. Employs: 100-249.

Chicago Joes
775 W Bijou St, Colorado Springs CO 80905-1314. 719/6335637. Employs: 100-249.

Chilis Grill & Bar
3240 Youngfield St, Wheat Ridge CO 80033-5243. 303/2384229. Employs: 50-99.

Chilis Hamburger Grill & Bar

14197 E Exposition Ave, Aurora CO 80012-2523. 303/3646668. Employs: 50-99.

Colacci's Restaurant
816 Main St, Louisville CO 80027-1832. 303/6739400. Employs: 50-99.

Coopersmith Brewing Co
5 Old Town Sq, Fort Collins CO 80524-2466. 303/4980483. Employs: 50-99.

Crestwood Restaurant
819 W Littleton Blvd, Littleton CO 80120-2301. 303/7955500. Employs: 100-249.

Dennys Restaurant
9930 W 49th Ave, Wheat Ridge CO 80033-2281. 303/4230716. Employs: 50-99.

Dominos Pizza
11098 W Jewell Ave, Lakewood CO 80232-6123. 303/9884795. Employs: 100-249.

Duggans
5151 S Federal Blvd, Littleton CO 80123-7780. 303/7951081. Employs: 100-249.

El Rancho Restaurant
El Rancho Postal, Golden CO 80401. 303/5260661. Employs: 50-99.

Family Restaurants Inc
5000 S Quebec St Suite 640, Denver CO 80237-2705. 303/7739898. Employs: 100-249.

Farmers Wings
2265 W 84th Ave, Westminster CO 80030. 303/4269464. Employs: 50-99.

Fresh Fish Company
7800 E Hampden Ave, Denver CO 80231-4862.   303/7409556.
Employs: 100-249.

Gemini Restaurant
4300 Wadsworth Blvd, Wheat Ridge   CO   80033-4622.
303/4214990. Employs: 100-249.

Golden Buff Restaurant
1725 28th St, Boulder CO 80301-1003. 303/4422800. Employs: 50-99.

Greenstreets Restaurant
505 Popes Bluff Tr, Colorado Springs   CO   80907-3509.
719/5997727. Employs: 50-99.

Grisantis Restaurant
11951 E Iliff Ave, Aurora CO 80014-4925.   303/7458822.
Employs: 50-99.

Grisantis Restaurant
7920 Wadsworth Blvd, Arvada CO 80003-2110.   303/4244227.
Employs: 100-249.

H Brinkers
7209 S Clinton St, Englewood CO 80112-3614.   303/7920285.
Employs: 100-249.

Hardees Restaurant
1340 N Cleveland Ave, Loveland CO 80537. 303/6692922. Employs: 50-99.

Harvest Express
2006 Broadway St, Boulder CO 80302-5255.   303/4496225.
Employs: 100-249.

Harvest Restaurant & Bakery
430 S Colorado Blvd, Denver CO 80222-1207.   303/3996652.
Employs: 100-249.

Holly Inn General Offices

6000 E Evans Ave Suite 260, Denver   CO   80222-5406.
303/7568361. Employs: 100-249.

King Soopers
4271 S Buckley Rd, Aurora CO 80013-2952.   303/6808690.
Employs: 100-249.

KM Concessions Inc
Train Station Cty Pk, Denver CO 80203. 303/3212760. Employs: 50-99.

Last American Diner
1955 28th St, Boulder CO 80301-1101. 303/4471997. Employs: 50-99.

Marie Callenders Restaurant
3535 S Yosemite St, Denver CO 80237-1806.   303/7790216.
Employs: 100-249.

Marriott In Flight Services
8000 Smith Rd, Denver CO 80207-1721. 303/3985460. Employs: 100-249.

McDonald's
595 US Hwy 287, Broomfield CO 80020-1731.   303/4669764.
Employs: 50-99.

McDonald's Restaurants
3000 Youngfield St Suite 320, Lakewood   CO   80215-6552.
303/2323390. Employs: 100-249.

McDonald's Restaurants
450 Hwy 105, Monument CO 80132-9125.   719/4880044.
Employs: 50-99.

McDonald's Restaurants
5550 W Dartmouth Ave, Littleton CO 80127. 303/9860814. Employs: 50-99.

McDonald's Restaurants
1800 28th St, Boulder CO 80301-
1004. 303/4434700. Employs: 50-
99.

McDonald's Restaurants
3994 E 120th Ave, Denver CO
80233-1606.   303/4500428.
Employs: 50-99.

McDonald's Restaurants
501 Big Thompson Ave, Estes Park
CO 80517. 303/5863434. Employs:
50-99.

McDonald's Restaurants
1809   W   Eisenhower   Blvd,
Loveland   CO   80537-3132.
303/6694211. Employs: 50-99.

Mr Steak Inc
7400 E Caley Ave, Englewood CO
80111-6711.   303/8507231.
Employs: 100-249.

Ogden Allied Arena Club
1635 Clay St, Denver CO 80204-
1799. 303/8932582. Employs: 100-
249.

Old Chicago Restaurant
1102 Pearl St, Boulder CO 80302-
5112. 303/4435031. Employs: 50-
99.

Old Spaghetti Factory
1215 18th St, Denver CO 80202-
1401. 303/2951864. Employs: 100-
249.

Perkins Restaurants
2222   W   Eisenhower   Blvd,
Loveland   CO   80537-3148.
303/6631944. Employs: 50-99.

Polo Club Bar & Grill
7290   Commerce   Center   Dr,
Colorado Springs CO 80919-2629.
719/5999100. Employs: 100-249.

Racines Restaurant

850   Bannock   St,   Denver   CO
80204-4026.   303/5950418.
Employs: 100-249.

Rossmoor Inc
120 Plaza Del Sol Ter, Colorado
Springs   CO   80907-8127.
719/5985457. Employs: 50-99.

Simms Landing
11911 W 6th Ave, Golden CO
80401-4705.   303/2370465.
Employs: 100-249.

Sizzler Buffet Court & Grill
7900 W Quincy Ave, Littleton CO
80123-1350.   303/9720806.
Employs: 50-99.

**Sizzler   Steak   &   Seafood
Restaurant**
7995 Sheridan Blvd, Arvada CO
80003-2653.   303/4288495.
Employs: 50-99.

Sky Chef Flight Kitchens
8650 Smith Rd, Denver CO 80207-
1727. 303/3985382. Employs: 100-
249.

Strings
1700 Humboldt St, Denver CO
80218-1109.   303/8317310.
Employs: 50-99.

Stuart Andersons Black Angus
3000 S Havana St, Aurora CO
80014-2621.   303/7515985.
Employs: 50-99.

Taco Bell
2401 8th Ave Suite 222, Greeley
CO   80631-7034.   303/3565341.
Employs: 50-99.

The Black Eyed Pea
7095 W 88th Ave, Broomfield CO
80021-6401.   303/4254442.
Employs: 50-99.

The Boulder Theatre
2032 14th St, Boulder CO 80302-5303. 303/4443600. Employs: 100-249.

The Chili Pepper
2150 Bryant St, Denver CO 80211-5117. 303/4338406. Employs: 50-99.

The Fort
19192 Highway 8, Morrison CO 80465-8731.   303/6974771. Employs: 50-99.

The Sandwich Board
5445 Dtc Pky, Englewood CO 80111-3045.   303/7739537. Employs: 50-99.

Three Thieves Steak House
1020 E Fillmore St, Colorado Springs   CO   80907-6317. 719/6347908. Employs: 50-99.

Village Inn Pancake House
535 Garden Of The Gds Rd, Colorado Springs CO 80907. 719/5985331. Employs: 50-99.

Village Inn Pancake House
247 Wolfenberger Rd, Castle Rock CO 80104-1564. 303/6883200. Employs: 50-99.

Village Inn Pancake House
222 Columbine St, Denver CO 80206-4723.   303/3991748. Employs: 50-99.

Village Inn Pancake House
15200 E Iliff Ave, Aurora CO 80014-4516.   303/7508288. Employs: 50-99.

Wellshire Inn Inc
3333 S Colorado Blvd, Denver CO 80222-6603.   303/7593333. Employs: 100-249.

Wendys   Old   Fashioned Hambrgrs

1555 S Nevada Ave, Colorado Springs   CO   80906-2219. 719/6302295. Employs: 100-249.

Wendys Old Fashioned Hmbrgrs
132 W Mountain Ave Suite 150, Fort Collins CO 80524-2823. 303/2210345. Employs: 50-99.

Western Restaurant Systems Inc
410 S 8th St Suite E, Colorado Springs   CO   80905-1822. 719/6357262. Employs: 100-249.

Western Sizzlin Steak House
221 S 8th St, Colorado Springs CO 80905-1630.   719/6338000. Employs: 50-99.

White Fence Farm
6263 W Jewell Ave, Lakewood CO 80232-7113.   303/9355945. Employs: 50-99.

Jackson Ice Cream Co
400 Yuma St, Denver CO 80204-4820. 303/5341922. Employs: 50-99.

McDonalds Restaurant
10950 S Parker Rd, Parker CO 80134-7440.   303/8418214. Employs: 50-99.

Holiday Inn-Greeley
609 8th Ave, Greeley CO 80631-3915. 303/3563000. Employs: 50-99.

DRINKING PLACES

Baby Does Matchless Mine Inc
2520 W 23rd Ave, Denver CO 80211-4808.   303/4333386. Employs: 100-249.

Bennigans
2203 S College Ave, Fort Collins CO 80525-1418. 303/4847974. Employs: 100-249.

Brittany Hill
9350 Grant St, Denver CO 80229-4325. 303/4519035. Employs: 100-249.

Charco Broiler
1716 E Mulberry St, Fort Collins CO 80524-3524. 303/4821472. Employs: 50-99.

Chilis Grill & Bar
2070 E County Line Rd, Littleton CO 80126-2403. 303/7970681. Employs: 50-99.

Chilis Grill & Bar
5807 N Academy Blvd, Colorado Springs CO 80918-3414. 719/2601788. Employs: 50-99.

Chilis Hamburger Grill & Bar
8450 W Cross Dr, Littleton CO 80123-2209. 303/9735863. Employs: 50-99.

Chilis Hamburger Grill & Bar
7475 W 88th Ave, Westminster CO 80030. 303/4672218. Employs: 50-99.

Embassy Suites Hotel
10250 E Costilla Ave, Englewood CO 80112-3716. 303/7920433. Employs: 50-99.

Hooters Restaurant
1390 S Colorado Blvd, Denver CO 80222-3302. 303/7820232. Employs: 50-99.

Jacksons Hole & Saloon
10001 Grant St, Denver CO 80229-2000. 303/4572100. Employs: 50-99.

Jose Muldoons
222 N Tejon St, Colorado Springs CO 80903-1314. 719/6362311. Employs: 50-99.

Jose Osheas

385 Union Blvd, Lakewood CO 80228-1502. 303/9887333. Employs: 100-249.

Peppermill Restaurant
5959 S Willow Way, Englewood CO 80111-5119. 303/7411626. Employs: 100-249.

Red Lobster
2885 23rd Ave, Greeley CO 80631-7957. 303/3306200. Employs: 50-99.

Red Lobster Inn
264 Union Blvd, Lakewood CO 80228-1806. 303/9873789. Employs: 50-99.

Red Robin Burger & Spirits
1410 Jamboree Dr, Colorado Springs CO 80920-3942. 719/5982473. Employs: 50-99.

The Armadillo
3161 Walnut St, Boulder CO 80301-2511. 303/4434292. Employs: 50-99.

West End Tavern
926 Pearl St, Boulder CO 80302-5109. 303/4443535. Employs: 50-99.

Writers Manor
1730 S Colorado Blvd, Denver CO 80222-4001. 303/7568877. Employs: 100-249.

Econo-Lodge Burlington
450 S Lincoln St, Burlington CO 80807-2107. 719/3465555. Employs: 100-249.

HOTELS AND MOTELS

Aircoa Hotel Partners L P
4600 S Ulster St, Denver CO 80237-2870. 303/2202000. Employs: 100-249.

Airport Denver Plaza
7201 E 49th Av, Commerce City CO 80022-4714. 303/2877548. Employs: 50-99.

American Motel
10101 I 70 Frontage Rd N, Wheat Ridge CO 80033-2228. 303/4227200. Employs: 50-99.

Best Western Landmark Inn
455 S Colorado Blvd, Denver CO 80222-8002. 303/3885561. Employs: 50-99.

Best Western Palmer House
3010 N Chestnut St, Colorado Springs CO 80907-5010. 719/6365201. Employs: 50-99.

Best Western Ramkota Inn
701 8th St, Greeley CO 80631-3956. 303/3538444. Employs: 100-249.

Broker Inn Hotel
555 30th St, Boulder CO 80303-2309. 303/4443330. Employs: 100-249.

Burnsley Hotel
1000 Grant St, Denver CO 80203-2910. 303/8301000. Employs: 50-99.

Cherry Creek Inn
600 S Colorado Blvd, Denver CO 80222-1503. 303/7573341. Employs: 100-249.

Clarion Hotel
7770 S Peoria St, Englewood CO 80112-4138. 303/7907770. Employs: 50-99.

Coast To Coast Resorts
64 Inverness Dr E, Englewood CO 80112-5101. 303/7902267. Employs: 50-99.

Colorado Springs Hilton Inn
505 Popes Bluff Trl, Colorado Springs CO 80907-3509. 719/5994550. Employs: 50-99.

Denver Airport Hilton Inn
4411 Peoria St, Denver CO 80239-4817. 303/3735730. Employs: 100-249.

Doubletree Hotel
13696 E Iliff Ave, Aurora CO 80014-1319. 303/3372800. Employs: 100-249.

Embassy Suites Hotel
1881 Curtis St, Denver CO 80202-1902. 303/2978888. Employs: 50-99.

Embassy Suites Hotel
7525 E Hampden Ave, Denver CO 80231-4804. 303/6966644. Employs: 50-99.

Fort Collins Marriott Hotel
350 E Horsetooth Rd, Fort Collins CO 80525-3130. 303/2265200. Employs: 100-249.

Hilton Inn South
7801 E Orchard Rd, Englewood CO 80111-2508. 303/7796161. Employs: 100-249.

Holiday Inn
4040 Quebec St, Denver CO 80216-6619. 303/3216666. Employs: 50-99.

Holiday Inn
1975 Bryant St, Denver CO 80204-1718. 303/4338331. Employs: 50-99.

Holiday Inn
15500 E 40th Ave, Denver CO 80239-5701. 303/3719494. Employs: 100-249.

Holiday Inn Downtown
1450 Glenarm Pl, Denver CO
80202-5019.   303/5731450.
Employs: 100-249.

Holiday Inn Lakewood
7390 W Hampden Ave, Denver CO
80227-5127.   303/9809200.
Employs: 100-249.

Holiday Inn North
3125 Sinton Rd, Colorado Springs
CO   80907-5076.   719/6335541.
Employs: 50-99.

Holiday Inn Northglenn
10 E 120th Ave, Denver CO
80233-1002.   303/4524100.
Employs: 100-249.

Holiday Inn Of Estes Park
101 S St Vrain Ave, Estes Park CO
80517.   303/5344775.   Employs:
100-249.

Hotel Boulderado
2115 13th St, Boulder CO 80302-
4801. 303/4424344. Employs: 100-
249.

Hyatt Regency Technical Center
7800 E Tufts Ave, Denver CO
80237-3001.   303/7791234.
Employs: 100-249.

Loews Giorgio Hotel
4150 E Mississippi Ave, Denver
CO   80222-3045.   303/7829300.
Employs: 100-249.

Marriott Hotel Inc
4710 Pearl East Cir, Boulder CO
80301-2472.   303/4404700.
Employs: 50-99.

Quality Inn North Of Denver
110 W 104th Ave, Denver CO
80234-4102.   303/4511234.
Employs: 100-249.

Raintree Inn

314 W Bijou St, Colorado Springs
CO   80905-1307.   719/4718680.
Employs: 100-249.

Ramada Inn
8773 Yates Dr, Westminster CO
80030-3678.   303/4274000.
Employs: 100-249.

Sheraton Inn
360 Union Blvd, Lakewood CO
80228-1503.   303/9872000.
Employs: 100-249.

The Ailines Airport Hotel
6090 Smith Rd, Denver CO 80216-
4630. 303/3884051. Employs: 100-
249.

The Comfort Inn
401 17th St, Denver CO 80202-
4005. 303/2960400. Employs: 50-
99.

University Park Holiday Inn
425 W Prospect Rd, Fort Collins
CO   80526-2064.   303/4822626.
Employs: 100-249.

Westin Hotel
1672 Lawrence St, Denver CO
80202-2010.   303/5729100.
Employs: 100-249.

Allaire Timbers Inn
9511 Hwy 9/S Main, Breckenridge
CO 80424. 303/4537530. Employs:
50-99.

Classic Inn
540 Silverthorne Ln, Silverthorne
CO 80498. 303/4680800. Employs:
50-99.

High Country Lodge & Breakfast
5064 Ski Hill Rd, Breckenridge CO
80424. 303/4539843. Employs: 50-
99.

Luxury Inn
1205 N Summit Blvd, Frisco CO
80443. 303/6683220. Employs: 50-
99.

Rodeway Inn Denver West
11595 W 6th Ave, Lakewood CO
80215-5537.   303/2387751.
Employs: 50-99.

1st Inn
361 Blue River Pkwy, Silverthorne
CO 80498. 303/4685170. Employs:
50-99.

Best Western Lake Dillon Lodge
I-70 Exit 203, Frisco CO 80443.
303/8257423. Employs: 50-99.

Cedar Lodge
99 Granite, Frisco CO 80443.
303/6680777. Employs: 50-99.

Frisco Bay Inn
117 Main, Frisco CO 80443.
303/6685222. Employs: 50-99.

Galena Street Mountain Inn
106 Galena, Frisco CO 80443.
303/6683224. Employs: 50-99.

Skier's Edge Lodge
4192 Hwy 9, Breckenridge CO
80424. 303/4530700. Employs: 50-
99.

The Breckenridge Wayside Inn
165 Tiger Rd, Breckenridge CO
80424. 303/4535540. Employs: 50-
99.

Club Mediterranee
0050 Beeler Pl, Frisco CO 80443.
303/9682161. Employs: 50-99.

Keystone Resort Ski Conditions
Hwy 6, Dillon CO 80435.
303/4684111. Employs: 100-249.

Summit Mountain Rental

200 Royal Tiger Rd, Breckenridge
CO 80424. 303/4537370. Employs:
50-99.

Swan Mountain Resort
0059 Soda Ridge Rd, Dillon CO
80435. 303/4686595. Employs: 50-
99.

**Swan   Mtn   Homeowners
Association Inc**
0059 Soda Ridge Rd, Dillon CO
80435. 303/5959625. Employs: 50-
99.

Waterford Townhomes
2025 Walton Creek Rd, Steamboat
Spr CO 80487-9006. 303/8799300.
Employs: 50-99.

Cotten House Bed & Breakfast
102 S French, Breckenridge CO
80424. 303/4535509. Employs: 50-
99.

Gore Range Bed & Breakfast
396 Tanglewood Ln, Silverthorne
CO 80498. 303/4685786. Employs:
50-99.

Granny's Inn
5435 Montezuma Rd, Breckenridge
CO 80424. 303/4689297. Employs:
50-99.

One Wellington Square
PO Box 2967, Breckenridge CO
80424-2967.   303/4536196.
Employs: 50-99.

Ridge Street Inn
212 N Ridge, Breckenridge CO
80424. 303/4534680. Employs: 50-
99.

Ski Tip Lodge
Montezuma Rd, Dillon CO 80435.
303/4684202. Employs: 50-99.

Williams House Bed & Breakfast
303 N Main, Breckenridge CO
80424. 303/4532975. Employs: 50-
99.

Days Inn
580 Silverthorne Ln, Silverthorne
CO 80498. 303/4688661. Employs:
50-99.

Holiday Inn
I-70 Exit 203, Frisco CO 80443.
303/5736345. Employs: 50-99.

Holiday Inn-Lake Dillon
1129 N Summit Blvd, Frisco CO
80443. 303/6685000. Employs: 50-
99.

**RECREATIONAL VEHICLE
PARKS AND CAMPSITES**

Mobile Home Communities Inc
116 Iverness Dr East, Englewood
CO 80112-5125. 303/7922166.
Employs: 50-99.

**ORGANIZATIONAL HOTELS
AND LODGING HOUSES, ON
MEMBERSHIP BASIS**

Kappa Alpha Theta
1020 Wood Ave, Colorado Springs
CO 80903. 719/6348072. Employs:
50-99.

Gamma Phi Beta
2233 S Josephine St, Denver CO
80210-4805. 303/7442879.
Employs: 50-99.

For more information on career opportunities in hospitality - hotels and
restaurants:

Associations

**American Hotel and Motel
Association**
1201 New York Avenue NW,
Washington DC 20005-3931
202/289-3100

**COUNCIL ON HOTEL,
RESTAURANT AND
INSTITUTIONAL EDUCATION**
1200 17th Street NW, Washington
DC 20036. 202/331-5990.

**THE EDUCATIONAL
FOUNDATION OF THE
NATIONAL RESTAURANT
ASSOCIATION**
250 South Wacker Drive, 14th
Floor, Chicago IL 60606. 312/715-
1010.

**HOSPITALITY SALES AND
MARKETING ASSOCIATION
INTERNATIONAL**

1300 L Street NW, Suite 800,
Washington DC 20005. 202/789-
0089.

**NATIONAL RESTAURANT
ASSOCIATION**
1200 17th Street NW, Washington
DC 20036. 202/331-5900.

Directories

**DIRECTORY OF CHAIN
RESTAURANT OPERATORS**
Business Guides, Inc., Lebhar-
Friedman, Inc., 3922 Coconut Palm
Drive, Tampa FL 33619-8321.
813/664-6700.

**DIRECTORY OF HIGH-
VOLUME INDEPENDENT
RESTAURANTS**
Lebhar-Friedman, Inc., 3922
Coconut Palm Drive, Tampa FL
33619-8321. 813/664-6700.

Magazines

CORNELL HOTEL AND RESTAURANT ADMINISTRATION QUARTERLY
Cornell University School of Hotel Administration, 327 Statler Hall, Ithaca NY 14853. 607/255-2093.

HOTEL AND MOTEL MANAGEMENT
120 West 2nd Street, Duluth MN 55802. 218/723-9440.

INNKEEPING WORLD
Box 84108, Seattle WA 98124. 206/362-7125.

NATION'S RESTAURANT NEWS
425 Park Avenue, New York NY 10022. 212/756-5200.

INSURANCE

The fastest-growing segment of the insurance industry will be in annuities. Premiums of property-casualty insurers should increase by about 5 percent, according to the Bureau of Labor Statistics. Competition and mergers will increase, while life insurance companies are expected to experience further problems. The industry as a whole has been trimming back through layoffs, although the worst may be over.

AETNA LIFE AND CASUALTY
P.O. Box 24683, Denver CO 80224. 303/793-1501. **Contact:** Personnel Office. **Description:** A regional office for the national insurance company. This office houses operations for three divisions: personal lines property and casualty insurance; commercial lines property and casualty insurance; and group benefits insurance. **Common positions:** Claim Representative; Management Trainee; Marketing Specialist; Underwriter. **Educational backgrounds sought:** Business Administration; Communications; Finance; Liberal Arts. **Special programs:** Training programs; internships. **Benefits:** medical, dental, and life insurance; pension plan; tuition assistance; disability coverage; daycare assistance; savings plan. **Corporate headquarters:** Hartford, CT. **Operations at this facility:** regional headquarters.

ATLANTIC & PACIFIC CORPORATION
P.O. Box 260007, Littleton CO 80126-0007. 303/792-9507. **Contact:** Personnel. **Description:** A Denver corporation involved in finance and insurance underwriting.

BLUE CROSS & BLUE SHIELD OF COLORADO
700 Broadway, Denver CO 80273. 303/831-2033. **Contact:** Human Resources. **Description:** Multiple area locations, including Colorado Springs, Grand Junction, and Greeley. A non-profit health care insurance organization, Blue Cross provides hospitalization insurance coverage to individuals and groups; Blue Shield provides a variety of group and individual insurance coverages for professional medical services from doctors, dentists, psychiatrists, and other medical professionals. **Corporate headquarters:** This location.

J. DEBELLA STATE FARM INSURANCE
720 Kipling Street, Suite 100, Lakewood CO 80215. 303/232-3202. **Contact:** Personnel Department. **Description:** A multiple line insurance firm.

GREAT WEST LIFE ASSURANCE COMPANY
8515 East Orchard Road, Englewood CO 80111. 303/689-3020. **Contact:** Mike Morris, Personnel Manager. **Description:** A Denver insurance agency.

GUARANTY NATIONAL INSURANCE COMPANY
P.O. Box 3329, Englewood CO 80155. 303/790-8200. **Contact:** Patrice Van Vleet, Hiring Administrator. **Description:** A property and casualty insurance company. **Common positions:** Accountant; Actuary; Claim Representative; Computer Programmer; Customer Service Representative; Financial Analyst; Branch Manager; Department Manager; Marketing Specialist; Personnel and Labor Relations Specialist; Purchasing Agent; Systems Analyst; Underwriter; Examiner; Adjuster; Clerical Supervisor. **Educational backgrounds sought:** Business Administration. **Benefits:** medical insurance; dental insurance; life insurance; tuition assistance; disability coverage; profit sharing; savings plan. **Corporate headquarters:** This location. **Operations at this facility:** regional headquarters; divisional headquarters; administration; service.

INSURANCE ASSOCIATES
2955 Belmont Street, Suite 100, Boulder CO 80301. 303/449-1500. **Contact:** Personnel Director. **Description:** A local insurance agency.

METROPOLITAN LIFE INSURANCE COMPANY
PENSION AND SAVINGS CENTER
1331 17th Street, P.O. Box 1019, Denver CO 80202-1019. 303/295-0505. **Contact:** Personnel Department. **Description:** A Denver-based life insurance company.

NATIONAL FARMER'S UNION INSURANCE CO.
10065 E. Harvard Avenue, Denver CO 80251. 303/337-5500. **Contact:** Assistant Vice President/Human Resources. **Description:** A medium-sized regional insurance company, specializing in coverage for farmers.

THE TALBERT CORPORATION

P.O. Box 9364, Denver CO 80209-0364. 303/722-7776. **Contact:** Judith Howard, Vice President. **Description:** An independent agency specializing in surety bonds and commercial insurance. **Common positions:** Customer Service Representative; Insurance Agent/Broker. **Educational backgrounds sought:** Business Administration; Insurance. **Benefits:** medical insurance; life insurance; disability coverage; profit sharing; savings plan. **Corporate headquarters:** This location. **Operations at this facility:** administration; service; sales.

VAN GILDER INSURANCE COMPANY

700 Broadway, Suite 1035, Denver CO 80203. 303/837-8500. **Contact:** Personnel Department. **Description:** Insurance agency with brokerage services.

WESTERN FARM BUREAU
LIFE INSURANCE COMPANY

P.O. Box 5087, Denver CO 80217. 303/861-8100. **Contact:** Leo Perino, Vice President/Personnel. **Description:** A Colorado insurance agency specializing in life, health, and accident insurance needs.

Additional large employers: 250+

LIFE INSURANCE

Security Life Of Denver
1290 Broadway, Denver CO 80203-5601. 303/9871230. Employs: 500-999.

HOSPITAL AND MEDICAL SERVICE PLANS

HMO Colorado Inc
700 Broadway St, Denver CO 80203-3421. 303/8314114. Employs: 1,000+.

Medical Network
555 E Pikes Peak Ave, Colorado Springs CO 80903-3641. 7194755602. Employs: 250-499.

INSURANCE AGENTS, BROKERS, AND SERVICE

Capitol Life Insurance
1331 17th St Suite 900, Denver CO 80202-1559. 303/8614065. Employs: 250-499.

Comprecare Inc
12100 E Iliff Ave Suite 200P, Aurora CO 80014-1249. 303/6956685. Employs: 250-499.

Continental Insurance
5690 Dtc Blvd, Englewood CO 80111-3232. 303/2206800. Employs: 250-499.

Farmers Insurance Group
3500 N Nevada Ave, Colorado Springs CO 80907-5333. 7196302000. Employs: 500-999.

Lincoln National Life Insurance
1125 Kelly Johnson Blvd, Colorado Springs CO 80920-3960. 7195315111. Employs: 250-499.

Metropolitan Group Sales
6251 Greenwood Plaza Blvd, Englewood CO 80111-4908. 303/7795420. Employs: 250-499.

Safeco Insurance Co Of America
12499 W Colfax Ave, Lakewood CO 80215-3731. 303/2326622. Employs: 250-499.

State Farm Insurance Companies
3001 8th Ave, Greeley CO 80631-8400. 303/3515000. Employs: 500-999.

Travelers Insurance Company
7600 E Orchard Rd, Englewood CO 80111-2518. 303/7401600. Employs: 250-499.

Additional small to medium sized employers: 50-249

LIFE INSURANCE

Rocky Mountain Life Insurance
700 Broadway Suite 1117, Denver CO 80203-3444. 303/8313085. Employs: 50-99.

ACCIDENT AND HEALTH INSURANCE

Cigna Healthplan Of Colorado
5970 Greenwood Plaza Blvd, Englewood CO 80111-4703. 303/7213000. Employs: 100-249.

HOSPITAL AND MEDICAL SERVICE PLANS

Kaiser Permanente
4803 Ward Rd, Wheat Ridge CO 80033-1902. 303/4673444. Employs: 100-249.

Insured Benefit Plans
6455 S Ivy Ct, Englewood CO 80111-4311. 303/7210317. Employs: 50-99.

J & R Group Benefits
2103 S Wadsworth Blvd, Denver CO 80227-2400. 303/9699019. Employs: 100-249.

Metropolitan Life Insurance Co
Westminster Mall, Westminster CO 80030. 303/4267100. Employs: 50-99.

NWN Group Marketing Service Colorado
1331 17, Denver CO 80202. 303/2956467. Employs: 100-249.

FIRE, MARINE, AND CASUALTY INSURANCE

Co Farm Bureau Mutual
2211 W 27th Ave, Denver CO 80211-4300. 303/4554553. Employs: 50-99.

St Paul Companies Inc
12250 E Iliff Ave Suite 400, Aurora CO 80014-1253. 303/6967500. Employs: 100-249.

TITLE INSURANCE

Denver Abstract Co
2620 S Parker Rd, Aurora CO 80014-1608. 303/6951919. Employs: 50-99.

Land Title Guaranty Company
3033 E 1st Ave Suite 600, Denver CO 80206-5625. 303/3211880. Employs: 50-99.

Transamerica Title Insurance
1800 Lawrence St, Denver CO 80202-1806. 303/2914800. Employs: 50-99.

PENSION, HEALTH, AND WELFARE FUNDS

First Trust Corp
717 17th St, Denver CO 80202-3330. 303/7442944. Employs: 100-249.

Public Employees Retirement
1300 Logan St, Denver CO 80203-2309. 303/8329550. Employs: 100-249.

MISC. INSURANCE CARRIERS

Federal Deposit Insurance Corp
707 17th St Ste 3000, Denver CO 80202-3430. 303/2964703. Employs: 100-249.

INSURANCE AGENTS, BROKERS, AND SERVICE

A L Williams & Associates
1980 Dominion Way, Colorado Springs CO 80918-1475. 719/5901141. Employs: 100-249.

Allstate Insurance Companies
6400 S Fiddlers Green Cir, Englewood CO 80111-4950. 303/7793700. Employs: 100-249.

Copic Insurance Company
7800 E Dorado Pl # 200, Englewood CO 80111-2306. 303/7790044. Employs: 100-249.

Crum & Forester Insurance Co
5445 Dtc Pky Suite 400, Englewood CO 80111-3049. 303/7732000. Employs: 100-249.

Equifax Company
7100 E Belleview Ave Suite 303, Englewood CO 80111-1654. 303/2200200. Employs: 50-99.

Firemans Fund America Life
7600 E Eastman Ave, Denver CO 80231-4376. 303/7520020. Employs: 50-99.

Geico Criterion Insurance Co
7551 W Alameda Ave, Lakewood CO 80226-3205. 303/2341636. Employs: 100-249.

Hartford Insurance Group

4643 S Ulster St Suite 800-P, Denver CO 80237-2862. 303/7794500. Employs: 100-249.

Home Insurance Company
6000 Greenwood Plaza Blvd, Englewood CO 80111-4816. 303/7401900. Employs: 50-99.

Kemper Group
10375 E Harvard Ave Ste 500, Denver CO 80231-5971. 303/6961441. Employs: 50-99.

Lincoln National Hlth Care Inc
5725 Mark Dabling Blvd Ste 108, Colorado Springs CO 80919-2228. 719/5945413. Employs: 100-249.

Maryland Casualty Insurance Co
14001 E Iliff Ave Suite 301, Aurora CO 80014-1426. 303/3697703. Employs: 50-99.

Morrison & Associates
190 E 29th St, Loveland CO 80538-2724. 303/6636921. Employs: 50-99.

Nationwide Insurance Company
9110 E Nichols Ave Suite 100, Englewood CO 80112-3448. 303/7994141. Employs: 100-249.

New York Life Insurance Co
3200 Cherry Creek Sth Dr, Denver CO 80209. 303/7442000. Employs: 100-249.

Northwestern Natl Insurance
5670 Greenwood Plaza Blvd, Englewood CO 80111-2448. 303/7709451. Employs: 50-99.

Pacific Indemnity Insurance Co
6400 S Fiddlers Green Cir, Englewood CO 80111-4950. 303/7708700. Employs: 50-99.

Prudential Insurance Co
4643 S Ulster St Suite 1000, Denver CO 80237-2887. 303/7966161. Employs: 100-249.

Safeco Insurance Companies
12499 E Colfax Ave, Aurora CO 80015. 303/2390251. Employs: 100-249.

Sedgwick James Of Colorado Inc
2000 S Colorado Blvd Suite 500, Denver CO 80222-7907. 303/6911300. Employs: 100-249.

State Farm Insurance Companies
8021 W 92nd Ave, Broomfield CO 80021. 303/4313300. Employs: 50-99.

State Mutual Life Assurance Co
44 Cook St Suite 900, Denver CO 80206-5899. 303/3885911. Employs: 50-99.

Transamerica Insurance Group
5660 Greenwood Plaza Blvd # 30, Englewood CO 80111-2416. 303/7717150. Employs: 50-99.

US States Fidelity & Guarantee
370 17th St Suite 2800, Denver CO 80202-5628. 303/8931166. Employs: 100-249.

Western Farm Bureau Life Insurance
1200 Lincoln St, Denver CO 80203-2121. 303/8618100. Employs: 100-249.

J H Silversmith Inc
4500 Cherry Crek Sotuh Dr, Denver CO 80222. 303/7532000. Employs: 50-99.

State Farm Insurance Companies
4380 S Syracuse St, Denver CO 80237-2607. 303/7963362. Employs: 50-99.

For more information on career opportunities in insurance:

Associations

ALLIANCE OF AMERICAN INSURERS
1501 Woodfield Road, Suite 400 West, Schaumburg IL 60173-4980. 708/330-8500.

AMERICAN COUNCIL OF LIFE INSURANCE
1001 Pennsylvania Avenue NW, 5th Floor South, Washington DC 20004-2599. 202/624-2000.

AMERICAN INSURANCE ASSOCIATION
1130 Connecticut Avenue NW, Suite 1000, Washington DC 20036. 202/828-7100.

HEALTH INSURANCE ASSOCIATION OF AMERICA
1025 Connecticut Avenue NW, Suite 1200, Washington DC 20036-3998. 202/223-7780.

INSURANCE INFORMATION INSTITUTE
110 William Street, New York NY 10038. 212/669-9200.

LIFE INSURANCE RESEARCH AND MARKETING ASSOCIATION
8 Farm Springs Road, Farmington CT 06032. 203/677-0033.

NATIONAL ASSOCIATION OF LIFE UNDERWRITERS
1922 F Street NW, Washington DC 20006-4387. 202/331-6000.

SOCIETY OF ACTUARIES
475 North Martingale Road, Suite 800, Schaumburg IL 60173-2227. 708/706-3500.

Directories

INSURANCE ALMANAC
Underwriter Printing and Publishing Co., 50 East Palisade Avenue, Englewood NJ 07631. 201/569-8808.

INSURANCE MARKET PLACE
Rough Notes Company, Inc., P.O. Box 564, Indianapolis IN 46206. 317/634-1541.

INSURANCE PHONE BOOK AND DIRECTORY
121 Chanlon Road, New Providence NJ 07974. 800/521-8110.

Magazines

BEST'S REVIEW
A. M. Best Co., A. M. Best Road, Oldwick NJ 08858. 908/439-2200.

INSURANCE JOURNAL
80 Southlake Avenue, Suite 550, Pasadena CA 91101. 818/793-7717.

INSURANCE REVIEW
Journal of Commerce, 2 World Trade Center, 27th Floor, New York NY 10048. 212/837-7000.

LEGAL SERVICES

The legal profession is undergoing a major adjustment, largely due to the rapid rise in the number of lawyers over the past two decades. In the 70's the number of lawyers doubled, and in the 80's the number rose by another 48 percent. Meanwhile, a decline in civil litigation, coupled with the recent economic downturn, has led to a "produce or perish" climate. Law schools are reporting a 10-20 percent decline in placements, and firms are laying off associates, freezing rates, and firing unproductive partners.
Graduates of prestigious law schools and those who rank high in their classes will have the best opportunities.

HOLLAND & HART
5517th Street, Suite 2900, Denver CO 80202. 303/295-8000. **Contact:** Personnel Director. **Description:** A Denver law firm.

SHERMAN & HOWARD
633 17th Street, Suite 3000, Denver CO 80202. 303/297-2900. **Contact:** Sue Mrva, Human Resources. **Description:** A Denver law firm.

Additional large employers: 250+

LEGAL SERVICES

Davis Graham & Stubbs Attorneys
370 17th St Suite 4700, Denver CO
80202-5682.   303/8929400.
Employs: 500-999.

Hall & Evans Attorneys
1200 17th St Suite 1700, Denver
CO 80202-5800. 303/6283300.
Employs: 250-499.

John M Husban Esq
555 17th St Suite 2900, Denver CO
80202-3979.   303/2958228.
Employs: 250-499.

Sheridan Ross & McIntosh Attorneys
1700 Lincoln St Suite 35 Fl,
Denver CO 80203-1014.
303/8639700. Employs: 500-999.

Additional small to medium sized employers: 50-249

LEGAL SERVICES

Ballard Spahr Andrews Ingers
1225 17th St Suite 2300, Denver
CO 80202-5596. 303/2922400.
Employs: 50-99.

Berenbaum & Weinshienk Attorneys
3773 Cherry Creek Nrth Dr # 88,
Denver CO 80209-3804.
303/3880800. Employs: 50-99.

Gehler & Merrigan Attorneys
6755 E 72nd Ave, Commerce City
CO 80022-2101. 303/2872563.
Employs: 100-249.

Ireland Stapleton Pryor Pascle
1675 Broadway Suite 2600, Denver
CO 80202-4685. 303/6232700.
Employs: 50-99.

Kelly Stanfield & Odonnell
1225 17th St Ste 2600, Denver CO
80202-5526.   303/8253534.
Employs: 50-99.

Kirkland & Ellis Attorneys
1999 Broadway Suite 4000, Denver
CO 80202-5749. 303/2913000.
Employs: 100-249.

Kutak Rock & Campbell Attorneys
707 17th St Suite 2400, Denver CO
80202-3494.   303/2972400.
Employs: 100-249.

Legal Aid Society
1905 Sherman St Suite 400, Denver
CO 80203-1181. 303/8371313.
Employs: 50-99.

Menin & Menin Attorneys
3300 E 1st Ave Suite 500, Denver
CO 80206-5808. 303/3995612.
Employs: 50-99.

Retherford Mullen Rector
415 Sahwatch St, Colorado Springs
CO 80903-3841. 719/4752014.
Employs: 50-99.

Baker & Hostetler
303 E 17th Ave, Denver CO
80203-1253.   303/8610600.
Employs: 50-99.

Faegre & Benson
370 17th St Ste 2500, Denver CO
80202-5665.   303/5925900.
Employs: 100-249.

Friedrich Weller Ward & Andrew
100 Fillmore St, Denver CO 80206-4921. 303/3229100. Employs: 50-99.

Gorsuch Kirgis Campbell Walker
1401 17, Denver CO 80202. 303/5341200. Employs: 50-99.

Haligman and Lottner Pc
7887 E Belleview Ave, Englewood CO 80111-6015. 303/8507887. Employs: 50-99.

Hughes Clikeman Attorneys
4155 E Jewell Ave, Denver CO 80222-4504. 303/7580680. Employs: 50-99.

Isaacson Rosenbaum Woods
633 17, Denver CO 80202. 303/2925656. Employs: 50-99.

Long & Jaudon Attorneys Pc
1600 Ogden St, Denver CO 80218-1414. 303/8321122. Employs: 50-99.

Machol Davis & Michael Pc
1640 Grant St, Denver CO 80203-1640. 303/8300075. Employs: 50-99.

McClearn & Hart Attorneys
555 17, Denver CO 80202. 303/2958162. Employs: 50-99.

Miller & Leher Pc
1901 W Littleton Blvd, Littleton CO 80120-2058. 303/7982525. Employs: 50-99.

Montgomery Ltl Yng Campbell
5445 Dtc Pky, Englewood CO 80111-3045. 303/7738100. Employs: 50-99.

Pendleton & Sabian Pc
303 E 17th Ave, Denver CO 80203-1253. 303/8391204. Employs: 50-99.

Pryor Carney & Johnson Pc
6200 S Syracuse Way, Englewood CO 80111-4737. 303/7716200. Employs: 100-249.

Tilly & Graves Pc
3773 Cherry Creek North Dr, Denver CO 80209-3804. 303/3218811. Employs: 50-99.

For more information on career opportunities in legal services:

Associations

AMERICAN BAR ASSOCIATION
North Lake Shore Drive, Chicago IL 60611. 312/988-5000.

FEDERAL BAR ASSOCIATION
1815 H. Street NW, Suite 408, Washington DC 20006. 202/638-0252.

NATIONAL ASSOCIATION FOR LAW PLACEMENT
1666 Connecticut Avenue, Suite 450, Washington DC 20009. 202/667-1666.

NATIONAL ASSOCIATION OF LEGAL ASSISTANTS
1601 South Main Street, Suite 300, Tulsa OK 74119. 918/587-6828.

NATIONAL FEDERATION OF PARALEGAL ASSOCIATIONS
P.O. Box 33108, Kansas City MO 64114-0108. 816/941-4000.

NATIONAL PARALEGAL
ASSOCIATION

P.O. Box 629, 6186 Honey Hollow
Road, Doylestown PA 18901.
215/297-8333.

MANUFACTURING: CONSUMER   MISCELLANEOUS

Because the consumer products industry is so diversified, industry outlooks depend more on specific product categories. Here's a sampling: Soaps and Detergents: One of the biggest trends in this category has been to move away from the environmentally damaging phosphates used in detergents. In fact, about 40 percent of the nation has banned phosphates altogether, instead using natural soaps made of tallow and tropical oils. Overall, employment in this area will be increasing. Household Products: The short-term prognosis depends on consumer confidence.

Although disposable incomes have risen slightly, many consumers are replenishing savings and paying off debts instead of buying expensive new items. A recovery in housing and the aging baby-boom generation should contribute to the long-term health of this segment.

ALLEN-LEWIS MANUFACTURING COMPANY
P.O. Box 16546, Denver CO 80216. 303/295-0196. **Contact:** Personnel Department. **Description:** Wholesale souvenirs, gifts, and novelties.

AMERICAN CANVAS COMPANY
4004 Grape Street, Denver CO 80216. 303/399-3342. **Contact:** Personnel Department. **Description:** A Denver manufacturer of canvas products.

JACK BARTON & COMPANY, INC.
1201 Auraria Parkway, Denver CO 80204. 303/571-5123. **Contact:** Personnel. **Description:** A retail furniture company.

BRASS SMITH INC.
2625 Walnut, Denver CO 80205. 303/296-8520. **Contact:** Personnel Department. **Description:** A Denver-based manufacturer of ornamental brass work.

CAREFREE OF COLORADO
2145 West 6th Avenue, Broomfield CO 80020. 303/469-3324. **Contact:** Personnel Department. **Description:** Manufactures a variety of recreational vehicle-associated products, including awnings, add-a-rooms, and lawn furniture and related accessories. A subsidiary of Scott Fetzer Company (Lakewood, OH). **Corporate headquarters:** This location.

DESKS INC.
1385 South Santa Fe Drive, Denver CO 80223. 303/777-8880. **Contact:** Iris Hartley, Human Resources Manager. **Description:** Manufactures office furniture.

DIAMOND VOGEL PAINT
P.O. Box 16388, Denver CO 80216-0388. 303/534-5191. **Contact:** Peter Lelong, Office Manager. **Description:** Produces a variety of paints, stains, and resins. **Corporate headquarters:** This location.

EASTMAN KODAK/COLORADO DIVISION
9952 Eastman Park Drive, Windsor CO 80551-1386. 303/686-7611. **Contact:** Personnel Office. **Description:** A manufacturer of photographic and medical X-ray films.

GERRY BABY PRODUCTS
12520 Grant Drive, Thornton CO 80241. 303/457-0926. **Contact:** John Lopresti, Vice President of Human Resources. **Description:** Manufactures juvenile products, baby strollers and baby carriers. A subsidiary of Huffy Corporation. **Common positions:** Accountant; Buyer; Customer Service Representative; Draftsperson; Industrial Engineer; Industrial Designer; Operations/Production Manager; Marketing Specialist; Purchasing Agent. **Educational backgrounds sought:** Accounting; Business Administration; Engineering; Finance; Liberal Arts; Marketing. **Benefits:** medical, dental, and life insurance; pension plan; tuition assistance; disability coverage; profit sharing; employee discounts; savings plan. Divisional headquarters location. **Corporate headquarters:** Dayton, OH. **Listed on:** New York Stock Exchange (Huffy Corporation).

HEAD RACQUET SPORTS
4801 North 63rd Street, Boulder CO 80301. 303/530-2000. **Contact:** Laura Alberts, Personnel Director. **Description:** A well-known manufacturer of tennis and other racquets. **Corporate headquarters:** This location. A subsidiary of Minstar Corporation.

HUGHES & COMPANY
500 East 76th Avenue, Denver CO 80229. 303/289-2211. **Contact:** Personnel Department. **Description:** Denver-based mill-shop specializing in manufacturing store fixtures such as showcases and cabinets.

NER DATA PRODUCTS, INC.

5125 Race Court, Denver CO 80216. 303/297-9900. **Contact:** Cynthia Eck, Manager of Employee Relations. **Description:** A manufacturer of office supplies, primarily ribbons and printing cartridges for typewriters, word-processors and computers, and injection-molded plastic products. Founded in 1906. **Corporate headquarters:** Glassboro, NJ.

PENTAX CORPORATION

35 Inverness Drive East, Englewood CO 80112. 303/799-8000. **Contact:** Personnel. **Description:** A well-known manufacturer of cameras, camera supplies, and related photographic products. **Corporate headquarters:** This location.

REDFIELD COMPANY

5800 East Jewell Avenue, Denver CO 80224. 303/757-6411. **Contact:** Jan Stanton, Personnel Department. **Description:** Manufactures and sells precision magnification scopes for rifles and pistols, used for hunting and target shooting. Also manufactures scope mounts. A subsidiary of The Brown Group (St. Louis, MO). **Corporate headquarters:** This location.

SAMSONITE CORPORATION

11200 East 45th Avenue, Denver CO 80239. 303/373-7479. **Contact:** Gypsy Twillman, Manager of Employment. **Description:** Manufactures and markets luggage and business cases. **Common positions:** Accountant; Blue-Collar Worker Supervisor; Buyer; Computer Programmer; Credit Manager; Customer Service Representative; Draftsperson; Industrial Engineer; Mechanical Engineer; Financial Analyst; Sales Representative. **Educational backgrounds sought:** Accounting; Art/Design; Business Administration; Computer Science; Engineering; Marketing. **Benefits:** medical insurance; dental insurance; pension plan; life insurance; tuition assistance; disability coverage; employee discounts; savings plan. **Corporate headquarters:** This location. **Operations at this facility:** regional headquarters; divisional headquarters; manufacturing; research and development; administration; service; sales.

SPRING AIR MATTRESS COMPANY

1055 South Jason Street, Denver CO 80223. 303/777-6683. **Contact:** Office Manager. **Description:** A manufacturer of mattresses.

STAINLESS FABRICATING CO. INC.

2401 South Delaware, Denver CO 80223. 303/733-2417. **Contact:** Personnel Department. **Description:** A manufacturer of custom kitchen equipment.

WRIGHT & McGILL

P.O. Box 16011, Denver CO 80216. 303/321-1481. **Contact:** Vicki Paradise, Vice President of Administration. **Description:** Produces a line of fishing rods and tackle. **Corporate headquarters:** This location.

Additional large employers: 250+

CARBON PAPER AND INKED RIBBONS

Aspen Imaging Intl Inc
555 Aspen Ridge Dr, Lafayette CO
80026-9333.   303/6665750.
Employs: 250-499.

SIGNS AND ADVERTISING SPECIALTIES

Ball Communications Sys
10 Longs Peak Dr, Broomfield CO
80021-2510.   303/4602180.
Employs: 250-499.

MISC. MANUFACTURING INDUSTRIES

Atmel Corp
1150 E Cheyenne, Colorado
Springs CO 80906. 7195763300.
Employs: 500-999.

The Bullibutton Shop
4220 Tennyson St, Denver CO
80212-2306.   303/4330444.
Employs: 250-499.

Additional small to medium sized employers: 50-249

WOOD HOUSEHOLD FURNITURE, EXCEPT UPHOLSTERED

Harris Of Pendelton
255 Sw 42nd St, Loveland CO
80537-7517.   303/6676724.
Employs: 50-99.

Pillow Kingdom
13300 E 38th Ave, Denver CO
80239-3550.   303/3930059.
Employs: 100-249.

Tuffy
1100 Simms St, Golden CO 80401-
4438. 303/2339801. Employs: 50-
99.

MATTRESSES, FOUNDATIONS, AND CONVERTIBLE BEDS

The Ohio Mattress Company
6275 Lake Shore Ct, Colorado
Springs CO 80915-1609.
719/5746944. Employs: 100-249.

WOOD OFFICE AND STORE FIXTURES, PARTITIONS, SHELVING, AND LOCKERS

Hughes & Company
500 E 76th Ave, Denver CO
80229-6216.   303/2892211.
Employs: 100-249.

Woodworkers Of Denver Inc
1475 S Acoma St, Denver CO
80223-3222.   303/7777656.
Employs: 50-99.

OFFICE AND STORE FIXTURES, PARTITIONS, SHELVING, AND LOCKERS, EXCEPT WOOD

Engineered Data Products
2550 W Midway Blvd, Broomfield
CO 80020-1633. 303/4652800.
Employs: 100-249.

DRAPERY HARDWARE AND WINDOW BLINDS AND SHADES

Hunter Douglas Inc
1 Duette Dr, Broomfield CO 80020-1090.   303/4661848. Employs: 100-249.

MISC. FURNITURE AND FIXTURES

Shafer Commercial Seating Inc
4101 E 48th Ave, Denver CO 80216-3206.   303/3227792. Employs: 100-249.

GAMES, TOYS, AND CHILDREN'S VEHICLES, EXCEPT DOLLS AND BICYCLES

Chessex
826 S Lincoln St, Longmont CO 80501-6317.   303/7765103. Employs: 50-99.

Skynasaur Inc
726 Front St, Louisville CO 80027-1805. 303/6664499. Employs: 50-99.

Stuart Entertainment Inc
400 E Mineral Ave, Littleton CO 80122-2604.   303/7952625. Employs: 100-249.

MISC. SPORTING AND ATHLETIC GOODS

Harloff Manufacturing Company
650 Ford St, Colorado Springs CO 80915-3712.   719/6370300. Employs: 50-99.

Lt Helmets Inc
517 Chestnut St, Leadville CO 80461-3903.   8007482738. Employs: 100-249.

Mountainsmith Inc

15866 W 7th Ave, Golden CO 80401-3966.   303/2795930. Employs: 50-99.

LEAD PENCILS, CRAYONS, AND ARTISTS' MATERIALS

Dreamworks Inc
1275 S Sherman, Longmont CO 80501. 303/7722400. Employs: 50-99.

SIGNS AND ADVERTISING SPECIALTIES

CGF Sign Inc
2930 W 9th Ave, Denver CO 80204-3713.   303/6296121. Employs: 50-99.

Sachs Lawlor Company
1717 S Acoma St, Denver CO 80223-3603.   303/7777771. Employs: 50-99.

Skyline Electric Sign Company
2845 Delta Dr, Colorado Springs CO 80910-1010. 719/3924228. Employs: 50-99.

MISC. MANUFACTURING INDUSTRIES

Capitol Color Imaging
1463 W Alameda Ave, Denver CO 80223-2042.   303/7777550. Employs: 50-99.

Protogenesis
157 Talamine Ct, Colorado Springs CO 80907-5163. 719/5789729. Employs: 50-99.

Radix Microelectronics Inc
2304 Broadway St, Colorado Springs CO 80904-3732. 719/4717752. Employs: 50-99.

Starpak Inc
237 22nd St, Greeley CO 80631-7212. 303/3526800. Employs: 100-249.

Ultimate Support Systems Inc

2506 Zurich Dr, Fort Collins CO 80524-1425. 303/4934488. Employs: 50-99.

Wat Shop
5741 Arapahoe Ave Suite 4, Boulder CO 80303-1341. 303/4430552. Employs: 50-99.

For more information on career opportunities in consumer manufacturing:

Associations

ASSOCIATION OF HOME APPLIANCE MANUFACTURERS
20 North Wacker Drive, Chicago IL 60606. 312/984-5800.

NATIONAL ASSOCIATION OF MANUFACTURERS
1331 Pennsylvania Avenue, NW, Suite 1500, Washington DC 20004. 202/637-3000.

NATIONAL HOUSEWARES MANUFACTURERS ASSOCIATION
6400 Schafer Court, Suite 650, Rosemont IL 60018. 708/292-4200.

ASSOCIATION FOR MANUFACTURING TECHNOLOGY
7901 Westpark Drive, McLean VA 22102. 703/893-2900.

SOAP AND DETERGENT ASSOCIATION
475 Park Avenue South, New York NY 10016. 212/725-1262.

Directories

APPLIANCE MANUFACTURER ANNUAL DIRECTORY
Corcoran Communications, Inc., 29100 Aurora Road, Suite 200, Solon OH 44139. 216/349-3060.

HOUSEHOLD AND PERSONAL PRODUCTS INDUSTRY BUYERS GUIDE
Rodman Publishing Group, 17 South Franklin Turnpike, Ramsey NJ 07446. 201/825-2552.

Magazines

APPLIANCE
1110 Jorie Boulevard, Oak Brook IL 60522-9019. 708/990-3484.

COSMETICS INSIDERS REPORT
Advanstar Communications, 7500 Old Oak Boulevard, Cleveland OH 44130. 216/243-8100.

HOUSEWARES
Harcourt Brace Jovanovich, 1 East First Street, Duluth MN 55802. 714/231-6616.

MANUFACTURING: INDUSTRIAL

MISCELLANEOUS

Trend to watch for: In the machinery manufacturing segment, many of the biggest company names will continue to disappear due to mergers and buy outs. While hundreds of U.S. companies still make machine tools, materials handling equipment, and compressors for American factories, the fastest-growing machinery markets are now overseas. This means that U.S. firms will have to build overseas presences just to survive. In fact, foreign orders for a number of American-made tools remain strong.

Although mergers are often followed by layoffs, workers who survive these cuts should be better positioned for the long-term. Many manufacturers are giving workers a much greater degree of across-the-board involvement, with team-based product management allowing individual workers to gain training in a number of different job functions.

B & B MACHINE GRINDING
303 West Evans Avenue, Denver CO 80223. 303/744-2751. **Contact:** Personnel Department. **Description:** Manufactures miscellaneous machine products, except electrical.

BRAND-IT-IDEX INC.
4799 Dahlia Street, Denver CO 80216. 303/320-4555. **Contact:** Mr. Bob Smallwood, Vice President of Manufacturing. **Description:** Manufactures clamps, fittings for hoses, and brackets.

COLORADO CRYSTAL CORPORATION
2303 West 8th Street, Loveland CO 80537. 303/667-9248. **Contact:** Maggie Bedford, Personnel Director. **Description:** Manufactures quartz crystals for a variety of original equipment manufacturers. **Corporate headquarters:** This location.

COORS CERAMICS COMPANY
2449 River Road, Grand Junction CO 81505. 303/245-4000. **Contact:** Personnel. **Description:** A manufacturer of ceramics. For hiring information, contact corporate headquarters at 303/277-5514 (Golden, CO).

DANA CORPORATION
ENGINE PRODUCTS DIVISION
P.O. Box 835, Pueblo CO 81002. 719/948-3311. **Contact:** Personnel Department. **Description:** A manufacturer of aluminum pistons and bell housings. **Common positions:** Accountant; Blue-Collar Worker Supervisor; Computer Programmer; Industrial Engineer; Mechanical Engineer; Operations/Production Manager; Personnel and Labor Relations Specialist; Quality Control Supervisor. **Educational backgrounds sought:** Accounting;

Engineering. **Benefits:** medical insurance; dental insurance; pension plan; life insurance; tuition assistance; disability coverage; savings plan. **Corporate headquarters:** Toledo, OH. **Operations at this facility:** Manufacturing. **Listed on:** New York Stock Exchange.

DIETRICH STANDARD CORPORATION

P.O. Box 9000, Boulder CO 80301. 303/530-9600. **Contact:** Personnel Department. **Description:** Produces a wide range of flow and process control equipment, including sensors, automatic valve devices, and metering equipment. A subsidiary of Dover Corporation (New York, NY), a Fortune 500 manufacturing company engaged in the production of elevators, oil well equipment, special valves, couplings and pumps, fluid dispensing nozzles, automotive lifts, pressure sealing devices, liquid filtration equipment, flow measurement devices, toggle clamps, food servicing and processing equipment, welding guns, and many other products. **Common positions:** Blue-Collar Worker Supervisor; Buyer; Computer Programmer; Customer Service Representative; Draftsperson; Electrical Engineer; Mechanical Engineer; Department Manager; Operations/Production Manager; Personnel and Labor Relations Specialist; Sales Representative. **Educational backgrounds sought:** Accounting; Engineering; Marketing. **Benefits:** medical, dental, and life insurance; pension plan; tuition assistance; disability coverage; profit sharing; savings plan. **Corporate headquarters:** This location. **Parent company:** Dover Corp. **Operations at this facility:** manufacturing; research/development; administration; service; sales.

GENERAL CABLE COMPANY

5600 West 88th Avenue, Westminster CO 80030. 303/427-3700. **Contact:** Edward J. Hvizda, Division Employee Relations Manager. **Description:** Manufacturer of aerial lifts, cable pressurization systems and ventilatory heaters. **Common positions:** Accountant; Blue-Collar Worker Supervisor; Buyer; Draftsperson; Electrical Engineer; Mechanical Engineer; Operations/Production Manager; Marketing Specialist; Sales Representative. **Educational backgrounds sought:** Accounting; Business Administration; Engineering; Marketing. **Benefits:** medical insurance; dental insurance; pension plan; life insurance; tuition assistance; disability coverage; savings plan. **Corporate headquarters:** Cincinnati, OH. A subsidiary of Penn Central Corp. **Operations at this facility:** divisional headquarters; manufacturing; research and development; administration; service; sales. **Listed on:** New York Stock Exchange.

ICE-O-MATIC

P.O. Box 39487, Denver CO 80239. 303/371-3737. **Contact:** Human Resources Department. **Description:** Manufactures automatic ice-making and dispensing equipment.

MICRO MOTION, INC.

7070 Winchester Circle, Boulder CO 80301. 303/530-8400. **Contact:** Human Resources Director. **Description:** A manufacturer of industrial flo-meters.

MOLI-INTERNATIONAL
1150 West Virginia Avenue, Denver CO 80223. 303/777-0364. **Contact:** Herb Laib, Personnel. **Description:** A manufacturer of miscellaneous industrial equipment.

MORSE INDUSTRIAL CORPORATION
EMERSON ELECTRIC COMPANY
4650 Steele Street, Denver CO 80216. 303/825-7134. **Contact:** Industrial Relations Manager. **Description:** Manufacturer of industrial power transmission products, specializing in worm gear reducers, helical shaft mount reducers, and other industrial gearing products. Divisional headquarters location. **Operations at this facility:** manufacturing. **Corporate headquarters (Morse):** Ithaca, NY. **Common positions:** Accountant; Blue-Collar Worker Supervisor; Buyer; Computer Programmer; Customer Service Representative; Draftsperson; Industrial Engineer; Mechanical Engineer; Financial Analyst; Industrial Designer; Department Manager; General Manager; Operations/Production Manager; Personnel and Labor Relations Specialist; Purchasing Agent; Quality Control Supervisor. **Educational backgrounds sought:** Accounting; Business Administration; Computer Science; Engineering; Finance. **Benefits:** medical insurance; dental insurance; pension plan; life insurance; tuition assistance; disability coverage; employee discounts; savings plan.

NORGREN
5400 South Delaware Street, Littleton CO 80120. 303/795-6200. **Contact:** Personnel Department. **Description:** Manufactures accessory and component parts for pneumatic systems. **Common positions:** Accountant; Blue-Collar Worker Supervisor; Computer Programmer; Customer Service Representative; Industrial Engineer; Department Manager; Operations/Production Manager; Purchasing Agent; Quality Control Supervisor. **Benefits:** medical, dental, and life insurance; pension plan; tuition assistance; disability coverage; savings plan. **Corporate headquarters:** This location.

POWER APPLICATION & MANUFACTURING CO.
10777 East 45th Avenue, P.O. Box 39068, Denver CO 80239. 303/371-0330. **Contact:** Susan Ripsam, Human Resources Supervisor. **Description:** Manufacturer of diesel engines and oil pumps. **Benefits:** medical, dental, and life insurance; pension plan; tuition assistance; disability coverage; profit sharing; savings plan. **Corporate headquarters:** This location. **Parent company:** AWT. **Operations at this facility:** manufacturing; research/development; administration; service; sales. **Employees:** 250. **Projected hires for the next 12 months:** 15. **Listed on:** American Stock Exchange.

RAGSDALE MACHINERY OPERATIONS
4535 South Santa Fe Drive, P.O. Box 1687, Englewood CO 80110. 303/781-4401. **Contact:** Cardell Webster, Personnel Manager. **Description:** Manufactures can-making and printing machinery, and provides related machine shop services and products. A division of Alcoa Packaging Machinery, Inc. (Pittsburgh, Pennsylvania). **Operations at this facility:** manufacturing; research/development; administration; service; sales. **Corporate headquarters:** This location. **Listed on:** New York Stock Exchange. **Common positions:** Accountant; Administrator; Blue-Collar Worker Supervisor; Buyer; Computer

Programmer; Credit Manager; Customer Service Representative; Draftsperson; Engineer; Electrical Engineer; Industrial Engineer; Mechanical Engineer; Manager; Department Manager; General Manager; Operations/Production Manager; Personnel and Labor Relations Specialist; Purchasing Agent; Quality Control Supervisor; Sales Representative. **Educational backgrounds sought:** Accounting; Business Administration; Computer Science; Engineering; Liberal Arts; Marketing. **Benefits:** medical insurance; dental insurance; pension plan; life insurance; tuition assistance; disability coverage; employee discounts; savings plan.

SAFETRAN TRAFFIC SYSTEMS INC.
1485 Garden of the Gods Road, Colorado Springs CO 80907. 719/599-5600. **Contact:** Georgine Fries, Personnel Manager. **Description:** Manufactures a broad range of traffic control products. **Corporate headquarters:** This location.

SILVER ENGINEERING WORKS INC.
14800 East Moncrieff Place, Aurora CO 80011. Mailed inquiries only. **Contact:** Human Resources. **Description:** Fabricators of heavy machinery for the food processing industry. **Common positions:** Draftsperson; Electrical Engineer; Industrial Engineer; Mechanical Engineer; Management Trainee; Machinists: CNC and Conventional. **Benefits:** medical insurance; dental insurance; life insurance; tuition assistance; disability coverage; savings plan. **Parent company:** Ingersoll-Rand (Woodcliff Lake, NJ). **Operations at this facility:** manufacturing; service; sales.

STANLEY AVIATION CORPORATION
2501 Dallas Street, Aurora CO 80010. 303/340-5200. **Contact:** John M. Morgan, Human Resources Representative. **Description:** Manufactures structural sheet metal and metal tube fabrications for the aircraft industry; couplings used in aircraft and missiles; structural ground support equipment for airlines; and large metal containers. **Common positions:** Accountant; Draftsperson; Mechanical Engineer; Department Manager; Marketing Specialist; Sales Representative. **Benefits:** medical insurance; dental insurance; pension plan; life insurance; tuition assistance; daycare assistance; profit sharing; savings plan; disability coverage. **Corporate headquarters:** This location. **Parent company:** Flight Refueling Ltd. **Operations at this facility:** manufacturing; research/development; administration; sales. **Revenues (1991):** $40 million. **Employees:** 285. **Projected hires for the next 12 months:** 20.

TRANSLOGIC CORPORATION
10825 East 47th Avenue, Denver CO 80239. 303/371-7770. **Contact:** Dave Lawson, Employee Relations Manager. **Description:** Produces pneumatic-powered conveying systems.

A.R. WILFLEY & SONS, INC.
P.O. Box 2330, Denver CO 80201. 303/779-1777. **Contact:** Bill Wilbur, Personnel. **Description:** Manufactures centrifugal pumps.

WILKERSON CORPORATION
1201 West Mansfield Avenue, Englewood CO 80110. 303/761-7601. **Contact:** Human Resources Administrator. **Description:** Manufactures fluid power equipment, air dryers, filters, regulators, lubricators. **Common positions:**

Accountant; Blue-Collar Worker Supervisor; Buyer; Commercial Artist; Computer Programmer; Customer Service Representative; Draftsperson; Engineer; Electrical Engineer; Industrial Engineer; Mechanical Engineer; Financial Analyst; Operations/Production Manager; Personnel and Labor Relations Specialist; Purchasing Agent; Quality Control Supervisor; Systems Analyst. **Educational backgrounds sought:** Accounting; Business Administration; Computer Science; Economics; Engineering; Finance; Liberal Arts; Marketing; Mathematics; Physics. **Benefits:** medical insurance; dental insurance; life insurance; tuition assistance; disability coverage; profit sharing. **Corporate headquarters:** This location. **Operations at this facility:** manufacturing; research/development; administration; service; sales.

Additional large employers: 250+

MACHINE TOOLS, METAL CUTTING TYPES

Esab Automation Inc
1941 Heath Pky, Fort Collins CO 80524-2722. 303/4841244. Employs: 250-499.

MEASURING AND DISPENSING PUMPS

Sundstrand Fluid Handling
14845 W 64th Ave, Arvada CO 80004. 303/4250800. Employs: 250-499.

FLUID POWER CYLINDERS AND ACTUATORS

Maxcor Manufacturing Inc
4240 N Nevada Ave, Colorado Springs CO 80907-4306. 7195984606. Employs: 250-499.

Texas Instruments Inc
5825 Mark Dabling Bl, Colorado Springs CO 80919-2210. 7195935151. Employs: 500-999.

FLUID POWER PUMPS AND MOTORS

A R Wilfley & Sons Inc

P O Box 2330, Denver CO 80201-2330. 303/7791777. Employs: 250-499.

MISC. INDUSTRIAL AND COMMERICAL MACHINERY AND EQUIPMENT

Electron Corp
5101 S Rio Grande St, Littleton CO 80120-1001. 303/7944392. Employs: 500-999.

INDUSTRIAL INSTRUMENTS FOR MEASUREMENT, DISPLAY, AND CONTROL OF PROCESS VARIABLES; AND RELATED PRODUCTS

Micro Motion Inc
7070 Winchester Cir, Boulder CO 80301-3506. 303/5308400. Employs: 250-499.

INSTRUMENTS FOR MEASURING AND TESTING OF ELECTRICITY AND ELECTRICAL SIGNALS

Honeywell Incorporated
4800 E Dry Creek Rd, Littleton CO 80122-3701. 303/7734700. Employs: 250-499.

Additional small to medium sized employers: 50-249

FARM MACHINERY AND EQUIPMENT

Hydro Gate Corp
6101 Dexter St, Commerce City CO 80022-3126. 303/2887873. Employs: 50-99.

Merritt Equipment Company
9339 US Hwy 85, Henderson CO 80640-8229. 303/2877527. Employs: 100-249.

Noffsinger Mfg & Supply Co
500 6th Ave, Greeley CO 80631-2419. 303/3520463. Employs: 100-249.

California Pellet Mills
1510 Glen Ayr Dr, Lakewood CO 80215-3051. 303/7972733. Employs: 50-99.

CONSTRUCTION MACHINERY AND EQUIPMENT

Wagner Equipment Company
18000 Smith Rd, Aurora CO 80011-3511. 303/3667700. Employs: 100-249.

MINING MACHINERY AND EQUIPMENT, EXCEPT OIL AND GAS FIELD MACHINERY AND EQUIPMENT

Brunner & Lay Inc
333 E Fillmore St, Colorado Springs CO 80907-6305. 719/6348803. Employs: 50-99.

Hydraulics Unlimited Mfg Co
600 Oak St, Eaton CO 80615. 303/4542291. Employs: 100-249.

John Clark Inc
4955 Bannock St, Denver CO 80216-1815. 303/8925800. Employs: 50-99.

INDUSTRIAL TRUCKS, TRACTORS, TRAILERS, AND STACKERS

Bemis Master Palletizer
14603 E Moncrieff Pl, Aurora CO 80011-1212. 303/3713377. Employs: 50-99.

SPECIAL DIES AND TOOLS, DIE SETS, JIGS AND FIXTURES, AND INDUSTRIAL MOLDS

Complex Tooling & Molding Co
4600 Nouthkal Ct S, Boulder CO 80301. 303/5302094. Employs: 100-249.

Plastec Products Inc
1418 E Magnolia Ct, Fort Collins CO 80524-2754. 303/4840343. Employs: 50-99.

J W Reffel Metals Foundry Inc
2650 S Tejon, Denver CO 80223. 303/9345679. Employs: 50-99.

MISC. SPECIAL INDUSTRY MACHINERY

Denver Equip Co
621 S Sierra Madre St, Colorado Springs CO 80903-4021. 719/4713443. Employs: 100-249.

The Hotsy Corporation
21 E Inverness Way, Englewood CO 80112-5707. 303/7925200. Employs: 100-249.

AIR AND GAS COMPRESSORS

Vac-Tec Systems Inc
6101 Lookout Rd, Boulder CO 80301-3359. 303/5302700. Employs: 50-99.

INDUSTRIAL AND COMMERCIAL FANS AND BLOWERS AND AIR PURIFICATION

Puritan Bennett Corp
4865 Sterling Dr, Boulder CO 80301-2307. 303/4433550. Employs: 50-99.

AIR-CONDITIONING AND WARM AIR HEATING EQUIPMENT AND COMMERCIAL AND INDUSTRIAL REFRIDGERATION EQUIPMENT

Apm Marketing
1008 S Evanston Way, Aurora CO 80012-3785. 303/7450902. Employs: 100-249.

Mile High Equipment
11000 E 45th Ave, Denver CO 80239-3004. 303/3713737. Employs: 100-249.

Sno Star Pipelines Inc
2525 Arapahoe Ave, Boulder CO 80302-6720. 303/9399457. Employs: 100-249.

MISC. SERVICE INDUSTRY MACHINERY

Windsor Industries
1351 W Stanford Ave, Englewood CO 80110-5533. 303/7621800. Employs: 100-249.

SCALES AND BALANCES, EXCEPT LABORATORY

Denver Instruments Co
6542 Fig St, Arvada CO 80004-1042. 303/4317255. Employs: 100-249.

MISC. INDUSTRIAL AND COMMERCIAL MACHINERY AND EQUIPMENT

Colorado Sintered Metals
835 Emory Cir, Colorado Springs CO 80915-3401. 719/5960110. Employs: 100-249.

Zimmerman Metals Inc
201 E 58th Ave, Denver CO 80216-1304. 303/2940180. Employs: 50-99.

Goldco Industries Inc
5605 Goldco Dr, Loveland CO 80538-8956. 303/6634770. Employs: 100-249.

Lane Bros Mfg
101 E 5th St, Loveland CO 80537-5503. 303/6671270. Employs: 50-99.

SEARCH, DETECTION, NAVIGATION, GUIDANCE, AERONAUTICAL, AND NAUTICAL SYSTEMS AND INSTRUMENTS

Mid West Machine Products
6255 Joyce Dr, Golden CO 80403-7541. 303/4225388. Employs: 50-99.

Tycho Technology Inc
2990 Center Green Ct, Boulder CO 80301-5420. 303/4432378. Employs: 50-99.

INDUSTRIAL INSTRUMENTS FOR MEASUREMENT, DISPLAY, CONTROL OF PROCESS VARIABLES; AND RELATED PRODUCTS

Anatel Corp
2200 Central Ave, Boulder CO 80301-2841. 303/4425533. Employs: 50-99.

Granville-Phillips Co
5675 E Arapahoe Ave, Boulder CO
80303-1332.   303/4437660.
Employs: 50-99.

Superflow Corp
3512 N Tejon St, Colorado Springs
CO   80907-5222.   719/4711746.
Employs: 50-99.

TOTALIZING FLUID METERS AND COUNTING DEVICES

Dieterich Standard Corporation
5601 71st St, Boulder CO 80301.
303/5309600. Employs: 50-99.

INSTRUMENTS   FOR MEASURING AND TESTING

OF   ELECTRICITY   AND ELECTRICAL SIGNALS

Colorado Data Systems
3301 W Hampden Ave Suite C,
Englewood   CO   80110-1800.
303/7621640. Employs: 50-99.

Westward Electronic Inc
5963 Wcr # 16, Frederick CO
80530.   303/8333303.   Employs:
100-249.

PHOTOGRAPHIC EQUIPMENT AND SUPPLIES

Pentax Corporation
35 Inverness Dr E, Englewood CO
80112-5404.   303/7998000.
Employs: 100-249.

For more information on career opportunities in industrial manufacturing:

<u>Associations</u>

APPLIANCE PARTS DISTRIBUTORS ASSOCIATION
228 East Baltimore Street, Detroit
MI 48202. 313/875-8455.

NATIONAL ASSOCIATION OF MANUFACTURERS
1331 Pennsylvania Avenue, NW,
Suite 1500, Washington DC 20004.
202/637-3000.

ASSOCIATION FOR MANUFACTURING TECHNOLOGY

7901 Westpark Drive, McLean VA
22102. 703/893-2900.

NATIONAL SCREW MACHINE PRODUCTS ASSOCIATION
6700 West Snowville Road,
Breckville OH 44141. 216/526-
0300.

NATIONAL TOOLING AND MACHINING ASSOCIATION
9300 Livingston Road, Fort
Washington MD 20744. 301/248-
1250.

MISCELLANEOUS SERVICES

ALLIED PAINT & DECORATING COMPANY
8250 East. 40th Avenue, Denver CO 80207. 303/333-2318. **Contact:** Mr.
Eugene Ardel, President. **Description:** A paint contractor.

AMERICOLD
5151 Bannock Street, Denver CO 80216. 303/292-4221. **Contact:** Corky Davie, Personnel Director. **Description:** A Denver cold storage warehousing company.

AUTOMATIC LAUNDRY COMPANY
P.O. Box 39365, Denver CO 80239. 303/371-9274. **Contact:** Personnel Department. **Description:** Leases laundry room space and installs coin-operated laundry equipment in apartment complexes.

BUTLER RENTALS
4455 E Virginia, Denver CO 80222. 303/388-5971. **Contact:** Jack Bown, Owner. **Description:** Party, meeting, and convention equipment rental and leasing services.

CALCO HAIR, INC.
5475 East Evans Avenue, Denver CO 80222. 303/757-3021. **Contact:** Personnel Department. **Description:** A Denver beauty salon which also retails hair and skin care supplies.

CHILDREN'S WORLD LEARNING CENTERS
573 Park Point Drive, Golden CO 80401. 303/526-1600. **Contact:** Human Resources Department. **Description:** A national provider of child care and early childhood education with 480 centers in 21 states. Corporate headquarters serves as administrative office for all centers, as well as headquarters for company-wide development, human resources, marketing, program and purchasing functions. **Common positions at corporate headquarters include:** Accounting Specialist; Administrator; Buyer; Computer Programmer; Early Childhood Education Specialist; Financial Analyst; Marketing Specialist; Personnel Specialist; Purchasing Agent. **Common positions at the operations level include:** Classroom Teacher; Lead Teacher; Assistant Center Director; Center Director; District Manager. **Educational backgrounds sought at corporate level:** Accounting; Business Administration; Computer Science; Early Childhood Education; Finance; Marketing. **Educational backgrounds sought at the operations level:** Business Administration; Early Childhood Education or related field. **Benefits:** medical insurance; dental insurance; pension plan; life insurance; tuition assistance; disability coverage; employee discounts; daycare assistance; profit sharing. **Parent company:** ARA Services.

EQUITEX, INC
7315 East Peakview Avenue, Englewood CO 80111. 303/796-8940. **Contact:** Henry Fong, President. **Description:** A business development company.

EXPRESS MESSENGERS
1200 West Evans, Denver CO 80223. 303/936-0200. **Contact:** Personnel. **Description:** A Denver messenger service.

HACH COMPANY
5600 Lindbergh Drive, Box 389, Loveland CO 80539. 303/669-3050. **Contact:** Personnel Department. **Description:** Hach Company is a world leader in developing and manufacturing water analysis systems. **Common positions:** Chemist; Computer Programmer; Electrical Engineer; Mechanical Engineer; Marketing Specialist; Technical Writer/Editor. **Educational backgrounds**

sought: Chemistry; Computer Science; Engineering. **Benefits:** medical insurance; dental insurance; life insurance; tuition assistance; disability coverage; profit sharing; savings plan. **Corporate headquarters:** This location. **Operations at this facility:** manufacturing; research/development; administration; sales

INVENTORY AUDITORS INCORPORATED
4301 Broadway, Denver CO 80216. 303/294-0317. **Contact:** President. **Description:** Company providing inventory services.

JONAS BROTHERS
1037 Broadway, Denver CO 80203-2707. 303/534-7400. **Contact:** Mike Drake, Controller. **Description:** A local taxidermist and furrier.

LAUREN GEOPHYSICAL PROCESSING SERVICES
910 15th Street, Suite 200, Denver CO 80202. 303/893-1344. **Contact:** Tom McGovern, Personnel Manager. **Description:** A geophysical data research and processing company.

MILLWRIGHT AND MACHINERY ERECTORS
900 West Milky Way, Denver CO 80221. 303/427-2834. **Contact:** Irvin Kruger, Personnel Director. **Description:** An area labor union.

NATIONAL CATTLEMEN'S ASSOCIATION
P.O. Box 3469, Englewood CO 80155. 303/694-0305. **Contact:** Earl Peterson, Vice President of Finance and Operations. **Description:** The mission of the National Cattlemen's Association is to advance the economic, political, and social interests of the U.S. cattle industry.

PINKERTON SECURITY & INVESTIGATIONS
4701 Peoria Street, #124, Denver CO 80239. 303/371-8154. **Contact:** Tim Buckner, Personnel Manager. **Description:** The regional office of the well-known private protection company that employs guards, investigators, and branch-office staff. **Common positions:** Security Officers; Investigators; Security Management; Public Relations Specialist; Security Officers. **Educational backgrounds sought:** Criminal Justice; Law Enforcement; Military. **Special programs:** Training programs. **Benefits:** medical, dental, and life insurance; stock options. **Corporate headquarters:** Van Nuys, CA. **Operations at this facility:** administration; service; sales.

STEINER CORPORATION
AMERICAN INDUSTRIAL SERVICE
1850 South Acoma, Denver CO 80223. 303/722-4661. **Contact:** Personnel Department. **Description:** A Denver laundry service.

UNIVERSAL FINANCIAL CORPORATION
2084 South Milwaukee, Denver CO 80210. 303/756-3300. **Contact:** Department of interest. **Description:** A Denver corporation dealing in machinery and equipment finance leasing.

WASTE MANAGEMENT OF DENVER SOUTH
2400 West Union Avenue, P.O. Box 1238, Englewood CO 80150. 303/797-1600. **Contact:** Randy Circle, Controller. **Description:** A waste disposal company, specializing in the hauling of waste materials.

Additional large employers: 250+

MISC. ADVERTISING

US West Direct
2500 S Havana St Suite 1-S, Aurora CO 80014-1622. 303/3378223. Employs: 1,000+.

The Denver Post
1650 Broadway, Denver CO 80202-4837. 303/8201010. Employs: 1,000+.

MISC. BUILDING CLEANING AND MAINTENANCE SERVICES

Janitronics Inc
4925 E Pacific Pl, Denver CO 80222-4822. 303/7592250. Employs: 250-499.

Varsity Contractors
7100 Broadway Suite 5P, Denver CO 80221-2923. 303/4283199. Employs: 250-499.

Porter Industries
418 E 4th St, Loveland CO 80537-5637. 303/6675239. Employs: 250-499.

HELP SUPPLY SERVICES

Prn Inc
1325 S Colorado Blvd Suite 016, Denver CO 80222-3303. 303/7599213. Employs: 250-499.

COMPUTER INTEGRATED SYSTEMS DESIGN

Litton Data Systems Divisions

425 E Fillmore St, Colorado Springs CO 80907-6307. 7194757220. Employs: 500-999.

INFORMATION RETRIEVAL SERVICES

Alexander Data Service Inc
300 E Hampden Ave Suite 324, Englewood CO 80110-2659. 303/7617256. Employs: 250-499.

Information Handling Services
15 Inverness Way E, Englewood CO 80112-5704. 303/7900600. Employs: 500-999.

Petroleum Information Corp
4100 E Dry Creek Rd, Littleton CO 80122-3729. 303/7407100. Employs: 250-499.

Shareholders Service Inc
3410 S Galena St, Denver CO 80231-5078. 303/6713587. Employs: 500-999.

Standard & Poors Compustat Service
7400 S Alton Ct, Englewood CO 80112-2310. 303/7716510. Employs: 250-499.

DETECTIVE, GUARD, AND ARMORED CAR SERVICES

Pinkerton Inc
4500 Havana St Suite 104, Denver CO 80239-2936. 303/3718154. Employs: 250-499.

SECURITY SYSTEMS SERVICES

Andy Frain Services
3333 Quebec St Suite 7550, Denver CO 80207-2329. 303/3881551. Employs: 250-499.

Apg Security Inc
12000 E 47th Ave Suite 105, Denver CO 80239-3115. 303/3735840. Employs: 250-499.

MISC. BUSINESS SERVICES

Citicorp Retail Services Inc
5889 Greenwood Plaza Bl, Englewood CO 80111-2505. 303/7793500. Employs: 250-499.

Consumer Health Services Inc
5720 Flatiron Pky, Boulder CO 80301-5728. 303/4421111. Employs: 250-499.

Diners Club US
183 Inverness Dr W, Englewood CO 80112-5203. 303/7999000. Employs: 500-999.

Neodata Services Group
833 W South Boulder Rd, Louisville CO 80027-2452. 303/6667000. Employs: 250-499.

Pioneer Teletechnologies
1750 Greeley Mall, Greeley CO 80631-8512. 303/3525500. Employs: 250-499.

Unipac Service Corp
3015 S Parker Rd, Aurora CO 80014-2904. 303/6969600. Employs: 250-499.

Attorneys Arbitration Med Ctr Inc
6200 S Syracuse Way, Englewood CO 80111-4737. 303/7737133. Employs: 250-499.

Additional small to medium sized employers: 50-249

CROP PLANTING, CULTIVATING AND PROTECTING

Air Dusters Inc
6458 Weld County Rd #73, Roggen CO 80652. 303/7324569. Employs: 50-99.

CROP HARVESTING, PRIMARILY BY MACHINE

Berger & Company
200 S 2nd St, La Salle CO 80645-4103. 303/2845506. Employs: 50-99.

VETERINARY SERVICES FOR ANIMAL SPECIALTIES

Csu Veterinary Teaching Hsptl
300 W Drake Rd, Fort Collins CO 80526-2866. 303/2214535. Employs: 100-249.

LANDSCAPE COUNSELING AND PLANNING

Beardsley Miller Construction
19 Inverness Way E, Englewood CO 80112-5706. 303/7904181. Employs: 50-99.

Dye Designs Lease Services
5500 E Yale Ave, Denver CO 80222-6930. 303/7592411. Employs: 50-99.

LAWN AND GARDEN SERVICES

Sabells Landscape Maintenance
2901 S Santa Fe Dr, Englewood CO 80110-1411. 303/7880208. Employs: 100-249.

Swingle Inc
8585 E Warren Ave, Denver CO 80231-3315. 303/3376200. Employs: 100-249.

ORNAMENTAL SHRUB AND TREE SERVICES

Shrub Care Chemlawn Tree Service
12445 N Dumont Way, Littleton CO 80125-9756. 303/7911444. Employs: 50-99.

POWER LAUNDRIES, FAMILY AND COMMERCIAL

Silver State Cleaners & Laundry
11505 E Colfax Ave, Aurora CO 80010-2703. 303/3661576. Employs: 100-249.

LINEN SUPPLY

American Linen Supply
5090 Cook St, Denver CO 80216-2428. 303/2957631. Employs: 100-249.

National Linen & Uniform Service
3850 Elm St, Denver CO 80207-1030. 303/3885391. Employs: 50-99.

Snow White Linen Service
110 S 25th St, Colorado Springs CO 80904-3003. 719/6342866. Employs: 50-99.

COIN-OPERATED LAUNDRIES AND DRYCLEANING

City Elite Laundry
2701 Lawrence St, Denver CO 80205-2226. 303/2979979. Employs: 50-99.

DRYCLEANING PLANTS, EXCEPT RUG CLEANING

Esquire Valet
3875 Newport St, Denver CO 80207-1539. 303/3229181. Employs: 50-99.

CARPET AND UPHOLSTERY CLEANING

Building Service Systems Inc
3255 Prairie Ave, Boulder CO 80301-2507. 303/4433836. Employs: 100-249.

BEAUTY SHOPS

JC Penney
Twin Peaks Mall, Longmont CO 80501. 303/7763763. Employs: 50-99.

FUNERAL SERVICES AND CREMATORIES

Olinger Mortuaries
16th & Boulder, Denver CO 80211. 303/4553663. Employs: 100-249.

MISC. PERSONAL SERVICES

Consumer Credit Counseling
5250 Leetsdale Dr Suite 205, Denver CO 80222-1435. 303/3218988. Employs: 50-99.

Smiling Moose Banquet Room
2501 11th Ave, Greeley CO 80631-6927. 303/3567010. Employs: 50-99.

MISC. ADVERTISING

Rocky Mountain News
4680 Edison Ave, Colorado Springs CO 80915-4105. 719/5500406. Employs: 50-99.

ADJUSTMENT AND COLLECTION SERVICES

Consolidated Collections Co
910 15th St Suite 400, Denver CO 80202-2938. 303/6233636. Employs: 100-249.

Professional Recovery Services Inc
2000 S Colorado Blvd, Denver CO 80222-7900. 303/7580520. Employs: 50-99.

PHOTOCOPYING AND DUPLICATING SERVICES

Cain T Square
1625 Blake St, Denver CO 80202-1323. 303/5727905. Employs: 50-99.

Kinkos Copies
1717 Walnut St, Boulder CO 80302-5520. 303/4497100. Employs: 50-99.

Word Processing Professionals
333 W Drake Rd # 133, Fort Collins CO 80526-2883. 303/4933912. Employs: 50-99.

Xerox Reproduction Center
1625 Broadway St Suite 200, Denver CO 80202-4702. 303/5924500. Employs: 50-99.

SECRETARIAL AND COURT REPORTING SERVICES

The Office
1401 Blake St # 200, Denver CO 80202-1330. 303/3318973. Employs: 50-99.

MISC. BUILDING CLEANING AND MAINTENANCE SERVICES

American Maid
2123 E Saint Vrain St, Colorado Springs CO 80909-4723. 719/6300777. Employs: 50-99.

B G Maintenance Services
1045 W Garden Of The Gods Ste, Colorado Springs CO 80907. 719/2601011. Employs: 50-99.

Barela & Sons Inc
1050 S Academy Blvd Suite 100, Colorado Springs CO 80910-3922. 719/5973977. Employs: 100-249.

Butefish Maintenance Ltd
1780 S Bellaire St, Denver CO 80222-4307. 303/7571231. Employs: 100-249.

Danas Housekeeping
363 S Harlan St # 109, Lakewood CO 80226-3552. 303/9371984. Employs: 100-249.

Floor Brite Guardsman
3608 N Stone Ave, Colorado Springs CO 80907-5316. 719/4713851. Employs: 50-99.

Greenwood Service Company
6200 S Syracuse Way, Englewood CO 80111-4737. 303/7799753. Employs: 100-249.

Maintenance Management Inc
1391 N Speer Blvd, Denver CO 80204-2552. 303/6290610. Employs: 100-249.

Master Klean Janitorial Inc
3900 S Wadsworth Bl Ste 30, Denver CO 80235-2203. 303/9883170. Employs: 100-249.

Metropolitan Building Mntnc
420 S Forest St, Denver CO 80222-8110. 303/3210703. Employs: 50-99.

New Pride Inc
635 E 16th Av, Denver CO 80203-2015. 303/8301439. Employs: 50-99.

Norex Service Systems
7388 S Revere Pky Ste 708, Englewood CO 80112-3995. 303/7909496. Employs: 100-249.

Ogden Allied Maintenance Services
1960 W 12th Pl, Denver CO 80204-3425. 303/5347000. Employs: 50-99.

Pedus Services Inc
621 17th St Suite 950, Denver CO 80293-0901. 303/2970192. Employs: 100-249.

Star Housekeeping Inc
7500 Fort Carson Rd, Colorado Springs CO 80913. 719/5760035. Employs: 50-99.

Summit Janitorial Inc
747 Sheridan Blvd Suite 1A, Denver CO 80214-2551. 303/2340610. Employs: 50-99.

Sunshine Bldg Maintenance Inc
1658 Cole Blvd Suite 70, Golden CO 80401-3304. 303/2770095. Employs: 100-249.

Young Janitorial Services Of Co
415 S Weber St, Colorado Springs CO 80903-2130. 719/6332621. Employs: 100-249.

Interclean Service System Inc
12075 E 45th Ave, Denver CO 80239-3123. 303/3730533. Employs: 100-249.

Maintenance Unlimited
600 S Cherry St, Denver CO 80222-1702. 303/3772835. Employs: 100-249.

Metro General House Cleaning
1902 S Michigan Way, Denver CO 80219-5256. 303/9370507. Employs: 50-99.

EMPLOYMENT AGENCIES

Avatrac
7700 Cherry Creek Sth Dr, Denver CO 80231-3217. 303/7556800. Employs: 50-99.

Forty Plus Of Colorado Inc
5800 W Alameda Ave, Lakewood CO 80226-3564. 303/8303040. Employs: 100-249.

HELP SUPPLY SERVICES

Hlj Management Group Inc
Building 1818 Ste 1818, Colorado Springs CO 80913. 719/5767576. Employs: 100-249.

Medistaff
9101 Harlan St, Westminster CO 80030-2924. 303/4300730. Employs: 50-99.

Midwest Services
2040 S Clay St, Denver CO 80219-5526. 303/4588826. Employs: 100-249.

Ready Men Labor
965 E 22nd Ave, Denver CO 80205-5106. 303/8308304. Employs: 100-249.

Resources Unlimited
2060 Broadway St, Boulder CO 80302-5216. 303/4497656. Employs: 100-249.

Western Temporary Services Inc
1025 9th Ave, Greeley CO 80631-4000. 303/3562070. Employs: 50-99.

COMPUTER INTEGRATED SYSTEMS DESIGN

Automation Research Systms Ltd
2327 Fort Carson, Colorado Springs CO 80913. 719/5764964. Employs: 100-249.

Consolink
1840 Industrial Cir, Longmont CO 80501-6524. 303/6512014. Employs: 50-99.

Prairie Tek
2120 Miller Dr, Longmont CO 80501-6744. 303/7724011. Employs: 50-99.

Precision Visual Inc
6260 Lookout Rd, Boulder CO 80301-3336. 303/5309000. Employs: 100-249.

QC Data Collectors
777 Grant St Suite 111, Denver CO 80203-3533. 303/8371444. Employs: 50-99.

INFORMATION RETRIEVAL SERVICES

Ags Information Services Inc
1331 17th St Suite 600, Denver CO 80202-1556. 303/2970234. Employs: 50-99.

Americom Direct Marketing Inc
10600 E 54th Ave Suite D, Denver CO 80239-2135. 303/3714400. Employs: 50-99.

Eds Federal Corporation
700 Broadway Suite 1011, Denver CO 80203-3443. 303/8313051. Employs: 50-99.

First Seismic Corp

600 Seventeenth St, Denver CO 80202-5401. 303/5730200. Employs: 50-99.

Mountain Bell
1260 Well County Rd 58 Ste 58, Greeley CO 80631. 303/3393001. Employs: 100-249.

Sp Info Services Corp
1401 Del Norte St, Denver CO 80221-6910. 303/4308881. Employs: 100-249.

United Banks Service Company
5700 Dtc Pky, Englewood CO 80111-3226. 303/7702400. Employs: 100-249.

COMPUTER RENTAL AND LEASING

Capital Associates Inc
7175 W Jefferson Ave, Denver CO 80235-2318. 303/9801000. Employs: 100-249.

DETECTIVE, GUARD, AND ARMORED CAR SERVICES

American Protective Services
14211 E 4th Ave Suite 330, Aurora CO 80011-8728. 303/3449502. Employs: 100-249.

Burns International Security
8000 E Prentice Ave Suite D-3, Englewood CO 80111-2728. 303/2900420. Employs: 100-249.

Commercial Guard Inc
155 S Madison St Suite 201, Denver CO 80209-3013. 303/3201058. Employs: 100-249.

Cpp Pinkertons Inc
5050 Edison Ave, Colorado Springs CO 80915-3540. 719/5916522. Employs: 100-249.

Firstwatch Security Services
1395 S Platte River Dr, Denver CO
80223-3467.   303/8710606.
Employs: 100-249.

Guardsmark Inc
3773 Cherry Creek Nrth Dr # 52,
Denver   CO   80209-3804.
303/3882800. Employs: 100-249.

Wackenhut Corporation
15290 E 6th Ave # 250, Aurora CO
80011-8833.   303/3414433.
Employs: 50-99.

Wells Fargo Armored Service Co
970 Yuma St, Denver CO 80204-
3836. 303/8250376. Employs: 100-
249.

Apg Security
325 E 7th St, Loveland CO 80537-
4872. 303/6695176. Employs: 100-
249.

Wells Fargo Guard Services
5961 E 38th Ave, Denver CO
80207-1252.   303/3334258.
Employs: 50-99.

SECURITY   SYSTEMS
SERVICES

Allied Security Inc
1675 Carr St Suite 210-N,
Lakewood   CO   80215-3159.
303/2396319. Employs: 50-99.

Contemporary Services Corp
6900 E Belleview Ave Suite 300,
Englewood   CO   80111-1630.
303/8500500. Employs: 100-249.

Stanley Smith Security Inc
2460 W 26th Ave Suite 430C,
Denver   CO   80211-5405.
303/4774441. Employs: 100-249.

The Alert Centre
6160 S Syracuse Way, Englewood
CO   80111-4700.   303/7794286.
Employs: 100-249.

PHOTOFINISHING
LABORATORIES

Royal Color Lab
2480 W 4th Av Ste A, Denver CO
80223-1059.   303/7783205.
Employs: 50-99.

Vivid Color Corp
4909 Oakland St, Denver CO
80239-2719.   303/5721110.
Employs: 50-99.

MISC. BUSINESS SERVICES

Bethesda Support Line
4400 E Iliff Ave, Denver CO
80222-6019.   303/7581123.
Employs: 50-99.

Career Track Seminars Inc
3085 Center Green Dr, Boulder CO
80301-5408.   303/4472323.
Employs: 100-249.

Desks Inc
1385 S Santa Fe Dr, Denver CO
80223-3233.   303/7778880.
Employs: 50-99.

Lear Siegler Measurement Contr
74 Inverness Dr E, Englewood CO
80112-5102.   303/7923300.
Employs: 100-249.

Original Publication Service
6425 Wadsworth Blvd Suite 306,
Arvada   CO   80003-4441.
303/4317435. Employs: 50-99.

Rgis Inventory Specialists
10200 E Girard Ave Suite C-243,
Denver   CO   80231-5513.
303/6956805. Employs: 100-249.

Time Life Libraries
999 18th St Suite 2250, Denver CO
80202-2422.   303/2987523.
Employs: 50-99.

Telecheck
3025 S Parker Rd, Aurora CO
80014-2911.   303/7525860.
Employs: 50-99.

May Telemarketing Inc
724 Whalers Way, Fort Collins CO
80525-3314.   303/2234811.
Employs: 100-249.

MISC. ELECTRICAL AND ELECTRONIC REPAIR SHOPS

GE Consumer Service
5855 Stapleton Dr N, Denver CO
80216-3312.   303/3930862.
Employs: 50-99.

MISC. REPAIR SHOPS AND RELATED SERVICES

Matsushita Services Company
1640 S Abilene St Suite C, Aurora
CO   80012-5819.   303/7522024.
Employs: 50-99.

Qmc Technologies Inc
660 Compton St, Broomfield CO
80020-1635.   303/4668297.
Employs: 50-99.

Team Managers Ski & Bike Co
1121 N Summit Blvd, Frisco CO
80443. 303/6683174. Employs: 50-99.

MISC. SERVICES

Ctl Thompson Inc
1971 W 12th Ave, Denver CO
80204-3436.   303/8250777.
Employs: 50-99.

Minproc
5600 S Quebec St Suite 300-C,
Englewood   CO   80111-2210.
303/7219111. Employs: 100-249.

Northern Geophysical America
7076 S Alton Way Suite H,
Englewood   CO   80112-2014.
303/7413700. Employs: 100-249.

NEWSPAPER PUBLISHING

Throughout the recession, the newspaper industry has been suffering from a severely shrinking share of advertising dollars. Classified advertising was especially hard hit, and recovery will depend on improvement in the retail, automotive, and real estate industries, as well as on a growing employment market. For the long-term, look for newspaper companies to target specific readers in order to attract advertisers.
Lifestyle, health care, and business sections will grow in importance.

BARNUM PUBLISHING COMPANY INCORPORATED
314 Federal Boulevard, Denver CO 80219. 303/936-2345. **Contact:** Personnel Director. **Description:** Publishing company involved in newspaper printing.

BOULDER COUNTY BUSINESS REPORT
4885 Riverbend Road, Suite D, Boulder CO 80301. 303/440-4952. **Contact:** Jerry Lewis, Editor. **Description:** A monthly business newspaper covering Boulder County, Colorado. **Common positions:** Advertising Worker; Reporter/Editor. **Educational backgrounds sought:** Business Administration; Communications; Liberal Arts; Journalism/Advertising. **Benefits:** medical insurance; dental insurance. **Operations at this facility:** sales.

DAILY CAMERA
P.O. Box 591, Boulder CO 80306. 303/442-1202. **Contact:** Ms. Dani Ross, Director of Human Resources. **Description:** Publishes a daily newspaper with a circulation of more than 40,000. A subsidiary of Knight-Ridder Newspapers (Miami, FL). **Corporate headquarters:** This location. **Common positions:** Accountant; Advertising Worker; Computer Programmer; Credit Manager; Customer Service Representative; Personnel and Labor Relations Specialist; Reporter/Editor; Sales Representative. **Educational backgrounds sought:** Accounting; Journalism. **Special programs:** Training programs and internships. **Benefits:** medical insurance; dental insurance; pension plan; life insurance; disability coverage; savings plan.

THE DENVER POST
1560 Broadway, Denver CO 80202. 303/820-1820. **Contact:** Human Resources Department. **Description:** Publishes a daily newspaper, with a weekday circulation of more than 230,000, and a Sunday circulation of 440,000. **Common positions:** Accountant; Advertising Salesperson; Blue-Collar Worker Supervisor; Commercial Artist; Computer Programmer (Hewlett Packard); Customer Service Representative; Reporter/Editor; Financial Analyst. **Educational backgrounds sought:** Journalism; Accounting; Art/Design; Communications; Computer Science; Finance; Marketing; Political Science. **Special programs:** Training programs and internships. **Benefits:** medical insurance; dental insurance; pension plan; life insurance; disability coverage; employee discounts. **Corporate headquarters:** Houston, TX. **Parent company:** Media News Group. **Operations at this facility:** divisional headquarters.

GREELEY DAILY TRIBUNE
P.O. Box 1138, Greeley CO 80632. 303/352-0211. **Contact:** Ed Otte, Managing Editor. **Description:** Publishes a daily newspaper with a circulation of more than 22,000. **Corporate headquarters:** This location.

ROCKY MOUNTAIN NEWS
400 West Colfax Avenue, Denver CO 80204. 303/892-5000. **Contact:** Donald Livingston, Personnel Manager. **Description:** Publishes a daily newspaper, with a daily circulation of more than 300,000; 320,000 on Sunday. Part of the Scripps-Howard Newspapers group (Cincinnati, OH).

STAR-JOURNAL PUBLISHING CORPORATION
P.O. Box 4040, Pueblo CO 81003. 719/544-3520. **Contact:** Managing Editor. **Description:** Publishes a number of area newspapers: The Morning Chieftain (circulation: 39,800); The Evening Star-Journal (circulation 11,400); The Saturday Chieftain and Star-Journal; and the Sunday Star-Journal and Sunday Chieftain. Independently owned. **Corporate headquarters:** This location.

Additional large employers: 250+

NEWSPAPERS: PUBLISHING, OR PUBLISHING AND PRINTING

Denver Publishing
400 W Colfax Ave, Denver CO 80204-2607. 303/8925000. Employs: 1,000+.

Ft Collins Newspapers Inc
1212 Riverside Ave, Fort Collins CO 80524-3230. 303/4936397. Employs: 250-499.

Gazette Telegraph
30 S Prospect St, Colorado Springs CO 80903-3638. 7196325511. Employs: 500-999.

Times Call Publ Co
717 4th Ave, Longmont CO 80501-5415. 303/7762244. Employs: 250-499.

Additional small to medium sized employers: 50-249

NEWSPAPERS: PUBLISHING, OR PUBLISHING AND PRINTING

Bingo Journal
4105 E Florida Ave, Denver CO 80222-3620. 303/7591764. Employs: 50-99.

Denver Blade
1160 Ogden St, Denver CO 80218-2851. 303/8618606. Employs: 50-99.

Electronic Classified Cooperative
7114 W Jefferson Ave, Denver CO 80235-2309. 303/9882600. Employs: 50-99.

Handicapped Coloradan
946 Pearl St, Boulder CO 80302-5109. 303/9388288. Employs: 50-99.

La Times Western News
1700 Lincoln St, Denver CO 80203-1014. 303/8301975. Employs: 50-99.

La Voz Newspaper
2885 W 3rd Ave, Denver CO 80219-1609. 303/9368556. Employs: 50-99.

Loveland Daily Reporter
450 N Cleveland, Loveland CO 80537. 303/6695050. Employs: 50-99.

Out Front Magazine
700 E Speer Blvd, Denver CO 80203-4215. 303/7441333. Employs: 50-99.

Out Front Magazine
600 Grant St, Denver CO 80203-3524. 303/8608994. Employs: 50-99.

Pueblo Star Journal & Chieftain
State Capitol Bldg, Denver CO 80203. 303/8617202. Employs: 50-99.

Sentinel Publishing
3501 E 46th Ave, Denver CO
80216-4214.   303/2925551.
Employs: 100-249.

Steamboat Pilot & Today
1041 Lincoln, Steamboat Spr CO
80487. 303/8791502. Employs: 50-
99.

The Colorado Gambler
3888 E Mexico Ave, Denver CO
80210-3813.   303/7334870.
Employs: 50-99.

The Downtown Walker

444   17,   Denver   CO   80202.
303/6290990. Employs: 50-99.

The Mountain Ear
20 Lakeview Dr, Nederland CO
80466. 303/2587075. Employs: 50-
99.

The Weekly Issue Hispania
2865 W 44th Ave, Denver CO
80211-1473.   303/4809945.
Employs: 50-99.

Westword
1621 18th St Suite 150, Denver CO
80202-1266.   303/2967744.
Employs: 50-99.

For more information on career opportunities in newspaper publishing:

Associations

**AMERICAN NEWSPAPER
PUBLISHERS ASSOCIATION**
Newspaper Center, 11600 Sunrise
Valley Drive, Reston VA 22091.
703/648-1000.

**AMERICAN SOCIETY OF
NEWSPAPER EDITORS**
P.O. Box 17004, Washington DC
20041. 703/648-1144.

**THE DOW JONES
NEWSPAPER FUND**
P.O. Box 300, Princeton NJ 08543-
0300. 609/520-4000.

**INTERNATIONAL
CIRCULATION MANAGERS
ASSOCIATION**
P.O. Box 17420, Washington DC
20041. 703/620-9555.

**NATIONAL NEWSPAPER
ASSOCIATION**
1627 K Street NW, Suite 400,
Washington DC 20006. 202/466-
7200.

NATIONAL PRESS CLUB

529 14th St. NW, 13th Floor,
Washington DC 20045. 202/662-
7500.

THE NEWSPAPER GUILD
Research and Information
Department, 1125 15th Street NW,
Washington DC 20005. 301/585-
2990.

Directories

**EDITOR & PUBLISHER
INTERNATIONAL
YEARBOOK**
Editor & Publisher Co. Inc., 11
West 19th Street, New York NY
10011. 212/675-4380.

**JOURNALISM CAREER AND
SCHOLARSHIP GUIDE**
The Dow Jones Newspaper Fund,
P.O. Box 300, Princeton NJ 08543-
0300. 609/520-4000.

Magazines

EDITOR AND PUBLISHER
Editor & Publisher Co. Inc., 11
West 19th Street, New York NY
10011. 212/675-4380.

NEWS, INC.
49 East 21st Street, New York NY
10010. 212/979-4600.

PAPER AND PACKAGING/GLASS AND FOREST PRODUCTS

The next few years hold both promise and problems for the paper industry. If the economy strengthens and export markets regain the momentum lost during the last few years, the industry should see revenues grow about 10 percent by the end of 1996. Technological advances should strengthen the industry both at home and abroad. In addition, environmental concerns should give the paper packaging segment the upper hand over plastics.

ALPINE LUMBER COMPANY
P.O. Box 21470, Denver CO 80221. 303/458-4740. **Contact:** General Manager. **Description:** A Denver-area lumber company. **Corporate headquarters:** This location.

AMERICAN LUMBER COMPANY, INC.
5920 Lamar Street, Arvada CO 80003. 303/424-7716. **Contact:** Jim Audiss, General Manager. **Description:** A Denver-area lumber company.

BOISE CASCADE CORPORATION
4565 Indiana, Golden CO 80403. 303/279-5511. **Contact:** Personnel Department. **Description:** A corrugated container plant, doing business as a division of the well-known forest products, office supplies, and can manufacturing company. **Corporate headquarters:** Boise, ID.

COACH HOUSE GIFTS
420 East 58th Avenue, Denver CO 80216. 303/292-5537. **Contact:** Mary Boyd, Director of Personnel. **Description:** Manufactures and distributes gifts, cards, and papergoods.

COORS COMPANY/GLASS DIVISION
10619 West 50th Avenue, Wheat Ridge CO 80033. **Contact:** Personnel. **Description:** A manufacturer of aluminum beer cans, glass beer bottles, six-pack bottle carriers, and bottle labels. For hiring information, contact corporate headquarters at 303/277-5514 (Golden, CO).

COORS PORCELAIN DIVISION
600 9th Street, Golden CO 80401. 303/278-4000. **Contact:** Employment Center. **Description:** A manufacturer of glass beverage bottles. For hiring information, contact corporate headquarters at 303/277-5514 (Golden, CO).

DENVER LUMBER COMPANY
1490 South Cherokee Street, Denver CO 80223. 303/733-5543. **Contact:** Scott Yates, General Manager. **Description:** A Denver lumber company.

DIXON PAPER COMPANY
3900 Lima Street, Denver CO 80239. 303/371-7510. **Contact:** Helga Mahaffey, Personnel Coordinator. **Description:** A wholesale distributor of paper and paper-related products. **Common positions:** Accountant; Blue-Collar Worker Supervisor; Buyer; Computer Programmer; Credit Manager; Customer Service Representative; Financial Analyst; Branch Manager; Department Manager; General Manager; Management Trainee; Operations/Production Manager; Marketing Specialist; Purchasing Agent; Sales Representative; Systems Analyst; Transportation and Traffic Specialist. **Educational backgrounds sought:** Accounting; Business Administration; Computer Science; Finance; Marketing. **Benefits:** medical insurance; dental insurance; pension plan; life insurance; tuition assistance; disability coverage; savings plan. **Corporate headquarters:** This location. **Parent company:** International Paper. **Operations at this facility:** administration; service; sales.

GUMP GLASS COMPANY INCORPORATED
1265 South Broadway, Denver CO 80210. 303/778-1155. **Contact:** Personnel Department. **Description:** A company dealing in the wholesale and retail of glass.

MAIL WELL ENVELOPE COMPANY
3500 Rockmont Drive, Denver CO 80202. 303/455-3505. **Contact:** Christi Levine, Personnel Manager. **Description:** Manufactures and markets envelopes in a wide range of sizes and styles. **Corporate headquarters:** This location.

MAIL WELL ENVELOPES, INC.
23 Inverness Way East, Englewood CO 80112. 303/790-8023. **Contact:** Personnel Department. **Description:** An envelope manufacturer; a subsidiary of Great Northern Nekoosa Corporation, a major coal mining company and manufacturer of paper products. **Corporate headquarters:** Stamford, CT.

PACKAGING CORPORATION OF AMERICA
5501 Brighton Boulevard, Commerce City CO 80022. 303/288-2601. **Contact:** Kevin Browner, Plant Foreman. **Description:** Production facility of the major packaging and paperboard products manufacturer. Company also produces corrugated containers, folding cartons, and molded pulp products.

PARADE PACKAGING MATERIALS COMPANY
2907 Huron Street, Denver CO 80202-1029. 303/297-3711. **Contact:** Kent Smith, Controller. **Description:** A Denver producer of assorted plastic bags.

SAGEBRUSH SALES INC.
P.O. Box 1447, Montrose CO 81402. 303/249-6616. **Contact:** Juan Velazquez, Personnel Director. **Description:** A wholesale lumber distributor. **Corporate headquarters:** This location.

STONE CONTAINER
5050 East 50th Avenue, Denver CO 80216. 303/399-0494. **Contact:** Human Resources. **Description:** Manufactures corrugated paper cartons.

Additional large employers: 250+

MILLWORK

Denver Window Corp
5961 E 64th Ave, Commerce City CO 80022-3316. 303/2874111. Employs: 250-499.

SETUP PAPERBOARD BOXES

Adolph Coors Co
17755 W 32nd Ave, Golden CO 80401-1299. 303/2773810. Employs: 1,000+.

Additional small to medium sized employers: 50-249

TIMBER TRACTS

US Forest Service
11177 W 8th Ave, Lakewood CO 80215-5515. 303/2369431. Employs: 100-249.

LOGGING

Louisiana-Pacific Corporation
350 County Rd 17, Walden CO 80480. 303/7238231. Employs: 50-99.

SAWMILLS AND PLANNING MILLS

Louisiana-Pacific Corp
1509 Hwy 9, Kremmling CO 80459. 303/7243467. Employs: 100-249.

MILLWORK

Pella Products Inc

4500 Grape St, Denver CO 80216-6403. 303/3880884. Employs: 50-99.

WOOD KITCHEN CABINETS

Innovative Co Inc
4401 Innovation Dr, Fort Collins CO 80525-3404. 303/2237779. Employs: 100-249.

Mastercraft Kitchens
3550 Odessa Way, Aurora CO 80011-8168. 303/3758220. Employs: 50-99.

Riviera Cabinets Inc
618 Garden Of The Gds Rd, Colorado Springs CO 80907. 719/5985254. Employs: 100-249.

Whirlpool Kitchens Incorporate
3550 Odessa Wa, Aurora CO 80011-8168. 303/3417300. Employs: 100-249.

MISC. STRUCTURAL WOOD MEMBERS

Crissey Fowler Lumber
117 W Vermijo Ave, Colorado Springs CO 80903-3824. 719/4732411. Employs: 50-99.

MOBILE HOMES

Titan Homes
2221 Clayton Ln, Berthoud CO 80513. 303/5322632. Employs: 100-249.

PREFABRICATED WOOD BUILDINGS AND COMPONENTS

Advanced Component Sys Inc
1201 S Boulder, Lafayette CO 80026. 303/6666800. Employs: 50-99.

Continental Manufacturing Inc
999 N Van Buren Ave, Loveland CO 80537-4456. 303/6676423. Employs: 50-99.

CORRUGATED AND SOLID FIBER BOXES

Boise Cascade Container Corp
4565 Indiana St, Golden CO 80403-1850. 303/2795511. Employs: 50-99.

Capitol Packaging
11333 E 55th Ave, Denver CO 80239-2029. 303/3750880. Employs: 50-99.

Colorado Container Corp
4221 Monaco St, Denver CO 80216-6605. 303/3310400. Employs: 50-99.

Deline Box Windows Inc
1201 Cornerstone Dr, Windsor CO 80550-5531. 303/6867600. Employs: 50-99.

Inland Container Corporation
5000 Oak St, Wheat Ridge CO 80033-2221. 303/4227700. Employs: 50-99.

Packaging Corp Of America
1377 S Jason St, Denver CO 80223-3407. 303/7773300. Employs: 100-249.

Tharco Containers Inc
13400 E 39th Ave, Denver CO 80239-3533. 303/3731860. Employs: 100-249.

Western Packaging Inc
10854 Leroy Dr, Denver CO 80233-3614. 303/4523556. Employs: 50-99.

FOLDING PAPERBOARD BOXES, INCLUDING SANITARY

Apex Die & Box Company
230 Yuma St, Denver CO 80223-1002. 303/6980100. Employs: 100-249.

MISC. COATED AND LAMINATED PAPER

Cal Emblem Labels
1455 S Platte River Dr, Denver CO 80223-3463. 303/7786777. Employs: 50-99.

ENVELOPES

Federal American Envelopes
5000 Kingston St, Denver CO 80239-2522. 303/3735900. Employs: 100-249.

Niagara Envelope Company
14101 E 33rd Pl Suite A, Aurora CO 80011-1613. 303/3731780. Employs: 50-99.

MISC. CONVERTED PAPER AND PAPERBOARD PRODUCTS

American Precision Plastics
11060 Irma Dr, Denver CO 80233-3611. 303/4572400. Employs: 100-249.

Software Labels Corporation
7925 E Harvard Ave, Denver CO 80231-3821. 303/7502990. Employs: 50-99.

Peter Mangone Inc
12687 W Cedar Dr, Lakewood CO 80228-2010. 303/9865447. Employs: 50-99.

FLAT GLASS

Cherry Creek Enterprises Inc
3500 Blake St, Denver CO 80205-2408. 303/2951010. Employs: 50-99.

Satellite Glass Inc
754 S Briscoe Ln Suite C, Castle Rock CO 80104-1944. 303/6880675. Employs: 50-99.

MISC. PRESSED AND BLOWN GLASS AND GLASSWARE

Particle Measuring Sys Inc
1855 57th Ct S, Boulder CO 80301-2809. 303/4437100. Employs: 100-249.

For more information on career opportunities in the paper, packaging, glass, and forest products industries:

Associations

AMERICAN FOREST COUNCIL
1250 Connecticut Avenue NW, Washington DC 20036. 202/463-2455.

AMERICAN PAPER INSTITUTE
260 Madison Avenue, New York NY 10016. 212/340-0600.

FOREST PRODUCTS RESEARCH SOCIETY
2801 Marshall Court, Madison WI 53705. 608/231-1361.

NATIONAL FOREST PRODUCTS ASSOCIATION
1250 Connecticut Avenue NW, Washington DC 20036. 202/463-2700.

NATIONAL PAPER TRADE ASSOCIATION
111 Great Neck Road, Great Neck NY 11021. 516/829-3070.

PAPERBOARD PACKAGING COUNCIL
1101 Vermont Avenue NW, Suite 411, Washington DC 20005. 202/289-4100.

TECHNICAL ASSOCIATION OF THE PULP AND PAPER INDUSTRY
P.O. Box 105113, Atlanta GA 30348. 404/446-1400.

Directories

DIRECTORY OF THE FOREST PRODUCTS INDUSTRY
Miller Freeman Publications, Inc., 600 Harrison Street, San Francisco CA 94107. 415/905-2200.

LOCKWOOD-POST'S DIRECTORY OF THE PAPER AND ALLIED TRADES
Miller Freeman Publications, Inc., 600 Harrison Street, San Francisco CA 94107. 415/905-2200.

POST'S PULP AND PAPER DIRECTORY
Miller Freeman Publications, Inc., 600 Harrison Street, San Francisco CA 94107. 415/905-2200.

Magazines

FOREST INDUSTRIES
Miller Freeman Publications, Inc., 600 Harrison Street, San Francisco CA 94107. 415/905-2200.

PAPERBOARD PACKAGING
Advanstar Communications, 1 E. First Street, Duluth MN 55802. 218/723-9200.

PULP AND PAPER WEEK
Miller Freeman Publications, Inc., 600 Harrison Street, San Francisco CA 94107. 415/905-2200.

PRINTING/GRAPHIC ARTS

As the U.S. economy improves, accompanied by growth in print advertising, the printing industry should begin to rebound. The price of paper is expected to remain soft, with paper mill capacity outstripping demand. The printing industry's employment levels will rise.

AUTREY INVESTMENTS
1250 South Parker Road, Suite 200, Denver CO 80231. 303/320-4113. **Contact:** Julie Miceli, Personnel Manager. **Description:** Two Denver-area locations and a location in Phoenix, AZ. A printing firm specializing in distinctive quality high school and college graduation announcements and similar accessories, cap and gown sales and rental, high school and college ring sales, business cards, letterheads, envelopes, company logos, and employee recognition programs. Uses Virkotype and engraved printing presses. **Corporate headquarters:** This location. **Operations at this facility:** manufacturing; administration; sales. **Common positions:** Accountant; Commercial Artist; Computer Programmer; Credit Manager; Customer Service Representative; Industrial Engineer; Operations/Production Manager; Marketing Specialist; Personnel Representative; Systems Analyst; Press Operator; Engraver. **Educational backgrounds sought:** Accounting; Art/Design; Business Administration; Engineering; Marketing. **Benefits:** medical insurance; life insurance; tuition assistance; disability coverage; profit sharing; employee discounts.

CAIN T-SQUARE
1625 Blake Street, Denver CO 80202. 303/572-7990. **Contact:** Personnel Department. **Description:** A Denver-area reprographics company.

EAGLE DIRECT
5105 East 41st Avenue, Denver CO 80216. 303/320-5411. **Contact:** Personnel Department. **Description:** A company which handles commercial and lithographic printing and design.

FREDERIC PRINTING

14701 East 38th Avenue, Aurora CO 80011. 303/371-7990. **Contact:** Personnel. **Description:** Provides a wide range of commercial printing services, from camera-ready art through binding. **Operations at this facility:** manufacturing; administration; sales. **Corporate headquarters:** This location. **Common positions:** Accountant; Blue-Collar Worker Supervisor; Buyer; Computer Programmer; Credit Manager; Customer Service Representative; Electrical Engineer; Mechanical Engineer; Department Manager; Management Trainee; Purchasing Agent; Sales Representative. **Benefits:** medical insurance; dental insurance; life insurance; tuition assistance; disability coverage; profit sharing.

GOLDEN BELL PRESS INCORPORATED

2403 Champa, Denver CO 80205. 303/296-1600. **Contact:** Personnel Department. **Description:** Publisher of periodicals and offset printing.

HIBBERT/WEST

1601 Park Avenue West, Denver CO 80216. 303/297-1601. **Contact:** Gordon Penley, Controller. **Description:** Provides commercial printing services, including offset printing. A subsidiary of the Hibbert Company (Trenton, NJ). **Corporate headquarters:** This location.

INFORMATION HANDLING SERVICES

15 Inverness Way East, Englewood CO 80150. 303/790-0600. **Contact:** Human Resources Services. **Description:** Assimilates and indexes technical, engineering, federal, and regulatory information which it delivers on microform and by electronic media. **Common positions:** Accountant; Computer Programmer; Customer Service Representative; Electrical Engineer; Industrial Engineer; Mechanical Engineer; Industrial Manager; Operations/Production Manager; Marketing Specialist; Sales Representative; Systems Analyst; Technical Writer/Editor; Transportation and Traffic Specialist. **Benefits:** medical, dental, and life insurance; pension plan; tuition assistance; disability coverage; savings plan. **Corporate headquarters:** This location. **Parent company:** Information Handling Services Group. **Operations at this facility:** divisional headquarters; manufacturing; administration.

KISTLER INC.

P.O. Box 5467, Denver CO 80217. 303/399-0900. **Contact:** Toni Balsley, Human Resources Administrator. **Description:** An area commercial printer, whose services include computerized typesetting, lithography, offset printing, letterpress services, and others. **Corporate headquarters:** Topeka, KS. **Common positions:** Accountant; Blue-Collar Worker Supervisor; Computer Programmer; Credit Manager; Customer Service Representative; Operations/Production Manager; Purchasing Agent; Sales Representative; Systems Analyst; Pressman. **Educational backgrounds sought:** Accounting; Business Administration; Communications; Computer Science; Finance; Marketing. **Benefits:** medical, dental, and life insurance; tuition assistance; disability coverage; 401K plan. **Parent company:** CGF Industries. **Operations at this facility:** manufacturing. **Employees:** 135.

ROCKY MOUNTAIN BANK NOTE

10455 West 6th Avenue, Lakewood CO 80215. 303/233-8080. **Contact:** Anthony W. Brown, Manager, Employee Relations. **Description:** Supplier of checks and financial forms, selling primarily to financial institutions. There are 23 different operating units across the western half of the United States. **Corporate headquarters:** Lakewood, CO. **Common positions:** Accountant; Engineer; Industrial Engineer; Financial Analyst; Department Manager; General Manager; Management Trainee; Marketing Specialist; Human Resources Positions; Public Relations Worker; Purchasing Agent; Sales Representative; Systems Analyst. **Common positions at manufacturing/imprinting facilities include:** Production Supervisor; Customer Service Representative; Department Manager; Operations/Production Manager; Quality Control Supervisor. **Educational backgrounds sought:** Accounting; Art/Design; Business Administration; Computer Science; Engineering; Finance; Marketing; Printing Management (manufacturing/imprinting facilities). **Benefits:** medical insurance; dental insurance; vision insurance; flexible benefits plan; pension plan; life insurance; tuition assistance; disability coverage; employee discounts; 401K plan; vacation; paid holidays (10).

SUN CHEMICALS

11925 East 49th Avenue, Denver CO 80239. 303/373-2655. **Contact:** Betty Osborne, Office Manager. **Description:** A Denver manufacturer of printing ink.

TYPOGRAPHY PLUS

2137 South Birch Street, Denver CO 80222. (303) 759-5951. **Contact:** Donald Guntenaar, Personnel Department. **Description:** An advertising typographer in Denver, using Multiset, Varityper 6400, and Macintosh Systems. **Common positions:** Typesetter; Desktop Publisher Specialist. **Benefits:** medical and life insurance; profit sharing.

U.S. WEST MARKETING RESOURCES CO.

P.O. Box 455, Loveland CO 80539-0455. 303/667-0652. **Contact:** Human Resources. **Description:** Produces directories, including telephone directories, city directories, and others, primarily on a contractual basis. **Corporate headquarters:** This location.

WOEHRMYER BUSINESS FORMS

13801 East Smith Drive, Suite E, Aurora CO 80011. 303/341-5550. **Contact:** Personnel Director. **Description:** Produces a variety of business forms.

Additional large employers: 250+

COMMERCIAL PRINTING, LITHOGRAPHIC

AB Hirschfeld Press Inc
5200 Smith Rd, Denver CO 80216-4525. 303/3208500. Employs: 250-499.

Walter Drake & Sons Inc
4510 Edison Ave, Colorado Springs CO 80915-4103. 7195963140. Employs: 250-499

Additional small to medium sized employers: 50-249

COMMERCIAL PRINTING, LITHOGRAPHIC

Bei Graphics Corp
3550 Frontier Ave, Boulder CO
80301-2410. 303/4498010.
Employs: 100-249.

Communigraphics Corp
2010 W Dartmouth Ave,
Englewood CO 80110-1323.
303/7616081. Employs: 50-99.

Intermountain Color Inc
1840 Range St, Boulder CO 80301-
2717. 303/4433800. Employs: 50-
99.

COMMERCIAL PRINTING, GRAVURE

Norwest Publishing Co
259 30th St, Greeley CO 80631-
7425. 303/3568352. Employs: 100-
249.

MISC. COMMERCIAL PRINTING

Charles A Redpath Jr Attorney
PO Box 616, Englewood CO
80151-0616. 303/7610238.
Employs: 100-249.

Jl Printing
102 W 4th St, Loveland CO 80537-
5523. 303/6676062. Employs: 50-
99.

Leanin' Tree Publishing Co
6055 Longbow Dr, Boulder CO
80301-3203. 303/5301442.
Employs: 100-249.

Mtn West Printing
1150 W Custer Pl, Denver CO
80223-2317. 303/7443313.
Employs: 50-99.

Westview Press
5500 Central Av, Boulder CO
80301-2847. 303/4443541.
Employs: 50-99.

Williams Printing
5075 Centennial Blvd, Colorado
Springs CO 80919-2401.
719/5983808. Employs: 50-99.

MANIFOLD BUSINESS FORMS

Damon Graphics
1516 E Fremont Cir S, Littleton
CO 80122-1480. 303/7985099.
Employs: 50-99.

Data Documents Inc
10700 E 45th Ave, Denver CO
80239-2906. 303/3714050.
Employs: 100-249.

Denver Forms Company
2829 S Santa Fe Dr, Englewood
CO 80110-1410. 303/7612314.
Employs: 50-99.

Rocky Mountain Bank Note Co
4990 Iris St, Wheat Ridge CO
80033-2244. 303/4258833.
Employs: 100-249.

Standard Register
4701 Colorado Blvd, Denver CO
80216-3218. 303/3889293.
Employs: 50-99.

BLANKBOOKS, LOOSELEAF BINDERS AND DEVICES

Deluxe Check Printers
8420 S Sangre De Cristo Rd,
Littleton CO 80127-4201.
303/9733366. Employs: 100-249.

John Harland Co
21100 E 33rd Dr, Aurora CO
80011-8158.   303/3758862.
Employs: 50-99.

TYPESETTING

Johnson Publ Co
1880 57th Ct S, Boulder CO
80301-2809.   303/4431576.
Employs: 100-249.

**PLATEMAKING   AND
RELATED SERVICES**

Boulder County Enterprises
3482 Broadway St, Boulder CO
80304-1824.   303/4491632.
Employs: 50-99.

Spectrum Color Center
6275 Joyce Dr, Golden CO 80403-
7541. 303/4250400. Employs: 50-
99.

T&R Engraving
2535 17th St, Denver CO 80211-
3935. 303/4580626. Employs: 50-
99.

For more information on career opportunities in printing and graphic arts:

Associations

**AMERICAN INSTITUTE OF
GRAPHIC ARTS**
1059 3rd Avenue, New York NY
10021. 212/752-0813.

**ASSOCIATION OF GRAPHIC
ARTS**
330 7th Avenue, 9th Floor, New
York NY 10001-5010. 212/279-
2100.

**BINDING INDUSTRIES OF
AMERICA**
70 East Lake Street, Suite 300,
Chicago IL 60601-5905. 312/372-
7606.

GRAPHIC ARTISTS GUILD
11 West 20th Street, New York NY
10011. 212/463-7730.

**INTERNATIONAL GRAPHIC
ARTS EDUCATION
ASSOCIATION**
4615 Forbes Avenue, Pittsburgh
PA 15213. 412/682-5170.

**NATIONAL ASSOCIATION OF
PRINTERS AND
LITHOGRAPHERS**
780 Pallisade Avenue, Teaneck NJ
07666. 201/342-0700.

**PRINTING INDUSTRIES OF
AMERICA**
100 Dangerfield Road, Arlington
VA 22314. 703/519-8100.

**TECHNICAL ASSOCIATION
OF THE GRAPHIC ARTS**
Box 9887, Rochester NY 14623.
716/272-0557.

Directories

**GRAPHIC ARTISTS GUILD
DIRECTORY**
Madison Square Press, Ten East
23rd Street, New York NY 10010.
212/505-0950.

GRAPHIC ARTS BLUE BOOK
A.F. Lewis & Co., 79 Madison
Avenue, New York NY 10016.
212/679-0770.

Magazines

AIGA JOURNAL
American Institute of Graphic Arts,
1059 Third Avenue, New York NY
10021. 212/752-0813.

GRAPHIC ARTS MONTHLY
249 West 49th Street, New York
NY 10011. 212/463-6836.

GRAPHIS

141 Lexington Avenue, New York
NY 10016. 212/532-9387.

PRINT
104 Fifth Avenue, New York NY
10011. 212/463-0600.

RESEARCH AND DEVELOPMENT

Science technicians with good technical skills should experience excellent employment opportunities in the next decade, largely due to the increased emphasis on research and development of technical products.

KAMAN SCIENCES CORPORATION
P.O. Box 7463, Colorado Springs CO 80933. 719/599-1500. **Contact:** Diana Shuck, Employment Manager. **Description:** Kaman Sciences Corporation serves defense, energy, and communications markets with research and development services in weapons effects, computer systems, space systems, C3I, SDI, range testing, and instrumentation. **Common positions:** Aerospace Engineer; Ceramics Engineer; Electrical Engineer. **Educational backgrounds sought:** Computer Science; Engineering; Mathematics; Physics. **Benefits:** medical, dental, and life insurance; pension plan; tuition assistance; disability coverage; savings plan. **Corporate headquarters:** This location. **Parent company:** Bloomfield, CT

VEREX LABS
14 Inverness Drive East, Building D, Suite 100, Englewood CO 80112. 303/799-4499. **Contact:** James Dunn, President. **Description:** A research organ of the pharmaceutical industry.

Additional large employers: 250+

COMMERCIAL, PHYSICAL, AND BIOLOGICAL RESEARCH

AT&T Bell Laboratories
11900 Pecos St, Denver CO 80234-2703. 303/5384307. Employs: 500-999.

Ford Aerospace
1250 Academy Park Loop Ste 112, Colorado Springs CO 80910-3706. 7195973571. Employs: 500-999.

Additional small to medium sized employers: 50-249

COMMERCIAL, PHYSICAL, AND BIOLOGICAL RESEARCH

Clifford Consulting & Research
4108 Stargrass Dr, Colorado Springs CO 80918-4420. 719/5998883. Employs: 50-99.

General Dynamics
1250 Academy Park Loop Ste 132, Colorado Springs CO 80910-3706. 719/5914242. Employs: 50-99.

Hager Laboratories Inc
5930 McIntyre St, Golden CO 80403-7430. 303/2783400. Employs: 50-99.

Hazen Research Inc
4601 Indiana St, Golden CO 80403-1848. 303/2794501. Employs: 100-249.

Immune Response Inc
7305 E Peakview Ave, Englewood CO 80111-6701. 303/7968940. Employs: 50-99.

Pinnacle Micro R & D
1670 Newport Rd N, Colorado Springs CO 80916-2750. 719/5914500. Employs: 50-99.

Science Applications International Corp
2860 S Circle Dr, Colorado Springs CO 80906-4115. 719/5762181. Employs: 100-249.

Solar Energy Research Institut
1617 Cole Blvd, Golden CO 80401-3393. 303/2311000. Employs: 100-249.

Synergen Inc
1885 33rd St, Boulder CO 80301-2546. 303/4427094. Employs: 100-249.

Biotransformations Inc
1321 Aeroplaza Dr, Colorado Springs CO 80916-2247. 719/5500555. Employs: 50-99.

Daily Planet Option Store
14 E Bijou St, Colorado Springs CO 80903-1302. 719/6337163. Employs: 50-99.

Environmental Recycle Systems
108 E Cheyenne Rd, Colorado Springs CO 80906-2549. 719/4711225. Employs: 50-99.

M H Services Inc
1717 S 8th St, Colorado Springs CO 80906-1926. 719/4752643. Employs: 50-99.

National Environment Film Resource Center
324 N Tejon St, Colorado Springs CO 80903-1224. 719/5785549. Employs: 50-99.

Risk Sciences
6190 Lehman Dr # 108, Colorado Springs CO 80918-3445. 719/5316782. Employs: 50-99.

Black Forest Techniks
3125 N El Paso St # A, Colorado Springs CO 80907-5414. 719/4954315. Employs: 50-99.

Ceram Inc
2260 Executive Cir, Colorado Springs CO 80906-4136. 719/5408500. Employs: 50-99.

PWS Inc
5144 N Academy Blvd, Colorado Springs CO 80918-4002. 719/5990129. Employs: 50-99.

TESTING LABORATORIES

Barringer Labs Inc
15000 W Sixth Ave, Golden CO 80401. 303/2771687. Employs: 50-99.

Rocky Mountain Analytical Lab

4955 Yarrow St, Arvada CO 80002-4517.   303/4216611. Employs: 100-249.

Hazardous Waste Technology Inc
1180 Brittany Cir, Colorado Springs   CO   80918-3108. 719/5980475. Employs: 50-99.

RUBBER AND PLASTICS

During the next five years, the demand for plastics is expected to be slow, and the U.S.' share of the world's plastics trade will continue to fall. The rubber industry, especially the synthetic rubber segment, will do much better. The highest growth rates will be for high-value, small-volume elastomers. In fabricated rubber, the big trend is toward customized production. Jobseekers with experience in Computer Aided Design and Manufacturing will reap the benefits of this trend.

THE GATES RUBBER COMPANY
P.O. Box 5887, Denver CO 80217-5887. 303/744-1911. **Contact:** Jill Carvalho, Supervisor/Employee Services. **Description:** An international developer, manufacturer, and distributor of a broad range of rubber and plastic products used by consumer and industry; also operates area subsidiaries engaged in the production of automotive and heavy-duty batteries. **Common positions:** Accountant; Chemist; Computer Programmer; Customer Service Representative; Draftsperson; Chemical Engineer; Electrical Engineer; Mechanical Engineer; Metallurgical Engineer; Management Trainee; Marketing Specialist; Personnel and Labor Relations Specialist; Physicist; Purchasing Agent; Quality Control Supervisor; Reporter/Editor; Sales Representative; Statistician; Systems Analyst; Technical Writer/Editor; Transportation and Traffic Specialist; Rubber-Related Engineer. **Educational backgrounds sought:** Accounting; Business Administration; Chemistry; Communications; Computer Science; Engineering; Finance; Liberal Arts; Marketing; Mathematics; Physics. **Benefits:** medical, dental, and life insurance; pension plan; tuition assistance; disability coverage; employee discounts; savings plan; 401K. **Corporate headquarters:** This location. **Operations at this facility:** divisional headquarters; research/development; administration; service; sales.

MIDWEST RUBBER & SUPPLY COMPANY
6404 East 39th Avenue, Denver CO 80207. 303/321-2800. **Contact:** Dennis Jones, General Office Manager. **Description:** A Denver industrial rubber distributor.

Additional large employers: 250+

MISC. PLASTICS PRODUCTS

PDM Molding

1955 S Cherokee St, Denver CO 80223-3914.   303/7917866.
Employs: 250-499.

Additional small to medium sized employers: 50-249

PLASTIC   MATERIALS, SYNTHETIC   RESINS,   AND NONVULCANIZABLE ELASTOMERS

Custom Vinyl Compounding
66 W Springer Dr, Littleton CO 80126-2316.   303/7913214.
Employs: 50-99.

Parade Packaging Materials
2907 Huron St, Denver CO 80202-1029. 303/2973711. Employs: 50-99.

RUBBER   AND   PLASTICS HOSE AND BELTING

National Products Inc
900 S Broadway, Denver CO 80209-4010.   303/7445111.
Employs: 50-99.

PLASTIC FOAM PRODUCTS

Plastics Design & Mfg Inc
1955 S Cherokee St, Denver CO 80223-3914.   303/6981313.
Employs: 50-99.

Styro Molders
1100 Garden Gods, Colorado Springs CO 80907. 719/5980602.
Employs: 50-99.

MISC. PLASTICS PRODUCTS

B & R Plastics Inc

4999 Kingston Street, Denver CO 80239-2516.   303/3730710.
Employs: 50-99.

Communications   Packaging Corp
2635 S Santa Fe Dr, Denver CO 80223-4429.   303/7581113.
Employs: 100-249.

New Systems Molding Corp
512 E County Rd 8, Berthoud CO 80513-9232.   303/6633930.
Employs: 100-249.

Plasticrafts Division
600 W Bayaud Ave, Denver CO 80223-1802.   303/7443700.
Employs: 50-99.

Technology Products Inc
805 S Lincoln St, Longmont CO 80501-6316.   303/4430402.
Employs: 50-99.

Unisys Cad Com
PO Box 9014, Boulder CO 80301-9014. 303/4491138. Employs: 50-99.

Watersaver Co Inc
5870 E 56th Ave, Commerce City CO   80022-3932.   303/2891818.
Employs: 50-99.

PTA Corporation
7343 Mineral Rd, Longmont CO 80503-7201.   303/6522500.
Employs: 100-249.

For more information on career opportunities in the rubber and plastics industries:

Associations

SOCIETY OF PLASTICS ENGINEERS
14 Fairfield Drive, Brookfield CT 06804. 203/775-0471.

SOCIETY OF PLASTICS INDUSTRY
355 Lexington Avenue, New York NY 10017. 212/351-5410.

TRANSPORTATION

Aviation: The airlines are about as closely linked with the overall economy as any industry. Competition between airlines will remain brutal. Increasingly, the industry will be dominated by three companies -- American, Delta, and United, with others at risk of falling by the wayside. With fewer major players, fewer jobs will be available. On a brighter note, according to the U.S. Labor Department, the hiring picture will improve over the long-term.

ACME DISTRIBUTION
18101 East Colfax, Aurora CO 80011. 303/340-2100. **Contact:** Personnel Department. **Description:** A company involved in local trucking and storage.

ALLIED CARRIERS EXCHANGE INCORPORATED
4242 Delaware Street, Denver CO 80216. 303/455-0075. **Contact:** Personnel Department. **Description:** A motor carrier corporation.

ASPEN DISTRIBUTION INCORPORATED
540 Oswego Street, P.O. Box 39108, Denver CO 80239. 303/371-2510. **Contact:** Personnel. **Description:** A local trucking and public warehouse.

ATWOOD TRUCK LINE INCORPORATED
P.O. Box 29190, Thornton CO 80229. 303/287-2882. **Contact:** Personnel Department. **Description:** A long-distance trucking company.

CONTINENTAL EXPRESS
Hangar 6/Stapleton International Airport, Denver CO 80207. 303/388-8585. **Contact:** Human Resources. Send resumes to: 15333 JFK, Gateway II-600, Houston TX 77032. **Description:** A regional commercial airline operated by Rocky Mountain Airways. **Common positions:** Airline and Airline Management. **Benefits:** medical insurance; dental insurance; pension plan; life insurance; tuition assistance; disability coverage; profit sharing; employee

discounts; savings plan. **Corporate headquarters:** This location. **Parent company:** Texas Air Corporation. **Operations at this facility:** Regional Headquarters; Divisional Headquarters; Administration; Service; Sales.

GREASE MONKEY INTERNATIONAL, INC.
216 Sixteenth Street, Suite 1100, Denver CO 80202. 303/534-1660. **Contact:** Personnel Department. **Description:** Denver company providing automotive services. **Common positions:** Accountant; Administrator; Advertising Worker; Attorney; Buyer; Computer Programmer; Customer Service Representative; Branch Manager; Department Manager; Operations/Production Manager; Management Trainee; Marketing Specialist; Purchasing Agent; Technical Writer/Editor. **Educational backgrounds sought:** Accounting; Art/Design; Business Administration; Finance; Marketing. **Special programs:** Training programs and internships. **Benefits:** medical, dental, and life insurance; pension plan; tuition assistance; disability coverage; profit sharing; employee discounts; savings plan; stock options. **Corporate headquarters:** This location. **Operations at this facility:** administration; sales. **Employees:** 293. **Projected hires for the next 12 months:** increase 5%. **Listed on:** NASDAQ.

PONY EXPRESS COURIER CORPORATION
5478 North Washington, Denver CO 80216. 303/296-0617. **Contact:** Personnel Director. **Description:** A Denver messenger service.

Additional large employers: 250+

RAILROADS, LINE-HAUL OPERATING

Denver & Rio Grande Western RR
1515 Arapahoe St, Denver CO 80202-2118. 303/6295533. Employs: 250-499.

LOCAL AND SUBURBAN TRANSIT

Regional Transportation District
1600 Blake St, Denver CO 80202-1399. 303/6289000. Employs: 500-999.

TAXICABS

Yellow Cab
3455 Ringsby Ct, Denver CO 80216-4919. 303/2926464. Employs: 500-999.

LOCAL TRUCKING WITHOUT STORAGE

NW Transport Service Inc
5601 Holly St, Commerce City CO 80022-3901. 303/2893500. Employs: 250-499.

TRUCKING, EXCEPT LOCAL

Edsen Express
9351 Grant St, Denver CO 80229-4358. 303/4509600. Employs: 250-499.

Garrett Freightlines Inc
1819 Denver West Dr Suite 26, Golden CO 80401-3112. 303/2789900. Employs: 250-499.

Longmont Foods
100 Emery St, Longmont CO 80501-5950. 303/7766611. Employs: 500-999.

COURIER SERVICES, EXCEPT BY AIR

Coors Transportation Company
5101 York St, Denver CO 80216-2249. 303/2930816. Employs: 250-499.

GENERAL WAREHOUSING AND STORAGE

Acme Distribution Centers
P O Box 17729, Denver CO 80217-0729. 303/3402100. Employs: 250-499.

AIR TRANSPORTATION, SCHEDULED

Covia
10949 E Peakview Ave, Englewood CO 80111-6804. 303/3973350. Employs: 250-499.

United Airlines
Stapleton Airport, Denver CO 80207. 303/3984577. Employs: 250-499.

United Airlines
5350 S Valentia Way, Englewood CO 80111-3102. 303/7792101. Employs: 500-999.

TRUCKING, EXCEPT LOCAL

Federal Express
5550 Tech Center Dr, Colorado Springs CO 80919-2308. 7195994700. Employs: 250-499.

AIRPORTS, FLYING FIELDS, AND AIRPORT TERMINAL SERVICES

Saint Anthony Central Airport
4231 W 16th Ave, Denver CO 80204-1335. 303/6293911. Employs: 250-499.

Stapleton International Airport
3200 Syracuse St, Denver CO 80207-2409. 303/3983844. Employs: 250-499.

Additional small to medium sized employers: 50-249

MISC. TRANSPORTATION EQUIPMENT

Murray Equipment Co
PO Box 16506, Denver CO 80216-0506. 303/4849377. Employs: 50-99.

RAILROADS, LINE-HAUL OPERATING

Burlington Northern Railroad
373 Inverness Dr S, Englewood CO 80112-5816. 303/4806200. Employs: 100-249.

LOCAL AND SUBURBAN TRANSIT

Airport Express
521 N Link Ln, Fort Collins CO 80524-2737. 303/3534557. Employs: 50-99.

Gold Camp Express Ltd
5921 N Nevada Ave, Colorado Springs CO 80918-3549. 719/5288190. Employs: 50-99.

RTD Corp
1325 S Colorado Bl, Denver CO 80222-3303. 303/7786000. Employs: 100-249.

Cripple Creek Express Inc
102 W Colorado Ave, Colorado Springs CO 80903-1606. 719/6300542. Employs: 50-99.

MISC. LOCAL PASSENGER TRANSPORTATION

Ambulance Service Company
2057 Downing St, Denver CO 80205-5209. 303/8395151. Employs: 100-249.

Broomfield Ambulance
18 Garden Office Ctr, Broomfield CO 80020-1730. 303/4661046. Employs: 50-99.

Reed Ambulance Service Inc
1805 S Bellaire St Suite 520, Denver CO 80222-4325. 303/7581584. Employs: 100-249.

Colorado Gamblers Express Inc
611 N Nevada Ave, Colorado Springs CO 80903-1005. 719/5785232. Employs: 50-99.

Resort Express Limousine Service
273 Warren Av, Silverthorne CO 80498. 303/4687600. Employs: 50-99.

INTERCITY AND RURAL BUS TRANSPORTATION

RTD Boulder
1707 Exposition Dr, Boulder CO 80301-2606. 303/4430100. Employs: 100-249.

BUS CHARTER SERVICE, EXCEPT LOCAL

Mayflower Contract Services
30 S Raritan St, Denver CO 80223-1220. 303/7787008. Employs: 100-249.

LOCAL TRUCKING WITHOUT STORAGE

Don Ward & Company
241 W 56th Ave, Denver CO 80216-1619. 303/2979779. Employs: 100-249.

HVH Transportation Inc
5630 Franklin St, Denver CO 80216-1518. 303/2923656. Employs: 50-99.

North Park Transportation Co
5150 Columbine St, Denver CO 80216-2305. 303/2950300. Employs: 50-99.

TRUCKING, EXCEPT LOCAL

ABF Freight System Inc
5871 Broadway, Denver CO 80216-1024. 303/2951561. Employs: 100-249.

Edson Express Inc
5300 E 56th Ave, Commerce City CO 80022-3827. 303/2894431. Employs: 100-249.

Leprino Transport Co
6655 York St, Denver CO 80229-7324. 303/2893800. Employs: 50-99.

Miller Brothers
6540 Washington St, Denver CO 80229-7013. 303/2867117. Employs: 50-99.

Navajo Shippers Inc
5863 Monaco St, Commerce City CO 80022-4020. 303/2873800. Employs: 100-249.

Pebble Haulers Inc
2630 Delta Dr, Colorado Springs CO 80910-1008. 719/3929026. Employs: 50-99.

Roadway Express Incorporated
14700 Smith Rd, Aurora CO 80011-2417. 303/3639881. Employs: 100-249.

Santa Anna Trucking
5135 York St, Denver CO 80216-2249. 303/2951117. Employs: 50-99.

Texas Intermountain Transport
6591 Brighton Blvd, Commerce City CO 80022-2321. 303/2892350. Employs: 50-99.

Trans Western Express Ltd
3110 N Stone Ave Suite B, Colorado Springs CO 80907-5306. 719/6346512. Employs: 50-99.

Viking Freight System Inc
5375 E 56th Ave, Commerce City CO 80022-3828. 303/2891303. Employs: 50-99.

Yellow Freight Systems Inc
15950 Smith Rd, Aurora CO 80011-2506. 303/3439770. Employs: 100-249.

LOCAL TRUCKING WITH STORAGE

City Storage & Transfer Inc
3625 Walnut St, Boulder CO 80301-2521. 303/4472440. Employs: 50-99.

Weicker Allied Moving & Storage
2900 Brighton Blvd, Denver CO 80216-5013. 303/2979797. Employs: 50-99.

COURIER SERVICES, EXCEPT BY AIR

Air Source Express Inc
4890 Ironton St, Denver CO 80239-2419. 303/3759800. Employs: 100-249.

Petco Inc Interstate
7627 Dahlia St, Commerce City CO 80022-1465. 303/2880755. Employs: 50-99.

Trans Western Express Ltd
5231 Monroe St, Denver CO 80216-2444. 303/2966969. Employs: 100-249.

United Parcel Service
5020 Ivy St, Commerce City CO 80022-4403. 303/2895311. Employs: 100-249.

GENERAL WAREHOUSING AND STORAGE

Fort Carson Class Six Storage
1524 Fort Carson, Colorado Springs CO 80913. 719/5766531. Employs: 50-99.

Colorado Denver Express
7170 Dahlia St, Commerce City CO 80022-1831. 303/2895566. Employs: 50-99.

MISC. SPECIAL WAREHOUSING AND STORAGE

Joseph T Ryerson & Son Inc
6600 Hwy 85, Denver CO 80216. 303/2870101. Employs: 50-99.

AIR TRANSPORTATION, SCHEDULED

Continental Airlines
1605 California St, Denver CO 80202-3701. 303/3983000. Employs: 100-249.

Continental Airlines
Stapleton Intern'L Airport, Denver CO 80207. 303/2701300. Employs: 100-249.

Continental Airlines
2 N Cascade Ave, Colorado Springs CO 80903-1614. 719/4737580. Employs: 50-99.

Delta Air Lines Inc
8850 Smith Rd, Denver CO 80207-1731. 303/3932552. Employs: 100-249.

Delta Air Lines Inc
1570 Court Pl, Denver CO 80202-5107. 303/6961322. Employs: 100-249.

Delta Airlines Inc
Stapleton Airport, Denver CO 80207. 303/3932500. Employs: 100-249.

Mesa Airlines
Colorado Springs Airport, Colorado Springs CO 80910. 719/5916211. Employs: 50-99.

Trans World Airlines
Stapleton Airport, Denver CO 80207. 303/3983552. Employs: 50-99.

TWA Ticket Sales
1574 Court Pl, Denver CO 80202-5107. 303/5347003. Employs: 100-249.

United Airlines
Colorado Springs Airport, Colorado Springs CO 80910. 719/6350570. Employs: 50-99.

AIR COURIER SERVICES

Emory Aviation
1245 Aviation Way # A, Colorado Springs CO 80916-2715. 719/5919487. Employs: 100-249.

Overseas Courier Service Denver
1512 Larimer St, Denver CO 80202-1610. 303/8931820. Employs: 100-249.

TNT Skypak
12445 E 39th Ave, Denver CO 80239-3453. 303/3732556. Employs: 100-249.

Cargo Inc
4195 Oneida St, Denver CO 80216-6618. 303/3887974. Employs: 100-249.

Corporate Air
2121 Valentia St, Denver CO 80220-2131. 303/3985007. Employs: 100-249.

Greyhound Bus Lines
Stapleton International Airprt, Denver CO 80207. 303/3984795. Employs: 100-249.

Lakin Intermodal Express Inc
5800 Franklin St, Denver CO 80216-1249. 303/2967522. Employs: 100-249.

M-K Trucking Inc
4040 Holly St, Denver CO 80216-4550. 303/3337452. Employs: 100-249.

Pak Air
6753 E 4M Av Dr, Denver CO 80216. 303/3551230. Employs: 100-249.

Precision Air Cargo
6405 E 48th Ave, Denver CO 80216-5306. 303/2892814. Employs: 100-249.

US Express Corporation
Stapleton International Airprt, Denver CO 80207. 303/3985300. Employs: 100-249.

AIR TRANSPORTATION, NONSCHEDULED

Air Methods Corporation
7301 S Peoria St, Englewood CO 80112-4133. 303/7900587. Employs: 50-99.

Continental Airlines Inc Cargo
9300 Smith Rd, Denver CO 80207-1733. 303/3983200. Employs: 100-249.

AIRPORTS, FLYING FIELDS, AND AIRPORT TERMINAL SERVICES

Allied Aviation Service Colorado
Stapleton Airport Suite B-5, Denver CO 80207. 303/3985367. Employs: 100-249.

AMR Combs Inc
2390 Syracuse St, Denver CO 80207-3650. 303/3985600. Employs: 100-249.

Air Care Maintenance Inc
Stapleton Int'Nal Airport, Denver CO 80207. 303/3885052. Employs: 50-99.

Airborne Hydraulics
4880 Ironton St, Denver CO 80239-2418. 303/3714325. Employs: 50-99.

United Aero Dynamics Corp
4665 Paris St, Denver CO 80239-3117. 303/3751111. Employs: 50-99.

TRAVEL AGENCIES

AAA Travel Agency
4100 E Arkansas Ave, Denver CO 80222-3405. 303/7538800. Employs: 100-249.

May D & F Travel Bureau
15 S Steele St, Denver CO 80209-2829. 303/3210305. Employs: 100-249.

MISC. ARRANGEMENT OF PASSENGER TRANSPORTATION

ATL Reserve Network Travel & Tours
11072 N Hwy 9, Breckenridge CO 80424. 303/4539237. Employs: 50-99.

ARRANGEMENT OF TRANSPORTATION OF FREIGHT AND CARGO

Express Messenger Systems
1200 W Evans Ave, Denver CO 80223-4025. 303/9364755. Employs: 50-99.

Transportation Services Inc
PO Box 5482, Denver CO 80217-5482. 303/2987005. Employs: 100-249.

Union Pacific
3620 Wazee St, Denver CO 80216-3642. 303/2918332. Employs: 100-249.

MISC. COMMUNICATION SERVICES

Cellular Inc
Orchard Pl IV Greenwood Pl, Englewood CO 80111. 303/6943234. Employs: 50-99.

Colorado International Communications Ctr
20 W 84th Ave, Denver CO 80221-4812. 303/4294945. Employs: 50-99.

For more information on career opportunities in transportation:

<u>Associations</u>

AMERICAN BUREAU OF SHIPPING

2 World Trade Center, 106th Floor, New York NY 10048. 212/839-5000.

AMERICAN MARITIME ASSOCIATION
485 Madison Avenue, New York NY 10022. 212/319-9217.

AMERICAN SOCIETY OF TRAVEL AGENTS
1101 King Street, Alexandria VA 22314. 703/739-2782.

AMERICAN TRUCKING ASSOCIATION
2200 Mill Road, Alexandria VA 22314-4677. 703/838-1700.

ASSOCIATION OF AMERICAN RAILROADS
50 F Street NW, Washington DC 20001. 202/639-2100.

INSTITUTE OF TRANSPORTATION ENGINEERS
525 School Street SW, Suite 410, Washington DC 20024. 202/554-8050.

MARINE TECHNOLOGY SOCIETY
1828 L Street NW, Suite 906, Washington DC 20036. 202/775-5966.

NATIONAL ASSOCIATION OF MARINE SERVICES
5024-R Campbell Boulevard, Baltimore MD 21236. 410/931-8100.

NATIONAL MARINE MANUFACTURERS ASSOCIATION
401 North Michigan Avenue, Suite 1150, Chicago IL 60611. 312/836-4747.

NATIONAL MOTOR FREIGHT TRAFFIC ASSOCIATION
2200 Mill Road, Alexandria VA 22314. 703/838-1700.

NATIONAL TANK TRUCK CARRIERS
2200 Mill Road, Alexandria VA 22314. 703/838-1700.

SHIPBUILDERS COUNCIL OF AMERICA
4301 N. Fairfax Drive, Suite 330, Arlington VA 22203. 703/276-1700.

TRANSPORTATION INSTITUTE
5201 Authway Street, Camp Springs MD 20746. 301/423-3335.

Directories

MOODY'S TRANSPORTATION MANUAL
Moody's Investors Service, Inc., 99 Church Street, New York NY 10007. 212/553-0300.

NATIONAL TANK TRUCK CARRIER DIRECTORY
2200 Mill Road, Alexandria VA 22314. 703/838-1700.

OFFICIAL MOTOR FREIGHT GUIDE
1130 South Canal Street, Chicago IL 60607. 312/939-1434.

Magazines

AMERICAN SHIPPER
P.O. Box 4728, Jacksonville FL 32201. 904/355-2601.

DAILY TRAFFIC WORLD
The Traffic Service Corporation, 1325 G Street, Washington DC 20005. 202/626-4533.

FLEET OWNER
707 Westchester Avenue, White Plains NY 10604-3102. 914/949-8500.

HEAVY DUTY TRUCKING
Newport Communications, P.O.
Box W, Newport Beach CA 92658.
714/261-1636.

**MARINE DIGEST AND
TRANSPORTATION NEWS**
P.O. Box 3905, Seattle WA 98124.
206/682-3607.

OCEAN INDUSTRY

Gulf Publishing Co., P.O. Box
2608, Houston TX 77252. 713/529-
4301.

SHIPPING DIGEST
51 Madison Avenue, New York
NY 10010. 212/689-4411.

TRANSPORT TOPICS
2200 Mill Road, Alexandria VA
22314. 703/838-1772.

UTILITIES

The major forces shaping the U.S. utilities industry are decreased regulation and competition from newly emerging alternative energy sources. Job prospects for those entering the utilities industry vary by sector; the best is electric, and at the bottom is the stagnant nuclear industry.

PUBLIC SERVICE COMPANY OF COLORADO
1730 Blake Street, Denver CO 80202. 303/571-7563, Jobline. **Description:** An operating public utility engaged in the generation, purchase, transmission, distribution, and sale of electricity; and in the purchase, transmission, distribution, and sale of natural gas. Provides service to a population of 2.5 million people, all within Colorado. **Corporate headquarters:** This location. **Listed on:** New York and American Stock Exchanges. **Common positions:** Accountant; Computer Programmer; Customer Service Representative; Draftsperson; Chemical, Civil, Electrical, and Mechanical Engineer. **Educational backgrounds sought:** Accounting; Business Administration; Computer Science; Engineering. **Benefits:** medical, dental, and life insurance; pension plan; tuition assistance; disability coverage; profit sharing; employee discounts; savings plan. **Operations at this facility:** administration.

TRI-STATE GENERATION & TRANSMISSION
Box 33695, Denver CO 80233. 303/452-6111. **Contact:** Jerry Jacobson, Personnel Manager. **Description:** An area utility dealing in electrical power.

WESTERN AREA POWER ADMINISTRATION
P.O. Box 3402, Building 18, 1627 Cole Boulevard, Golden CO 80401. 303/231-1502. **Contact:** Personnel. **Description:** Responsible for the power marketing and transmission functions in 15 Central and Western states, encompassing a 1.3-million-square-mile geographic area; sells power to over 550 wholesale customers, primarily cooperatives, municipalities, public utility districts, private utilities, federal and state agencies, and irrigation districts. A federal agency

operated by the Department of Energy. **Common positions:** Attorney; Civil Engineer; Electrical/Electronic Engineer; Power Dispatcher. **Educational backgrounds sought:** Engineering. **Benefits:** standard federal government benefits.

Additional large employers: 250+

NATURAL GAS TRANSMISSION

Colorado Interstate Gas Co
N Nevada Ave, Colorado Springs CO 80903. 7194732300. Employs: 1,000+.

MIXED, MANUFACTURED OR LIQUEFIED PETROLEUM GAS PRODUCTION AND/OR DISTRIBUTION

Western Gas Processors
12200 Pecos St, Denver CO 80234-3439. 303/4525603. Employs: 250-499.

ELECTRIC AND OTHER SERVICES COMBINED

Fort Collins Light & Power
700 Wood St, Fort Collins CO 80521-1945. 303/2216700. Employs: 500-999.

SEWERAGE SYSTEMS

Metro Denver Sewage
6450 York St, Denver CO 80229-7407. 303/2895941. Employs: 250-499.

Additional small to medium sized employers: 50-249

ELECTRIC SERVICES

Basin Electric Power Cooperative
11479 N Pine Dr, Parker CO 80134-8050. 303/8410130. Employs: 100-249.

Colorado Power Partnership
303 E 17th Ave, Denver CO 80203-1253. 303/8601110. Employs: 50-99.

Intermountain Rural Electric Association
13404 Old US Hwy 285, Conifer CO 80433. 303/8385583. Employs: 50-99.

Intermountain Rural Electric Association

P O Drawer A, Sedalia CO 80135-0220. 303/6883100. Employs: 100-249.

K-C Electric Association
422 3rd Ave, Hugo CO 80821. 719/7432431. Employs: 50-99.

K-C Electric Association
425 Hwy 385, Cheyenne Wls CO 80810. 719/7675525. Employs: 50-99.

K-C Electric Association
281 Main St, Stratton CO 80836-1106. 719/3485318. Employs: 50-99.

Loveland Light and Power
200 N Wilson, Loveland CO 80537. 303/9623000. Employs: 50-99.

Morgan County REA
6975 Weld County Rd 69, Keenesburg CO 80643. 303/7324525. Employs: 50-99.

Mountain Parks Electric Inc
636 Main, Walden CO 80480. 303/7234500. Employs: 50-99.

Mountain Parks Electric Inc
417 S 3rd, Kremmling CO 80459. 303/7243314. Employs: 50-99.

Mountain Parks Electric Inc
908 Park, Kremmling CO 80459. 303/7249377. Employs: 50-99.

Platte River Power Authority
Timberline Hstth Rd, Fort Collins CO 80525. 303/2264000. Employs: 50-99.

Poudre Valley Rural Electric
4809 S College Ave, Fort Collins CO 80525-3724. 303/6677324. Employs: 50-99.

Public Service Co Of Colorado
810 9th St, Greeley CO 80631-1104. 303/3531144. Employs: 50-99.

Public Service Co Of Colorado
5139 W 120th Ave, Broomfield CO 80020-5608. 303/6655511. Employs: 50-99.

Public Service Company Of Co
16805 Weld County Rd 19-1/2, Platteville CO 80651. 303/7856471. Employs: 50-99.

Public Service Company Of Co
1730 Harrison Ave, Leadville CO 80461-3337. 719/4861110. Employs: 50-99.

Public Service Company Of Co
200 W 6, Silverthorne CO 80498. 303/4680613. Employs: 100-249.

Public Service Co Of Colorado

681 County Rd 308, Dumont CO 80436. 303/5672293. Employs: 50-99.

Public Service Co Of Colorado
1901 E Horsetooth Rd, Fort Collins CO 80525-2941. 303/2254010. Employs: 50-99.

Tri State Generation & Transportation Association
28136 U S Hwy 40, Kremmling CO 80459. 303/7243510. Employs: 50-99.

Tri State Generation & Transportation
21889 County Road 50, Burlington CO 80807-9580. 719/3465528. Employs: 50-99.

United Power
Hwy 72, Golden CO 80403. 303/6427921. Employs: 50-99.

Western Gas Supply Co
1050-17th St, Denver CO 80265-0101. 303/5341261. Employs: 100-249.

NATURAL GAS DISTRIBUTION

Greeley Gas Co
1200 11th Ave, Greeley CO 80631-3828. 303/3527171. Employs: 50-99.

Public Service Company Of Co
422 Main St, Windsor CO 80550-5130. 303/6862291. Employs: 50-99.

Public Service Company Of Co
13-1/2 S Parish Av, Johnstown CO 80534. 303/5874671. Employs: 50-99.

MIXED, MANUFACTURED OR LIQUEFIED PETROLEUM GAS PRODUCTION AND/OR DISTRIBUTION

Greeley Gas Co
1301 Pennsylvania, Denver CO 80203-5011. 303/8618080. Employs: 100-249.

ELECTRIC AND OTHER SERVICES COMBINED

Public Service Co Of Colorado
1123 W 3rd Ave, Denver CO 80223-1351. 303/5713927. Employs: 100-249.

MISC. COMBINATION UTILITIES

Public Service Co Of Colorado
209 S Meldrum St, Fort Collins CO 80521-2603. 303/4825922. Employs: 100-249.

WATER SUPPLY

Boulder City Utilities
1739 Broadway Suite 306, Boulder CO 80302-6241. 303/4413240. Employs: 50-99.

Consolidated Mutual Water Co
12700 W 27th Ave, Lakewood CO 80215-7088. 303/2380451. Employs: 50-99.

Highlands Ranch Water District
62 Plaza Dr, Littleton CO 80126-2304. 303/7910430. Employs: 50-99.

Northern Col Water Conservancy
1250 N Wilson Ave, Loveland CO 80537. 303/6672437. Employs: 50-99.

REFUSE SYSTEMS

Browning Ferris Industry Of Co
5590 E 55th Ave, Commerce City CO 80022-3833. 303/2878043. Employs: 100-249.

Disposal & Recycling Inc
6091 Brighton Blvd, Commerce City CO 80022-3631. 303/2892345. Employs: 50-99.

Laidlaw Waste Systems
6015 E 58th Ave, Commerce City CO 80022-3915. 303/2885558. Employs: 100-249.

Packers Sanitation Service Inc
710 11th Ave, Greeley CO 80631-3200. 303/3524729. Employs: 100-249.

US Recycling Industries
2441 Broadway, Denver CO 80205-2116. 303/2966116. Employs: 100-249.

Waste Management
80 Chambers St, Colorado Springs CO 80907-5220. 719/6328877. Employs: 50-99.

Waste Management Of Aurora Inc
3995 Nome St, Denver CO 80239-3342. 303/3716622. Employs: 50-99.

Waste Management Of Denver North
380 W 62nd Ave, Denver CO 80216-1016. 303/4276200. Employs: 50-99.

Waste Tech Services Inc
18400 W 10th Ave, Golden CO 80401-6000. 303/2799712. Employs: 100-249.

For more information on career opportunities in the utilities industry:

<u>Associations</u>

AMERICAN WATER WORKS ASSOCIATION
6666 West Quincy Avenue, Denver CO 80235.
303/794-7711.

ADIA PERSONNEL SERVICES
55 Madison Street
Suite 103
Denver CO 80206
303/399-7706

Contact: Sandy Mazur, Area Vice President. Employment agency; temporary help service. Appointment requested. Founded 1957. Specializes in the areas of: Accounting and Finance; Banking; Clerical; Insurance; Legal; Technical and Scientific; Data Processing; Secretarial; Word Processing. Positions commonly filled include: Administrative Assistant; Bookkeeper; Claim Representative; Computer Operator; Customer Service Representative; Data Entry Clerk; Demonstrator; Factory Worker; General Laborer; Legal Secretary; Light Industrial Worker; Medical Secretary; Office Worker; Public Relations Worker; Receptionist; Secretary; Typist; Word Processing Specialist. Company pays fee. Number of temporary placements per year: 501-1000. Number of permanent placements per year: 50.

PROFESSIONAL SEARCH & PLACEMENT INC.
4901 East Dry Creek Road
Suite 101
Littleton CO 80122
303/779-8004

Contact: John Turner, President. Employment agency. Appointment requested. Specializes in the areas of: Computer Hardware and Software; Engineering; MIS/EDP. Positions commonly filled include: Aerospace Engineer; Biomedical Engineer; Computer Operator; Computer Programmer; EDP Specialist; Electrical Engineer; Industrial

Engineer; Mechanical Engineer; Systems Analyst. Company pays fee. Number of placements per year: 201-500.

CAREER FORUM
4350 Wadsworth Boulevard
Suite 300
Wheatridge CO 80033
303/425-8721
Contact: Stan Grebe, President. Employment agency; temporary help service. Appointment requested. Founded 1969. Specializes in the areas of: Accounting and Finance; Advertising; Banking; Clerical; Computer Hardware and Software; Engineering; Insurance; Legal; Manufacturing; Personnel and Human Resources; Printing and Publishing; Sales and Marketing; Technical and Scientific. Positions commonly filled include; Accountant; Administrative Assistant; Advertising Worker; Architect; Bank Office/Manager; Bookkeeper; Chemical Engineer; Chemist; Civil Engineer; Claim Representative; Computer Operator; Computer Programmer; Credit Manager; Customer Service Representative; Data Entry Clerk; Draftsperson; Electrical Engineer; Financial Analyst; General Manager; Insurance Agent/Broker; Legal Secretary; Marketing Specialist; Mechanical Engineer; Medical Secretary; Office Worker; Public Relations Worker; Purchasing Agent; Receptionist; Sales Representative; Secretary; Stenographer; Technician; Typist; Underwriter. Company pays fee; individual pays fee. Number of placements per year: 501-1000.

CHUCK'S CONTRACT LABOR SERVICE, INC.
Box 46224
Denver CO 80201
303/295-7336
Contact: Chuck Harbargh, President. Temporary help agency. No appointment required. Founded 1976. Top-quality unskilled workers, generally within the hour. No minimum charge, no charge for permanent hire. Free pre-screening. Telephone dispatch from home. Specializes in the areas of: Construction; Food Industry; Manufacturing. Positions commonly filled include: Clerk; Construction Worker; Driver; Factory Worker; General Laborer; Light Industrial Worker; Receptionist; Typist. Number of placements per year: 1000+.

DUNHILL OF FORT COLLINS, INC.
2120 South College Avenue
Suite 3
Fort Collins CO 80525
303/221-5630
Contact: Jerold Lyons, President. Employment agency. Appointment requested. Founded 1976. Specializes in the areas of: Banking; Engineering; Health Care; Sales and Marketing; Semiconductor Industry; Wire and Cable Industry. Positions commonly filled include: Bank Officer/Manager; Electrical Engineer; Mechanical Engineer; Nurse. Company pays fee. Number of placements per year: 51-100.

JFI JOBS FOR INDUSTRY
1888 Sherman Street
Suite 500
Denver CO 80203
303/831-0048
Contact: Kevin Courtney, President. Fax: 303/832-3401. Specializes in the areas of: distribution (customer service; inventory control; logistics; materials handling; operations; planning; traffic; transportation); entry level (management trainees; support staff); manufacturing/production (factory automation; plant management; quality control; supervisory; technicians); packaging (manufacturing).

LANGLEY ASSOCIATES
P.O. Box 3668
Littleton CO 80161
303/798-8929
Contact: Carol Langley, President. Employment agency. Appointment required; unsolicited resumes accepted. Founded 1982. Specializes in the areas of: Accounting; Administration, MIS/EDP; Advertising; Architecture; Banking; Broadcasting; Computer Hardware and Software; Construction; Engineering; Finance; General Management; Health and Medical; Legal; Manufacturing; Mortgage Banking and Lending; Oil and Gas; Personnel and Human Resources; Printing and Publishing; Procurement; Real Estate; Sales and Marketing; Technical and Scientific; Women. Contingency. Number of searches conducted per year: 26-50.

MARGARET HOOK'S PERSONNEL
7800 East Union Avenue
Suite 120
Denver CO 80237
303/770-2100
Contact: Manager. Fax: 303/770-6620. Specializes in the area of: office administration (administrators; clerks; receptionists; secretaries; word processing).

PERSONNEL PLUS
770 West Hampton
Suite 310
Englewood CO 80110
303/781-1659
Contact: Joe Armbruster, Owner. Temporary help service. Appointment requested. Specializes in the area of: Clerical. Positions commonly filled include: Administrative Assistant; Bookkeeper; Clerk; Computer Operator; Customer Service Representative; Data Entry Clerk; Demonstrator; EDP Specialist; Factory Worker; General Laborer; Legal Secretary; Light Industrial Worker; Marketing Specialist; Office Worker; Receptionist; Secretary; Stenographer; Typist; Word Processing Specialist. Company pays fee. Number of placements per year: 201-500.

PREFERRED LEADS, INC.
1660 South Albian Street
Suite 812
Denver CO 80222
303/782-5447
Contact: Manager. Fax: 303/830-6783. Specializes in the area of: real estate (asset/portfolio management; finance; property management; rentals; sales)

SOS/STAFF RESOURCES
6595 South Dayton Street
Suite 1000
Englewood CO 80111
303/790-7823
Contact: Katherine Ferguson, Office Manager. Employment agency; temporary and permanent help service. Appointment requested. Specializes in the areas of: Accounting and Finance; Banking; Clerical;

Computer Hardware and Software; Engineering; Health and Medical; Insurance; Legal; MIS/EDP; Personnel and Human Resources; Printing and Publishing; Real Estate; Sales and Marketing; Technical and Scientific. Positions commonly filled include: Accountant; Actuary; Administrative Assistant; Advertising Worker; Aerospace Engineer; Agricultural Engineer; Architect; Attorney; Bank Officer/Manager; Biochemist; Biologist; Biomedical Engineer; Bookkeeper; Buyer; Ceramics Engineer; Chemist; Civil Engineer; Claim Representative; Clerk; Commercial Artist; Computer Operator; Computer Programmer; Construction Worker; Credit Manager; Customer Service Representative; Data Entry Clerk; Dietician; Demonstrator; Draftsperson; Driver; EDP Specialist; Economist; Electrical Engineer; Financial Analyst; Food Technologist; General Manager; Hotel Manager/Assistant Manager; Industrial Designer; Industrial Engineer; Insurance Agent/Broker; Legal Secretary; Light Industrial Worker; MIS Specialist; Marketing Specialist; Mechanical Engineer; Medical Secretary; Metallurgical Engineer; Mining Engineer; Model; Nurse; Office Worker; Operations/Production Specialist; Personnel and Labor Relations Specialist; Petroleum Engineer; Physicist; Public Relations Worker; Purchasing Agent; Quality Control Supervisor; Receptionist; Reporter/Editor; Sales Representative; Secretary; Statistician; Stenographer; Systems Analyst; Technical Writer/Editor; Technician; Typist; Underwriter; Word Processing Specialist. Company pays fee; individual pays fee. Number of placements per year: 201-500.

SUNNY SIDE INC./TEMP SIDE

210 University Boulevard
Suite 550
Denver CO 80206
303/320-5361
Contact: Mary Ann Padilla, Owner. Specializes in the areas of: office administration (administrators; clerks; receptionists; secretaries; word processing); temporary services (accounting/bookkeeping; secretaries; word processing).

TEMP FORCE OF DENVER

1888 Sherman Street
Suite 550
Denver CO 80203
303/831-1096
Contact: Debbie Vernon, Manager. Temporary help service. No appointment required. Founded 1965. Branch offices located in: Alabama; Arkansas; California; Colorado; Conneticut; Florida; Illinois; Indiana; Kansas; Maryland; Massachusetts; Michigan; Mississippi;

Nevada; New Jersey; New Mexico; New York; Ohio; Oklahoma; Pennsylvania; Tennessee; Utah; Vermont; Virginia. Nonspecialized. Positions commonly filled include: Accountant; Bookkeeper; Clerk; Computer Operator; Computer Programmer; Customer Service Representative; Data Entry Clerk; Demonstrator; Driver; Factory Worker; General Laborer; Legal Secretary; Light Industrial Worker; Medical Secretary; Office Worker; Purchasing Agent; Receptionist; Secretary; Statistician; Stenographer; Typist; Word Processing Specialist.

TEMP FORCE OF PUEBLO
201 West 8th Street
Suite 306
Pueblo CO 81003
719/545-8148
Contact: Manager. Temporary help service. No appointment required. Founded 1965. Branch offices located in: Alabama; Arkansas; California; Colorado; Conneticut; Florida; Illinois; Indiana; Kansas; Maryland; Massachusetts; Michigan; Mississippi; Nevada; New Jersey; New Mexico; New York; Ohio; Oklahoma; Pennsylvania; Tennessee; Utah; Vermont; Virginia. Nonspecialized. Positions commonly filled include: Accountant; Bookkeeper; Clerk; Computer Operator; Computer Programmer; Customer Service Representative; Data Entry Clerk; Demonstrator; Driver; Factory Worker; General Laborer; Legal Secretary; Light Industrial Worker; Medical Secretary; Office Worker; Purchasing Agent; Receptionist; Secretary; Statistician; Stenographer; Typist; Word Processing Specialist.

TERRY PERSONNEL
9191 Sheridan Boulevard
Suite 101
Westminster CO 80030
303/427-4633
Contact: Marilyn D. Terry, President. Employment agency; temporary help agency. No appointment required. Specializes in the areas of: Clerical and Secretarial; Construction; Manufacturing. Positions commonly filled include: Administrative Assistant; Bookkeeper; Clerk; Credit Manager; Data Entry Clerk; Executive Secretary; General Laborer; Legal Secretary; Light Industrial Worker; Receptionist; Secretary; Stenographer; Typist; Word Processor. Individual pays fee. Number of placements per year: 201-500.

INTERIM PERSONNEL SERVICES OF BOULDER
3000 Pearl Street
Suite 200
Boulder CO 80301
303/442-8677
Contact: Ron Rohr, Branch Manager. A member of Victor Temporary Services. Appointment requested. Founded 1954. Victor Temporary Services has over 100 offices throughout the United States. Nonspecialized. Positions commonly filled include: Bookkeeper; Clerk; Computer Operator; Customer Service Representative; Data Entry Clerk; Demonstrator; Draftsperson; Electronic Assembler; Factory Worker; General Laborer; Legal Secretary; Light Industrial Worker; Medical Secretary; Office Worker; Receptionist; Secretary; Stenographer; Technician; Typist; Word Processing Specialist. Company pays fee. Number of placements per year: 1001+.

INTERIM PERSONNEL SERVICES OF DENVER
4155 East Jewell Avenue
Suite 1018
Denver CO 80222
303/758-8677
Contact: Office Manager. A member of Victor Temporary Services. Appointment requested. Founded 1954. Victor Temporary Services has over 100 offices throughout the United States. Nonspecialized. Positions commonly filled include: Bookkeeper; Clerk; Computer Operator; Customer Service Representative; Data Entry Clerk; Demonstrator; Draftsperson; Electronic Assembler; Factory Worker; General Laborer; Legal Secretary; Light Industrial Worker; Medical Secretary; Office Worker; Receptionist; Secretary; Stenographer; Technician; Typist; Word Processing Specialist. Company pays fee. Number of placements per year: 1001+.

INTERIM PERSONNEL SERVICES OF LAKEWOOD
441 Wadsworth
Suite 220
Lakewood CO 80226.
303/232-3883. A member of Victor Temporary Services. Appointment requested. Founded 1954. Victor Temporary Services has over 100 offices throughout the United States. Nonspecialized. Positions commonly filled include: Bookkeeper; Clerk; Computer Operator; Customer Service Representative; Data Entry Clerk; Demonstrator; Draftsperson; Electronic Assembler; Factory Worker; General Laborer;

Legal Secretary; Light Industrial Worker; Medical Secretary; Office Worker; Receptionist; Secretary; Stenographer; Technician; Typist; Word Processing Specialist. Company pays fee. Number of placements per year: 1001+.

INTERIM PERSONNEL
318 Main Street
Longmont CO 80501
303/678-0551
Contact: Office Manager. A member of Victor Temporary Services. Appointment requested. Founded 1954. Victor Temporary Services has over 100 offices throughout the United States. Nonspecialized. Positions commonly filled include: Bookkeeper; Clerk; Computer Operator; Customer Service Representative; Data Entry Clerk; Demonstrator; Draftsperson; Electronic Assembler; Factory Worker; General Laborer; Legal Secretary; Light Industrial Worker; Medical Secretary; Office Worker; Receptionist; Secretary; Stenographer; Technician; Typist; Word Processing Specialist. Company pays fee. Number of placements per year: 1001+.

UNITED EMPLOYMENT
2141 North Academy Boulevard
Colorado Springs CO 80909
719/574-2101
Contact: Jim Goodman, Owner. Employment agency. No appointment required. Founded 1977. Nonspecialized. Positions commonly filled include: Accountant; Bookkeeper; Buyer; Civil Engineer; Clerk; Computer Operator and Computer Programmer; Credit Manager; Data Entry Clerk; Draftsperson; Driver; EDP Specialist; Factory Worker; General Laborer; Insurance Agent/Broker; Legal Secretary; Light Industrial Worker; Mechanical Engineer; Medical Secretary; Nurse; Office Worker; Public Relations Worker; Receptionist; Sales Representative; Secretary; Stenographer; Typist. Individual pays 90% of fee. Number of placements per year: 201-500.

JULIE WEST AND ASSOCIATES
3801 East Florida Avenue
Suite 400
Denver CO 80210
303/759-1622
Contact: Julie West, Owner. Employment agency. Appointment required. Founded 1984. A small, selective personnel agency geared to in depth servicery, both client companies and qualified candidate.

Specializes in the areas of: Accounting; Banking and Finance; Legal; Real Estate; Secretarial and Clerical. Positions commonly filled include: Administrative Assistant; Bank Officer/Manager; Bookkeeper; Clerk; Computer Programmer; Credit Manager; Customer Service Rep; Data Entry Clerk; Draftsperson; Executive Secretary; General Manager; Legal Secretary; Medical Secretary; Personnel Director; Receptionist; Secretary; Stenographer; Systems Analyst; Typist; Word Processor. Company pays fee. Number of placements per year: 51-100.

EXECUTIVE SEARCH FIRMS OF DENVER

THE BUXTON GROUP LIMITED
3307 South College
Suite 200
Fort Collins CO 80525
303/449-0021
Contact: Gary Buxton, C.P.C., E.V.P. Executive search firm. Appointment required; unsolicited resumes accepted. Founded 1978. Specializes in the areas of: Accounting; Banking; Chemicals; Data Processing (hardware and software); Finance; Office Equipment; Packaging; Printing and Publishing; Sales and Marketing. Contingency; noncontingency. Number of searches conducted per year: 101-200.

COMPUSEARCH OF BOULDER
P.O. Box 4657
Boulder CO 80306
303/447-9900
Contact: Sharon Hunter, General Manager. Executive search firm. Appointment required; no phone calls; unsolicited resumes accepted. Founded 1965. World's largest contingency search firm. Five hundred offices nationwide, doing business under the names "Management Recruiters", "Sales Consultants", "CompuSearch" and "OfficeMates5". Specializes in mid-management/professional positions, $25,000-75,000 per annum. Specializes in the areas of: Accounting; Administration, MIS/EDP; Advertising; Affirmative Action; Architecture; Banking and Finance; Chemicals and Pharmaceuticals; Communications; Computer Hardware and Software; Construction; Design, Industrial and Interior; Electrical; Engineering; Food Industry; General Management; Health and Medical; Human Resources; Insurance; Legal; Manufacturing; Operations Management; Printing and Publishing; Procurement; Real Estate; Retailing; Sales and Marketing; Technical and Scientific; Textiles; Transportation. Contingency.

MANAGEMENT RECRUITERS OF COLORADO
3090 S. Jamaica Court
Wedgwood Building
Suite 100
Aurora CO 80014
303/337-4434
Contact: Kent Milius, President. Executive search firm. Appointment required; no phone calls; unsolicited resumes accepted. Founded 1965. World's largest contingency search firm. Five hundred offices nationwide, doing business under the names "Management Recruiters", "Sales Consultants", "CompuSearch" and "OfficeMates5". Specializes in mid-management/professional positions, $25,000-75,000 per annum. Specializes in the areas of: Accounting; Administration, MIS/EDP; Advertising; Affirmative Action; Architecture; Banking and Finance; Chemicals and Pharmaceuticals; Communications; Computer Hardware and Software; Construction; Design, Industrial and Interior; Electrical; Engineering; Food Industry; General Management; Health and Medical; Human Resources; Insurance; Legal; Manufacturing; Operations Management; Printing and Publishing; Procurement; Real Estate; Retailing; Sales and Marketing; Technical and Scientific; Textiles; Transportation. Contingency.

DUNHILL PERSONNEL OF BOULDER
1790 30th Street
Suite 230
Boulder CO 80301
303/444-5531
Contact: Ron Knox, Owner. Executive search firm. Specializes in the areas of: Computer Hardware and Software; Engineering; Scientific and Technical.

ALPHA GROUP INC.
201 Centennial Street
Suite 303
Glenwood Springs CO 81601
303/945-2336
Contact: Jim Astrach, President. Executive search firm. Specializes in the areas of: Electronics; Engineering; Scientific and Technical.

EXECUTIVE RESOURCE MANAGEMENT
2134 South Eagle Court
Aurora CO 80014
303/337-5588
Contact: Monty C. McCurry, President. Executive search firm. Appointment required. Founded 1985. Specializes in the areas of: Architecture; Commercial Office Furniture; Computer Hardware and Software; Construction; Distribution; Health and Medical; Manufacturing; Paper; Printing and Publishing; Real Estate; Sales and Marketing. Positions commonly filled include: Financial Analyst; General Manager; Management Consultant; Marketing Specialist; Project Manager; Real Estate Developer; Sales/Marketing Manager; Sales Representative. Company pays fee. Number of placements per year: 0-50.

MANAGEMENT RECRUITERS OF COLORADO SPRINGS
6760 Corporate Drive
Suite 220
Colorado Springs CO 80919
719/599-9400
Contact: Mark Merriman, Manager. Executive search firm. Appointment required; no phone calls; unsolicited resumes accepted. Founded 1965. World's largest contingency search firm. Five hundred offices nationwide, doing business under the names "Management Recruiters", "Sales Consultants", "CompuSearch" and "OfficeMates5". Specializes in mid-management/professional positions, $25,000-75,000 per annum. Specializes in the areas of: Accounting; Administration, MIS/EDP; Advertising; Affirmative Action; Architecture; Banking and Finance; Chemicals and Pharmaceuticals; Communications; Computer Hardware and Software; Construction; Design, Industrial and Interior; Electrical; Engineering; Food Industry; General Management; Health and Medical; Human Resources; Insurance; Legal; Manufacturing; Operations Management; Printing and Publishing; Procurement; Real Estate; Retailing; Sales and Marketing; Technical and Scientific; Textiles; Transportation. Contingency.

MANAGEMENT RECRUITERS OF DENVER
3090 South Jamaica Court
Wedgwood Building
Suite 100
Aurora CO 80014-2978
303/337-4434
Contact: Kent Milius or Gregg Milius, Co-Managers. Executive search firm. Appointment required; no phone calls; unsolicited resumes accepted. Founded 1965. World's largest contingency search firm. Five hundred offices nationwide, doing business under the names "Management Recruiters", "Sales Consultants", "CompuSearch" and "OfficeMates5". Specializes in mid-management/professional positions, $25,000-75,000 per annum. Specializes in the areas of: Administrative and Clinical Health Care; Insurance; Pensions and Trusts; Telecommunications Sales and General Management. Contingency. Number of searches conducted per year: 501+.

MANAGEMENT RECRUITERS OF GOLDEN HILL
12600 West Colfax Avenue
Suite C-440
Lakewood CO 80215-3736
303/233-8600
Contact: Rodney D. Bonner, Manager. Executive search firm. Appointment required; no phone calls; unsolicited resumes accepted. Founded 1965. World's largest contingency search firm. Five hundred offices nationwide, doing business under the names "Management Recruiters", "Sales Consultants", "CompuSearch" and "OfficeMates5". Specializes in mid-management/professional positions, $25,000-75,000 per annum. Specializes in the areas of: Accounting; Administration, MIS/EDP; Advertising; Affirmative Action; Architecture; Banking and Finance; Chemicals and Pharmaceuticals; Communications; Computer Hardware and Software; Construction; Design, Industrial and Interior; Electrical; Engineering; Food Industry; General Management; Health and Medical; Human Resources; Insurance; Legal; Manufacturing; Operations Management; Printing and Publishing; Procurement; Real Estate; Retailing; Sales and Marketing; Technical and Scientific; Textiles; Transportation. Contingency. Number of searches conducted per year: 501+.

PROFESSIONAL SEARCH & PLACEMENT INC.
4901 East Dry Creek Road
Suite 101
Littleton CO 80122
303/779-8004
Contact: John Turner, President. Executive search firm. Appointment requested. Specializes in the areas of: Data Processing and Software Engineering; MIS/EDP. Positions commonly filled include: Aerospace Engineer; Data Base Administrator; DP Manager; EDO Specialist; Programmer/Analyst; Software Engineer; Systems Analyst. Company pays fee. Number of placements per year: 201-500 nationally.

ROTH YOUNG PERSONNEL
9725 East Hampden Avenue
Suite 204
Denver CO 80231
303/755-0075
Contact: Irv Rimehart, President. Executive search firm. Appointment requested; unsolicited resumes accepted. Founded 1972. Specializes in the areas of: Administration, MIS/EDP; Fashion; Finance; Food Industry; Hospitality (Hotel/Motel/Clubs); Restaurants; Retail; Supermarket/Wholesale Grocery. Contingency. Number of searches conducted per year: 201-500.

SALES CONSULTANTS OF DENVER
3033 South Parker Road
Suite 304, Aurora CO 80014
303/752-2550
Contact: Manager. Executive search firm. Appointment required; no phone calls; unsolicited resumes accepted. Founded 1965. World's largest contingency search firm. Five hundred offices nationwide, doing business under the names "Management Recruiters", "Sales Consultants", "CompuSearch" and "OfficeMates5". Specializes in mid-management/professional positions, $25,000-75,000 per annum. Specializes in the areas of: Accounting; Administration, MIS/EDP; Advertising; Affirmative Action; Architecture; Banking and Finance; Chemicals and Pharmaceuticals; Communications; Computer Hardware and Software; Construction; Design, Industrial and Interior; Electrical; Engineering; Food Industry; General Management; Health and Medical; Human Resources; Insurance; Legal; Manufacturing; Operations Management; Printing and Publishing; Procurement; Real

Estate; Retailing; Sales and Marketing; Technical and Scientific; Textiles; Transportation. Contingency.

R.W. SWANSON AND ASSOCIATES, INC.
10200 E. Girard Avenue
Suite 351C
Denver CO 80231
303/695-0978
Contact: Richard Swanson, President. Executive search firm. Appointment required; unsolicited resumes accepted. Founded 1978. The firm provides a comprehensive program of job finding and career development skills specializing in top executive positions. All counselors are ex-top executives. Specializes in all Managerial, Professional and Executive positions. Noncontingency. Number of searches conducted per year: 201-500.

J.Q. TURNER & ASSOCIATES, INC
11940 East Bates Circle
Suite 200, Aurora CO 80014-3105
303/671-0800
Fax 303/671-0559
Contact: Jim Turner, President. Professional search firm. Appointment requested. Founded 1982. Specializes in the areas of: Experienced degreed (BS, MS, PhD, MBA, PA) Engineers and other Technical disciplines in Research and Development, Product Design/Development, Manufacturing, Quality Control, Test, and Customer Support. Typical Industries covered are: Biomedical, Computers and Computer Peripherals, Telecommunications, Scientific Instrumentation, Micro- and Opto-Electronics, Optics, Robotics, Aerospace and Defense, Electronics, Chemisty and Plastics. Company pays fee. Number of placements per year: up to 50.

INDEX TO PRIMARY EMPLOYERS

NOTE: Below is an alphabetical index of Denver's primary employer listings, as included in this book. Those employers in each industry that fall under the headings "Additional Large Employers" or "Small to Medium Sized Employers" are not indexed here.

A

B

C

D

E

F

G

H

I

L

M

S

T

U

V

Z

INDEX TO EMPLOYMENT SERVICES

H

I

J

L

M

P

R

S

T

U

W

AVAILABLE AT YOUR LOCAL BOOKSTORE

Knock 'em Dead

The Ultimate Job Seeker's Handbook

The all-new 1993 edition of Martin Yate's classic now covers the entire job search. The new edition features sections on: Where the jobs are now and where they will be tomorrow, how best to approach companies; keeping the financial boat afloat; how to recharge a stalled job hunt; "safety networking" to protect your job regardless of the economy; why corporate resume databases and electronic bulletin boards are the new wave for the career savvy; and bridging the gender gap in salary negotiations. Of course, the new addition also includes Yate's famous great answers to tough interview questions. When it comes to proven tactics that give readers the competitive advantage, Martin Yate is the authority to turn to. 6x9 inches, 312 pages, $7.95.

Resumes that Knock 'em Dead

Martin Yate reviews the marks of a great resume: what type of resume is right for each applicant, what always goes in, what always stays out, and why. Every single resume in *Resumes that Knock 'em Dead* was actually used by a job hunter to successfully obtain a job. No other book provides the hard facts for producing an exemplary resume. 8-1/2x11 inches, 216 pages, $7.95.

Cover Letters that Knock 'em Dead

The final word on not just how to write a "correct" cover letter, but how to write a cover letter that offers a powerful competitive advantage in today's tough job market. *Cover Letters that Knock 'em Dead* gives the essential information on composing a cover that wins attention, interest, and job offers. 8-1/2x11 inches, 184 pages, $7.95.

ALSO OF INTEREST...

The JobBank Series

There are now 20 *JobBank* books, each providing extensive, up-to-date employment information on hundreds of the largest employers in each job market. Recommended as an excellent place to begin your job search by *The New York Times, The Los Angeles Times, The Boston Globe, The Chicago Tribune,* and many other publications, *JobBank* books have been used by hundreds of thousands of people to find jobs.

Books available: *The Atlanta JobBank--The Boston JobBank--The Carolina JobBank--The Chicago JobBank--The Dallas-Ft. Worth JobBank--The Denver JobBank--The Detroit JobBank--The Florida JobBank--The Houston JobBank--The Los Angeles JobBank--The Minneapolis JobBank--The New York JobBank--The Ohio JobBank--The Philadelphia JobBank--The Phoenix JobBank--The St. Louis JobBank--The San Francisco JobBank--The Seattle JobBank--The Tennessee JobBank--The Washington DC JobBank.* Each book is 6x9 inches, over 300 pages, paperback, $15.95.

If you cannot find a book at your local bookstore, order it directly from the publisher. Please send payment including $3.75 for shipping and handling (for the entire order) to: Bob Adams, Inc., 260 Center Street, Holbrook, MA 02343. Credit card holders may call 1-800-USA-JOBS (in Massachusetts, 617-767-8100). Please check first at your local bookstore.